W9-AKH-006

Family Capital

Family Capital

Working with Wealthy Families to Manage Their Money across Generations

GREGORY CURTIS

WILEY

Published by John Wiley & Sons, Inc., Hoboken, New Jersey.

Published simultaneously in Canada.

Library of Congress Cataloging-in-Publication Data:

Names: Curtis, Gregory, 1947- author.
Title: Family capital : working with wealthy families to manage their money across generations / Gregory Curtis.
Description: 1 | Hoboken : Wiley, 2016. | Includes bibliographical references and index.
Identifiers: LCCN 2015036772 (print) | LCCN 2015045963 (ebook) | ISBN 9781119094135 (hardback) | ISBN 9781119094111 (ePDF) | ISBN 9781119094128 (ePub)
Subjects: LCSH: Finance, Personal. | Wealth—United States. | Investments—United States. | Finance—United States.
Classification: LCC HG179 .C848 2016 (print) | LCC HG179 (ebook) | DDC 332.02400973—dc23
LC record available at http://lccn.loc.gov/2015036772

Cover Design: Wiley
Cover Image: gold tree © Marinamik/iStockphoto

Printed in the United States of America

10 9 8 7 6 5 4 3 2 1

Contents

Preface

I've written two investment books—*Creative Capital* (iUniverse Press, 2004) and *The Stewardship of Wealth* (John Wiley & Sons, 2013). When I sat down to think about my third book, I naturally considered how it might be improved over the first two. I paged through both books and tried to think what topics I'd overlooked, where advances in our understanding of the investment process had occurred that needed to be addressed. I reviewed many other investment books.

But then I stepped back and asked myself a different question. Suppose, I thought, wealthy families had asked me what the best way was to learn the business of managing capital. Or suppose colleagues in the wealth advisory world had asked me how they might best improve their skills to stay at the top of their professions. What would I have told them?

In both cases, I would have said something like this: "The best way to learn about managing capital or staying at the top of the wealth management business is to observe thoughtful families and skilled advisors meeting and discussing the challenges presented by managing capital."

But what does that answer have to do with writing a third investment book? At first, I thought the answer was "nothing whatever." But one day, as I was flying to New York to meet with a family client, I had an epiphany. Wait, I said to myself! Here you are on your way to a client meeting. You attend at least 40 such meetings every year and you've been doing it for nearly 40 years. That's a whole lot of family meetings.

Over the course of those four decades and more than 1,500 meetings, I've learned a huge amount about what tends to work and what doesn't in the wealth management space. I've learned from my wealth management colleagues—especially my partners at Greycourt & Co., Inc. But I've learned even more from all those clients over all those years.

Why not, I thought, reproduce some of the best of those meetings and let my readers come to their own conclusions about what constitutes sound capital management and what constitutes best practices in the wealth advisory business?

THE TITAN FAMILY

Of course, client confidentiality prevents me from *literally* reproducing the discussions between families and advisors. So, instead, I've created a fictitious American family—the Titan family. We learn who this family is and how they made their money. We watch as, over the years and across the generations, the family and its advisors grapple with the many challenges involved in managing great wealth. Sometimes the family succeeds and sometimes they fail. Sometimes their advisors do a terrific job and sometimes they let the family down.

Throughout, I don't *tell* you what happened, I *show* you what happened. We actually listen in on the meetings the various family members have with their advisors. Some of the conversations are almost verbatim from meetings I've had with my own clients. Others are reproduced based on reports of meetings my partners have had with families they work with. When I'm not reporting conversations exactly as they occurred, it's mainly due either to lapse of memory or to the need to maintain client confidentiality. (I'm quite sure that some of my clients will recognize themselves in these pages, though I hope no one else recognizes them.)

Finally, in some cases I've invented conversations out of whole cloth in order to make a point that seemed important. Even in these cases, I've tried to organize the conversation and the dialogue so that they sound as realistic as possible.

When the Titan family members speak, I've tried to make them speak like real people. They sometimes get things right and they sometimes don't. They lose their patience and they keep their cool. They have individual personalities, and those personalities affect the way they think.

I've tried to make the meetings as realistic as possible, too. Sometimes the family and its advisors stick to their agendas and sometimes they don't. Some of these detours are simply timewasters (I've eliminated most of those), but most are very much the opposite. I've tried to make the point repeatedly that when an agenda is hijacked by the family, it's almost always for a good reason. They are departing from the set agenda because something is on their minds and the advisors in the room need to address that topic.

The net result is that this book may seem to the reader more like a novel—one with a lot of dialogue—or a screenplay than a traditional investment book. Let's face it—investment books can be terminally dry. Trying to tell people how to invest their capital doesn't result in the most riveting prose. I hope that by transcribing dialogue as it actually happened, some of this dreariness will be dissipated and readers will recognize themselves and their families in the conversations.

ORGANIZATION OF THE BOOK

The chapters in this book follow each other largely in the order that most families will encounter the various challenges involved in managing private wealth. Consequently, the book is designed to be read straight through from the preface to Chapter 11. However, there is no reason a family or advisor couldn't decide simply to read an individual chapter, say, the chapter on setting investment objectives. In that case, the reader may wish to review the Titan family tree, which appears at the front of the book, in order to keep the family members straight.

The book is organized as follows:

Prologue. In the prologue I introduce the Titan family, founded by a poor Italian immigrant named Georgio Titano. Over the course of a remarkable lifetime, Georgio will launch a business, change his name to the more American-sounding George Titan, marry a pretty Scots-Irish girl named Ellie, father two children who lived to adulthood, and die quite a wealthy man. We will also meet George's children and grandchildren and some of his later descendants.

Chapter 1. In Chapter 1 we fast-forward to the mid-1970s. I chose that period for two reasons. First, it's the most remote investment decade that people now alive will well remember, and hence in some sense it represents the beginning of the "modern era" of investing. Second, the mid-1970s were dominated by the terrible Bear Market of 1973–1974, an event seared in the minds of anyone, including myself, who lived through it. In the late summer of 1974, George Titan III, grandson of the original George Titan, will make a catastrophic investment mistake that will eventually result in the loss of his wealth. Shirtsleeves-to-shirtsleeves in three generations is the normal outcome for wealthy families, and George III's branch of the Titan family proves to be no exception.

Chapter 2. We are now well into the modern era. It is 2005, and Ned Titan and Rose (Titan) Wainwright, fifth-generation descendants of the original George Titan, join the family investment committee and begin to learn the business of managing capital. When their father suffers a second stroke, he steps down from his role at the family office and Ned and Rose succeed him as stewards of the family fortune. We observe their interactions with the advisory firm their father had engaged and watch as they make at least one serious investment error. As the great Financial Crisis of 2008 settles across the land, Ned and Rose find themselves floundering. Unhappy with their current advisor, they find out, almost fortuitously, that there are other, more interesting advisory options available to them.

Chapter 3. Here we follow Ned and Rose Titan as they search for and ultimately engage a new financial advisor. The Titans meet with various firms, put together a request for proposal, interview the finalists, and hire a firm we will call Spenser Advisors. Over the years the Titan family had progressed through string of satisfactory and unsatisfactory advisors: a local trust company, a bank, a brokerage firm, and, finally, Spenser—an independent, employee-owned, open-architecture firm.

Chapter 4. In Chapter 4 the Titans meet for the first time with their new advisor. The purpose of this meeting is to discuss governance issues and investment policies, but the real purpose of the meeting is for the family and their new advisor to become acquainted. We meet the lead advisor for the Titan account, Clarissa (Carrie) Knowlton.

Chapter 5. The creation of an investment policy statement for a family is all-too-often glossed over. Many advisors simply pull out their standard-form policy statement and change the name at the top of the first page. But Spenser Advisors considers the policy statement to be a crucially important document. Moreover, Spenser believes that the process of creating the policy statement is itself a very important learning experience for both the family and the advisor. As a result, the entire Jake Titan branch of the family attended this meeting, and we meet Ned and Rose's children, who are all young adults. Carrie Knowlton sensibly brought along to the meeting a younger advisor from Spenser named Roger Epperson, since she believed that the Titan children might relate better to a younger person.

Chapter 6. As with the creation of an investment policy statement, the establishment of appropriate investment objectives is a crucial task. If the investment objectives for the family are improperly understood or incorrectly articulated, all else will fail. Carrie Knowlton and Roger Epperson had managed to involve the Titan children in the process of setting objectives, viewing this approach as being more likely to capture the interest and attention of the younger family members.

Chapter 7. As all advisors know, asset allocation is a vital part of the capital management process. Unfortunately, asset allocation often seems impenetrable to family members. Carrie and Roger devoted a very long meeting to describing the process and answering the family's questions about it.

Chapter 8. Most investors, especially including family investors, dramatically overestimate the impact that investment managers will have on their portfolio returns. In this meeting, the Spenser advisors do their best to put managers in the proper context, pointing out to the Titans that many other aspects of the investment process will probably have a larger impact on their returns.

Chapter 9. Once an advisory relationship is up and running, most of the meetings between a family and its advisors will center on performance reporting. In Chapter 9, we listen in on the initial performance reporting meeting between the Titans and Spenser, as Carrie Knowlton and Roger Epperson walk the family through the nature of performance reporting and the actual performance reports.

Chapter 10. This chapter assembles in one place a variety of topics that are more or less directly related to investing capital, but which don't require the full treatment of a dedicated chapter. Spenser and the family discuss family investment education, how value is added to portfolios through the portfolio management process, the use of investment committees, and socially responsible investing.

Chapter 11. In the course of any long and close advisory relationship, many topics arise that are not directly related to investing but that can nonetheless have a dramatic impact on whether the family remains wealthy across many generations. This chapter isn't meant to represent an exhaustive list of these types of topics, but only a representative list. The Titans and Spenser discuss, for example, hiring an asset custodian, using family limited partnerships, philanthropy, the family office, how much money to leave the kids, and, finally, the delicate topic of economic inequality in America. Inequality is a major concern to all Americans, but it has a special resonance for families who aren't just in the 1%, but in a tiny fraction of the 1%.

Throughout the book I make periodic observations, commenting on the discussions that are going on. Most of these comments are designed for wealth advisors, but they may be of interest to families as well.

A NOTE TO MIDDLE-INCOME INVESTORS

This book describes a very wealthy family as it struggles to manage its wealth and to discharge its stewardship obligations to future generations. More than anything else, the Titan family is striving to avoid the usual outcome for the rich: shirtsleeves-to-shirtsleeves in three generations.

On the other hand, the issues the Titan family grapples with are, for the most part, the issues every family faces in managing its money. We tend to think that "the rich are different," but in my experience, Hemingway was right: they just have more money. If you read through these chapters, you will likely recognize not just rich people talking, but your own family making its way through the selfsame struggles.

It's certainly true that government rules prevent middle-income investors from benefiting from some of the best investments available—hedge funds and private equity. (Write your congressional representative!) Otherwise, investing is investing, and what a wealthy family needs to know is quite similar to what you need to know.

■ ■ ■

I don't know whether the unusual approach of this book will prove helpful to families and their advisors. I certainly hope it will, and it's been fun for me to write it, basically reliving so many interesting client meetings and discussions. But aside from the format, my main hope is that the book will help families improve their management of capital and help advisors improve their skills at helping families.

In a free market economic system, private wealth is the engine of prosperity. It fuels entrepreneurship, philanthropy, and the arts, it pays the great bulk of taxes, and it greases the skids of the capital markets, making the world safe for all investors. Wealthy families face enormous headwinds in the battle to remain wealthy. If this book reduces those headwinds by even a small fraction, it will redound not merely to the wealth of many families, but also to their happiness.

Gregory Curtis
Pittsburgh
August 3, 2015

Acknowledgments

This book opens with the stock market crash of 1973–1974 and it closes with the challenges of navigating a central banker–fueled bull market in the summer of 2015. Over the course of those 41 years I've had the extraordinary good fortune to work with hundreds of remarkable American and non-American families.

In 1974, I was a young lawyer slaving away in the bowels of a very large corporate law firm, one that today is among the 25 largest law firms in the world. In those days I was utterly ignorant of the challenges faced by families of wealth, but I quickly got a baptism of fire—a stock market that, on an inflation-adjusted basis, dropped more than 50% in less than two years.

Five years later, I joined the family office of one of America's most iconic families—the Mellons of Pittsburgh. That family had established its first family office in 1868, and so far as I know it is the oldest continually operating family office in the world.

In the mid-1980s, I organized my own firm, Greycourt, which has now served wealthy families with distinction for 30 years. My first 12 clients were all European families, an experience that very much broadened and deepened my horizons. Non-American families tend to think quite differently about the world and about their capital than do American families.

In America, stock markets have operated largely uninterrupted since the Buttonwood Agreement of 1792—123 years of securities trading activity. But it's important to understand how fantastically unusual that experience is. Our European cousins have seen their stock markets destroyed again and again, most recently in World War I and World War II. And even the European experience is a rock of stability compared to the calamities faced by families in Latin America, the Middle East, and elsewhere.

Private capital faces all the usual headwinds: taxes, inflation, high fees, price volatility, and human error. But, in addition, it must withstand war, revolution, financial panic, global depression, expropriation, and terrorist attack. It's no mystery why shirtsleeves-to-shirtsleeves in three generations is the norm. What is remarkable is how many families escape this trap and remain not just wealthy but vibrant and happy into their eighth generation and beyond.

To have the opportunity to work with such families and to generate deep and lasting friendships with many of them has been one of the genuine pleasures of my life. This book could not have been written without those families. I wish I could name them all and specify from which I learned this lesson and from which I learned that. But one of the first lessons of the wealth advisory world is that confidentiality is paramount. Still, they know who they are and I hope they know how much they have taught me.

Aside from the families, I've been privileged to work for nearly 30 years with a remarkable group of people at Greycourt. Turnover at the firm has been so extraordinarily low that almost everyone who joined the firm either is still with us or has retired.

I should thank every one of the employees at Greycourt, but in the interests of time and space let me single out my fellow managing directors: Greg Friedman, CEO; Jim Foster, CIO; Mark Laskow; David Lovejoy; Roy Nichol; and Matt Litwin. Gretchen Shoup, our COO, and Jamie Linhart, who oversees performance reporting. Liz Jones, whose client service operation has freed up our time to deal with larger issues. The Administration Group (and my own assistant, Dana Schmitt), who keep the trains running on time. Chris Fineburg and Tom Moore, who handle much of the day-to-day work on so many of my clients. Jeff Moyer, manager of the Greycourt Partners Fund, which handles my own capital. Chad Cribbs, Stephanie Halpern, and Brian LaBore in manager research.

In a very real sense, it is the families and my colleagues at Greycourt who have provided the material for this book. I've merely been the scrivener. Thanks to one and all.

GC
August 3, 2015

Prologue: The Titan Family in America

PREPARATION AND USE

Georgio Titano arrived in America in the late spring of 1854 from Abruzzo, a then-impoverished region in southern Italy. As a third son—and seventh child—Georgio's prospects were not good in the Old World, and Georgio determined to emigrate to the New World.

As it happened, Georgio had a second cousin who'd been in America for several years. Benedetto worked in a coal mine not far from Wheeling, West Virginia, and so that's where Georgio headed. The pay was good in the mines, but Georgio suffered from a touch of claustrophobia and as a result he hated coal mining. When he heard about a bricklayer who needed an assistant, Georgio leaped at the chance.

Somewhat to his own surprise, Georgio was good at laying brick. Mostly, of course, he was simply a laborer, hauling mortar and bricks and doing whatever his boss told him to do. But as time went by, Georgio began laying brick himself, essentially apprenticing under his boss. In no time at all, Georgio's walls were straighter and his mortar more even than the boss's work.

One day in the early fall of 1854, Georgio and his boss were working quickly, trying to finish off a wall before a rainstorm hit. The boss lost his footing and fell from the top of the wall, breaking his neck and dying instantly. Georgio was devastated. He'd liked his boss, despite the man's grumpy ways, and now he'd be unemployed. In fact, the man who'd contracted for the wall asked Georgio if he could finish it himself. Startled but happy, Georgio assured the man it would be no problem. And in fact, it *was* no problem. The man was so happy with the wall that he promptly hired Georgio to handle the brickwork on a small factory he was building outside Steubenville, Ohio.

After less than 18 months in America, Georgio Titano owned his own bricklaying business. As his business grew, he hired other workers and found that he liked being the boss. He was good with numbers, and when he quoted a job, the owner knew it would come in on time and as-bid.

In 1860, now relatively prosperous by the standards of new immigrants, Georgio decided it was time to become a real American. He changed his name officially from Georgio Titano to George Titan. He liked the sound of that name, and he knew that a "titan" was a person of great importance.

Shortly afterward, now that he considered himself a true American, George Titan determined to marry. He had the girl in mind: a pretty Scots-Irish lass he'd walked out with a few times while on a job in Waynesburg, Pennsylvania. Unfortunately, the girl's parents happened to know that George Titan was really Georgio Titano, and they wanted no part of an Italian son-in-law. These Scots-Irish parents had higher aspirations for their only daughter. But, unfortunately for the parents, the girl was of age and she and George eloped.

Over the course of the next ten years, George and Ellie (as his wife was called), née McCabe, produced five children, though only two of them, George Titan, Jr. and Andrew Titan, lived to adulthood. Meanwhile George was reinvesting nearly every penny into his business, continuing to grow it rapidly.

As the American Civil War dragged on, the economy had collapsed and George, who was already overextended, found himself in deep trouble. He got some work contracting with the Union army, but it didn't begin to replace the civilian work that had disappeared.

In those days men and women occupied different spheres of life, the men working out in the world and the women dominating the home front. That was mostly the way it was in the Titan family, too, but on really important issues, whether they related to business or family, George and Ellie tended to pool their minds and talents. In this case, George advocated closing the business down, finding a job, and waiting out the war. But Ellie had other ideas. She knew her husband to be a good businessman and she wasn't ready to throw in the towel. She suggested that they move to the rapidly growing city of Pittsburgh, about 50 miles to the north, where even during the war commerce went on and there was likely to be work for a talented man like George Titan.

Neither in the Old Country nor in America had George, or, for that matter, Ellie, ever been to a city, much less and to a wild, chaotic, frontier city like Pittsburgh. At first they were simply overwhelmed by the chaos, but gradually George found the energy in the town to be exciting.

Once back on his feet, George began to contemplate the future. He and Ellie would go for long walks along the banks of the Allegheny River, watching the busy river traffic and talking about what the future might hold for America, for Pittsburgh, for the Titan family. The conclusion they came to—a remarkable one—was that despite that the hardships of the war, when it finally ended there was likely to be a major economic expansion. What

George needed to do was to position himself to take advantage of it. And so he did. While his competitors were cutting back and keeping their heads down, George not only expanded his bricklaying business, he expanded into related work, including general contracting.

When the war finally ended, Titan Industries, as George now called his firm, was well-positioned, and throughout the 1870s and 1880s the company grew alongside Pittsburgh, which was then the fastest-growing city in America. Between 1870 and 1910, while the population of the United States was more than doubling, Pittsburgh grew six-fold from about 85,000 to over 530,000.[1]

At the peak of the Industrial Revolution, Pittsburgh was America's Silicon Valley, boasting vast industries in such diversified fields as steel (Carnegie Steel), coal (Consolidation Coal), glass (Pittsburgh Plate Glass), oil and gas (Gulf Oil), electronics (Westinghouse), aluminum (Alcoa), food (Heinz), and so on. During the late nineteenth century and for most of the twentieth century, Pittsburgh boasted more corporate headquarters than any American city except New York and Chicago. And each of these industries had a voracious appetite for brickwork for their factories and for general contractors who could build those factories.

■ ■ ■

Titan Industries continued to prosper right through the end of the nineteenth century. Of their two sons, only one, George Jr., went permanently into the business. George Sr. died in 1915 and Ellie soon followed—the two really *were* inseparable. But by that time George Jr. had been CEO for a few years and the firm barely skipped a beat.

When Titan Industries was finally sold, fortunately just before the Great Depression, the Titan family members found themselves to be moderately rich. They took stock in the acquiring company—an architectural-engineering firm called Smythson Brothers—for half the value of the sale, and cash for the balance. But the sale also meant that the Titans no longer had jobs. George Jr. was kept on by Smythson for a year, but after that he, too, was unemployed.

It was a strange world for the Titans, being owners of capital rather than owners of an operating business. After two generations of working hard every day to build Titan Industries, suddenly there was little to do. They would wake up in the morning and instinctively begin to think about everything that had to be done that day, only to find that the answer was, "very little."

After a lost period of groping their way forward, George Jr. asked the family to come together at their estate in Ligonier, in the highlands east of

Pittsburgh, to talk about their new lives and how best to move forward. There was a lot of unfocused chatter, but they didn't seem to be getting anywhere. It was all too new, this world they now lived in.

Over dinner, however, they heard from a friend of George Jr.'s named Bill Wilkins, whose family had gone through a similar transition about a decade earlier. Wilkins assured the Titans that the Wilkins family had gone through exactly the same awkward period and that it was all perfectly normal. However, he cautioned them that they needed to pass beyond this phase and begin to take control of their new lives. The Titans, he pointed out, were no longer managers of a business, they were managers of capital, and they needed to get good at it. Specifically, he encouraged the Titans to form what was called a "family office."

In those days family offices were still a fairly new concept. The Mellons—another, much wealthier, Pittsburgh family—had established a family office called T. Mellon & Sons way back in 1868, and the Rockefellers had followed suit a year later.

At first, Lawburn (as the family office was called, named after Ellie's family's ancestral home in Scotland, which none of the Titans had ever seen), was a modest affair. George Jr. had an office there, from which vantage point he oversaw the family's investment portfolio, but otherwise Lawburn was more a name on the door than anything else.

■ ■ ■

Before we move forward, we should step back and introduce the other branch of the Titan family. George and Ellie had another child who survived into adulthood, Andrew. Unlike George Jr., Andrew was a sickly boy who grew into a sickly man. He died young, at age 40, but before he did he married and produced a line of remarkable progeny that will be the main focus of the rest of this book.

Andrew's only child, Jack, known as Jake, may not have been a large, robust fellow like his uncle, George Jr., and his cousin, George III (see below), but he was a remarkable fellow nonetheless. Jake took after his mother—light-brown hair, slim figure, and large, thoughtful eyes. Most days, while other boys were outside roughhousing, Jake could be found inside, curled up with a book by the fire.

Like his cousin, Jake joined the family company when he graduated from high school, but unlike his brothers, Jake hated the work. Hauling heavy loads of brick in a wheelbarrow in rotten weather wasn't Jake's idea of fun, and after a few dreary years of this Jake quit and headed off to college.

George Titan Sr., then near the end of his life, was appalled—no one in the Titan family had ever attended college and George didn't see any reason why any of them ever should. There might have been serious trouble between grandfather and grandson, except that Ellie took Jake's side. She'd have loved to attend college when she was young, she told George, and she was proud of Jake for wanting to try it out.

And try it out Jake did. Never in his life had he found anything so compelling. He loved his courses and quickly became a darling of the faculty. But after two years Jake left college to pursue yet another dream—Jake had decided to become an attorney.

Although the Law School at Harvard University had opened its doors back in 1817, most young men (they were virtually all men in those days) entered the profession by reading law under the tutelage of an experienced lawyer. Because of his excellent academic record, Jake was able to attach himself to the already-legendary Pittsburgh firm of Knox & Reed. Knox & Reed represented such luminaries as Andrew Mellon, Andre Carnegie, Charles Schwab, and many other titans of industry in the city.

Most young lawyers who had the opportunity to join a firm as prestigious as Knox & Reed would have leaped at the chance. But no sooner had Jake passed the bar exam with the highest score in the state that year than he left Knox & Reed and hung up his own shingle:

J. Titan & Partners
Business Law Only

There were in fact no partners, but Jake had big plans for the future and didn't wish to have to change his sign as he grew. While at Knox & Reed Jake had realized that the senior partners at the firm hadn't gotten rich charging legal fees—they'd made their money by investing in the companies launched by their wildly successful clients, often taking stock in lieu of legal fees, and otherwise simply buying the stock whenever they could do so.

The clients of Knox & Reed, however, were of an older generation, men who'd built great fortunes in the second half of the nineteenth century. Jake wanted to represent the young men of the coming twentieth century who, he hoped, would soon be building new fortunes.

While Jake didn't resemble his grandfather in many ways, in one way they were very much alike: both were astute judges of character. Jake seemed to know intuitively when a young man had the right stuff to build a company and when he didn't. And if the young man with the wrong stuff nonetheless had a good business idea, Jake considered it part of his legal duty to find men who could take the idea and run with it. Sometimes the young men kept an ownership interest in their ideas, but sometimes they didn't, and Jake rather quickly became known as a man who didn't hesitate to make hard decisions, a man not to be trifled with.

When Jake died of cancer in 1945, he headed a small but very successful law firm. More important for his heirs, he owned important pieces of more than 30 companies, and he had nearly surpassed his grandfather in the accumulation of capital.

THE EXTENDED TITAN FAMILY

We won't need to know all the members of the Titan family down through the years, but we do need to know a couple of the family groups, as we will be observing them as they grapple with various investment issues.

George Titan Jr. and His Family

Nearly everybody who met George Jr. remarked on the resemblance between father and son. George looked like his father and talked like his father. He moved and thought like his father. And consequently, it was no surprise that when it came time for George Sr. to step down as CEO of Titan Industries, it would be George Jr. who took over.

Unfortunately, despite the superficial similarities between the two Georges, the younger man lacked his father's vision and creativity. Perhaps even worse, he lacked a partner like his mother had been to his father. George Jr. was married late in life to a much younger woman. It was a good marriage, but a very traditional one. Even worse, George Jr. became CEO somewhat prematurely, upon the death of George Sr., and, of course, the son no longer had the father around to mentor him.

During the years that George Jr. ran Titan Industries, Pittsburgh's growth rate slowed considerably. In retrospect, Titan Industries should have expanded into more rapidly growing regions of the country, but George Sr. had kept Titan focused on Pittsburgh and George Jr. didn't see any reason to change that. As a result, instead of remaining independent and family-owned, Titan Industries would eventually be forced to sell itself, although this wouldn't become obvious for some years.

George Jr. and his wife, Mary, had three children: daughters Ellie and Grace, and a son, George III. Ellie, named for her grandmother, died of typhus in her teens, but Grace and George III lived to adulthood. George Jr. was an older father and a largely absent one, spending most of his time at the office and the rest at the Duquesne Club, Pittsburgh's renowned business club. This had a particular effect on George III, who resented his father's absence from his life.

Grace, however, proved to be a remarkable young woman. She seemed to most people to be a throwback to her grandmother, Ellie Titan, not so much in looks (she unfortunately resembled her grandfather, George Sr.) but in her lively personality and quick mind.

Upon graduating from Pennsylvania College for Women, known as PCW, now Chatham University, Grace went directly to work for Titan Industries, intending to work her way up through the firm as her father had done. She started in the typing pool, but was quickly noticed by one of the junior executives and she moved up to be secretary to the assistant comptroller at Titan.

After four years, Grace moved up again, this time to be secretary to the comptroller himself, an older, gentle, soft-spoken man, but also a very traditional male of that era. Much as he enjoyed having a secretary as competent as Grace, he was constantly telling her she was wasting her time working all day long and that she should focus on finding a man, getting married, and raising children. Grace, however, had little interest in these suggestions, and after several more years working in the comptroller's office she complained to her father about her slow progress in moving up the ladder.

George Jr. was astonished by Grace's complaints—he, too, had wondered when she was going to settle down and start a family. Father and daughter had a long and awkward conversation about the role of women in the world and about the role of Grace in particular at Titan Industries, the result of which was that Grace quit in a huff.

But she didn't quit to start a family; Grace quit to join a firm across town called Lawson & Dyer Engineering, known by everyone as L&D. She had majored in math at PCW, which offered no engineering courses, but she'd taken courses in mechanical and electrical engineering at the University of Pittsburgh.

The men at L&D were bemused to encounter this young woman who was interested in an engineering career, and under most circumstances Grace would probably never have been hired. Why, the men at L&D would have asked, should a good job go to a young woman who didn't need it and who would probably quit after a few years to raise her kids, when there were so many men who needed to support their families?

But L&D was growing so rapidly that they were willing to hire just about anybody, and Grace got her job. She stayed at L&D for 30 years, never marrying, and at the end retired as the firm's senior engineer. Along the way, L&D had merged with the much larger firm of Smythson Brothers—the very firm that would eventually acquire Titan Industries.

The career of George III was not such a happy one. He joined Titan Industries, as expected, starting in the brickyard and working his way up. George III wasn't a particularly capable fellow, but he was willing to work, and under ordinary circumstances would probably have found a useful place for himself at Titan. But because his father was the CEO, George rose up through the ranks too fast—far faster and far higher than his limited capabilities warranted. This caused endless problems for Titan and, much more important for our purposes, endless problems for George III.

Eventually, when Titan Industries was sold to Smythson-L&D, George was eased out of his role as a vice-president-without-portfolio and he never worked again. He did, however, continue to manage the family's liquid portfolio, with results that were, as we shall see, unfortunate.

Jake Titan and His Family

Jake Titan turned out to be the most successful member of his generation in the Titan family, using his small law firm as a vehicle to build very significant wealth for himself. Along the way, however, Jake alienated many people in Pittsburgh with his hard-charging ways and he struggled to build his law firm because he found it impossible to delegate authority or to allow younger lawyers to have any significant responsibility for the management of the firm.

As a result, it was Jake Jr., Jake's son, who actually built J. Titan & Partners into a serious law firm. Jake Jr. had begun his legal life working for a Pittsburgh law firm that competed with J. Titan & Partners. But when Jake Sr. became ill, Jake Jr. moved over to J. Titan and ultimately became one of its most dominant partners.

The long hours at the law office didn't leave Jake Jr. much time for a social life, but he did finally marry just after World War II, and his son—and only biological child—Edward (Ned) Titan was born in 1948. Unfortunately, Jake's wife died in childbirth, leaving Jake as a single father. (From this point forward, "Jake" will refer to the son, technically Jake Jr.)

This made Jake one of the most eligible bachelors in Pittsburgh, and mothers across the city were soon angling for advantage. Jake began to think that if he attended one more dinner party at which an eager, young, unattached woman happened to be seated next to him, he was going to scream.

Then Jake did something completely unexpected—he courted and married an older woman, a widow named Margaret Ellison who already had four children of her own. Margaret was five years older than Jake and had settled into what she thought of as a permanent widowhood. When she realized the young lawyer was actually interested in her, she considered the matter to be little more than amusing.

But Jake was nothing if not persistent. He bided his time, never pressing Margaret too hard, but never leaving her alone for too long, either. On

Sundays they would have tea together in the ornate lobby of the William Penn Hotel, lingering for hours, Jake regaling Margaret with stories of the clients whose affairs he handled. Since Jake was now the managing partner of J. Titan & Partners, and since the firm was growing rapidly once again, Jake had many stories to tell.

On one of these occasions, Margaret expressed disagreement with Jake about how he was about to proceed on a matter. Astonished, and at first annoyed, Jake demanded to know how Margaret would handle the case. Patiently, and a little delicately, Margaret told him. The essence of the matter was that Jake was representing a young man named Eldridge who was hoping to build a better barge, barges being critical to Pittsburgh's reputation as America's then-busiest inland port. The ideas young Eldridge had come up with were quite interesting—they promised to shorten the time required to complete a barge by nearly 50%—but the young man himself was too much of a dreamer ever to put his ideas to work.

Jake's plan was to ease the fellow out of his own newly formed company by merging the firm into a holding company controlled by Jake and several of his clients. Margaret objected, not so much because she thought it was unfair, but because she felt that if Jake continued to follow in his father's footsteps, that is, developing a growing reputation as a sharp dealer, both Jake and his law firm would eventually suffer.

Jake could hardly believe his ears. Who was Margaret Ellison to give business advice to Jake Titan? But as the conversation continued, Margaret remaining completely unflappable in the face of Jake's irritation, Jake found himself coming around to her point of view. His father *did* have a reputation for engaging in sharp practices—not precisely dishonest dealings, but *barely* honest ones. And Jake had learned some of these practices all too well. He'd already noticed, though he'd mainly tried to ignore it, that many young entrepreneurs were taking their business elsewhere.

Impressed with Margaret's insight, Jake asked her to marry him on the spot. And on the spot, Margaret agreed that she would think about it.

They did eventually marry, of course. By that time Jake's son, Ned, was four years old, as was Margaret's youngest daughter, Rose. Ned and Rose would grow up almost as twins, remaining remarkably close throughout their lives. Ned would eventually become the managing partner at J. Titan & Partners. Rose would marry a young client of J. Titan, a fellow named Landon Wainwright, who'd started a business offering commercial laundry services to hospitals, hotels, and similar businesses.

THE TITAN FAMILY TREE

George Titan Branch

George Titan, 1834–1915 (m. Ellie McCabe)
George Titan Jr., 1868–1938
Ellie Titan, 1901–1908
Grace Titan, 1902–1978
George Titan III, 1904–1981
(Other descendants, no longer wealthy)

Jake Titan Branch

George Titan, 1834–1915 (m. Ellie McCabe)
Andrew Titan, 1869–1919
Jake Titan Sr., 1891–1945
Jake Titan Jr., 1921–2007
Ned Titan, 1948–
Suzy, 1984–
Geoffrey, 1991–
Rose Titan Wainwright, 1949–
Ellen, 1983–
Billy, 1987–

SUMMARY

Now that we've introduced the first three generations of one branch of the Titan family (the one now headed by George Titan III), and five generations of another branch (the one now headed by Ned Titan and Rose Wainwright), we'll move on to their various adventures with managing their capital.

But before we do, I would emphasize the importance of a family's history and background to a financial advisor's ability to succeed with the family. You can't really know the man or woman without knowing something about their parents and grandparents. It's not always easy to get this kind of information, but it's worth going after it.

NOTE

1. See William S. Dietrich II, *Eminent Pittsburghers: Profiles of the City's Founding Industrialists* (Lanham, MD, Taylor Trade, 2011), 7–8.

CHAPTER 1

George Titan III and His Catastrophic Mistake

PREPARATION AND USE

George Titan III was the third child and only son of George Titan Jr. and his wife, Mary (see Chapter 1). George had a difficult career at Titan Industries, and was let go by Smythson Brothers following its acquisition of Titan. However, when his father died George became the patriarch of that branch of the family and inherited responsibility for its investment portfolio. His sister, Grace, would probably have been a better choice, but in those days it was assumed that the males in the family would handle business and investment matters.

And this is an important point. In some families in the early and mid-twentieth century, the brains of the family happened to fall mainly on the female side. But decision-making responsibilities continued to lie in the male line, right up until fairly recently. This meant that those families were fielding second-string players instead of their best, and sometimes that situation would come back to bite them. As we will see, such was the case with the George Titan III branch of the family.

HOW NOT TO MANAGE YOUR FAMILY'S MONEY

For decades, the capital of the children of George Titan Jr. had been managed by a local Pittsburgh trust company, the one selected by George Titan Jr. years earlier. But shortly after World War II the trust company was acquired by a local bank, and over the years that bank decided it wanted to become a world-class investment manager and to compete globally for investment business.

Up to that point, the family's portfolio had been managed very cautiously, with half the capital always invested in bonds. But as time went by, and as their bank advisor developed many new products, they sold those products to George III, convincing him to invest more and more aggressively.

QUICK NOTE

This episode illustrates the danger of a family behaving too passively in the face of industry changes. The acquisition of the trust company by a bank completely changed the identity and nature of George Titan's advisor, but he went along with it without, apparently, realizing how consequential the change was.

Note that there is nothing wrong with investing aggressively. Many families have done it with great success for many years. But aggressive investing leaves precious little margin for error. If you're driving your car at 40 miles per hour, a lot of bad things can happen on the road and you'll still have plenty of time to adjust. But at 80 miles per hour, you'd better be on high alert at all times. George III thought of himself as a far-above-average investor, but as we will see, he was confusing brilliance with a bull market.

The American Stock Market Turns Sour

The late 1960s had seen strong equity markets in the United States, but the year is now 1974 and it is mid-July. George III is 70 years old and has been overseeing the family investment portfolio from his office at Lawburn (the Titan family office) for many years.

George III considered himself to be an astute investor, and both under the local trust company and, later, under the bank, George believed that the family's capital had been well-managed. Following the Allied victory in World War II, the United States had become the world's most powerful country. It's main competitors at the time—Germany, Japan, and Britain—had all been devastated in the war and the U.S. economy expanded rapidly.

The American stock market had kept pace with this growth, so that even net of the family's rather heavy spending—about 5% of the capital's value every year—the portfolio had continued to grow in both nominal and real terms. Basically, since the end of World War II the U.S. stock market had been on a consistent upward march. During the decade of the 1950s, for example, the Dow rose from just over 200 to over 600. The surge slowed a bit in the 1960s, but even so the Dow rose to 800 during that decade, and there were several official bull markets late in the decade (1962–1966 and 1967–1968).

In 1972, the Dow Jones Industrial Average had gained 15%, and most investors believed that the good times would continue. The 1970s would be at least as good as the 1960s, and maybe as good as the 1950s. *Time* magazine, for example, in early January 1973, predicted that 1973 was "shaping up as a gilt-edged year."[1]

But the prognosticators were badly off-target. On January 11, 1973, the Dow began a dive that would result in one of the worst bear markets in history. Over the following 699 days, through December 1974, the Dow dropped 45%. Making matters worse, inflation, which had been just over 3% in 1972, jumped to 12.3% in 1974. In other words, in inflation-adjusted terms the losses were even greater. And while the market was crashing, so was the U.S. economy, where GDP growth dropped from +7.2% in 1972 to −2.1% in 1974. (Matters were even worse elsewhere. The London FT 30 Index, a predecessor of today's FT 100 Index, dropped 73% during the bear market.)

All this stunned George III who, as noted earlier, had presided over two decades of excellent returns and who had forgotten that those returns were driven mainly by strong market conditions and not by his excellent investment judgment. As the markets continued to sink throughout 1973 and into 1974, George began to raise hell with his bank investment managers.

But those advisors believed that investors should think long term. Sure, the market was currently in a bear phase, their thinking went, but that wasn't a permanent condition. Sooner or later, the market would turn up again, and when it did, families like the Titans needed to be heavily exposed to stocks in order to take advantage of the rebound.

But the result of this thinking was that the bank was continually "averaging down," as George indignantly put it, selling good bonds to buy bad stocks. Whatever the bank bought, it promptly went down.

QUICK NOTE

Here is a case of the family's advisor giving them reasonably good advice, but not couching it in terms the family could accept. Quarter-after-quarter of "averaging down" convinced George Titan that the bank didn't know what it was doing, that it was just operating on automatic pilot.

By the first quarter of 1974, George was getting questions from his wife and (adult) children about what was going on in the portfolio. They were naturally concerned that, as the value of their capital plummeted, their spending might have to be cut. In an effort to keep the pressure off, George III didn't cut the family's spending, but as a result, that spending grew and grew as a percentage of the capital that supported it.

As noted earlier, at the end of the 1960s the George III branch of the family had been spending 5% of its capital every year. This was too high, but George III was analogizing his family to the endowments of the nonprofit organizations on whose boards he served, most of which spent about 5% per year. But George had forgotten that nonprofit endowments don't pay taxes and that, typically, they are large enough to pay much lower investment management fees than families pay. Moreover, endowed institutions have a fallback in the event of poor outcomes: they can go out and raise more money. Try *that* as a family.

George's family should have been spending more like 3% of their capital each year, even in good times. But as the value of the portfolio plummeted throughout 1973 and 1974, and as the family's spending remained constant, the percentage they were spending grew and grew, causing the capital to decline even faster. By early summer of 1974, the George III branch of the Titan family was spending more than 8% of the portfolio's value.

The family's account managers at the bank were alarmed by the high spending, and they would sometimes (very gently) raise the issue with George III. But the patriarch's view was that it was none of the bank's business how much the family spent, and so the conversation went nowhere.

George III Makes a Fateful Decision

As his family's losses deepened, George III found himself losing sleep. He became difficult to live with, snapping at Mary and avoiding his friends. Finally, at the end of June 1974, George III took a room at the Rolling Rock Club, locked his door, and spent the better part of three days reviewing the performance of the family's portfolio under his management—going all the way back to World War II.

As he worked his way forward from the war years to the present day, George noticed something he'd never focused on before. As mentioned above, immediately after the war everything went America's way. But this was because our competitors in Europe and Japan had been flattened in the war while America was hardly touched.

By the 1960s, while things still looked good in America and while the market was still moving up, albeit not so sharply, it was obvious to George that looks were deceiving. Europe and Japan were recovering rapidly, thanks in many cases to generous help from America, and competition from those quarters was beginning to bite. Already steel from Germany and Japan was beginning to show up in the United States, and it was not only cheaper than our own steel, it was in many cases of better quality.

American investors, lulled into somnolence by two decades of easy money, had been asleep at the switch. But in the early 1970s those investors woke up and realized that America had fallen behind Europe and Japan, to say nothing of a resurgent Soviet Union. Suddenly, no one wanted to own stocks.

George returned to his office and scheduled a family meeting for mid-July. That meeting would also be held at the Rolling Rock Club, a tony country club founded by Pittsburgh's Mellon family. George had reserved a secluded meeting room behind the Card Room, most easily accessed by a secret door through the bookcases. George wanted to be sure no one would hear what he had to say except his own family. His advisors at the bank weren't invited, and only one young lawyer from the family's law firm would be there to take notes.

When the family was assembled and drinks had been served, George rose to his feet and made a long and impassioned speech. That speech clocked in at 37 minutes, but we'll look at an edited version of it here. The essence of the matter was that, the very next day, George planned to instruct the bank to sell every stock in the family portfolio. Because some of the positions were large and thinly traded, it would be the end of August before the family was completely out of stocks, but after that the family would own not a single equity security.

There were a few gasps around the table when George announced this decision, but the patriarch held up his hand for silence.

"I want to be quite clear about this," he said. "All across the world investors are dumping their stocks because of the bear market. But that's not what's driving my decision. No one likes to lose money, of course, and no one especially likes to lose money month in and month out for eighteen months.

"But long-term investors know that bear markets come and go, just as bull markets come and go. To pull out of the stock market just because stocks are going down is a very foolish thing to do. And that's not what I'm doing.

"If I continued to have confidence in American industry—indeed, in America itself—I would simply hold on, knowing that sooner or later the markets will turn and we will be making money again. But—and I say this in sadness and regret—I've lost that confidence."

George went on to describe how American businesses had thrived after the war, and how they appeared to be continuing to thrive during the 1960s. But that was just surface momentum and investor hardheadedness. In fact, it was in the 1960s that America began to lose its way.

"I don't have to remind you what was happening on our college campuses in the Sixties," George said, glancing pointedly at his grandchildren. "Hippies everywhere, antiwar activists blowing up buildings, administrators who should know better throwing in the towel and capitulating to the demonstrators.

"And you all know what happened to us in Vietnam. America had never lost a war before, but in Southeast Asia we cut and ran. The American public has no stomach for war anymore, and keep in mind that that's when Rome began to decline, too.

"How many of you in this room have waited in a long line to buy gas?" Hands went up. "Do you know why? Because America allowed itself to become dependent on oil from the Middle East, that's why. When we backed Israel in the Yom Kippur War, the Arabs embargoed our oil and forced us to our knees. We made Israel back down because we were desperate for oil, for oil at any price! We used to pay about three dollars a barrel for oil, but now it's twelve dollars and no end in sight.

"And what about what's going on in the White House? I voted for Nixon, and I'm sure—I *hope* I'm sure—that many of you did, too. But God knows what he thinks he's been doing down there in Washington. I hear he could resign any day. Imagine that! A president of the United States forced out of office for possible criminal activities! It's unbelievable!" (In fact, President Nixon resigned less than a month after George III spoke, on August 9, 1974.)

George took a long swallow of his martini, shook his head in disbelief at what had happened to his country, and then continued.

"The worst of it all is what's happened to American industry. When my grandfather—your great-grandfather and great-great-grandfather—came to America, he came because we were the greatest country in the world, a country full of opportunity. American companies were the most competitive anywhere.

"When the United States Steel Company was organized right here in Pittsburgh just after the turn of the century, it was the largest and most powerful firm in the world. Imagine! The United States of America, barely a century old, had outdone all the countries of Europe and Asia.

"But look at U.S. Steel today—it's a pathetic shell of its former self. Sure, they've built themselves a fine new building, but they're not half as good at making steel as they are at building fancy headquarters.

"In fact," George continued, really warming to his message now, "I wouldn't even call it a company. It's more like a bureaucracy, like something you'd find in the government. There are so many layers of management at U.S. Steel they can never get anything done. No one can make a decision, and in the rare cases when a decision gets made it's impossible to know who was responsible for it.

"All U.S. Steel's management cares about is preserving labor peace, and they've bought it by selling out to the unions. Do you know that a young steelworker who's willing to work overtime can earn almost fifty thousand dollars a year? Do you know what a young lawyer, straight out of Harvard, makes a year?"

George looked around the room, but no one seemed to know the answer.

"Well, I'll tell you: twelve thousand. Yes! A Harvard-trained lawyer in Pittsburgh makes twelve thousand dollars a year, while an uneducated steelworker makes fifty thousand! How long do you think that's going to last? I predict the American steel industry'll be dead in twenty years, if not sooner. And where the steel industry goes, so goes the rest of American industry."

George looked around the room. Everyone was riveted, staring at him. He nodded his head at them and continued.

"If I had confidence in America, in American business, I wouldn't be selling stocks. No, I'd be a *buyer* at these prices! I'm not selling out because of the bear market, I'm selling out because the American Century is over. We've had our day in the sun, but just like every other great civilization, we rose and now we've fallen. Some of you might remember that Russian Premier Khrushchev told us way back in 1959, 'We will bury you!' Well, the Russians *have* buried us, not by beating us in war, but by beating us in peace. And Germany and Japan have beaten us, too.

"I don't say any of this out of anything but sadness, deep and abiding sadness for the country I love, for the *city* I love. But it's my family I have to think of first. We've lost a lot of money over the past year and a half—nearly forty percent of our capital, in fact. But we're still rich and I want to be sure we stay that way. By the end of next month we'll be entirely out of stocks. Our wealth will be secure. Thank you."

George set down and drained the rest of his martini, then ordered another. For a long moment there was silence around the table, but then someone started to clap. Others took up the applause and soon George Titan III was being given a standing ovation by his family.

QUICK NOTE

One important thing to note here is that George Titan stated that he wasn't exiting the stock market because he was in a panic over his losses. Instead, he couched his decision in broader terms. But note that when a family panics during a bear market, there will almost always be "broader terms." Often, the broader terms will have to do with not wanting the family's asset base to drop below a certain, usually arbitrary, point.

The Aftermath of George's Decision

The extraordinary thing about this episode in the Titan family is this: George III was right—or nearly right—about almost everything he said. And yet, the decision to sell all the family's stocks proved to be an utter debacle, destroying his family's capital almost entirely in one generation.

How could this be? The main problem was that George Titan III failed to consider the resilience of the American economy and the American people. He was correct that conditions were dire in the mid-1970s in America—a few years later, in 1979, President Carter would give his famous "malaise" speech in which he opined that Americans were suffering from a "crisis of confidence."

But Americans had faced far worse challenges over the prior 200 years: fighting for their freedom against Great Britain, then the most powerful country in the world; engaging in one of the most destructive civil wars in human history; entering World War I barely in time to turn the tide; surviving the Great Depression; leading the fight in World War II, where Americans were forced to battle powerful foes on two fronts thousands of miles away. George should have been able to put the current malaise in perspective, but he didn't.

Even as George was addressing his family at the Rolling Rock Club, the bear market was coming to an end. Stock prices would continue to jump around until December 1974, but looking back it's clear that the terrible downdrafts ended in August, a few weeks after George spoke to his family.

The Dow eventually settled near 578 on December 4, 1974, but in 1975 and 1976, the stock markets snapped back, as they usually do after a bear market, closing just above 1,000 at the end of 1976. By the end of 1980 the Dow was back where it had been at its peak in 1972.

But none of this mattered to George III's branch of the Titan family, because they were no longer invested in stocks. The family had ridden the bear market all the way to the bottom, then sold out (immortalizing their losses), paid heavy capital gains taxes, and then failed to reinvest.

Missing the 1975–1976 recovery was bad enough, but most of the family remained invested entirely in bonds throughout the 1980s and 1990s. George Titan III died in 1981, but he had run the family's capital entirely on his own for a very long time, and as a result no one else had any experience investing money. If bonds were good enough for their father, bonds were good enough for them. Besides, their spending needs were very great and stocks yielded very little.

The bank that was advising them had made a few timid suggestions to the effect that it might be a good idea to get back into the stock market, but it never happened. Stocks made the family uncomfortable, and the family patriarch had made it clear before his death that owning stocks was a fool's errand.

QUICK NOTE

Once it became clear that George Titan was not just exiting the stock market, which was bad enough, but that he planned to stay out indefinitely, query whether the bank shouldn't have resigned as his advisor. Note that if a lawyer's client refuses to take his advice, the lawyer may be required by the Code of Professional Responsibility to resign. A wealth advisor's ethical compass should be at least as sensitive.

In 1982, one of the great bull markets in history began, running almost uninterrupted until 1999, when investor enthusiasm slammed into the "tech bust" and prices collapsed. During those 17 years, many investors built large fortunes in the markets, but, again, the George Titan III family missed out on all of it.

Eventually, the combination of no portfolio growth and high spending made it clear even to the most unsophisticated family members that matters couldn't long continue. But by then a new generation of Titans had come along, and, while *per capita* spending did decline, *absolute* spending increased.

The end result was highly predictable: by the late 1990s, the George III branch of the family was no longer wealthy. From the end of World War II through the 1970s, that branch of the family had been one of Pittsburgh's most prominent. George III and his wife, Mary, sat on all the important boards in town and were members of all the right clubs. Everyone knew who they were and their opinions mattered. But by the end of the 1990s, the Titans were a middle-class family, struggling to avoid falling even further. No one knew who they were or cared. They had become the "poor" Titans.

THE MISTAKES GEORGE MADE

When a family's wealth is devastated through investment errors, there is usually more than one mistake in the picture. Let's walk through some of the mistakes George Titan III made in managing his family's money.

Failing to Learn and Grow

Although George Titan III had managed his family's portfolio for more than three decades, he knew very little more about the investment process in 1974 than he'd known in 1938. If we'd asked George about this, he would have dismissed the question—after all, George had advisors whose job it was to understand these sorts of things, and he paid them high fees to do so.

George would have viewed investment advice as similar to any other kind of advice or service he might need. For example, George knew very little about how his furnaces worked, but so what? He had a contractor who handled that sort of thing. Similarly, George saw no reason to learn about investing, because he had advisors who handled that sort of thing.

What George forgot was the difference in the *consequences* of failure. If his furnace failed, the only consequence was that George needed to buy a new one. This might be a serious annoyance if the furnace happened to fail in January, but it would hardly be a catastrophe.

But if George's portfolio failed, that would be a family tragedy that would haunt the George Titan III family members for generations. There are big differences between furnace failures and portfolio failures, but George never picked up on this important point.

What George should have done was to learn enough about the investment process at least to be a thoughtful client, a prudent overseer of his family's wealth. He could have achieved this objective by requiring his advisors to help teach him about the investment process. He could also have attended conferences and seminars at which investment issues are discussed. He could have read books on investing or he could have joined the local Pittsburgh affinity group of family offices, which offered regular investment seminars, as well as contacts with other family offices.

Unfortunately, George did none of this. He relied as heavily on his financial advisors as he did on his furnace contractor, and the results were very unfortunate.

Working with the Wrong Advisor

When the trust company that had managed the Titan portfolio was acquired by a bank, the nature of George Titan III's financial advisor changed radically. The bank was a very fundamentally different creature from the trust company and the chance that it would just happen to be appropriate for the family was very low. But George simply went along passively with the change. It's true, of course, that the trust company had been acquired by a Pittsburgh-based bank that George was somewhat familiar with and that many people he knew banked with. But George knew nothing about the bank's (rapidly evolving) money management capabilities.

As noted, the bank had decided to get into the investment business in a big way and had begun buying up money management firms and hiring scores of investment professionals. Today, in 2015, that bank manages billions of dollars for pension funds and individuals. But along the way the bank went through many difficult periods.

Building a global money management business almost from scratch is a huge undertaking. Many of the firms the bank acquired promptly produced dismal performance numbers. The investment professionals who had built those firms had just cashed out on the sale and no longer much cared about the hard work of managing money.

But since George knew nothing about the investment management business, it never occurred to him that, behind the scenes, things were not well at the bank. And since the bank was reporting on its own performance, it was usually able to sweep poor results under the rug. Those results were in the account statements somewhere, but George wasn't likely to find them on his own, and the bank had no incentive to point them out.

Being Sold Instead of Buying

Over the decades, the bank's advisory personnel managed to sell George just about every hot new product they could dream up. Some of these products were actually useful and appropriate for the Titans, but many were not. Inside the bank, George was notorious for his willingness to buy just about anything the bank had to sell.

But a family that hopes to do well in the investment of its capital should never, ever be *sold* anything. The family should, instead, be an active, knowledgeable and proactive *buyer* of investment services and products.

The way the process should work is that a family looks at the risk and return profile of its portfolio and decides that (let's say) it needs to reduce its risk but, hopefully, without reducing its returns by a similar amount. The family will then look around for ways to accomplish this and might (for example) decide to replace some of its long equity managers with long/short hedge fund managers. The family will look for the best long/short managers in the business and engage one or two of them.

But that's not how it worked with George Titan III. Instead, George would show up at a meeting with his advisors and find that they had a new idea for him. The bank had recently purchased a hedge fund, and the advisors thought the find would be a useful addition to the family's portfolio. The advisors would walk George through reams of data showing how terrific the hedge fund's returns had been, and eventually, with George lost in the details, he would tell the advisors, sure, let's give it a try.

Maybe the family's portfolio needed a hedge fund and maybe it didn't. George would never know. Maybe this was the best hedge fund for the family and maybe it wasn't (in fact, the odds were huge that it wasn't), but, again, George would never know.

Abandoning the Equity Markets

The biggest error George Titan III made was his decision to abandon the equity markets. A wealthy family, like it or not, is in the business of managing capital, and it's a tough business to be in. Families pay taxes, they pay investment management fees, they spend money from the portfolio, and, of course, inflation constantly eats away at the value of the capital. And as if all that weren't enough, families tend to compound faster than capital does, so that even successful families will likely see their *per capita* wealth drop across the generations.

Given all these headwinds, it's essential that family portfolios be growth-oriented, and that means owning stocks. George's rationale for selling equities may have resonated at the time, but longer term it was a calamitous, utterly destructive act. When George sold out, the family's portfolio had already declined by about 40%. Selling immortalized those losses. Then, with no growth assets in the portfolio, it was impossible for the family to recoup.

As noted previously, if George had simply held on for a few more months, the stock markets would have resumed their upward trend. The strong markets of 1975 and 1976 wouldn't have restored the family to its former wealth, but it would have been a nice start. Then, when the big bull market started in 1982, the family would have enjoyed 17 long years of mainly very strong markets. They would have been much wealthier in 1999 than they'd been in 1972, before the 1973–1974 bear markets.

But it wasn't to be. George Titan III's investment mistakes, and especially the devastating decision to abandon equities, destroyed his family's wealth.

WHAT A GOOD ADVISOR COULD HAVE DONE FOR THE TITANS

For advisors to wealthy families, there are many lessons here, but perhaps the main one is this: a successful wealth advisor must grapple with much more than capital markets. Let's examine some of the ways George Titan III's advisors might have helped prevent the very unfortunate outcome described earlier.

Putting the Client First

Advisors shouldn't even think about working with wealthy families unless they are willing to place the clients' interests above their own. This should be true of any financial advisor, but unfortunately the Securities and Exchange

Commission (SEC) has seen fit to allow most advisors to put their own interests first.

The first words on the SEC's website are these: "The mission of the U.S. Securities and Exchange Commission is to protect investors."[2] In fact, it would be more accurate to say, "The mission of the SEC is to protect large brokerage firms." The brokerage industry has lobbied the SEC hard to avoid having to put their clients' interests ahead of their own, and so far they have always succeeded.

As we'll see in the next chapter, some advisors are fiduciaries, meaning that, as a matter of law, they must elevate their clients' interests above their own. Mainly, these are so-called RIAs (registered investment advisors). But most financial advisors, including the ones George Titan III used, are *not* fiduciaries.

These other advisors, constituting the vast majority of financial advisory professionals, operate under a loosey-goosey rule known as the *suitability standard*. In other words, so long as an investment is "suitable" for the client, non-fiduciary advisors are free of any further obligations to their clients.

In the case of George Titan III, every investment product the bank's advisory professionals sold George was suitable. Since the Titans were a wealthy family, it's almost impossible to imagine an investment that would be *prima facie un*suitable. Yet many of those products were very expensive, poorly performing, tax-inefficient, and had no business being in George's portfolio. But under the SEC definition, they were certainly suitable.

Ideally, every advisor to a wealthy family would be, legally, a fiduciary. But if advisors are working in environments where they aren't technically fiduciaries, they should always *act* as though they are. Thus, stockbrokers, insurance agents, and advisors working inside banks should put aside the suitability standard and provide advice that would meet any fiduciary standard.

But that's not what happened with the Titan III family. The bank's advisors sold George everything they could think of to sell him. This made the bank a lot of money, but it also made a mockery of the idea that the bank's professionals were *advisors* in any useful sense of the word.

Educating the Client

The goal of every wealth advisor should be to ensure that the client is more knowledgeable about the investment process every year of the engagement. This means that in every interaction with the client the advisor needs to be sure the client understands what is being discussed. At every client meeting, opportunities for education should be seized. At least once a year, time should be set aside at meetings for both the client and the advisor to become better informed about some aspect of the investment process. This can be done by using guest speakers, for example.

But George Titan III's advisors wasted none of their time trying to educate George about the investment world—after all, an ignorant client was a much more profitable client. If George had clearly understood the investment process, for example, he would have clearly understood how full of conflicts of interest his bank advisors were. That in turn may have led George to terminate his relationship with the bank. Hence, why educate George?

One dire consequence of George's lack of understanding of capital markets was that he was able to convince himself that America and its industries were in a terminal state of decline. George didn't grasp the way capitalism works: when companies get fat and lazy, they become easy targets for people who want to turn them into lean competitors again, and a lot of money can be made doing this.

Beginning with the Reagan tax cuts and the deregulatory activity of the 1980s, the leveraged buyout (LBO) industry was born. Firms like Kolberg Kravis & Roberts would raise capital, leverage that capital with borrowings from banks, then buy up units of companies or even whole companies. They would then strip out redundant layers of management, eliminate excess employment, bring in new management, and provide strong incentives for those managers to deliver on profit targets.

As the value of the now-competitive companies rose, the LBO firm would take the companies public again (or sell them to larger firms) at much higher price multiples than they had originally paid. Add on the effect of leverage and the LBO firms—and their limited partner investors—made huge sums of money.

Thousands of uncompetitive firms were transformed in this manner, and thousands of other firms, observing that they were in the crosshairs of the LBO artists, transformed *themselves* rather than being taken out. By the 1990s, American industry, which had been moribund in the 1970s, had become fearsome, so much so that every developed country in the world had to respond or be crushed.

George, unfortunately, understood none of this. He saw American businesses becoming increasingly uncompetitive and he assumed that trend would go on forever. It was a deadly error.

Focusing on Spending

Many families overspend, and the George Titan III family was no exception. A driving force behind overspending is almost always a lack of appreciation by the family of the *consequences* of spending too much.

George III's advisors did, tentatively, raise the issue of spending on one or two occasions, but George shut them down and they never raised it again.

What the advisors could have done was to have prepared analyses showing the *impact* on the family's wealth of spending at various levels.

Consider, for example (this is a very simplified analysis), a family that spends 5% of the value of its capital every year, as the George Titan III family was doing even before the bear market hit. It doesn't take a rocket scientist to run through a simple calculation like this:

Expected *after-tax* return on the portfolio: 6%

Investment fees: (1%)

Inflation: (3%)

Portfolio growth before spending: 2%

Spending: 5%

Net portfolio growth: (3%)

George Titan III may not have been the best steward of his family's capital, but a chart like that, showing that over the three decades of his oversight the portfolio would decline very significantly or even disappear altogether, might well have gotten his attention.

Taking Private Capital Seriously

The bank that was advising the George Titan III family certainly took the *business* of advising private capital seriously. It spent lavishly to build its investment management business and also spent heavily to market it. For a bank, a large wealth management business offers important advantages.

The problem for banks is that lending is sometimes a good business and sometimes a bad business, depending on interest rate and economic conditions. Investors don't like earnings volatility, so a bank that generates its earnings mainly from its credit activities will sell at a relatively low price/earnings ratio.

A healthy wealth management business, on the other hand, provides a bank with an annuity-like stream of revenue and earnings, which investors prize. Such a bank will sell at a higher multiple of earnings. Therefore, for the bank's senior management, building a strong wealth management business made a lot of sense.

The problem was that the bank didn't take private capital *itself* seriously. The bank and its advisors viewed wealthy families essentially as prey. The idea was to hunt these families down, get them to engage the bank as their advisor, and then sell them everything they could sell and charge fees as high as they could get away with.

This lack of respect for private capital virtually ensured that any client of the bank that began to go off the rails would continue to go off the rails. The bank simply failed to understand the nature of private capital and the crucial role it plays in the American economy and way of life.

I've discussed this point in depth elsewhere, but here is the essence of the matter:

> *Private capital is critically important because it is the progenitor of all other forms of capital. Governments possess capital, but only because they tax it away from private individuals. Corporations possess capital, but only because individuals have voluntarily invested their capital in corporate stocks and bonds. Colleges and universities and charitable foundations and nonprofit groups of all kinds possess capital (in the form of endowments and operating funds), but only because private individuals have donated that capital.*[3]

Just to take one simple example, wealthier families pay roughly 80% of all federal income taxes. If all private capital went the way of the capital of the George Titan III family, taxes on middle-income people would have to skyrocket. More broadly, almost everything that makes America unique would cease to exist, and in terms of our economic, cultural, military, and financial characteristics we would look more like, say, the peripheral countries of Europe.

But no one at the bank ever thought about these matters. When the George Titan III family's capital disappeared, it was a catastrophe for the family, but it was no more than a minor annoyance to the bank. The family's capital was completely gone while the bank had merely lost a small portion of its annual revenue.

It's a dirty little secret in the wealth advisory business that many wealth advisors quietly despise their own clients. If we could have injected the bank's advisors with truth serum, we would have found that many of them resented George's wealth and his privileged status in the community. After all, they would have said, George III didn't make the money. Even George's father, George Titan Jr., didn't make it. The family fortune was made by George III's *grandfather*.

Let's face it, George Titan III wasn't a very sympathetic character. But so what? There are plenty of middle-income people who aren't very sympathetic, either, but that doesn't cause us to despise the middle class.

George III's advisors were making the mistake of confusing the importance of the *owner* of the capital with the importance of the *capital itself*. Private capital is what distinguishes America from other societies that are superficially similar, and it is what is largely responsible for American exceptionalism: the extraordinary success America has experienced versus its international competitors for more than 200 years.[4]

Advisors who allow their personal biases to color the quality of their advisory work simply shouldn't be in the business. Unfortunately, this describes all too many of the so-called professionals in the wealth advisory business today.

SUMMARY

The main point in this chapter is that advisors who aspire to work with wealthy families have an obligation to understand much more than capital markets. The kinds of mistakes families can make range from the trivial and easily rectified to the catastrophic. A competent wealth advisor needs to help families navigate these treacherous waters every step of the way.

In order to be successful, wealth advisors must first and foremost understand the important role private capital plays in America, and, therefore, the important role wealth advisors play. Private capital is enormously hard to create and, once created, it needs to persist for many generations if it is to do its work on America's behalf.

Beyond that, wealth advisors must put their clients' interests ahead of their own. Whatever platform advisors are working from, they need to conduct themselves as though they were fiduciaries, even if, technically, they are not.

Successful wealth advisors need to help their clients become better investors and help them understand the consequences of overspending and overpaying. Advisors who fall short of these goals are shortchanging their clients, of course, but they are also shortchanging themselves, their firms, and the reputation of the financial advisory business.

NOTES

1. Issue of January 8, 1973.
2. http://www.sec.gov/about/whatwedo.shtml#.VMggLcaIcqw.
3. Gregory Curtis, *The Stewardship of Wealth: Successful Private Wealth Management for Investors and Their Advisors* (Hoboken, NJ: John Wiley & Sons, 2013), 42 ff.
4. I discuss this important issue at great length in Part One of *The Stewardship of Wealth*, op. cit., note 3, pages 1–50.

CHAPTER 2

Ned and Rose Succeed Jake as Co-Heads of the Family

PREPARATION AND USE

Edward (Ned) Titan, as you may recall, was the only biological child of Jake Titan Jr. Ned's mother died in childbirth and, after Jake remarried, Ned became very close to his stepsister, Rose, who was exactly his age. Ned and Rose remained close throughout their lives, and when Jake relinquished control of their branch of the family's investment portfolio in 2005, Ned and Rose jointly took responsibility for it.

NED AND ROSE REACT TO GEORGE III'S DECISION TO SELL EQUITIES

Ned and Rose were only in their mid-twenties in 1974, when George Titan III made his fateful decision to sell all the stocks owned by his branch of the family. They were certainly aware of their uncle's action, but they didn't really understand it or its consequences. They experienced George's decision mainly through the eyes of their father, Jake Titan Jr.

Jake admitted that he was sympathetic with much of what George III had said to his family. Like George III, Jake had lost a lot of the family money in the 1973–1974 bear market, although, fortunately, his portfolio was down only about 30%, versus 40% for George III. This was because Jake had kept his portfolio more conservatively invested.

But, like George III, Jake also feared for the future of his country. Jake pointed out to Ned and Rose that the United States was then the only important country in the world that still followed a capitalistic, free market economy. Following the Russian Revolution, which had occurred just before Jake was born and which didn't seem like ancient history to him, the world entered a long period of struggle between forces of the far left—communism—and forces of the far right—fascism.

In Russia (and later in China and Eastern Europe), communism had prevailed, while in Germany (Hitler), Italy (Mussolini), and Spain (Franco), fascism had prevailed. But World War II had discredited fascism, which was defeated everywhere except in Spain, while communism emerged as victorious.

In the postwar era, virtually the entire world had moved leftward, adopting either communist or socialist economic models. All of Western Europe was socialist, as was India and much of Latin America. Russia, China, Eastern Europe, and North Korea were communist. Jake felt it was only a matter of time before the United States succumbed as well. After all, George III had been right about how many of America's largest companies had already become similar to large government bureaucracies, with many layers of management and no one charged with responsibility.

But Jake's opinion differed from that of his cousin in two ways. First, Jake had spent his entire legal career representing bright young people whose ideas were being carried out by enterprising companies that were nothing like the swollen bureaucracies George III described. Thus, Jake's view of American competitiveness was more nuanced than George III's.

Second, Jake believed that America was an energetic, resilient society that had the ability to recover from its mistakes. He had lived through the Great Depression—Jake had been only eight years old when the market crashed in 1929—but he had also lived to see America shake off the Depression and defeat Germany and Japan in World War II. He believed that somehow America would also shake off the malaise of the 1970s and return to its former greatness.

In the end, Jake had decided not to follow George III's example, and he held onto his stocks through the end of the bear market. As a result, Jake was still invested when the markets began their recovery in 1975 and 1976. And he continued to be invested throughout the legendary bull market that began in 1982 and persisted almost uninterrupted until the year 2000. This was an investment lesson Ned and Rose would not soon forget.

QUICK NOTE

Knowing something about a family's history and experience with investments and the capital markets can be very important in helping an advisor anticipate what the family might do during stressful times. In this case, of course, Ned and Rose Titan learned what *not* to do by observing their Uncle George's unfortunate decision.

JAKE PICKS NED AND ROSE AS CO-HEADS OF HIS BRANCH OF THE TITAN FAMILY

In mid-1999, Jake suffered a stroke. While he recovered, he realized that, like it or not, he wasn't going to live forever, and that he needed to begin transitioning authority over the family's investment portfolio to the next generation. It was natural for Jake to turn to his biological son, Ned. But Jake also did something unprecedented in the Titan family: he insisted that his stepdaughter, Rose, be co-head of the family.

As mentioned in Chapter 1, in most families, intelligence and other important traits tend to be evenly distributed between males and females. But in some families, the most capable family members turned out to be women. If those families continued to insist that major responsibility for family affairs rest with the men, they were fielding second-string players.

We observed this phenomenon with the George Titan III branch of the family. George III was a relatively unimpressive individual while his sister, Grace, was a remarkable woman. Yet, when George Titan Jr. gave up his responsibilities as head of the family, he turned not to Grace but to George III. The results turned out to be very unhappy for that branch of the family.

But the George III branch of the family had plenty of company in the middle of the twentieth century, as a great many wealthy American families continued to look only to the male line even when the female line was superior. The results weren't always as dramatic as they were for the George III branch of the family, but they were always substandard.

As far as Jake was concerned, there was nothing wrong with Ned. As a young man he had joined Jake's law office and had given a good account of himself. But Ned had in effect always worked for his father, and Jake feared that Ned would give too much weight to the way Jake had handled things, and not enough weight to how they actually needed to be handled under new circumstances.

Rose, on the other hand, was clearly the brightest person in the family. While Rose had never worked outside the home, she had always maintained a busy life as a volunteer. She was now in high demand by the region's non-profit organizations and was serving on several important boards.

Finally, Ned and Rose had been extremely close all their lives, and Jake knew he could count on them to work well together and to find ways to compromise when they disagreed.

Jake Begins to Train Ned and Rose in Investment Matters

On January 1, 2000, the beginning of the new century, Jake Titan formed an "investment committee" to oversee his branch of the family's money. The committee consisted of Jake, a stockbroker named Paul Winthrop, the family's attorney, Carl Schumacher, and Ned and Rose. The real purpose of the investment committee, in Jake's mind, was to help educate Ned and Rose in the complex business of managing the family's money.

At that point the money was being managed by a regional brokerage firm at which Paul Winthrop was the number-two executive. Winthrop had started his brokerage career at almost the same time that Jake had started his legal career. Winthrop would refer clients to Jake and Jake would reciprocate by sending business to Winthrop.

When the trust company that had been managing the Titan family money was acquired by the bank, Jake hadn't been happy. He liked the trust company and its cautious way of managing money while the bank was much more aggressive. Moreover, they were always trying to sell Jake whatever their hot new product was. Jake *hated* to be sold things, and he refused to buy almost everything the bank had on offer. Unfortunately, he refused to buy even when the product was actually a good one and would have played a useful role in the portfolio.

Eventually, Jake realized that he simply didn't trust the bank and that a change needed to be made. It was natural for him to turn his longtime friend, Paul Winthrop. Winthrop would also sell products to Jake, but he did it in an open and engaging manner, making it clear that he was profiting on the sale, but assuring Jake that he really believed in the product and that it would play a positive role in the portfolio.

The way the investment committee worked was that Ned and Rose pretty much kept their mouths shut during meetings. Jake had pointed out to them that Carl Schumacher was charging his usual hourly fees for attending investment committee meetings, and Jake didn't want those meetings extended unnecessarily while Carl's meter was running.

On the other hand, Jake encouraged Ned and Rose to take careful notes during the meeting, especially regarding anything they didn't understand. Then, after the meeting, Jake, Ned, and Rose would have their own meeting at which Jake would respond to their questions. This process worked so well that it wasn't long before Ned and Rose were carrying their own weight in the main meeting.

QUICK NOTE

Jake's decision to bring Ned and Rose onto the family investment committee and to begin their investment education was a good one. Unfortunately, it happened way too late. Ideally, a matriarch or patriarch should begin the investment education of the next generation far earlier and at a much younger age. As we will see, Ned and Rose's inexperience would come back to haunt them.

Ned and Rose Assume Full Responsibility and Don't Like What They See

In early 2005, Jake suffered another stroke, and his doctors insisted that he give up the stress of practicing law and managing his family's money. Jake had long ago stepped down as managing partner at his law firm, but he was still the senior partner, and at the age of 84 he still went into the office nearly every day.

But now Jake decided that, like it or not, it was time for him to retire. He gave up all his responsibilities at the law firm, merely keeping a small office and a secretary. He gave up his office at Lawburn (the Titan family office), which was remodeled into two offices for Ned and Rose.

When Jake stepped down, Paul Winthrop decided that the time had come for him to step down, as well. Winthrop was already semiretired from the regional brokerage firm, and at the end of 2005 he left the Titan account and asked a younger man, Frank Patterson, to take his place. At that time, then, the investment committee for the Jake Titan branch of the family consisted of Ned and Rose as co-chairs, Frank Patterson, representing the brokerage firm, and Carl Schumacher, the family lawyer.

Frank Patterson was an aggressive sales executive for the brokerage house, having parlayed his sales skills into making himself the firm's largest producer. He was given the Titan family account (Jake's branch) as a reward for a job well done. But Frank Patterson's relationship with Ned and Rose was very different from Paul Winthrop's relationship with Jake. What Frank should have done was to spend many months building an atmosphere of trust with the Titans. Unfortunately, though, Frank was too much of a salesman and too impatient.

At the very first meeting after he'd replaced Paul Winthrop, Frank Patterson recommended two new investment products to the Titans. "Both these managers," he told the investment committee, "have shot the lights out in recent years. You really can't go wrong with them."

"These managers have certainly had impressive performance," Ned responded. "But how'd they do back in the tech crash?"

The huge bull market that began in 1982 had finally hit the wall in 2000. All stocks were hard hit, but tech stocks took a particular pounding.

Frank looked at Ned blankly. He had no idea how they'd done. "I—I really don't know," he said. "But their three-year track record is great, and we usually look at three years of performance before we recommend a manager."

"You see," said Rose, "it might be that these two managers are terrific, but it also might be that they're just taking too much risk. And then, when the next bear market comes along, we'd lose an awful lot of money. That's why we're wondering how they did in, say, 2000 to 2002."

Back in his office at the brokerage firm, still licking his wounds, Frank learned that in fact the two managers he'd just presented to the Titans had produced dismal results during the tech crash. Both had loaded up on tech stocks for no better reason than that they were going up regularly. Frank realized that he'd gotten off on the wrong foot with his new client, but he was nothing if not resourceful.

At the next investment committee, Frank came better prepared. "This manager," he said, passing out summaries, "has done pretty well during the bull market, and he *really* did well during the bear market that started in 2000." Frank walked the investment committee members through the manager's results.

"Very impressive!" Rose remarked. "What's he charge?"

"One percent," Frank said, "like everybody else."

"And of that one percent," Ned asked, "how much goes to you?"

Frank Patterson was dumbstruck. In his entire career as a stockbroker, no one had ever inquired about the fee-sharing arrangements his firm negotiated with the managers they recommended. But Jake had taught Ned and Rose well. "I—I think those numbers are confidential," Frank stammered.

"The thing is," Ned continued, "we're wondering how objective your firm can be when it's being paid by the managers it recommends."

"On top of that, how many good managers are out there who we'll never see because they won't pay you?" Rose said.

"And, really, when you come to think about it," said Ned, "will you be willing to terminate this manager if he's underperforming? I mean, if you did, you'd lose your share of the fee."

Frank staggered out of the second investment committee meeting in even worse shape than he'd left the first meeting. After he'd left, Ned and Rose discussed whether they should keep their money with the brokerage firm, given the results of the last two meetings. But Carl Schumacher cautioned against any rash action. He pointed out that their father had retained the firm and obviously had confidence in it. In Carl's view, the committee should give Frank Patterson a chance to improve.

"Anyway," said Carl, "where would we go if we left the brokerage firm? All advisors have conflicts of interest, and at least Frank Patterson is the devil we know."

QUICK NOTE

It was almost certainly a mistake for Ned and Rose to remain with an advisor in whom they had lost confidence. But because they were still new at the investment game, and because Carl Schumacher had been around a long time and had been a confidant of their father's, they unfortunately deferred to Carl.

Ned and Rose agreed, albeit reluctantly, and no change was made. Over the next few years, however, Ned and Rose insisted that Frank Patterson be replaced on the account, and he was followed by a series of short-term advisors, none of whom impressed the investment committee.

However, the performance of the family's accounts was pretty good during those years. The markets were flat in 2005, but 2006 and most of 2007 were good years. As the summer of 2007 came along, the Titan family was working with a fellow named Reggie Clause, a senior broker at the regional brokerage firm. The Titans didn't know Clause terribly well, but he seemed to know his stuff.

In the spring of 2007, Carl Schumacher retired from J. Titan & Partners and, with that retirement, the investment committee for the Titan family essentially dissolved. Ned and Rose discussed reconstituting it, but they weren't sure who should be on the committee and so nothing was done.

The Titans and the Credit Crunch

The first hint of trouble came in the summer of 2007, with the so-called "credit crunch." An obscure corner of the financial markets—subprime mortgages—suddenly seized up. A couple of hedge funds at Bear Stearns had failed and Bear itself was reeling.

Ned and Rose had been co-heads of the Titan family office for only a short time, and the last thing they wanted to see was for the family's capital to melt away under their stewardship. At a specially called meeting Ned and Rose told Reggie Clause that they would like "to lighten up on risk." Reggie was perplexed. The family's portfolios had performed extremely well and a "little spot of trouble" at some hedge funds didn't seem to him to be worth worrying about.

After an extended conversation, Ned and Rose decided that a substantial amount of capital should be removed from the markets and put "somewhere safe." The amount they had in mind was $25 million. Reggie Clause agreed that he would confer with his partners at the brokerage firm and come back with a recommendation.

A few weeks later, Reggie sent to Ned and Rose what appeared to be a well-thought-out proposal. It identified which securities and funds should be liquidated to raise the $25 million, and it proposed to put the money in a "safe, money-market-like" account at Lehman Brothers. Reggie had included the paperwork required to establish such an account, along with investment guidelines that were complete gobbledygook to Ned and Rose. However, they liked the sound of a safe, money-market-like option, and so they signed the papers and sent them back to Reggie.

At the time, Ned and Rose were thinking that if they had a sizeable, very safe pool of capital set aside, they would be more comfortable riding out what surely looked to be choppy markets.

Unfortunately, the safe, money-market-like account Reggie Clause recommended—a fund highly touted by his firm—was actually an account that invested in "auction-rate notes." While a detailed description of these securities is beyond the scope of this chapter, their essence was that, although the notes had long maturities, the interest rate was reset every week or month via "Dutch auctions." Investors who wished to sell submitted to the auction the number of securities they wanted to auction off or the minimum yield they would accept to continue holding the securities. Buyers would specify the number of notes, in $25,000 denominations, they wished to buy and the lowest interest rate they would accept.

Issuers liked auction rate notes because bank loans were becoming quite expensive, and investors liked them because they paid higher interest than money market funds. Because the notes were issued with minimum denominations of $25,000, most of the individual investors who bought them were high-net-worth families like the Titans.

Unbeknownst to Ned and Rose, the SEC had already investigated the auction rate industry and had issued cease-and-desist orders. The Commission was particularly concerned that investors weren't being adequately warned about the possibility that the auctions could fail, resulting in sudden illiquidity for the investors. It was certainly true that nobody at Reggie Clause's firm, and nobody at Lehman Brothers, had mentioned anything about the fund freezing up. True, way back in the fine print was a disclosure about this supposedly remote possibility, but neither Ned nor Rose ever read that far.

Throughout the balance of 2007, the credit crisis continued, although it was largely out of sight of most investors—it affected mainly so-called "subprime mortgages" and securities linked to those credits. In June, two hedge funds managed by Bear Stearns faced huge losses, and Bear, highly leveraged against low-quality assets, would eventually be sold to JP Morgan for a song. By August, major players in the subprime market, such as Countrywide Financial, were on the verge of bankruptcy. Throughout the balance of the year, virtually every major bank and investment bank posted multibillion-dollar writedowns related to the credit crisis.

On January 22, 2008, the Federal Reserve, in a panic over conditions in the banking sector, cut interest rates by 75 basis points. A week later, the Fed announced another 50-basis-point cut. This was unprecedented, and it naturally alarmed Ned and Rose. Then matters got worse. In February, the Dutch auctions for the auction rate notes began to fail. Buyers could not be found, and the banks that had always backstopped the auctions as bidders-of-last-resort walked away. Suddenly, billions of dollars of safe, money-market-like securities—the auctionrate notes—became completely illiquid.

Stunned by this development, Ned and Rose summoned Reggie Clause to a meeting at Lawburn. When Clause arrived, he was distressed to notice that the Titans had brought a securities lawyer to the meeting. Clause expressed his own regret and bewilderment at the development with the auction rate account and promised to contact Lehman Brothers and find out what was going on. In the meantime, the $25 million that Ned and Rose had thought was invested in a safe manner simply could not be accessed.

QUICK NOTE

Although many family investors—and not a few institutional investors—were burned by auction-rate securities, none of this need have happened. As soon as Ned and Rose realized that they didn't understand what they were buying—that the investment guidelines were gobbledygook—they could have called a halt to the investment. They went ahead with it in part because of their inexperience and in part because they were overly impressed with the Lehman Brothers name. It was a hard and expensive lesson. But it's a lot to expect for investors to understand impenetrable disclosures. The real source of the problem was the greed of Lehman and the other brokers who sold auction-rate funds as substitutes for safe money market funds.

The Titans and the Financial Crisis

Stung by their disastrous investment in the auction-rate fund, Ned and Rose began to rethink their portfolio strategies. In a meeting with Reggie Clause and his team, Ned and Rose expressed deep concern about what was going on in the financial world. They asked Reggie to undertake a complete review of the Titan portfolios and to suggest ways to reduce risk. After all, the "safe" money they thought they had set aside turned out not to be safe at all.

Unfortunately, the Titan family portfolios were being managed more or less by the seat of the pants. Each portfolio had a brief, one-page "investment policy statement," but that statement offered no guidance on how to manage through a financial crisis. The statement contained targets for equities and fixed income (60% and 40%, respectively), but no minimums or maximums.

Several weeks later, as Bear Stearns was collapsing, Reggie Clause and his team returned to Lawburn. They suggested that the Titans reduce their equity exposure from 60% to 50%, and that they increase their bond exposure from 40% to 50%. This was done, resulting in substantial capital gains taxes. These taxes came on top of the taxes paid to raise the $25 million fund that was now locked up in auction-rate securities.

Early that summer, Reggie Clause reported back on his discussions with Lehman Brothers about the auction-rate securities that had been sold to the Titans. According to Clause, the SEC and several state attorneys general were nearing an accord under which banks and investment banks would agree to buy back auction-rate notes they had sold. In fact, Citi, Merrill JP Morgan, Morgan Stanley, UBS, and RBC all eventually agreed to the buyback, but Lehman was not included.

Furious about this, Ned and Rose filed a lawsuit against Lehman Brothers, claiming that they were fraudulently misled about the safety of the auction-rate notes. Many other lawsuits were also filed, although most were settled when the banks agreed to repurchase the auction-rate notes at par. Lehman, however, agreed to no such repurchase.

The likely reason for Lehman's refusal to repurchase the notes was that Lehman itself was on the brink of failure. More than a year and a half later, the U.S. Justice Department would launch a criminal investigation into Lehman's actions, looking into (among other things) whether Lehman had moved risky auction rate securities off of its own balance sheet and into client accounts.

Unfortunately for the Titans' lawsuit, in September 2008 Lehman Brothers filed for the largest bankruptcy in U.S. history. Even if the Titans prevailed in their lawsuit, the bankruptcy court took precedence over their litigation, and they would become unsecured creditors, ranking far behind senior and more secured creditors of the failed firm.

While all this was going on, the U.S. stock markets continued to melt down. On January 2, 2008, the Dow Jones Industrial Average stood at 13,338. By early November, it had dropped to 7449—a sickening, 5,889-point drop in less than a year (44%).

By early December, Ned and Rose were on the phone with each other several times a day. They knew they were supposed to remain calm, that bear markets happened but wouldn't last forever. But in their minds they had already lost the $25 million that was stuck in the auction rate securities fund. And now they seemed to be losing the rest of the capital that was under their stewardship.

At a meeting in mid-December with their financial advisors, Ned and Rose could see that Reggie Clause was as unnerved as they were. After all, it wasn't just the Titans who were nervous and calling him regularly—virtually all his clients were frightened and his life had become almost insupportable. He was afraid to answer his phone, afraid to return calls.

And, although Ned and Rose didn't know this at the time, Reggie Clause and his brokerage firm were in deep trouble over their own role in the auction rate securities debacle. Reggie was worried about losing his job, worried about his firm possibly failing. At this mid-December meeting, Ned and Rose told Reggie that they realized he was in a stressful situation, but that they needed his advice. What should they do?

"All I can suggest," Reggie said, "is that you sell everything. Go to cash—I mean, a true money market fund or Treasury bills—and wait for this to blow over."

QUICK NOTE

The suggestion to "sell everything" was obviously terrible advice and it was driven by Reggie Clause's private concerns about his personal career. Note (see Chapter 5) that a well-drafted investment policy statement will contain an appendix in which the family lays out how it will deal with a bear market environment.

Rose motioned to Ned and the two of them stepped out of the conference room. Ned followed Rose to her office down the hall at Lawburn and closed the door. "This is terrible," Rose said, stating the obvious.

"We need sound advice, Rose, and we're not getting it from Reggie and his firm."

"They're the ones who got us into the auction rate disaster."

"We probably should have sued *them*, as well as Lehman."

"So what do we do now?"

"First," suggested Ned, "let's fire these guys and then we can go find a better advisor."

"I'm all in favor of that," Rose said, "but what do we do with our portfolio in the meantime?"

Ned paced around Rose's office for a while, while Rose drummed her fingers on her desktop. "I honestly don't know," Ned said eventually.

"Me, neither. Reggie says to sell everything and wait it out."

"My guess," said Ned, "is that whatever Reggie says is probably wrong."

Rose gave a hollow laugh. "Well," she said, "first things first. Let's go fire our financial advisor."

Rose Learns about Another Option

In early January 2009, Rose found herself in New York City, where she was attending a charity dinner at the American Museum of Natural History.

Her dinner partner happened to be a well-known New Yorker we'll call Ralph. Among other things, Ralph managed his own family's money and also chaired the investment committee at a well-known college. Naturally, the talk turned to the disastrous stock market environment.

"I know it's none of my business, Ralph," Rose said, "but may I ask how you're handling your family's money and the college's money during all this turmoil?"

"Mostly," said Ralph, "I take a lot of antacids." Rose laughed. "I could recommend my brand of antacid to you," Ralph continued, "but somehow I don't think that's what you were getting at."

"It might help, though," said Rose.

"Before I answer," Ralph said, "can you tell me what you're doing with your own money?"

Rose sighed. "Pretty much nothing," she said. "We made some mistakes back in 2007, when the credit markets were falling apart. And then, when the stock market melted down we were pretty panicky."

"I don't blame you."

"At the recommendation of our financial advisor, we spent much of last year reducing our exposure to stocks, so we're now, I suppose, about 40% in stocks and the rest in bonds and cash. Maybe a little lower in stocks since the market's continued to decline."

Ralph looked down at Rose over his reading glasses—he'd been perusing the set menu—and said, "What was your stock exposure before you lightened up?"

"Sixty percent."

"I see. And your advisor recommended that you go down to forty percent?"

"Oh, no!" exclaimed Rose. "Our advisor recommended that we sell everything and go to cash and municipal bonds!"

Ralph set his menu down and removed his glasses. "In that case," he said, "I have one recommendation for you: Fire your advisor."

Rose laughed. "We did! Last month!"

"Better late than never," Ralph said drily.

"What basically happened to us is that my brother and I took over the portfolio management duties from our father just a few years ago. We weren't completely inexperienced—we'd been on the family investment committee for some time."

"Oh—you have an investment committee? And where was this committee when your advisor was panicking?"

Rose blushed. "My father dropped off after his second stroke about five years ago, and then the family lawyer retired and dropped off, and that just left my brother, Ned, and me. So the committee disintegrated."

"And you didn't reconstitute it?"

"We should have, I guess. Especially in retrospect. It would have been good to have had other people in the room in 2007 and 2008."

There was a silence as the salads were served.

"May I tell you a story, Rose?" Ralph said. "It's a bit long, but I think it's relevant here."

"Somewhere in this story will you be telling me how you're navigating these markets?"

"Yes, at the very end. In my view the way investors react to very bad market conditions depends on how well prepared they were before the bad conditions arose. By the time the bear market is here, it's too late."

"That sounds right to me," Rose said. "I'd love to hear your story."

■ ■ ■

"Way back in 1979," Ralph began, "when I wasn't yet forty years old, I attended a dinner in honor of a fellow named McGeorge Bundy. Do you know the name?"

Rose didn't follow politics closely, but she knew that Bundy had been in the Kennedy and Johnson White Houses and that he'd been an advocate of escalating America's involvement in Vietnam. This didn't endear Bundy to Rose, who had demonstrated against the war while she was in college. "I remember him," Rose said. "What did he do after he left the Johnson administration?"

"He became president of the Ford Foundation here in New York," Ralph said. "This would have been in the mid-Sixties."

"I was just a kid then," Rose said. "I graduated from college in 1970."

"Well, if you were in college in the Sixties, then I don't suppose you were a big fan of Mac's."

"If you mean McGeorge Bundy, you're right!"

"Yes, he went by 'Mac.' Anyway, my father had been invited to a dinner celebrating Mac's retirement from the Ford Foundation. Like I said, this was in 1979 or maybe early 1980, I can't remember which. Dad was very ill at the time—he died in '81—and so I went to the dinner in his place. Dad was a pretty prominent guy, and so I was seated at Bundy's table. Everyone else there was at least seventy years old!"

"Must have been an interesting evening, though."

"It was that. All through the dinner I was afraid to open my mouth, certain that I'd say something really stupid. But then I started thinking how dumb I looked just sitting there not saying anything."

"I remember dinners like that when I was young and insecure. They can be pretty dreadful."

"They can. But at least this one was interesting. In any event, the evening was almost over. All the toasts had been made, all the speeches finished, the dessert had been eaten and we were lingering over coffee. Half the people at our table had already made their goodbyes.

"Then, suddenly, a topic popped into my mind. My father was ill, as I said, and already I was being drawn into the management of our family's capital. I knew almost nothing about managing money, and here, right across the table from me, was the guy who'd been managing the capital of the largest foundation in the world for years!"

"You're right, Ralph, what an opportunity! Did you seize it?"

"My mouth was so dry I could hardly talk. Fortunately, I'd had a lot of wine by then ... "

"Ha! The universal tongue-loosener!"

"Exactly. So I said, 'Excuse me, Mr. Bundy, but I'm being asked to help manage my family's money. You've been managing billions for years. Do you have any advice for me?'

"Unfortunately, just as I began speaking, Bundy was standing up, getting ready to leave. I blushed profusely and began to stammer something about 'Never mind,' but Bundy came around the table and sat down beside me. He asked me about my family and about my father's health. He knew Dad, of course, and knew he was ill. I glanced around and realized that everyone else was leaving the room. The servers were removing the dessert plates and pretty soon we were the only two people still at our table."

"You and McGeorge Bundy! That's one for the family history book!"

Ralph nodded. "Mac told me that when he arrived at the Ford Foundation the entire endowment was managed by a large bank. He sat through meeting after meeting listening to the bank tell Ford how terrific they were, but he had to wonder if having all the Foundation's money with one organization was really smart. Could that one bank really have the best investment ideas and products in the world?"

"We had a bank managing our family money, too," Rose said. "But my father got annoyed at them for always trying to sell him their hot new products, so he fired them."

"Where'd you end up?" asked Ralph.

"With a regional brokerage firm in Pittsburgh," Rose said. "Father knew them well and had a friend who was a senior executive there."

Ralph gave Rose a sad smile. "I guess we know how that worked out," he said. Anyway, Mac asked me if I'd ever heard of something called ERISA."

"Well, *I* haven't heard of it," Rose said.

"No reason you should have. It's an obscure law governing corporate pension plans. ERISA stands for Employee Retirement Income Security Act. Congress passed it in 1974, after Mac had been at Ford for about eight years.

The key thing about ERISA was that it made it clear that trustees of pension plans were fiduciaries."

"Like trustees of private trusts," Rose said. "I'm a trustee of, oh, I don't even know how many trusts for our family."

"Exactly. But it turned out that trustees of pension plans knew almost nothing about investing. They'd just hire some bank or brokerage firm and hope for the best. But in 1974 they woke up and realized they could be surcharged if their financial advisor did a bad job."

"*Ouch!* Some of those pension plans must be huge!"

"In the billions. So everybody went into a big panic and didn't know what to do. But, this being America, some guys saw an opportunity and they started up firms called 'investment consultants.' You ever hear of them?"

"Never," said Rose. "What's an investment consultant do?"

"Well, the key thing is what they *don't* do. They don't have any proprietary products to sell you. They don't take money under the table from investment managers or other product vendors. Whatever you pay them, that's what they get. They sit on the same side of the table as you."

"I don't think I understand, Ralph. If they don't have any investment products, how do they manage the portfolio?"

"Here's how it works," said Ralph. "It was all new to me at the time, too, until I heard about it from Mac Bundy. So what these investment consultants do is, first, they design the portfolio that's right for you. You're not the Ford Foundation, and the Ford Foundation isn't you. So your portfolio and their portfolio had better look different."

"Yes, I see that."

"Mac said to me, 'If you were working with a bank or a broker, they'd be designing your portfolio with their own product list in mind.' But the consultants, since they don't have any products, design the portfolio objectively."

"So far, so good!"

"Next," said Ralph, "these consultants scour the world for the best money managers. They put them through the wringer, not looking just at their investment returns, but also their fees, how much risk they're taking, how long they've been in business, how compelling their investment ideas are, all that sort of thing. Then, when they have a list of the best of the best—what they call 'best-in-class' managers—those are the ones they recommend to their clients."

"Well, that all sounds pretty terrific. But how did you say these investment consultants make money?"

"They charge a small fee, based on the size of your portfolio."

"And that fee comes on top of what you pay the managers, right?"

"Right. But since the consultant's interests are aligned with yours, they're looking for the lowest-fee managers they can find who are also good. Mac Bundy told me that when Ford left the bank and went with the investment consultant, their overall investment costs went way down."

"That makes me wonder why everybody doesn't manage their money using these consultant people. Do you have to have billions of dollars to use them?"

"Not at all," said Ralph. "Even people with a couple hundred thousand dollars to invest can find a good fee-only financial planner, which is the retail version of the consultants. But if your family has enough money to have a lot of trusts, I'm sure the investment consultants would be happy to work with you."

QUICK NOTE

Obviously, not every family will have such a fortunate encounter with someone who can help them think about a new advisor. But Rose's experience does suggest the wisdom of asking around. Any one family can give you poor advice, but if you speak with enough families, a pattern of sound thinking will emerge.

Rose was so excited that she actually called Ned as soon as she returned to her hotel room. Ned, who'd been asleep, was still a little groggy, and he had trouble understanding just what an investment consulting firm was and why it might be interesting. But he could hear the excitement in Rose's voice, and they set up a meeting back in Pittsburgh to discuss the matter further.

Over the next few months, Ned and Rose talked to as many people as they could about investment consulting firms, and eventually they developed a list of five names they would start with. Over the course of the next few months, while the markets stopped going down and began climbing back up, Ned and Rose traveled around the country, meeting with each of the consulting firms on their list. They put together a series of questions to ask each firm, and those questions would become the basis of an RFP (request for proposal) that they would eventually put together and send out to the firms on their long list of prospective advisors.

In Chapter 3 we'll examine the Titan family's experience as they search for, interview, and engage an investment consulting firm to serve as their financial advisor.

WHAT THE REGIONAL BROKERAGE FIRM COULD HAVE DONE BETTER

Some of the mistakes the regional broker made in its relationship with the Titan family are obvious, but some are more subtle. One obvious mistake was assigning an aggressive salesman to be the lead advisor on the Titan account. Ned and Rose weren't used to dealing with pushy salesmen and they reacted negatively to Frank Patterson from the beginning.

Another mistake was underestimating the investment knowledge of Ned and Rose. There were probably investment professionals at the brokerage firm who could have handled the questions and concerns Ned and Rose raised with aplomb, but Frank Patterson wasn't one of them. As a result, Ned and Rose lost confidence in the entire firm, rather than just in Frank.

Of course, Frank Patterson was starting from a serious disadvantage in working with a wealthy family like the Titans: he worked for a firm with many conflicts of interest, and Ned and Rose picked up on those issues right away. As we've seen, Ned and Rose decided to solve the problem of conflicts by engaging an investment consulting firm that didn't have any.

The later shift from Patterson to Reggie Clause, while an improvement, eventually resulted in the brokerage firm losing the Titan family account. The firm had aggressively marketed the auction rate securities fund that ended up being such a disaster for the Titans and, undoubtedly, for many other clients.

As the bad press, angry clients, and lawsuits piled up, advisors like Reggie Clause lost their nerve. It seemed as though all the world had turned against them, and the market meltdown in 2008 proved to be the last straw. Instead of being a trusted advisor to the Titan family in their time of need, Reggie panicked.

At the core of the problems of the brokerage firm, and of Frank Patterson and Reggie Clause, were the firm's many conflicts of interest. The firm's (and its advisors') financial incentives led them in directions that diverged away from, and in many cases directly opposed, the clients' interests. Selling mediocre investment products, being nontransparent about sharing fees with managers, and touting a product—auction rate securities—that was highly defective, were only a few of the many ways the firm's interests were badly misaligned with the interests of its clients.

Still, many investment advisory professionals work in conflicted situations and still manage to provide sound and trusted advice to their wealthy clients. How do they do it? Here's how.

First, Always Provide Full Disclosure

Frank Patterson was used to working with much smaller clients than the Titans, what we would now call *mass affluent* families, those with $1 million to $5 million to invest. It's unfortunately the case that those investors tend to be less demanding than truly wealthy families, and less sensitive to conflicts of interest.

A wealthy family, as I said earlier and as I can't repeat frequently enough, *is in the business of managing capital.* Retail investors and even mass affluent investors are for the most part in the business of doing something else: working at their jobs, managing their professions, running their small companies, and so on. Therefore, wealthy families are going to be much more focused on their portfolios and consequently on any shortcomings in their professional relationships.

Frank's predecessor, Paul Winthrop, wasn't likely to underestimate Jake Titan, whom he'd known all his life, and therefore he always made full disclosure to Jake about the brokerage firm's interests. Jake knew exactly what share of each manager's fee the firm received and exactly how much of that was passed on to Winthrop. In addition, Winthrop would never have dreamed of showing up at a meeting unprepared to answer Jake's questions, even if it meant bringing several other investment professionals to the meeting with him.

Frank Patterson's failure to prepare carefully for meetings with the Titans, and his reluctance to disclose his personal and institutional interests in the recommendations he was making, were fatal to his hopes of retaining this or any other wealthy client.

Be Patient

Frank Patterson was such an aggressive salesman that he allowed his natural instincts to overwhelm his judgment. Instead of charging into the very first meeting with Ned and Rose with recommendations in hand, Frank should have spent time getting to know the Titans, getting to understand where they were coming from, allowing a relationship of trust to develop.

It's difficult for a professional like Frank to be patient, because patience doesn't increase his income—only selling something does. But this was shortsighted. By being impatient, by trying to sell something at his very first meeting with Ned and Rose, the trust Paul Winthrop had built up with the Titans over many years was destroyed very quickly. And that *certainly* didn't improve Frank's income, or his reputation at the brokerage firm.

Think Like a Consultant

Although Frank Patterson and Reggie Clause weren't investment consultants and certainly weren't fiduciaries with respect to their relationship with the

Titans, they could have *acted* like consultants and they could have *behaved* like fiduciaries. We'll be getting into what investment consultants do and how they think in much more detail in later chapters. But for now, instead of selling hard right out of the gate, and instead of wallowing in their conflicts of interest for short-term financial gain, here is how Frank and Reggie might have proceeded:

- **Focus on the family.** Frank Patterson showed up at his very first meeting with two manager recommendations. He thought this would impress the Titans, but it had exactly the opposite effect. Ned and Rose had serious concerns about the quality of those managers and, more important, there is no way that Frank could have known whether the managers were appropriate since he was very new to the Titan family account. Frank should have devoted the first three or four meetings to developing a broader understanding of the family and its needs. Then his manager recommendations would have been more compelling.
- **Look first at the overall portfolio strategy.** Frank and Reggie knew, as all serious investment professionals know, that the overall strategy a family follows will have vastly more effect on their investment outcomes than will other matters, like manager selection. But because an activity like a careful review of the Titans' asset allocation didn't result in direct compensation, they gave the overall strategy short shrift. When the financial crisis arrived in 2008, neither the Titans nor their advisors at the brokerage firm had an overall context for navigating that difficult and challenging market environment.
- **Recommend only appropriate managers.** The managers Frank recommended at his first meeting with the Titans were selected by him because they shared a larger portion of their revenue with the brokerage firm than other, similar managers. As we saw earlier, Ned and Rose reacted very negatively to these managers. (As well they should have. The very best managers don't have to share revenue with brokerage firms in order to build their client bases.) If Frank had waited until he knew the Titans better, and then recommended managers who met the tests of risk-adjusted returns and low fees, he would have gotten paid at that time. Instead, he not only didn't get paid on the first two managers, since the Titans declined to engage them, he ended up losing the entire account.
- **Be an advisor when it really matters.** When the credit crisis of 2007 was followed in quick succession by the financial crisis of 2008, Ned and Rose Titan were desperate for calm and sensible advice. But what they got from Reggie Clause was panic. Advisors who are only there for their clients during bull markets are not worthy of the name.

SUMMARY

Ideally, anyone who wishes to advise wealthy families on their investment portfolios should work from a completely objective platform that doesn't present conflicts of interest with their clients. In virtually every case, this will mean that the advisors are acting as fiduciaries with respect to their clients and legally must place their clients' interests above their own.

But let's face it—many wealth advisors don't work for objective, open-architecture firms, and probably don't want to. This makes their job—the job of becoming a long-term, trusted advisor to their clients—much harder, but not impossible.

Advisors like Frank Patterson and Reggie Clause are so common in the brokerage and banking industries that it's no wonder those firms have been losing ground to objective firms for many years. But it doesn't have to be the case. Large brokerage firms and large banking institutions offer many advantages to wealthy families: global investment research, credit facilities, institutional permanence, brand names, and so on. Advisors working for such firms, and who approach their wealthy clients with an objective, fiduciary mindset, can be very successful. But this requires a fierce determination to place clients first in spite of the fact that all the incentives are running the other way.

CHAPTER 3

The Titans Search for and Engage a New Financial Advisor

PREPARATION AND USE

Following Rose's serendipitous meeting with Ralph at the American Museum in New York, she and Frank gathered additional names of investment consulting firms and, over the next few months, visited with as many of the firms as they could manage to see.

Since Ned and Rose knew very little about investment consultants—or, for that matter, any kinds of advisors other than banks and brokerage firms—the first few meetings were quite confusing. After that, however, Ned and Rose put together a list of questions to ask each firm, and, as noted in Chapter 2, that list was eventually expanded into an RFP (request for proposal) that the Titan family sent to those consultants who seemed likely possibilities for their next advisor.

HOW THE TITANS CONDUCTED THEIR SEARCH

For a family that had never searched for a financial advisor before, the Titans did many things right—and a few things wrong. In this chapter we will follow along with Ned and Rose as they gradually learned more and more about investment consultants in particular and about financial advisory firms in general. One thing we will notice is that Ned and Rose were making it up as they went along. They had no models, no forms, and didn't know any families who used consulting firms. This turned out to be both an advantage and a disadvantage, as we will see.

Visiting with Consulting Firms

Today, families who are looking for advisors typically visit only the firms that make it to the final round, if that. Ned and Rose didn't do it this way.

Instead, they visited almost every firm on their list *before* they sent out an RFP, indeed before they had even prepared the RFP.

And this is a strategy other families would do well to emulate, especially if the family hasn't used an investment consulting firm in the past. Unlike, say, very large banks and brokerage houses, investment consulting firms tend to be quite different from one another. They are different in size, in the number of years they've been in business, in the way they are internally organized, and in their day-to-day cultures.

Thus, while all investment consultants engage in similar activities, the way those activities are carried out will depend heavily on the specific nature of the firm. When families make a mistake in engaging a new advisor, it's often because they have allowed the RFP process to overwhelm human judgment—and human judgment can't operate effectively just by looking at black-and-white answers to an RFP.

Thus, when Ned and Rose visited a firm, they had a list of key questions they wished to pose, but they were also interested in the culture of the firms. Was the firm rigidly hierarchical, with a few senior partners dominating the conversation, or was it more collegial, with employees on various levels expressing their opinions? Did the people at the firm seem to get along well with each other and enjoy working together, or was the atmosphere more formal? How well did the different functional sections of the firm (manager research, performance reporting, client advisory) communicate and interact? In the end, the intuitive sense the Titans had of each firm would matter more than many of the formal questions they asked in their RFP.

Questions Ned and Rose Asked

At each firm, there were a small number of questions Ned and Rose posed when they visited. These questions focused, naturally, on the issues that were of most importance to them and their family. Here are some samples:

- Can you outline for me the history of your firm? We're interested in who founded it, when it was founded, what changes it's gone through, and so on.
- How much of your business is advising families versus institutional clients? Please answer in terms of both assets under management and number of clients.
- Ideally, our family would like to work with an advisor that is objective and that will be acting as a fiduciary in its dealings with us. Please (a) outline any actual or potential conflicts of interest your firm has with its clients, and (b) state whether you will always, in every capacity, be acting as a fiduciary as you advise us.[1]

- Do you have any formal or informal relationships, including fee-sharing, with other firms, including broker/dealers and money managers?
- How do you charge for your services? Are you open to other fee arrangements?
- How can we best assess the intellectual capital of your firm? Do you publish books or papers? Do you speak widely at investment events?
- If our family engages your firm, and later decides to terminate the relationship, what complications will we encounter? In other words, is there a long notice period? Will we be invested in proprietary products that we can't exit from for a prolonged period?
- What are the two or three most important things about your firm we should take away from this visit?
- When a family considers you as their advisor but ultimately doesn't hire you, what is typically the reason?

The answers to some of these questions could eliminate a firm from consideration, of course. For example, as far as the Titans were concerned, a firm with obvious conflicts of interest was simply ruled out. But with most of the other questions, Ned and Rose were more interested in how the questions were answered rather than in the actual answers themselves.

For example, if the firm seemed baffled by the question about intellectual capital, that could mean that it didn't value keeping up with cutting-edge thinking in the field. If the firm was totally rigid about their fee arrangements, perhaps they were rigid about other things as well. As noted, the specific answers were often less important than how thoughtfully the answers were phrased.

The Titan Family's RFP

Today, RFPs can be daunting documents—and I'm not talking about daunting to the prospective advisors, I'm talking about daunting to the families who issue them. What has happened over the years is that the RFP process has become institutionalized even though the process is supposed to help *families*.

Institutions began to use RFPs long before families began to use them, and hence, when families looked around for model forms for an RFP, they naturally looked at the forms institutions were using. A family member might sit on the board of a college or university, for example, and they would simply take the form of RFP used by that institution and modify it (typically slightly) before sending it out.

Today, many RFPs ask more than 100 questions, especially when you consider that some questions have ten or more parts to them. This is typically not a problem for the advisory firms, because most firms have more or less automated the process of responding to RFPs.[2] However, it can be a big headache for the family.

Imagine that a family sends out RFPs to ten firms and that each RFP asks 100 questions. All ten firms respond, answering every question at length and also adding numerous addenda. Who is going to wade through all this? Institutions generally have in-house investment staff whose (miserable) job it is to go through all the RFP responses and prepare spreadsheets comparing the different firms and their answers. But families often have no investment staff at all, and sometimes hardly any paid employees. This leaves it to individual family members, few of whom are likely to be investment professionals, to try to make sense out of the mountain of responses they have received.

QUICK NOTE

It would be useful if someone—perhaps one of the family affinity groups—would put together a standard-form RFP, perhaps with annotations and commentary. In the foundation community, for example, many regional associations of grantmakers (RAGs) have developed common form applications for grants that are used by virtually all foundations in those regions of the country.[3]

The approach taken by the Titan family in preparing their RFP is superior. The Titans focused on a few key areas that were extremely important to them as a family and ignored the boilerplate kinds of questions that tend to make it into institutional RFPs. It's important to remember that institutional investors are very different from family investors, and the way institutions use investment consulting firms or other advisors is also very different. This is partly because institutional investors are far more like each other than families are like each other.

Although of course an institutional investor wants to end up with a good advisor, it's more important that the institution go through a thorough search that can withstand scrutiny by investment committee members, board members, donors, and so on. And if the thoroughness of the search actually interferes with the *quality* of the search, and the likelihood that the institution will end up with the best advisor, so be it.

In this sense, an advisory search is a bit similar to the way institutions look at their investment performance. Institutional investors tend to be *relative return* focused. That is, whether the return is high or low matters less than whether the return is similar to the returns achieved by similar institutions. If Institution A is down 45% in a particular year, that might be a good or a bad year depending on how other institutions performed. If the average peer institution was down 47%, then Institution A had a good year despite the horrific downdraft.

Families, on the other hand, are almost always *absolute return* oriented investors. Since every family is quite different from every other family, it matters almost not at all what returns other families are getting. What matters is whether the return is satisfactory on an absolute basis. As we have seen, a −45% year can be perfectly acceptable to an institution. But a −45% year would *never* be acceptable to a family.

It's also important to keep in mind how differently institutions tend to use their advisors from how families use them. Most larger institutions have investment professionals on staff, and these individuals perform many of the more important functions of an outside advisor, albeit often with the assistance of the advisor. Thus, for example, a college's in-house investment staff will perform much of the heavy lifting on asset allocation work and on deciding when to make tactical bets in the markets. The staff will, however, tend to outsource to the advisor such matters as performance reporting and manager selection. (That is, the advisor will bring recommended managers to the table and the finalists will then be interviewed by the college's investment committee.)

Very few families will have investment professionals on staff, and therefore they will need to rely on the advisor for almost all investment functions. If an institutional investor fails to hire the best advisor, the consequences are relatively modest; after all, all institutional advisors can handle performance reporting and have long lists of managers they follow.

But if a family makes a mistake in selecting its advisor, that mistake will resonate across the entire investment portfolio. Therefore, it's far more important for a family to make the right decision than it is for them to go through some process that appears to others to be thorough.

QUICK NOTE

I can't emphasize enough the importance for families of focusing on the *quality* of the questions in an RFP, rather than quantity of questions. Otherwise, the RFP process tends to degenerate into gamesmanship, and it's a game that advisors are far better at than families.

What the Titan RFP Got Right

The approach taken by the Titan family in the RFP was straightforward. The RFP (a version of which appears on the companion website for this book at www.wiley.com/go/familycapital) begins with a brief description of the Titan family, its decision makers, and (in a broad way) the beneficiaries of the family portfolio.

Note that some families skip this step out of privacy concerns. However, I strongly recommend it. It helps the prospective advisors tailor their responses to the RFP, and it allows the family to judge whether the advisor seems to understand or care about the family and its needs. If privacy is an issue, the prospective advisory firms can be asked to sign a confidentiality agreement, a version of which is available on the companion website for this book at www.wiley.com/go/familycapital.

The next section of the Titan RFP gives a quick overview of the family's portfolio, including a brief history of the advisors the family used over the years and what the Titans had liked and not liked about those advisors.

Following the description of the family and its portfolio, the RFP asked, right up front, the questions that really mattered to it. That way it was easy to eliminate advisors who were inappropriate and easy to compare and contrast the semifinalists. The Titans then asked the advisory firms to add anything they considered important but that the RFP hadn't addressed. However, because the family had limited resources, they imposed a strict page limit on additional material. This forced the advisors to focus on what they thought was really important about their firms rather than just throwing in everything but the kitchen sink.

In addition to the questions previously listed, which the family had tried to ask during its visits with the prospective advisors, the Titans were interested in issues such as these:

- **Risk versus return.** Like most wealthy families, the Titans were capital preservation–oriented investors. Capital preservation strategies made sense to them because, since they were already rich, the extreme outcomes of aggressive investing were asymmetrical. On the one hand, they might get even richer, which would be nice. On the other hand, they could go broke, which would be *catastrophic*. Capital preservation investing begins by thinking first about risk and only second about return, and this is what the Titans were trying to get at with this question. An advisor that bragged about its high returns was unlikely to be of interest. (The reasons why most wealthy families will want to be capital preservation–oriented investors are discussed in detail in Chapter 5.)

- **Asset allocation.** Advisory firms approach the asset allocation challenge in different ways. While there is no one right way to do it, there are many wrong ways, most obviously firms that offer only predesigned portfolios (e.g., a conservative strategy, a moderate strategy, and aggressive strategy). Predesigned portfolios might be necessary in the retail world, but they are completely unacceptable in the world of wealth management. Every family's portfolio needs to be custom-designed from the ground up. (We will observe the Titan family as it grapples with asset allocation in Chapter 7.)
- **Investment policy statement.** The Titans wanted to see a sample of an investment policy statement not because that sample would be appropriate for them, but simply to observe the thoughtfulness with which it was put together. (The Titan family will prepare a sound policy statement in Chapter 5.)
- **Manager research.** Like the question of asset allocation, there are many ways to go about manager research and monitoring. The Titans weren't hung up on any particular approach, but simply wished to understand how an advisor thought about the issue and whether the approach resonated with them as a family. Note that the RFP requested an example of a manager diligence report. (The Titans will take up manager selection in Chapter 8.)
- **Performance reporting.** The Titans had very much disliked the performance reports they had been receiving from the regional brokerage firm, and they were eager to see if another advisor might approach the problem in a more client-friendly way, hence their request for a sample performance report. (We will take a look at the performance reports Spenser prepared for the Titans in Chapter 9.)
- **Form of advisory agreement.** Perhaps because Jake Titan had been a prominent lawyer, the Titans were sensitive to what sort of agreement they would be expected to sign, and hence they asked for each advisor's form of agreement. Ideally, the advisory agreement the Titans would sign would be a simple document not weighed down with a lot of legalese. A sample advisory agreement in plain English is available on the companion website for this book at www.wiley.com/go/familycapital.

How the RFP Might Have Been Improved

For a family that had never issued an RFP to an investment advisor, the Titan RFP was a very strong document. It might have been improved, however, if some of the following issues had been addressed:

- **Custodianship.** At the regional brokerage firm, the firm that managed the money—the brokerage—also held custody of the assets. However, this is rarely a good practice. You don't want your investment manager and your custodian to go broke at the same time. The Titan RFP should have inquired about the advisors' views of asset custodians (typically large banks, but also brokers), which custodians they worked with, and what the pros and cons of different custody options might be. (Asset custody is discussed in Chapter 11.)

- **Discretion versus non-discretion.** At the regional brokerage firm the Titans made all the final decisions, albeit based (in most cases) on recommendations from the broker. But there is another model—fully discretionary advice—and the Titans might have inquired about it. Firms known as "outsourced chief investment officers" (OCIOs) actively manage the portfolio but within very strict guidelines approved by the client. Since neither Ned nor Rose was an experienced investor, and since both were busy people, a discretionary advisory relationship might have been an interesting option for them. (The OCIO option is discussed in Chapter 9.)
- **Getting from there to here.** The RFP should have asked how the advisors would transition the Titan portfolio from its current posture—as invested by the regional brokerage firm—to the new recommended portfolio. The issue is how sensitive would the advisor be to tax issues, market timing issues, and similar matters. For example, would the advisor be willing to keep a manager that had a large embedded gain? Would the advisor slow the transition to allow short-term gains to become long-term? Would the advisor move immediately from the old strategy to the new strategy even if it meant buying into overvalued markets or selling out of undervalued ones?

CONCLUDING THE SEARCH

A well-drafted RFP, and well-studied responses to the RFP, should make the final steps—meeting with advisor finalists and making the selection—a piece of cake. However, poorly drafted RFPs, or failure to carefully review the RFP responses, can complicate the process immeasurably.

Identifying and Interviewing Final Candidates

Most families interview far too many advisory candidates. There seems to be a sense that there must be a perfect firm out there that might be missed if a large number of firms aren't interviewed. But this is nonsense. There are no perfect firms; there are only firms that are more appropriate for what the family needs and firms that are less appropriate.

The more firms a family interviews, the more exhausting the interview process will be, the more prolonged it will be, and the less likely the family will be to make a sound decision. The purpose of the RFP process is to reduce the number of candidates to a manageable few; otherwise the process is a waste of time. A family that spends two long days interviewing eight advisory candidates is doing neither itself nor the advisors any favors.

QUICK NOTE

When a family insists on interviewing far too many prospective advisors, it puts advisory firms in an awkward position. The long list of candidates being interviewed makes it clear to the advisors that the family doesn't know what it's doing. In order to winnow the list of candidates down to a manageable size, the family will have to employ arbitrary criteria to eliminate most of the firms. Because the criteria for elimination are arbitrary, the firms remaining are unlikely to be the best candidates for the family and the resulting advisory relationship is likely to be rocky. As a result, when the list of firms being interviewed is too long, most of the firms are likely to send their B list of presenters, rather than their A list.

The Titans used the RFP process to select the two firms it felt were most appropriate for their needs and they invited those two firms to interview at Lawburn, their family office. Each firm was asked to bring to the interview the individuals who would be assigned to the family's account, plus no more than one additional person.

Both advisors were required to follow the same agenda and each meeting was to last no more than 90 minutes, preferably less:

1. Brief introduction of those present
2. Opening statement by the family, letting the advisor know where they stand in their search process[4]
3. Brief opening statement by the advisor, no more than 15 minutes, positioning itself however it wished
4. Discussion, led by the family, of issues raised in the RFP response
5. Meeting ends

This kept things short, sweet, unexhausting, and effective.

Making the Final Selection and Negotiating the Advisory Agreement

Fortunately, there were only two Titan family members involved in the advisory search process. When many family members are involved, it can prove exceedingly difficult to get consensus on a final selection. Ned and Rose did differ on some issues, but they both liked both the finalists and figured they couldn't go wrong either way.

Indeed, it's usually the case that, by the time a family has winnowed the advisory firms down to a final two, both firms will be satisfactory and the final decision will often come down to intangibles: Which individuals did the family feel more comfortable with? Who seemed to communicate better? Did the age ranges of the advisors more or less match the age range of the family members who would be making investment decisions? Was the chemistry good?

Ned and Rose decided to enter into fee negotiations with a firm we'll call Spenser Advisors. Unfortunately, fee negotiations are fraught with peril for clients and advisors alike. Clients, naturally, want to get the best fee deal they can get and they certainly don't want to overpay. Advisors, on the other hand, know very well that unless they can maintain reasonable profit margins they won't be in business very long. Indeed, the relatively short history of the wealth management business (about 30 years) is already littered with the carcasses of investment advisory firms that bought new business by underbidding on fees.

If the client side is led by G1 (the first generation of wealth, the one that made the money), that generation is likely to be adept at business dealings and negotiations and they will tend to drive a hard bargain. If the client side is led by subsequent generations (as in the case of Ned and Rose Titan), those individuals are likely to be highly sensitive to being taken advantage of. Wealthy people know all too well that when a vendor realizes it is dealing with a wealthy family, the price usually goes up. Thus, even when a client recognizes the advisor's need for healthy profit margins, the client is likely to feel that those margins should be built on the backs of other clients, not them. But this is shortsighted for several reasons.

First, as noted, many weak advisory firms survive for a time by underbidding stronger firms. They are able to build AUM (assets under management), but they are unable to build EBITDA (earnings before interest, taxes, depreciation and amortization). No sooner will the family become comfortable with such an advisor than it will disappear—selling out or simply dissolving. And as noted earlier in connection with the acquisition of the Titan family's trust company by a large bank, when a wealth advisor is sold, that's a new advisor and requires that a new search be conducted. The hard-negotiating family will find itself starting over.

Second, driving down the advisor's fee might give a client a short-term feeling of success, but clients need to keep in mind that advisors have ways to deal with lowballing clients and those ways aren't pretty. Let's look at a specific situation.

The Cheap family selected its advisor following an exhaustive search. According to the advisor's fee schedule, the Cheaps should be paying a fee of 35 basis points (a bit over 1/3 of 1 percent), or $350,000 on their asset base of $100 million. By dint of hard negotiating, the Cheaps managed to drive the fee down to $275,000, or about 28 basis points. The Cheaps felt pretty good about this, but let's look under the hood and watch what happened at the Cheaps' new advisory firm.

A well-managed advisory firm knows exactly what it costs to advise families in general, and almost exactly what it will cost to advise any specific family. Families differ widely in how complex and difficult the advisory relationship will be, depending on a variety of factors, including the number of different family units and entities (trusts, foundations, etc.), the required number of meetings annually, how active the family is in making one-off requests and unimportant inquiries, the complexity of performance reporting, and so on.

The Cheaps' advisor required that every client meet a minimum profit margin target, and the Cheaps were below that target. So what did the advisor do? They underworked the account. Although, nominally, a senior advisor was in charge of the account, in fact that advisor spent little time even thinking about the Cheaps' account until just before an upcoming meeting. Then he would sit down with the junior staff who had been handling matters and get briefed.

During one such briefing, the senior advisor noticed several issues. The Cheaps should have been moved out of an underperforming manager several months ago, but the juniors had overlooked this. Several sales had been made in the Cheap accounts even though, if the juniors had simply waited a few months, the gains on those securities would have moved from short-term (i.e., highly taxed) to long-term. Two investment products had been purchased, which was correct, but the Cheaps had been placed in the higher-priced retail versions of the products rather than the lower-priced institutional versions, which the Cheap accounts qualified for.

The senior advisor corrected these issues as much as he could, but in the meantime the Cheaps had overpaid for investment products, overpaid in taxes, and lost money due to manager underperformance. Most of this would never be known to the Cheaps, but similar issues arose every quarter due to the inattention of the senior advisor—he was busy working for clients who paid fairer fees.

In the long run, the 7 basis points the Cheaps were saving annually on the advisory fee were disappearing in the (very loud) noise of losses elsewhere, which averaged 22 basis points per year during the seven years the Cheaps worked with the advisor. Eventually, the Cheaps realized that they were being underserved by their advisor and they terminated the account. The advisor couldn't have been happier.

The point of all this is simple: Advisors shouldn't attempt to gouge clients on fees, as so many large, institutional advisory firms have been doing for generations. But, by the same token, clients shouldn't attempt to gouge advisors on fees, either. It's self-defeating in the long run. Instead, clients and advisors should talk openly about why fees are set as they are. If there are ways to reduce the fees without compromising the quality of the advice, those avenues should certainly be investigated. But simply charging high fees because the advisor can get away with it, or negotiating rock-bottom fees because the client can get away with it, are both stagecoach stops on the road to ruin.

QUICK NOTE

One lesson here for advisors is to be as flexible as possible in how fees are structured. Families differ in how they react to various fee structures, and it will therefore be in the advisor's interest to be as flexible as possible. Note that this does *not* mean underbidding on business or accepting business that will result in a loss for the advisor.

SUMMARY

Searching for a new advisor, preparing RFPs, reviewing RFP responses, interviewing finalists, selecting the best firm, and negotiating fees are nobody's idea of a good time. When a family has to go through an advisor search, they will want to do it right the first time and not have to do it all over again a few years later. Advisors can help with this process by being honest and transparent during the RFP process, by charging fair fees for the value they are bringing to the client, and by refusing to accept low-fee business rather than taking it on and then underserving the account.

Since most families will issue RFPs that are not user-friendly for either the family or the advisor, even smaller advisory firms should arrange to respond to the RFPs in as efficient a manner as possible. All RFPs ask (mostly) the same questions, perhaps in different words. Thus, by maintaining a template RFP response, one competent person in the firm can handle 90% of the work involved in responding to RFPs. The other 10% will need to be handled by senior professionals, and those professionals should also carefully review the most crucial questions and answers. But trying to respond to every RFP starting from ground zero is a good way to go broke—and crazy.

NOTES

1. Part (b) of this question is important because some firms are *dually registered*, that is, they are both RIAs (registered investment advisors, and in that capacity act as fiduciaries) and also brokers (and in that capacity can place their own interests above those of their clients). Dually registered firms all too often wear whichever hat (fiduciary or non-fiduciary) serves their own interests at the time.
2. That is, most firms have assigned the process of responding to RFPs to a small group of people who have access to model answers to virtually every question a family is likely to ask.
3. See, for example, the form devised by Philanthropy New York and the Council of New Jersey Grantmakers, available at https://philanthropynewyork.org/resources/nynj-area-common-application.
4. Many families skip this step, leaving advisors in the dark. This isn't a good way to get off on the right foot with the firm that will be advising you.

CHAPTER 4

First Meeting: Governance, Investment Strategy, and Other Introductory Matters

PREPARATION AND USE

From this point on we will be listening in on meetings the advisors at Spenser Advisors held with members of the Titan family. As we will see, the Spenser advisors were experienced and talented people who took their advisory work seriously and in general did a good job advising the Titans. No one is perfect, of course, and we will observe mistakes being made both by Spenser and by the Titans.

FIRST MEETING WITH THE TITANS' NEW ADVISOR

The move from a sales-oriented advisor to an objective, unbiased advisor was such a major change for Ned and Rose that at first it led to a certain amount of confusion. Let's listen in on excerpts from the first meeting Ned and Rose had with Clarissa (Carrie) Knowlton, the lead advisor on the Titan account for Spenser Advisors.

Investment Strategy

Carrie Knowlton I hope you don't mind my saying so, but I was surprised to see how cautiously your family's portfolio is invested. From reading your RFP, I would have expected a more balanced strategy.

[Ned and Rose glance at each other.]

Ned: We're pretty cautious investors, aren't we, Rose?
Rose: You bet.

Carrie: Well, that's good—you should be. But you also need to keep up with inflation in a portfolio that pays taxes, pays fees, and is diminished by spending.

Rose (sighing): The thing is, Carrie, we got very nervous during the financial crisis and we began selling stocks. We lost some money in a likely fraud situation. That made us even more nervous.

Ned: And our advisor wasn't much help. He was a nervous wreck himself. He was probably losing a lot of clients in those days, and he was the one who convinced us to put a lot of money in a fund that turned out not to be as safe as it was advertised to be.

Carrie: I certainly understand your nervousness, but an important part of being a good investor is doing things that seem uncomfortable, sometimes intensely so.

Ned: Like buying back into a stock market that just went down almost fifty percent!

Carrie: Well, yes. Of course, I'm not suggesting you jump back in with both feet. For all I know, the market is going to go down another twenty percent. What I do know is that your current equity exposure is too low, so maybe we could adopt a plan to gradually get you back to a reasonable risk level again.

Ned: Do you have a specific suggestion, Carrie?

Carrie: Yes. Since we don't know each other all that well, I suggest we go slow. We can always accelerate the process—or, for that matter, slow it down. How about if we aim for a sixty percent equity exposure target (I'd be more comfortable with sixty-five percent, actually), and that we get there between now and the end of 2009?

Rose: So over nine months.

Carrie: Right. If these numbers are correct, you're only at thirty-seven percent equity now, so we need to add twenty-eight percent. That would mean we should add, say, three or four percent a month until the end of the year.

Ned: What do you think, Rose?

Rose: It makes me nervous, to be honest.

Ned: Me, too. But we don't want to end up like Uncle George.

Carrie: Uncle George?

Ned: Long story, Carrie, but our uncle, George Titan III, sold all his stocks at the bottom of the bear market in, let's see, it would have been 1974.

Carrie: When did he get back into the market?

Rose: He didn't.

Carrie (staring at Rose): He never got back in? Never reinvested? Do you mean that he missed the entire bull market of the 1980s and 1990s?

Rose: I'm afraid so.

Ned: And that branch of the family always spent like drunken sailors. I believe they've spent through their entire fortune.

Carrie: Dear God. I'm so sorry to hear that.

Rose: Well, like you said, Ned, we don't want to end up like Uncle George, so let's take a deep breath and start buying back into the market.

Ned: Done.

QUICK NOTE

Carrie Knowlton was going way out on a limb by opening her first meeting with a new client by criticizing the portfolio. Of course, Carrie had met Ned and Rose during the RFP and interview process, and she felt that one reason they'd hired Spenser was to hear the truth. It's not always easy or comfortable to tell clients the truth—in this case, that the Titans' fears during the bear market had gotten the best of them—but if the truth is told in a palatable way, the client will almost always accept it and be glad they are working with an honest advisor.

Governance

Carrie: In your RFP, you said that the two of you make all the decisions for the family's investment portfolio, is that right?

Ned: Well, for our branch of the family, yes.

Carrie: There's no investment committee?

Rose: We had one, but Dad died and the other member of the committee got old and didn't want to do it anymore. Should we have one?

Carrie: It's not a bad practice when so much capital's at stake. But building a good investment committee for a family can be a challenge. It's not like an investment committee for, say, a college or university. In those cases, you have lots of alums who understand investments and who are happy to contribute their time to building the endowment for their alma mater. It's much tougher for a family.

Rose: You serve on some investment committees, don't you, Ned?

Ned: Just one these days, for the symphony.

Carrie: That's a good example. You support the symphony financially, I'm sure, and consider it an important part of the city's cultural scene. So you're happy to contribute your time and expertise to building their endowment. But a family is different. Not that many people want to volunteer their time to make the Titan family even richer than they are!

[Ned and Rose both laugh.]

Rose: I don't see why not!

Carrie: So, usually, the family's investment committee is made up of people you know and trust and who are already associated with the family in some way. Your family lawyer, for example, or accountant. Maybe a trustee. It could even be another family member—a cousin, let's say—if there are no confidentiality issues.

Ned: What would be the advantage of having an investment committee? Most of the people you've mentioned aren't really investment types.

Carrie: No, but they are presumably people with good judgment and people you trust. Just having more people in the room when you have to make difficult decisions can make you and possibly others in the family more comfortable making those decisions. Also, I assume that whenever the two of you disagree, nothing happens?

Ned: Right. It has to be unanimous.

Rose: There's no tie-breaker!

Carrie: That's another role the committee could play, then. If the two of you don't agree, but the rest of the committee is on one side, well, that tells you something.

Rose: I guess we could think about it.

Carrie: One suggestion would be for the two of you to make up a short list of people you might ask to be on such a committee, and then we can go from there.

QUICK NOTE

Governance—how investment and other family decisions get made—is a crucial aspect of successful capital management. As Carrie Knowlton suggested, many wealthy families will find it useful to have an investment committee, even if the committee members aren't skilled investment professionals. The existence of such a committee is also a good training ground for younger family members. (See Chapter 10.)

Family Education

Carrie: You each have two grown children?

Rose: Yes. My two are out of college and working, a daughter in New York and a son in Boston.

Ned: My daughter is also working in New York. In fact, she and Rose's daughter are rooming together in an awful third-floor walkup on East Twenty-Sixth Street. Terrible place!

[But Rose was beaming. She loved the idea that her daughter was living and working in New York. Indeed, she wished she'd done the same thing when she was younger.]

Carrie: And your son?

Ned: Finishing up graduate school at the university here in town. He wants to teach at the college level.

Carrie: What I'm thinking is, when would be a good time to start educating the kids about investment matters? All this will be their responsibility someday, I assume.

Rose: Yes, it certainly will, if Ned and I don't screw it up and lose all the dough! [Laughter.] But right now, they're very young and very busy getting their careers started.

Carrie: True, but they're likely to be busy for a long time. Most of them will probably get married, then have kids, and the first thing you know, twenty years has gone by.

Ned: You're right about that. Our father brought us onto the investment committee way too late. Fortunately, he lived long enough to teach us something. But how do we get the kids interested, motivated?

Carrie: Well, you know them better than I do, but one thing that often works is to give the kids an assignment, something important. They can work on it together and then come back to the two of you with a recommendation.

Rose: Did you have something in mind?

Carrie: Sure. How about charging the kids with preparing a first draft of your investment policy statement?

Rose: But isn't that an awfully important document to be turning over to people who know almost nothing?

Carrie: It's a *very* important document. But remember that they'll be working from a form my firm will supply. Actually, you saw a copy of it in our response to your RFP. And whatever the kids produce will just be a draft for the two of you to look at. The nice thing about having to produce a policy statement is that it touches on every important aspect of the investment process. By the time your kids have worked their way through it, they'll know a lot more than they do now, and they'll be ready to move on to more of the nitty-gritty details of investing.

QUICK NOTE

It might seem rash to think about asking extremely inexperienced young adults to undertake the first draft of a document as important as an investment policy statement. But Carrie is making the point that educating the next generation about the management of capital is vastly more important than almost anything else the family will do.

Ned (speaking to Rose): Maybe the kids could start on it over Labor Day.

Rose: Our family has a place in Vermont that we share with another branch of the family. Our branch has a long tradition of gathering there over a long Labor Day Weekend. All the kids will be there.

Ned: Plus, in all likelihood, a couple of boyfriends!

Carrie: Would there be some family-only time when we could discuss this?

Rose: Sure. Our place isn't far from Stowe. The boyfriends like to hike, so they could go climb the mountain while we talk.

Carrie: That's great. Why don't we plan to get the process started over Labor Day, with the idea that the kids would come back to you with a draft by, say, Christmas.

Rose: Perfect. The kids are all usually home for Christmas.

Ned: Plus boyfriends!

Investment Managers

Ned: Has your firm reviewed all our managers?

Carrie: We're working on it, Ned. Since we don't use any of these guys, we're starting from scratch with little information.

Rose: You don't use a single one of them?

Carrie: I'm afraid not. But I can tell you this much just off the top of my head—we're likely to recommend that you terminate all of them.

Ned: Everyone?

Carrie: All these managers were on your former advisor's wrap account platform.[1] As you may or may not know, that means "pay to play." The managers were paying the broker to recommend them to you. Really good managers rarely have to do that.

Ned: But we've already paid a lot of taxes, and won't exiting these managers just generate more?

Carrie: Probably. What we'll do is triage them. Some will be both awful and expensive, and those will need to go right away. Others will be either awful *or* expensive, so we can be a little more patient with them. Maybe exit them when there are losses elsewhere in the portfolio that we can use to offset against any gains they have. We can also move some of the gains into future tax years. That sort of thing.

Rose: And what about the new managers you'll be recommending to replace the old ones? How will we go about reviewing them?

Carrie: We can do it in one of two ways. For most of our institutional clients—universities, foundations—we'll put together a search book that contains three or four appropriate candidates. We'll discuss those with the institution's investment committee and narrow it down to one or two. Then the committee, or sometimes the investment staff, will interview the final candidates and make the selection.

Rose: Sounds complicated.

Ned: That's the way we do it at the symphony.

Carrie: And I suppose it makes sense in an institutional setting. The idea there is to get as many eyes on the managers as possible before a final selection is made. But all too often the point is to spread the responsibility widely, so nobody is stuck with the burden of having picked a manager who turns out to underperform.

Ned: Absolutely! *I* wouldn't want to be the guy everybody pointed at!

Carrie: But for almost all our family clients we do it differently. I usually bring one manager to the table and discuss it with you. If you're uncomfortable with the manager, of course, I'll find a different one. But otherwise, we're good. That way, the responsibility's on Spenser—on me—which is where it should be.

Ned: Sold. Let's do it that way.

QUICK NOTE

As we'll see when we get to the discussion of new managers for the Titan family's portfolio (see Chapter 8), one important client management issue for advisors is putting investment managers in the proper perspective. Clients almost always overestimate the importance of manager selection, for example. In this meeting Carrie is already beginning to deal with this issue by suggesting that Spenser be mainly in charge of selecting managers, with the family having a veto.

Performance Reporting

Carrie: So here's where we are and where we're headed. We'll gradually bring your equity exposure up over time. We'll get your children working on a first draft of the investment policy statement. Spenser will continue to evaluate your existing managers, although as I said we'll probably want to replace them all over time. What else?

Rose: When can we expect our first performance report?

Carrie: Good question. You saw our standard report in our RFP response. Does that work for you, or will we need to do some custom work?

[A sample investment performance report is available on the companion website for this book at www.wiley.com/go/familycapital.]

Ned (paging through the sample report) It's so different from what we're used to. Can you walk us through it quickly?

Carrie: Sure. We'll go over this in more detail at our performance reporting meeting, but, as you can see, it's in the form of a letter from Spenser to you, signed by me. The report contains these sections:

- For some clients—those who are most interested in the markets—we begin the performance report with an "executive summary." This section is a brief series of charts and graphs illustrating the most important aspects of current market conditions. The summary might also show so-called "performance attribution," that is, which factors added and which subtracted value during the quarter. If there are managers we're worried about, we'll list them on a "watch list." Finally, if the client owns a large position in one stock, we'll usually include a page summarizing how the stock performed that quarter.
- Following the executive summary, we have a brief section devoted to an overview of how the capital markets performed in general during the past quarter. As you can see, this is only three or four paragraphs long and touches only on the important points. That section isn't written for you specifically, but is the same for all our client letters.
- The next section is a high-level, plain-English view of how your portfolio performed. As you can see from this sample, it compares the overall portfolio performance to its benchmarks, then does the same for each sector of the portfolio: U.S. large cap stocks, U.S. small cap, international, and so on. Managers are mentioned only if they were outliers during the quarter, performing especially well or badly.
- The next section shows any major transactions in the portfolio during the quarter—moneys withdrawn, moneys added, capital calls, and so on.
- The section after that—the final plain-English section—contains whatever recommendations we have for that quarter. Moving money around tactically, terminating a manager, whatever.
- Then you have the quantitative section, showing the numbers for how the overall portfolio performed, how each sector performed, how each manager performed, all compared to the relevant benchmarks.

- After that are some charts that can be easily customized. The most important is the asset allocation chart, showing how your actual allocation compares to your targets, and also where you are relative to your upper and lower allocation limits.
- Questions? Thoughts about how the report could be improved for your use?

Ned: What do you think, Rose? It's so superior to what we used to get it's hard to think how it might be improved.

Rose: Like gilding the lily.

Ned: Maybe after we've worked with the report for a while we'll find ways to make it more useful for us. But for now, let's stick with this.

Carrie: Sounds good. Just keep in mind that some customization is easy—and free—while other customization is hard and we have to charge for it. The sooner you decide on any customization requests, the easier it will be for us to make the changes and do it cheaply.

QUICK NOTE

Obviously, wealth advisory firms differ on how they structure their performance reports and on how flexible the reports can be. The main issue, however, is to make the reports as client-friendly as possible. A state-of-the-art performance report with every bell and whistle imaginable might make the advisor feel good about itself. But if the client can't understand the report, it's a waste of time and money.

Post-Meeting Discussion

Rose: Ned, did it seem to you that there was something strange about the meeting with Carrie Knowlton?

Ned: Yes, I was just thinking the same thing. It wasn't like meeting with a vendor, it was like she was part of our team.

Rose: Like she was sitting on the same side of the table with us as we looked out at the investment world and tried to deal with it.

Ned: She didn't try to sell us anything.

Rose: And she seemed to know what she was talking about.

Ned: We should have hired Spenser Advisors years ago!

Rose: Better late than never! What say we walk over to the Duquesne Club. You can buy me a drink and we can and toast our good judgment.

Ned: You're on!

SUMMARY

A financial advisor who really cares about the client—as opposed to one who only cares about selling—will proceed in a profoundly different way in meetings with families. In this chapter we observed a client-centered advisor as she handled her first full meeting with the Titan family.

Carrie Knowlton, the advisor, did her best to establish herself as a valued part of the Titan family investment team. She focused on the high-level issues that would have the most impact on the family's fortunes over the long haul: an equity-oriented strategy, governance and decision making in the family, educating younger family members. Only then did Carrie move to short-term issues: manager selection and performance reporting.

And note that Carrie wasn't shy about giving her opinions. She actually opened the meeting by criticizing the too-cautious posture of the family's portfolio. Many advisors prefer to keep their opinions to themselves out of fear of alienating the client. But clients want to hear your opinion—that is part of why they hired you. An advisor who has no opinions is an empty suit.

So effective was Spenser's approach that after only one meeting Ned and Rose Titan were already celebrating their good sense in finding Spenser Advisors. But the specific firm they ended up with was less important than the *kind* of firm it was: an unbiased, client-focused firm that saw its job as working hand-in-hand with its clients to ensure their wealth would remain intact across the generations.

This is of central importance to the families, of course, but it also worked to the long-term advantage of Spenser, which was able to establish very long-term client relationships that provided in effect an annuity-like stream of revenue to the firm. The combination of a stable and growing income stream, and close attention to costs and appropriate fee levels, would over the long run allow Spenser Advisors to build a very valuable franchise.

NOTE

1. The term *wrap account* used by Carrie is industry lingo for *wrap-fee account*, an innovation that became extremely popular because it dispensed with the sales commissions stockbrokers usually charged. Instead, the broker charged a fee that wrapped around the account and covered advice, manager selection, and performance reporting. However, wrap fees were quite high—often starting at 3% per year—and the fact that the managers were sharing fees with the broker corrupted the broker's ability to give honest advice.

CHAPTER 5

The Titans Create an Investment Policy Statement

PREPARATION AND USE

Over a long Labor Day Weekend, the Titan family gathered at the house near Stowe, Vermont, that they shared with another branch of the family. Spenser Advisors was invited to attend the first day of the gathering to introduce themselves to Ned and Rose's children, to explain who they were and how they worked, and to launch the process of drafting an investment policy statement for the family.

As we will see as we listen in on these meetings, the family gathering was far more successful than anyone—even Spenser—could have imagined. But, first, let's learn a bit about the adult children of this branch of the Titan family, since they will be the ones mainly occupied with drafting the policy statement.

Ellen Wainwright. Ned Titan and Rose Wainwright, stepbrother and sister, each had two children, a son and a daughter. The eldest, Ellen, was Rose's daughter. Ellen had always been something of an unconventional child. A tomboy when young, Ellen had struggled at school, unable to sit still in class and having little apparent interest in her studies. Although she was never formally diagnosed with ADHD, she exhibited many similar symptoms.

Ellen had started as a kindergartener at the private girls' school her mother had attended. But in early middle school, with Ellen unhappy and not exactly flourishing, Rose moved Ellen to a coeducational school nearby. The change wasn't exactly magical, but it did allow Ellen to establish herself as a new personality at the new school, and at a school half filled with boys her high energy level didn't seem so unusual. By high school Ellen was doing much better, but she was never going to be a straight-A student—she simply didn't care that much and continued to view herself as something of a rebel.

After college, Ellen moved to New York City for no better reason than that she thought it was the most exciting city in the world and she wanted to be part of that. She convinced her cousin, Suzy (Ned's daughter, see ahead), to join her even though Suzy was a bit nervous about it. They roomed together, as Ned pointed out earlier, in a small, not-very-plush apartment on East 26th Street between Third Avenue and Lexington.

Ellen had no job when she moved to New York and, just to pay her rent, went to work for a small, organic grocery store on Second Avenue just around the corner from her apartment.

Billy Wainwright. Ellen's younger brother, William, known as Billy, was a happy, outgoing, cheerful sort of fellow who made friends easily and never seemed to be out of sorts. Rose always said that Billy would grow up to be a salesman, and she was right. After college, Billy got a job selling pharmaceuticals for a firm in Boston. The job required a lot of travel, but Billy was young and unattached and found that he enjoyed traveling to new towns and meeting new people. He quickly established himself as a valuable member of the firm's sales team.

It was well-known in the Titan family that Billy had a close girlfriend, but Billy never mentioned her, much less introduced her to his family. This made Rose nervous, but Billy was an adult who was earning his own living, and he was, Rose decided, entitled to make his own decisions in life.

Suzy Titan. Suzy was a pretty, popular girl who cruised through high school and the first couple of years of college, but then seemed to hit the wall. She lost interest in her studies, began experimenting with drugs, and found herself on academic probation. Ned was beside himself with worry about her, but there seemed to be little he and his wife could do.

Late one night, Suzy's car ran off the road, rolled over several times, and Suzy wound up in the hospital with a concussion and broken ribs. She had no memory of the accident, and little memory of anything between the time she'd left an off-campus party and when she woke up in the hospital. Suzy's blood alcohol level was well above the legal limit and she had a high reading for THC, indicating that she had recently been using marijuana. Fortunately, no one else was in the car.

Ironically, the traffic accident turned out to be a Godsend, as it shocked Suzy into realizing that she was headed down a very dangerous path. She dropped out of college for a semester and spent the time working on a Native American reservation in Arizona, then returned to college and got her degree, albeit a term late.

Not really sure what she wanted to do with her life, Suzy was willing, though not exactly eager, to join her cousin Ellen in New York. Suzy had visited New York several times, and while she enjoyed those visits, especially the part about going to Broadway shows, the size and pace of the city unnerved her. She went to work as a bank teller, found that she liked the work and was good with numbers, and was quickly promoted. At the time of the Titan family meeting in Vermont, Suzy was in the middle of a management training course at the bank and was enjoying the work and enjoying living in New York.

Geoffrey Titan. Geoffrey, Suzy's younger brother and the youngest of the children in this branch of the Titan family, was a quiet, studious boy who flourished in school and went on to the University of Pittsburgh, graduating with a degree in history. He was currently doing graduate work and was hoping to find a tenure-track position at a college or university when he completed his Ph.D.

Geoffrey was widely believed by the family to be its most intelligent member. On the other hand, while the other three cousins were outgoing and friendly, Geoffrey was bookish and tended to keep to himself. His sister and his cousins had made a project of drawing Geoffrey out, even going so far as to fix him up with suitable—and occasionally very *un*suitable—young women.

Geoffrey mainly took all this with good grace, but in fact he was happiest when he could be alone with his books. Because he was still in school, Geoffrey lived at home with Ned and his mother.

THE TITAN FAMILY MEETING

Ahead of the meeting over Labor Day Weekend, Carrie Knowlton had sent copies of the form of investment policy statement to each of the adult children, with copies to Ned and Rose. She asked the kids to look through the form, recognizing that not much of it would make sense to them at this point, and to note down any specific questions they had.

When they convened in Vermont, they were all seated around the large kitchen table over a buffet lunch: Ned, Rose, Ellen, Billy, Suzy, and Geoffrey. Carrie Knowlton was attending, representing Spenser Advisors, and she had brought with her a younger member of her firm, Roger Epperson. While Carrie was in her fifties, Roger was in his mid-thirties and Carrie felt the Titan kids might relate to him more easily.

When everyone was seated, and while the Titans were eating, Carrie opened the meeting as follows.

Carrie: It's very nice to meet the other members of the family, and thank you for having us with you today. Has everyone had a chance to look over the policy statement form we sent around?

Ellen: I looked it over, but I can't say I understood much of it.

Billy: I didn't understand *any* of it!

Carrie: That's all right, we're going to walk through each major section of the policy statement today and answer any questions you might have. Shall we start?

Rose: Should Ned and I stay? The first draft is the kids' responsibility.

Carrie: It's up to you. I suggest you stay for at least the first part of the meeting.

Suzy: But it would be easier for us to ask stupid questions if Dad and Aunt Rose weren't here to laugh at us.

[Laughter around the table.]

Ned: And it would be *really* embarrassing for the kids to hear the stupid questions Rose and I might ask!

[More laughter.]

Geoffrey: Shouldn't we let Carrie and Roger eat and then start?

Carrie: Roger can eat while I talk, and then I'll eat while he talks. I talk more than he does, and he eats more than I do!

Roger: Very funny!

Carrie: Okay, let's open to page one of the policy statement. By the way, I'll sometimes refer to this document as an "IPS," short for investment policy statement.

[A version of the investment policy statement is available on the companion website for this book at www.wiley.com/go/familycapital.]

The IPS: Description of the Family

Carrie: As you can see, the introduction to the policy statement addresses the purpose of the document, which is pretty much self-explanatory. Does anyone have a specific question about it?

[Heads shook and Billy said, "Nope."]

Carrie: Okay. Part One of the IPS calls for a description of the family. Keep in mind that one very important purpose of the policy statement is this: suppose something were to happen to Ned and Rose—a common accident, for example. Who would take over the management of the portfolio? It might be one or more of the four of you, but it might also be someone else, someone outside the family who might not know all that much about the family's background. So we want to write this section as though we're addressing that future person who might be assuming responsibility for the portfolio.

Billy: Part of this section is pretty straightforward, I think. Just listing the family members, their birthdays and ages, what they're up to at this moment in their lives. Any of us could write that part. And Mom and Uncle Ned could write the part about family trusts, I guess. But what about this first section, talking about the family's background and history? I don't know most of this stuff. Does anybody else?

Ellen: Don't look at me.

Suzy: Or me.

Geoffrey: I'm clueless.

[Carrie looks over at Ned and Rose, raising an eyebrow.]

Ned: I guess the history of our family isn't something we've ever talked much about.

Rose: But there's a reason for that. We wanted the kids to grow up like any other kids, not like there was something special about them.

Ned: It's really easy for children who come from money to get spoiled.

Rose: And entitled.

Ellen: Hey, we're not like that!

Rose: Maybe, Ellen, dear, that's because we've always treated you like you were just a regular, middle-class person.

Ellen: Oh, right! Like I'm blind!

Ned: What does that mean?

Billy: Come on, Uncle Ned, we live in a mansion practically. So do Suzy and Geoff.

Geoffrey: We all went to private schools and expensive colleges.

Suzy: You drive a Mercedes, Dad, and Aunt Suzy drives a Beamer.

Rose: Well, we did the best we could, given the circumstances. Are you suggesting we should all have moved to a trailer park?

[Laughter.]

Suzy: No, Aunt Rose, I don't think we'd be too happy in a trailer park. We're just making the point that the fact that we're rich isn't exactly news to us.

Carrie (intervening): Actually, you're all correct. Trying to raise kids as normally as possible is exactly the right approach for a wealthy family to take. But children know a lot more than they let on, and they sense even more than they know. If you live in the best neighborhood in town, in a very large house, and drive a Mercedes, well, it sort of speaks for itself.

Ellen: Exactly.

QUICK NOTE

This is an important point—many parents in wealthy families imagine that if they don't talk about their wealth to their kids, the kids will think they're just a normal, middle-class family. But children are far more insightful than that. In the case of the Titan family, the children grew to adulthood unspoiled and unentitled not because Ned and Rose didn't talk about money with them, but because Ned and Rose set an example by working hard and behaving modestly themselves.

Carrie: Probably more important than anything else is what the kids see the parents doing. If the parents are modest, hardworking people who don't put on airs, the kids will just naturally follow that lead. On the other hand, well, we all know wealthy families who flaunt it and whose kids are spoiled rotten.

Geoffrey: I'd really like to know more about the history of our family. I mean, we all know that our, uh, let's see, Great-Great-Great-Grandfather immigrated to America from Italy way back when.

Suzy: And that he started a business and made good.

Billy: But that's about all we know.

Ellen: Maybe our parents don't *want* us to know.

Geoffrey: Why would that be?

Ellen: You know what they say: behind every great fortune there's a great crime![1]

Rose: Ellen!

Ellen: I'm kidding, Mom. I think. But since no one ever talks about old George Titan, maybe there's something to hide there.

Ned: Okay, okay, let's just agree that maybe we should have spent more time talking to the kids about the history of our family. What I know about it, frankly, makes me very proud to be a Titan.

Rose: Me, too, even though I don't have a drop of Titan blood in me. Your Great-Great-Great-Grandfather must have been a really remarkable man. He came to America with nothing and when he died he was one of the richest men in Pittsburgh!

Geoffrey: Sort of like Andrew Carnegie.

Ned: Well, on a much smaller scale—Carnegie was the wealthiest man in the world!

Rose: And your grandfather and Great-Grandfather—the two Jakes—were no slouches, either.

Billy: They were both lawyers, weren't they, like Uncle Ned?

Ned: Well, yes, your Great-Grandpa was a lawyer, but he was much more than that. For one thing, he started his own law firm when he was your age, Billy, imagine that!

Rose: And Great-Grandpa Jake didn't get rich on legal fees. He specialized in representing young men who had ideas and wanted to build companies around them.

Ellen: Why only young *men*?

Ned (laughing): Fair point! But remember, in those days women didn't have as many opportunities as they do today. I can't remember Grandpa ever representing a woman, though maybe he did.

Rose: Actually, Ned, Great-Grandpa Jake worked closely with our Great-Aunt Grace when she was starting her career as an engineer, and then again when she changed jobs.

Ned: Well, that's right. I forgot about that. But my main point is that Grandpa made most of his money by buying stock in the companies these young men—young *people* were starting. And he added a lot of value to those companies over the years. He was much more than just their legal counsel.

Rose: Everyone in the extended Titan family has benefited from what George Titan accomplished, and our branch has benefited in addition from what the Jakes accomplished. We're a very lucky family. And, by the way, Ellen, your Great-Great-Great-Grandmother, Ellie, was a full partner in everything her husband did.

Ellen: You mean, she worked in the family company?

Rose: Well, no, she was a mom. What I mean is, from what little I heard from Grandpa, old George respected Ellie's advice and almost always took it. Pretty much every important decision George made in his life resulted from long conversations he had with Ellie.

Ned: Well, we're taking up way too much time with this family history stuff. Carrie and Roger will only be with us for another hour or two, so let's get back to the investment policy statement.

Geoffrey: But this is really interesting stuff!

Rose: How about this. Over dinner tonight Ned and I will tell you everything we know about the family history. It's interesting to us, too, you know. I only wish Grandpa had spent more time talking to us about it. There's a lot of family history that's probably lost now that everyone in Daddy's generation has passed on.

Geoffrey: What a shame!

Ned: Let's talk over dinner. Back to you, Carrie.

Carrie: Family stories are very important. Your family has a lot of money, but that money didn't just fall out of the sky. It was earned by people, your forebears, who did remarkable things. In fact, it sounds to me as though you had several generations of very talented forebears. Not many families can make that claim.

Roger: These stories are really interesting to me, and I'm not even related to you!

Carrie: Roger and I won't be here for dinner, but after you have your discussion, we'll look forward to seeing what you write in this section of the IPS. One reason family stories are meaningful is that they demonstrate the important things your family has accomplished over the years. It fleshes out the family culture and what you want your legacy to be. And, remember, that DNA is in your blood.

Rose: Well, not mine. I was adopted by Daddy.

Carrie: I didn't know that, Rose. I wondered what you meant when you said earlier that you didn't have a drop of Titan blood! But I don't mean "DNA" in its literal sense. I mean it in the sense of being a part of a really remarkable family, of rubbing shoulders with people who are closely connected with people who did remarkable things.

Rose: I agree. I'm very lucky to be part of all this.

Carrie: My guess is that some of the people around this table, and maybe their children, will also do remarkable things. It will be interesting to watch.

QUICK NOTE

Advisors sometimes make the mistake of viewing the families they work with as *clients* instead of as *families*. Families are flesh and blood and they have family histories that are often utterly fascinating. Advisors should learn about those histories and, to the extent the families themselves aren't already telling family stories, they should be encouraged to do so.

The IPS: Investment Objectives

Carrie: I'm going to ask Roger to lead the discussion on the next section of the IPS, so I can eat.

Roger: Sure, thanks, Carrie. And, again, thanks to all of you for allowing us to butt into your holiday weekend!

Geoffrey: So far, it's been a lot more interesting than I thought it would be!

Roger: I'm afraid things are going to get more complicated and maybe a little more boring. As you can see, this next section discusses the various family groupings, and specifies investment objectives for each of those groups. Each group is, basically, a generation or a coherent family *unit*. For example, Ned and his wife and the trusts of which they're beneficiaries might be one family unit that would have one overall set of investment objectives.

Ned: What about trusts with beneficiaries that span the generations, or even the family units? For example, what we call the "Grandchildren's Trust." That one was established for Rose and me—we're the "grandchildren" referred to in the name of the trust. Obviously, Rose and I are the heads of different family units. Also, if we don't spend all the corpus during our lifetimes …

Rose: Which I certainly hope we won't!

Ned: Right! If we don't spend it all, the kids become the next generation of beneficiaries.

Roger: Carrie can correct me if I'm wrong, but some of these kinds of issues can be relatively straightforward, and some can be complicated. For example, fiduciary rules require that multigenerational trusts be managed for the benefit of all the beneficiaries, not just the current beneficiaries. And those current and future beneficiaries can have conflicting interests.

Rose: Conflicting in what way, Roger?

Carrie: What Roger is referring to is the common situation where the current beneficiaries of a trust want as much income from the trust as possible, while future beneficiaries want to keep the spending down and invest for capital appreciation.

Rose: Yes, I see. But in this case Ned and I take nothing from the Grandchildren's Trust. We're entitled to the income if we need it, but since we don't it's simply being accumulated.

Carrie: Well, that simplifies matters somewhat. But, still, we have to consider the possibility that at some point you might need or want the income.

Rose: Fair enough. But I would still think the trust would be invested mainly for growth, right, Carrie?

Carrie: *Mmmff.* [Speaking with her mouth full, then swallowing.] Never fails. All I have to do is stuff my mouth and somebody asks me a question. But, yes, that's right. We'll get to the specific investment objectives for the trust in a minute. Are you finished with the discussion of the family groupings, Roger?

Roger: Almost. We'll depend on the family to guide us through the right family groups. But in a typical case, which you folks might not be, of course, we would expect to establish something like the following groupings:

- Ned and his wife and any trusts for their benefit. We would also include here any IRAs for Ned or his wife, pension accounts for their benefit, and so on.
- Rose and her husband, plus any trusts, IRAs, and so on for their benefit.
- We understand that each of the kids has a trust for his or her benefit, and I assume you each also have some personal assets. Thus, for Ellen, one group would include the trust or trusts for her benefit plus her personal assets.
- We'll establish a separate investment group for any trusts, like the Grandchildren's Trust, that span family units or generations.
- I understand there are two relatively small family foundations. Those would be in groups of their own.

Once we have the groups organized properly, we'll turn to the important task of establishing investment objectives for each group.

Ellen: How do you do that? Also—no laughing!—what's an "investment objective"?

Roger: Really, it's just the purpose of the capital. Suppose, for example, that Ned were to say to us, "Look, I have more assets than I'll likely ever need. I want to be able to support my lifestyle and to live without worrying constantly about my portfolio or that I'm somehow going to spend down my principal. Twenty years from now, I want my capital to be at least as large as it is now, that is, adjusted for inflation, net of all the draws on that capital. Draws like spending, taxes, and so on."

Ned: That *is* what I would say to you!

Carrie: I bring Roger along to these meetings because he can read the clients' minds.

[Laughter.]

Ned: Except I would probably add that I would like to leave as much as possible for Suzy and Geoffrey, and also enough to substantially increase the size of our family foundation. As Roger mentioned, it's currently small.

Roger: If you page ahead to the exhibits section of the IPS you can see that, for each (currently hypothetical) family unit, the investment objectives exhibits follow a standard pattern. We start with a description of that family unit or entity. Then, as you can see, the Investment Objectives section describes the objectives in simple English. Different family units, individuals, and entities will have different objectives, and those that are shown here are just illustrations of common objectives. Following that, we mention any other appropriate guidelines, then performance objectives. Sometimes there are both long-term objectives and shorter-term objectives. Then the asset allocation strategy for that entity is set forth, with targets and ranges, and, finally, we set forth the tax status—that is, which state the person is taxed in, any local taxes, whether the Alternative Minimum Tax is an issue, that sort of thing.

Carrie: But while we're on the subject of investment objectives, I want to mention something that is very important. I'm jumping ahead a bit, but since I mentioned it at the start of my very first meeting with Ned and Rose, I'll ring it up now. I'm talking about investing with a *capital preservation bias*. Does anyone know what that means?

[Roger raises his hand. Everyone laughs.]

Carrie: I sure *hope* you know, Roger! Anyway, investing with a bias toward preservation of the capital—as opposed, let's say, to trying to grow the capital very rapidly—is the way Spenser invests its client money. It's not specifically an investment objective, but more like a fundamental principal we follow.

Suzy: Am I the only one who's confused?

Carrie: Sorry. Let me see if I can explain it in simple terms. Investors who are only concerned with growing their capital as fast as possible will think mainly in terms of investment *returns*. They'll look out at the market and say, where can we get the highest returns in today's environment.

Billy: Isn't that what everybody does?

Carrie: Unfortunately, it is what most people do. But there's a serious problem with that approach. Does anyone know what it is? Not you, Roger!

Rose: Wait, I think I see what you're getting at. The investors you just described are likely to get into trouble because they didn't think about how much *risk* they were taking.

Carrie: Exactly! And at Spenser, we think about risk—think about it long and hard—long before we start worrying about return. There are a bunch of reasons for this, but two of the most important are—Roger?

Roger: One is that over anyone's investment lifetime, there are going to be huge market dislocations that can destroy your capital. In a very real sense, the core challenge of managing private capital is to prepare for those dislocations without undermining the long-term returns you need to generate.[2]

Carrie: That's right. Think of stock market returns over the course of many years. If you plot them on a chart, they form a bell curve.

[Carrie draws a bell curve on a piece of paper and holds it up for everyone to see. It looks like this:]

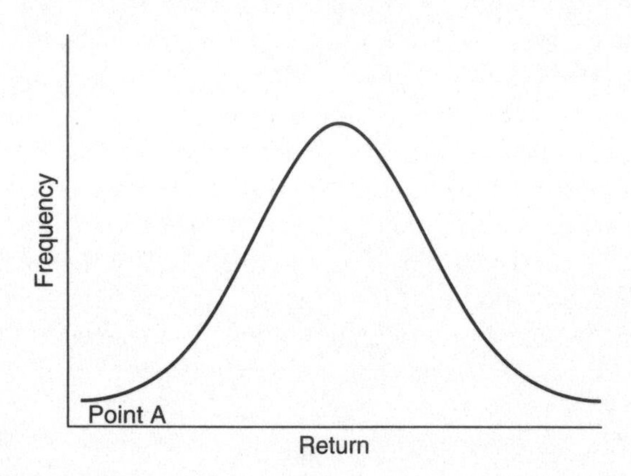

Carrie: At the peak of the curve is where the most common market returns fall. So for U.S. stocks, that would be in the eight-to-twelve percent range annually. As you go down the right side of the curve, you get years in which returns were higher, and then much higher, but these are relatively rare. As you go down the left side of the curve, you get some really bad markets, but those are also fairly rare.

Roger: But not as rare as they *should* be.

Carrie: Right. If you look at the left tail of the bell curve, around point A on the chart, those very bad market outcomes happen far more frequently than they would if outcomes were completely evenly distributed.

Rose: I see. So one reason for an investor to be capital preservation–oriented is that really lousy markets happen more often than they should.

Roger: That's right, Rose. And on top of that, the point Carrie is making is that, while market returns are mainly, but not perfectly, symmetrical, the outcomes for family capital tend to be very *a*symmetrical. There are three reasons for this. The first is what we would call a *behavioral* factor, that is, it doesn't have directly to do with the markets, but rather with how investors react—emotionally—to market turmoil.

Carrie: There are people who have devoted their lives to studying investor behavior in the face of powerful markets.[3] What this research tends to show is that, while investors like bull markets, they really, really hate bear markets. So there's one asymmetry right there—in general, people hate bear markets more than they love bull markets. In fact, people hate bear markets so much that they tend to panic and sell out near the bottom of bear markets. This immortalizes their losses.

Roger: Plus, now that they no longer own stocks, their portfolios don't have enough octane to recover from the loss. Lots of investors who panic and sell out during bear markets never recover their lost capital.

[Ned and Rose exchange a look.]

Ned: As we mentioned to Carrie earlier, I'm afraid we have an example of that in our own family.

Suzy: Really?

Ned (sighing): My Uncle George got so worried at the bottom of the bear market back in 1974–75 that he sold all his stocks.

Rose: And he never bought stocks again until the day he died. That branch of the family had no growth assets in their portfolio, and they ended up spending it all down.

Ned: We're now the so-called "rich" Titans and they're the "poor" Titans. It's a very bad situation.

Roger: I'm really sorry to hear that.

Rose: It's sad, but they brought it on themselves by selling out at the bottom and then never reinvesting. Unfortunately, it's caused a lot of family division.

Suzy: Our cousins are jealous of us and some of them don't even speak to us!

Billy: Like it was our fault, somehow.

Ned: Well, that's enough dirty linen for today! Anyway, your point about fearing bad markets and doing the wrong thing is something that resonates with us.

Carrie: We talk about these kinds of things at Spenser all the time, but we don't often run into real life catastrophes like that.

Roger: So that's the first reason Spenser worries so much about risk and therefore invests for capital preservation. The second asymmetry has to do with the simple mathematics of investment returns.

Carrie: Suppose you start by investing a million dollars. In the first year, your money appreciates fifty percent, but in the second year it drops fifty percent. What's happened to your capital?

Suzy: You're right back where you started.

Billy: Except you've had a really exciting ride along the way!

[Laughter.]

Roger: Actually, that's wrong. Not the excitement part, the back-where-you-started part. If we do the math, we started with one million dollars and after one year, up fifty percent, we now have $1,500,000, right? Now, in year two, we go down fifty percent. Fifty percent of $1,500,000 is $750,000, so we're down to $750,000.

Geoffrey: Egad! That's right. If you go up fifty percent and down fifty percent, you've actually lost $250,000!

Roger: Exactly. And it works the other way around, too. If you lose fifty percent of your million in year one, then gain fifty percent in year two, you're still down $250,000.

Suzy: I hate that math!

Roger: Everybody hates it, but it's an iron law of investing: losses hurt you more than gains help you. So that's reason number two that we focus on risk and try to avoid incurring steep losses. It's the asymmetry between the impact of losses versus gains. It's very, very difficult to recover from, say, a fifty percent loss of your capital.

Carrie: In fact, most families who experience such a big loss never recover from it. So, as Roger said, we try to structure portfolios so that losses on that level are extremely unlikely to happen.

Roger: And then, finally, there is a special asymmetry that mainly affects families who are already rich.

Rose: I think I see where you're headed with this. You're going to point out that if, as a family, we get even richer than we are, that's nice, but not especially important. It won't change our lives. But if we were to get *poor* …

Geoffrey: Like Great Uncle George's branch of the family …

Rose: Right. If we were to get poor, that would be a terrible outcome. So getting richer isn't as good as getting poor is bad.

Carrie: Bull's-eye, Rose. That's the third asymmetry and reason number three why we invest for preservation of the capital.

QUICK NOTE

Advisors who work with wealthy families should always be focused on the preservation of the families' capital. But when families are out looking for an advisor, they are often focused on which firm can get them the best returns. Advisors who emphasize the great returns they are getting will often get the business but will often undermine the families they work with. It's a conundrum every honest advisor and every family has to deal with.

Ellen: Okay, you've convinced us. But how does capital preservation investing work?

Carrie: We'll get into that in detail as we design and manage the portfolio, but we can give you an eighty-thousand-foot answer now, can't we, Roger?

Roger: Sure. As we mentioned, capital preservation investing begins by thinking first about risk and only second about return. So when prices are at historic lows, risk will also be low and we will want to own significant risk assets—stocks, for example. But as prices get higher and higher, we'll want lighten up on those kinds of assets, because the higher the price, the higher the risk of a serious market correction.

Carrie: That's right. I'm getting a bit down into the weeds, now, but one widely recognized metric of stock pricing is the ratio of its market price to its earnings per share. Say a company is selling at forty-five dollars a share and it's earning three dollars a share. That company's price/earnings ratio—or P/E ratio—would be fifteen.

Roger: Carrie used that example because stocks have historically tended to sell, on average, at a P/E of about fifteen.

Carrie: So let's say that the way we've designed your portfolio, U.S. large-capitalization stocks—that is, the big companies we've all heard of, like GE and Microsoft—will represent twenty percent of your assets. And let's also say that we are willing to go as high as twenty-five percent in large-company stocks, or as low as fifteen percent. Everybody with me?

[Heads nod.]

Carrie: Okay. Now, if the entire stock market, not just any random stock, is selling for an average P/E of fifteen, you can expect that your portfolio will be at its target allocation to large company stocks, in other words, twenty percent. But as prices begin to rise, we will gradually reduce your exposure to these stocks. In fact, if prices get much above twenty times earnings—a P/E of twenty—we'll likely be at our lower limit of fifteen percent.

Roger: In other words, as stocks get pricier, the room for additional appreciation gets smaller and the likelihood of a serious correction in the markets gets bigger. We really, really don't want to be *overexposed* to stocks when that correction comes. We want to be *underexposed* to them.

Carrie: Similarly, as stock prices fall, we will want to own more of them. In effect, they've gone on sale so we'll want to stock up. If pricing gets down around twelve or so—I mean, a P/E of twelve—we will likely be positioned at our maximum exposure to stocks. In this case, that would be twenty-five percent. Does everyone see how this works?

Billy: I see it, but why just bounce around inside that range you've set? If stocks get really expensive, why not just get out of stocks altogether? And if they get real cheap, why not buy them by the basketful?

Carrie: There are couple of reasons, Billy. One is that selling stocks generates capital gains taxes, so we don't want to sell if we don't have to. But the main reason is simply that we're not infallible. Spenser may think the market is outrageously expensive when stocks are selling for twenty-two times earnings, but that market could get a lot *more* expensive. Maybe prices would go to thirty times earnings, something like that. If we sold out at twenty-two times, we'd be leaving a lot of money on the table.

Roger: And it works the other way, too. Spenser might think the market's a screaming buy at ten times earnings. But the market could get a lot cheaper, going to, say, six or seven times earnings. So we'd be buying stocks way too soon. They'd keep going down after we bought them and our clients wouldn't be too happy. A famous economist, John Maynard Keynes, once said, "The markets can remain irrational longer than you can remain solvent."

Carrie: And, unfortunately, it's true. Markets can go crazy and stay crazy for a long time.

Ellen: In other words, all this is very complicated!

Carrie: And we've barely scratched the surface. I'll get off this subject in a second, but I want to mention one slight complexity about stock valuations. I mentioned price/earnings ratios and how they're calculated, which is the current price divided by the current dividend. That gives a snapshot of valuations, but when we're looking at the market as a whole it might be better to look at valuations on a longer-term basis.

Roger: Carrie is talking about so-called "Shiller P/Es."

Carrie: Right. A fellow named Robert Shiller has constructed valuations that are *normalized* by dividing the inflation-adjusted price level of large-company stocks by the moving average of the preceding ten years of real reported earnings. So sometimes you might see Spenser talking about short-term P/Es and sometimes we'll be looking at longer term, Shiller P/Es.[4] And this is just Capital Preservation Investing 101. You could get a Ph.D. in the subject!

The IPS: Asset Allocation

Carrie: As you can see in the IPS form, once we've established the family groups and set the investment objectives for each group, the next step is to design each group's portfolio. That's what we call *asset allocation*:

the decisions about which asset classes to include or exclude in each portfolio and how much of each asset class to own. This is a long and complicated and very important discussion, and we usually do it in a completely separate meeting. So for now I'm just going to outline briefly what asset allocation is all about. I'm happy to take questions, but keep in mind that we'll be doing a deep dive on this topic, probably at our next meeting.

[See Chapter 7 for the asset allocation meeting discussion.]

Billy: I think my brain is already full, anyway!
Carrie: But we still have a couple of topics to go!
Billy: Bio-break!

[Following the break, the meeting resumes.]

Carrie: Asset allocation is the process we go through to design your overall portfolios so they will meet your investment objectives. It's a complicated process, but in reality it's just a smart form of diversification. Right, Roger?
Roger: Exactly. "Don't put all your eggs in one basket."
Carrie: We divide all the possible investment assets in the world into *asset classes*, each asset class consisting of securities that tend to behave very much like each other. They have similar financial characteristics and are subject to the same rules, laws, and regulations. Very broad asset classes would be stocks, bonds, and cash.
Roger: But we actually break the groups down into finer categories: U.S. large-company stocks, U.S. small-company stocks, non-U.S. large-company stocks, and so on.
Ellen: Why do you do that? Doesn't it just make things more complicated?
Carrie: It sure does! But it very much improves the diversification of your portfolio. Also, a broad category like "stocks" is hard to deal with. There are so many different kinds of stocks all over the world.
Ned: But we're going to devote a separate meeting to this topic, right?
Carrie: Right.
Ned: Then in the interest of time, I suggest we move on, unless someone has a really burning question.
Suzy: I have one. Where's dessert?

[Laughter. Rose and Billy leave briefly to bring in the dessert, then the meeting continues.]

The IPS: Spending

Carrie: Our form of IPS has a section in it on spending. I know we're treading on delicate ground here. In a way, what your family spends is none of our or anybody else's business. The point of this section isn't to tell you how to live your lives, but only to point out the impact of spending on your capital.

Roger: When we're talking to institutional clients—organizations like college and university endowments, foundations, even pension plans—the spending issue is usually pretty simple. Institutions tend to spend roughly four to five percent of their asset value every year. Charitable foundations *have* to spend at least five percent, and most other institutions tend to follow that model, although the average is probably between four and five percent.

Roger: There's also a dirty little secret about institutional spending policies. When the stock markets have been weak for a while, institutional spending tends to go down. Everyone says, "We really shouldn't spend more than three or four percent per year or we'll go broke."

Carrie: And then, after a few years of strong markets, students, faculty, and administrations begin to demand more spending, so the institution thinks, "Well, we could easily spend five percent or so and still be fine."

Geoffrey: So which is right? Three, four, or five percent?

Carrie: My view is that four percent is probably the right number. But our main point is that institutional spending is more a political issue than a true investment issue.

Suzy: But does it matter?

Roger: Sure. It means that institutions reduce their spending just when they don't really need to—because the markets are likely to be strong looking forward. And they increase their spending just when they shouldn't—because markets are likely to be weak going forward.

Suzy: Oh, I see.

Carrie: For an institution, the issue should really come down to intergenerational equity. How much can the organization spend on today's needs and still be fair to future generations the institution is serving?

Roger: After all, if *past* generations hadn't been fair to future generations, the current generation wouldn't have any money to spend.

Carrie: It's very important to think about the rights and needs of future generations for two reasons. First, those future generations aren't around to speak for themselves, so the current generation of fund managers—boards and investment committees—have to protect their interests.

Roger: The second reason is that *every* generation imagines that the needs it's facing are urgent—more so than the needs of past or future generations. But that's rarely the case, right, Carrie?

Ned: Rose and I can speak to that issue. Every organization whose board I've served on, and I'm sure this is true for Rose as well, has imagined that it is facing urgent and complex issues. Left to their own devices, the staff would spend every dollar in the endowment.

Rose: I served for years on the board of our local community foundation. It's a wonderful organization, but every year all you hear is how important, how critical the issues are that the people of our community are facing. I often sit there and think, well, yes, these are important issues, and many people and organizations in our community are struggling. But what about during the Great Depression? What about during World War II? Now *those* were periods when people were *really* struggling, when our very civilization was at risk.

Ned: Exactly, but it's hard for dedicated people to have that long-term perspective. They see problems and needs everywhere and they want to address them. I can see that what Carrie and Roger are saying is exactly right. It's the role of the board and investment committee to say ...

Rose: In the nicest possible way ...

Ned (laughing): In the nicest possible way, that every generation faces major challenges, not just our own. And, therefore, annual spending has to acknowledge that.

Carrie: So with that introduction, let's turn to spending in families. And let me say again that this isn't Spenser trying to tell you how to run your lives.

Roger: And it's certainly not Carrie Knowlton and Roger Epperson trying to tell you how to run your lives!

[Laughter.]

Carrie: I started by talking about institutional investors for a specific reason: families also need to think intergenerationally. "Dynastically," if you will. If your ancestors had been heavy spenders, there wouldn't be any money left for you to spend. And, similarly, if you are heavy spenders, there won't be any money for your grandchildren to spend.

Roger: And like institutions, every generation of every family can find all sorts of ways to spend a lot of money.

Carrie: And like institutions, future generations of your family aren't around to speak up for themselves.

Ned: Rose and I face that issue in the trust context. We not only have to invest to meet the needs of current income beneficiaries, but also of future income beneficiaries. And, ultimately, of the beneficiaries that will one day inherit the principal.

Geoffrey: Talk about complicated!

Carrie: Ideally, each generation in a family should think of itself not as the owner of the family's capital, free to do with it as they please, but as *stewards* of that capital for the family, including current and future generations.

Rose: I like that formulation—we're not really *owners* of this capital at all. In fact, none of us around this table had anything to do with earning it. We're really just stewards of the capital for our generation and, especially, for our children, grandchildren, and more remote descendants.

Ellen: And for the broader community. Some of this money is earmarked for charity.

Carrie: That's a very good point, Ellen.

Rose: I agree. Any family that controls a large fortune has obligations to the broader community, and our family has been especially fortunate.

Ned: I'll say! Back in the nineteenth century, what other country would have allowed a poor Italian immigrant to become so successful?

Billy: And we're lucky to have been born in the United States ourselves. I mean, what if we'd been born in some awful place where the government confiscated our money?

Ned: That's true. George and Ellie were very smart, hardworking people, and so was Great-Grandpa Jake and Grandpa Jake, but that wouldn't have counted for much in a lot of countries. And, despite all the taxes we've paid over the years, we've been allowed to maintain our capital. So, as Rose says, we owe a lot to American society.

Carrie: It's wonderful to hear the family talking like that. No matter how wealthy a society is, there will always be people who are left out.

Ellen: People who never had a chance to build a good life, much less a fortune.

Carrie: Exactly. But I'd like to make another point. Private capital plays a huge role in America and in the world. Some people even argue that it is private capital, the kind that your family controls, that is at the root of America's success in its competition with other societies.[5]

Ned: But there are other people who argue that the money rich families have should just be confiscated and distributed to the poor.

Carrie: Fortunately, that's still a fringe opinion. But if wealthy families don't take their stewardship responsibilities seriously—and I mean stewardship both to the family and the broader community—confiscation could become a more popular idea.

Billy: There's a great ad that talks about this idea of stewardship. For a watch or something.

Ned: I've seen that ad. It shows a father and a son, and the father is holding a watch, showing it to the boy. The caption at the bottom says, "You never actually own a Patek Philippe. You merely look after it for the next generation." Something like that.

Ellen: It would have been better if it had a little girl in it. The French are so sexist.

Billy: Sorry, Ellen, Patek Philippe is a *Swiss* company.

Ellen: Oops. Well, the Swiss are sexists, too. Not to mention the Americans.

Ned: Okay, we're getting off the reservation.

[Laughter.]

Ned: In any event, I don't own a Patek Philippe watch, and if I did, the only way any of you would get it is to pry it off my cold, dead wrist!

[Raucous laughter.]

Carrie: It's a great ad, there really are some geniuses working on Madison Avenue. And it states the sentiment perfectly. Right now, Ned and Rose are stewarding the family's assets, just as, before them, Jake Jr. "looked after" them and, before him, Jake Sr., and so on. Soon, the mantle of stewardship will pass to the four kids, and after them, to their own kids and so on.

Geoffrey: It makes it sound like we're a dynasty!

QUICK NOTE

The use of the term *dynasty* has uncomfortable echoes of hereditary dynasties of the past. But it is actually important for families to think dynastically, that is, to view the family capital as a permanent endowment designed to benefit the current generation and many generations to come. And it's important for advisors to remind families of this way of thinking.

Carrie: You *are* a dynasty, but an American one, based on talent and accomplishment, rather than birth. If I count right, the kids around this table are the sixth generation of the Titan family in America. And because of the sound stewardship exercised by your forebears, and currently by Ned and Rose, you've beaten the odds—beaten them by a mile.

Suzy: What odds?

Roger: "Shirtsleeves-to-shirtsleeves in three generations."

Carrie: Exactly, if you were a normal American wealthy family, George and Ellie would have been rich, Andrew would have spent most of the money, and Jake Sr. would have spent the rest. You folks would be broke.

Roger: And it's not just an American phenomenon. As Jay Hughes has pointed out, almost every important civilization has a similar phenomenon and a similar saying.[6] Do you remember any of them, Carrie?

Carrie: "Rice-paddies-to-rice-paddies in three generations." That's the Chinese one.

Roger: Right. In other words, making money and losing it pretty quickly isn't just an American phenomenon, it's a human phenomenon.

Rose: Why does it happen so regularly, Carrie?

Carrie: Well, I'm no expert on it, Rose. We should invite Jay Hughes in to speak to the family at one of your meetings. But one reason families lose their wealth is simply that it's very hard to hang onto it. There are so many headwinds facing wealthy families: spending, taxes, fees, inflation. Plus, families compound faster than capital does. I notice that in the Ned and Rose generation, there are two Titans. But in the next generation there are four: Ellen, Billy, Suzy, and Geoffrey. You pretty much have to do everything right to have any chance of holding onto your money across the generations.

Ned: And, believe me, we know how easy it is to do things wrong. Rose and I happen to be very good at it!

[Laughter.]

Carrie: Oh, I don't know about that.

Rose: Well, let's see. We invested in that stupid auction-rate securities fund. Then ...

Billy: What's an auction-rate securities fund?

Ned: Don't ask. Just don't ever invest in one!

Rose: And then we got scared during the financial crisis and allowed our equity allocation to drop and drop. Now the market's recovering quickly and we're still way below where we should have been.

Ned: And while we didn't exactly pick a lousy advisor, we kept the one Dad left us because we didn't know any better.

Suzy: Grandpa Jake picked a bad advisor? That doesn't sound like him.

Rose: To be fair, when Daddy was in charge of things, the guy at the brokerage firm he was working with was pretty good. But that fellow retired and we've had nothing but bad luck ever since. We should have fired that firm years ago.

Carrie: Well, you did eventually fire them. And since then you've been utterly brilliant as stewards of your capital.

Ned: You mean, by hiring Spenser?

Carrie: Exactly!

[Laughter.]

Carrie: In any event, you're beating yourselves up too much. Every family will make mistakes. The question is, do you remedy them or keep making them? You eventually realized your advisor left a lot to be desired and you made a change. And I'm not just buttering you up, I really mean this—you've gotten the really important things right.

Rose: We have?

Carrie: Sure. You raised four good kids, you've kept your family spending under control, and you're working hard to get better and better at stewarding your capital. I'd say that puts you in the top one percent of wealthy families around the world.

Ned: Maybe we're not as dumb as we thought, Rose!

Rose: That's good!

Carrie: If I had to choose between a family that takes good care of its financial capital and a family that takes good care of its human capital, I'd choose the latter every time. If the human capital stays strong, the financial capital will take care of itself. But if the human capital dissipates, the financial capital won't be far behind.

Rose: That sounds very wise, Carrie. I hope we can keep it up!

Ned: You said that our spending is "under control," Carrie. What does that mean in numbers and dollars?

Carrie: Well, of all the many aspects of stewardship, sensible spending is one of the most important. It's probably the case that more families spend themselves into penury than mis-invest themselves into penury. What sort of guidelines should the family be thinking about, Roger?

Roger: Basically, you back into those guidelines. You start by figuring out, given your risk tolerance, how much return you can expect to make on your family's assets. Then you deduct taxes, investment fees, inflation, variance drain …

Billy: What's "variance drain"?

Carrie: Oh. We'll talk about this more later, but the term *variance drain* refers to the fact that the volatility of returns slows the growth of capital.

A simple example would be this: a portfolio that grew by ten percent per year with no volatility would be worth a lot more at the end of ten years than a portfolio with a ten percent return and ten percent volatility.

Billy: I see. It goes back to the fact that if you're up fifty percent and down fifty percent, you're not back to even.

Carrie: Well, yes, that's an aspect of how volatility hurts.

Ned: You were calculating how much we can spend.

Carrie: Right, So just to cut to the chase, no matter how you look at it, the best answer is that families shouldn't spend much above three percent of the value of their capital per year. You could argue for a little more, but you would have to take more risk than some family members would likely be comfortable with. A really prudent family will spend less than three percent

Suzy: So how are we doing, Dad and Aunt Rose?

[Ned and Rose exchange a perplexed glance.]

Ned: Well, no one ever talked about spending to us in this way. I don't actually know how much we spend as a percentage of our capital.

Rose: Me, neither. I mean, we keep track of how much we spend annually, and we know what our capital is worth, so we could figure it out.

Carrie: Why don't I send you what I think a reasonable range of spending would be and you can compare it with what you actually spend?

Rose: Perfect.

QUICK NOTE

It's always awkward for an advisor to be talking with a family about spending. But by sticking to the facts and backing into what a maximum spending level might be, the Spenser advisors are keeping emotion and character out of the conversation and basing it on what is reasonable in the real world.

The IPS: General Policies

Carrie: As you can see in the IPS example, every policy statement has a section where we include a variety of policies and practices that are to be applied to the portfolio. For example:

- **Asset allocation ranges.** Here we talk about how we set these ranges and what we will do if the ranges are breached.

- **Taxes and investment costs and fees.** In this section we talk about the importance of taxes, fees, and investment costs and how they will be approached in the management of the portfolios. You'll notice that, in general, we prefer to *optimize* costs rather than *minimize* them. Minimizing costs can all too often be pennywise and pound-foolish.
- **Time frame for performance measurement.** Investors should always guard against being too short-term oriented. If the portfolio underperforms for a year or two, or if a manager underperforms for a year or two, we should try to understand what's causing the underperformance, but we don't want to depart from our long-term strategies, or fire what might be a very good manager, just on the basis of short-term underperformance. Every portfolio and every manager will suffer periods of underperformance.
- **Commingling family investments.** Depending on the size of the various family portfolios, it might make sense to commingle them for investment purposes. Suppose that Rose and Ellen and Billy all want to invest in a particular hedge fund manager, or a particular private equity vehicle. If the manager has a very large minimum account size, which many good managers do, Rose might be able to meet the minimum but Ellen and Billy might not. So we could create a commingled account—usually in the form of a limited liability company, or LLC—and Rose and Ellen and Billy would all contribute capital to it and that capital would be invested with the manager. Or we could do it family-wide, including Ned, Suzy, and Geoffrey. We might have one family LLC for hedge funds and one for private equity funds.

The IPS: Periodic Review

Carrie: Finally, there's a section requiring that the policy statement be reviewed periodically. You don't want to be changing the IPS every quarter—it's a long-term document and shouldn't be amended every time the markets change. On the other hand, you don't want it to get stale and you don't want to forget about it. So, typically, we like to see the IPS reviewed annually.

QUICK NOTE

In reality, even an annual review of asset allocation is probably too frequent. It's useful, of course, to take a look around and see whether anything has changed with the family or the markets (a new asset class that might be worth looking at, for example). But the temptation will always be to make changes in what should be a very long-term strategy.

The IPS: Appendixes

Carrie: At the end of the policy statement there are some appendixes. These are optional and differ from family to family. The ones in our sample IPS are just that, samples. But let's take a quick look at them in case you might find them useful for your family. Roger?

Roger: Okay, the first one, Appendix A, is what we call an "Investment Committee Operating Manual." [A version of an operating manual is available on the companion website for this book at www.wiley.com/go/familycapital.] We can go more deeply into the purpose of this document later if you're interested, but for now …

Suzy: Excuse me, Roger, but what's the difference between an operating manual and a policy statement? Do we need both?

Roger: Good question. As we see it, a policy statement tells us where we want to be, while an operating manual tells us how to get there.

Carrie: Exactly. If you have a chance to look at the operating manual, you'll see that it's in effect a detailed agenda for meetings about the portfolio. It assumes you have an investment committee, but of course yours has been disbanded. On the other hand, Ned and Rose constitute a kind of informal investment committee, so you might find the manual to be useful.

Roger: Finally, there is an appendix that discusses how the family's money will be managed during periods of market extremes—on both the upside and downside.

Ned: I saw that appendix. I certainly understand why it might be needed for bear markets—we've had enough experience with wrong decisions in that environment! But why should we worry about bull markets? Are we really in any danger of doing something dumb then?

Billy: We'd be in danger of getting richer!

Carrie: Actually, Ned, I'm glad you asked that question, because it's Spenser's view that most of the worst investment mistakes investors make have their seeds in extreme *bull market*s, not bear markets.

Rose: Seriously?

Carrie: Yes, I'm serious. It's during bull markets that investors forget about risk. Everything is going up and investors begin to think they're extremely smart.

Roger: "Never confuse genius with a bull market."

Ned: Who said that, Roger?

Roger: I have no idea!

[Laughter.]

Carrie: Whoever said it was right. Bull markets don't make us smarter, they make us dumber. Let's suppose our target allocation to stocks, was say, sixty percent. At the end of a bull market we might be at seventy or even seventy-five percent. Then, when the bear market hits, we're a huge fat target. We get killed. That terrifies us and we bail out of the market. But while the mistake we made, bailing out of the market, happened during the bear market, its roots lay back in the bull market. If we'd have kept our stock allocation at sixty percent, we wouldn't have gotten killed so badly, and we wouldn't have been so terrified, and we wouldn't have bailed out.

Ned: Back when Dad was running the portfolio it was roughly fifty percent stocks and fifty percent bonds. But in 2006 and 2007 we let our profits run and we got up to—what was it Rose, about seventy percent stocks?

Rose: About that, yes.

Ned: So when the bad markets came around, starting in mid-2007, we were, as Carrie points out, fat targets.

Roger: It's the math that kills you. Suppose we had a market as bad as the one in 1973–74. If you had a fifty–fifty stock–bond mix, you'd lose twenty-five percent of your capital. But if you had a seventy–twenty-five stock–bond mix, you'd lose close to forty percent of your capital.

Suzy: Ouch!

Billy: Double ouch!

Carrie: So, just to repeat, it's during the bear market that the losses happen, but it was mistakes made during the bull market that allowed the bear market to cause so much damage.

Ned: You've convinced me! I hate bull markets!

[Loud laughter.]

QUICK NOTE

It's human nature for investors and their advisors to love bull markets. But the Spenser advisors are making a very important point and one that advisors need to emphasize to clients during bull markets: we can't afford to get all caught up in the money we're making. If we do, we'll allow our risk to ratchet up to staggering levels, and when the inevitable bear market comes along we'll lose all the money, and more, that we were so excited about.

Meeting Wrapup

Carrie (looking at her watch): Our time's about up, so let's wrap up. We've walked through the investment policy statement, and I hope everyone has a better idea of what it is and what each section means. I realize we've only touched the surface, but, really, it's been a very good discussion.

Roger: I'll say. It's really rare for a younger generation to take such an interest in learning about investment issues. Usually, we have to drag them kicking and screaming to the table!

Ellen: Mom and Uncle Ned *did* drag us kicking and screaming to the table!

[Laughter.]

Suzy: That's true, we all thought we had better things to do today. But, actually, I thought the conversation was really interesting. I might even semi-understand some of this stuff now!

Billy: Me, too.

Carrie: Well, that's great. But now the hard work starts. The four of you [indicating the adult children] now need to get to work changing this form so it meets your family's needs. You can divide up the work any way you want, and please don't hesitate to ask us for help. You can call or email Roger or me, or we can set up a conference call everyone can participate in.

Geoffrey: If nobody minds, I'd like to take the lead on the description of the family. I found that part really interesting. But I'll leave it to Dad and Aunt Rose to put together the family groupings.

Suzy: I guess we'll each have to draft our own language for the investment objectives section. But I'm not sure how to proceed for myself.

Carrie: If you look at the investment objectives samples in the draft IPS, you'll see they're written in investment-ese. That's so we can create target returns and so on. But what I suggest is that you draft your own objectives in plain English. Just put in your own words what you think about how you'd like your money to be managed. Then, when we get together to talk about asset allocation, we'll go over the drafts and, eventually, convert them into investment-ese.

Roger: And note in the IPS anything you don't understand, so we can pay special attention to those sections.

Ellen: Who's going to deal with the delicate issue of spending?

Rose: That would be Uncle Ned and me. But each of you will have to think about it for yourselves, too. I mean, you and Suzy are working and covering the costs of living in New York …

Suzy: Barely!

Rose: Right. But, still, it's nice that you're managing on your own. But neither of you has a car or a house.

Suzy: Or a husband. I hear husbands can be expensive.

[Laughter.]

Ned: Nothing like wives, though!

[Laughter and some hisses.]

Rose: Anyway, my point is that any sort of special purchase couldn't be covered by your incomes, so it would have to come out of your trusts.

Ellen: I have no idea how my trust is invested.

Suzy: Me, neither.

Ned: Well, that's part of what this meeting is all about, to bring you into the picture. We'll show you how the trusts are invested—they're all invested the same way, by the way—and as you gain understanding and experience you'll be able to manage your own money.

Rose: It will be good practice for the day when all the Titan money will fall to your management.

Suzy: That's a scary prospect!

Rose: It was scary for Ned and me, too, when Daddy first brought us into the investment committee meetings. But at least you have the advantage of coming into it much earlier and younger than we did. By the time Ned and I get put out to pasture, you'll be old pros.

Ned: Plus, you have the advantage of working with the folks at Spenser. The advisor your Grandpa Jake was using when Rose and I first got involved didn't believe in educating its clients.

Suzy: That's sort of weird.

Ned: The dumber the client, the better! That was their motto!

Geoffrey: How am I going to get started on the family history section? It's going to be like pulling teeth to get Dad and Aunt Rose to talk about our ancestors.

Ned: Hey! I said we'd talk over dinner tonight. That'll be a start, anyway.

Rose: Who knows, if we drink enough wine we might remember some really good stories!

[Laughter, meeting ends.]

SUMMARY

My guess is you're thinking that that was the most successful family-advisor meeting in the history of the investment advisory business. And you'd be right. But my goal here is to show what's possible. The Spenser advisors worked hard—and worked smart—to make the meeting with the Titan family a success. Conducting meetings with families, especially when it's a family-wide, multigenerational meeting, is an art form. To do it well, you would be wise to consult the experts on the subject, especially people like Dennis Jaffe and Stacy Allred,[7] Barbara R. Hauser,[8] Susan Shoenfeld,[9] and John Messervey.[10]

Ahead of the meeting, Spenser considered a variety of issues that would be important to making the meeting a success:

- **What were they trying to accomplish at the meeting?** The main goal of the meeting was to get the younger generation of Titans involved in the investment process. But Spenser actually managed to kill two birds with one stone: the adult children found themselves engaged in the conversation and at the same time vastly furthered their own investment knowledge and understanding. True, the Titan kids still have a long way to go, but in one meeting they made a great start.
- **What was the agenda?** Interestingly, Spenser didn't provide an agenda for the meeting. Instead, it allowed the various sections of the investment policy statement to serve as the organizing principle of the meeting. This outlined the meeting and also walked the client through the investment process itself, largely in the order it should be addressed.
- **Who should attend?** It seems obvious that the attendees should have been the parents and their children, but that's only obvious after the fact. Why not a meeting with just Ned and his kids, followed by a meeting with Rose and her kids? Why not separate meetings with the parents and then with the kids? What about the boyfriends? A lot of thought goes into the issue of selecting the attendees, and in this case Spenser got it right. Important considerations included the fact that Ned and Rose had worked together well for years as stewards of their family capital, and the fact that the cousins got along well. If the older generation were especially dominant—as often happens if the older generation is G1—it might be the case that the children would be reluctant to speak up. In this case, though, Ned and Rose were G5 and their children had little hesitation in speaking up. Excluding the boyfriends was an easy decision, as they weren't part of the family. But what about in-laws? What if, say, Suzy had just married her boyfriend? These issues can be extremely complex. Parents will naturally be worried about the possibility of divorce and a hostile ex-in-law running around telling family secrets. On the other hand, excluding in-laws can be offensive to the married family member, to say nothing of the in-law.
- **How long should the meeting last?** This might seem like a minor issue, but meetings that are too long or too short can seriously undermine their productivity. If the time set aside for the meeting is too brief—often at

the insistence of the client—the agenda will have to be foreshortened to avoid a sense that little was accomplished. If the meeting is too long, everyone's attention will wander and the younger generation will conclude, not unreasonably, that investment issues are boring.

- **When to talk and when to listen?** This is always a difficult issue. Let's face it; we like to hear ourselves talk, whether we are the advisor in the meeting or the client. And if we're the advisor, there is always the temptation to show off—to get way down in the weeds and impress the client with our knowledge. In the meeting we've just observed, the Spenser advisors tripped over this challenge once or twice, although for the most part they either kept their focus at a high level or dipped into the details only in response to indications that the client was interested in doing so.
- **Should they use the services of a facilitator?** This was a fairly straightforward meeting about investment issues, centered on a review of a sample investment policy statement. And the participants were friendly and relaxed around each other. But both these characteristics are often absent. If the meeting is likely to be sensitive, or if there are participants who don't get along, or if the family has already recognized that they can't communicate well with each other, the use of a facilitator can be a godsend. Facilitators are trained to deal with situations in which human emotions or family conflict can derail the conversation.
- **The importance of following up.** Too many family meetings, whatever the topic, seem to evaporate into thin air because nobody bothers to follow up. In this case, the Spenser advisors suggested to the Titan family that they should call or write with any questions or concerns that might arise as they worked their way through their assignments. In fact, Spenser should proactively follow up by (a) circulating at least brief notes of the minutes,[11] and (b) contacting the family members to see if they could use some help.

As noted, one important goal of the meeting was to bring the younger generation of Titans into the loop to get their investment education started. Spenser accomplished that by getting the parents, Ned and Rose, to agree to assign a specific, important task to the kids. In this case, it was preparing the initial draft of the investment policy statement.

Drafting the IPS for a wealthy family is a critically important step, so this wasn't make-work. And by assigning that task to the kids, Spenser was able to walk them through the basic IPS form the firm used, which touched on many of the larger, longer-term issues every family needs to work its way through.

Another reason Spenser was successful in this meeting was that Carrie Knowlton and Roger Epperson weren't insisting on coming out of the meeting with hard, short-term action plans. In one sense, there were no action items at all. No specific investment trades, no specific strategic or tactical changes in the portfolio, no managers to hire or fire. There were, however, family assignments. The adult children were assigned to prepare the initial draft of the IPS, while their parents were assigned the job of taking a hard look at family spending.

Despite the lack of immediate action items, if we look at the meeting on a longer-term basis, a great deal was accomplished. Most important, the next generation of Titans is now engaged in the portfolio management process. True, they are at a very early stage in their knowledge and understanding, but at least a start, and a good one, has been made.

Even for Ned and Rose, who are much more experienced, the meeting improved their understanding of issues they were rather dim on. They now feel much more confident in their ability to manage their capital, and it is a great relief to them to see their children taking an interest. Sooner or later those young adults will in fact succeed to the management of a lot of capital.

A bonus was the interest the adult children manifested in the history of their family. Like many families, the Titans had taken their family history for granted, whereas in fact it was both quite interesting and also iconic—a history of America in miniature from the Industrial Revolution to the modern era. Telling family stories is very important to the hard task of keeping families together across the generations. These stories keep earlier generations alive in the minds of their descendants. They build pride in the family's accomplishments and challenge younger generations to try to live up to the high standards set by their ancestors.

The Titans hadn't spent much time telling family stories, but they began the process over dinner after the Spenser advisors left, and the process continued every time the family gathered. Geoffrey Titan became so interested in the family's history that, later in life, he would write a family memoir, gathering together all the stories he had heard over the years and preserving them for later generations. This process would have been much easier if earlier generations had been interviewed while they were alive.

Obviously, I've spent a great deal of time going over a typical family investment policy statement. But it's almost impossible to spend too much time on this crucial document—and this crucial *process*. A meeting like the one the Spenser advisors had with the extended Titan family doesn't result in the sale of any investment products and it takes a great deal of the advisors' time. But it pays off both in the strengthening of the client's family and in the bond it builds between the family and the advisor.

Each advisory firm will have its own ideas about what a family investment policy statement should look like—the one the Spenser advisors showed to the Titans is merely an example. But it touches on all the important points, and I recommend it for your consideration.

NOTES

1. Ellen's statement of the quote from Balzac is the one people always mention. But in fact the full quote goes like this: "The secret of a great success *for which you are at a loss to account* is a crime that has never been discovered, because it was properly executed." [Emphasis supplied.] The line is spoken in Balzac's novel, *Père Goriot*, by a villain named Vautrin. In many corrupt societies great fortunes are in fact often the result of some great crime, but not in societies that are generally fair and law abiding. In those societies, fortunes have to be earned by doing something remarkable.
2. This point is powerfully made by Andrew Ang in the preface to his recent book, *Asset Management: A Systematic Approach to Factor Investing* (Oxford: Oxford University Press, 2014), which begins: "The two most important words in investing are 'bad times'" (p. ix).
3. The pioneers in the field of behavioral finance were Amos Twersky and Daniel Kahneman. Kahneman was awarded a Nobel Prize for his work in 2002. Twersky had died and was therefore ineligible.
4. Shiller P/Es are also known as the CAPE (cyclically adjusted price earnings ratio).
5. See, e.g., Gregory Curtis, *The Stewardship of Wealth: Successful Private Wealth Management for Investors and Their Advisors* (Hoboken, NJ: John Wiley & Sons, 2013). See also Gregory Curtis, *Creative Capital: Managing Private Wealth in a Complex World* (Bloomington, IN: iUniverse Press).
6. James E. Hughes Jr., *Family Wealth—Keeping It in the Family: How Family Members and Their Advisers Preserve Human, Intellectual, and Financial Assets for Generations* (New York: Bloomberg Press, 2004).
7. See especially the very useful working papers, *Talking It Through* (http://dennisjaffe.com/adminpanel/uploads/documents/1421866915 Talking%20it%20Through.pdf) and *A Handbook for Conducting Effective Multigenerational Family Meetings about Business and Wealth* (http://dennisjaffe.com/adminpanel/uploads/documents/1416250119 Handbook%20for%20Conducting%20Effective%20Multi-Gen%20 Family%20Meetings.pdf).

8. Barbara's resources are available on her website at http://brhauser.com/.
9. Susan is founder and CEO of Wealth Legacy Advisors LLC, http://wlallc.com/.
10. John is founder of the National Family Business Council and is especially effective in dealing with issues at the intersection of families and their businesses (http://privatefamilyadvisor.com/).
11. Circulating minutes can be especially important when the meeting is with trustees of a family trust. Years later, if a question arises about the fiduciary behavior of the trustees, these minutes can demonstrate that they discharged their responsibilities appropriately.

CHAPTER 6

Establishing the Titan Family's Investment Objectives

PREPARATION AND USE

The meeting at which the Spenser advisors discussed investment objectives with the Titan family was also a performance reporting meeting. Especially early in a relationship with a new client, when there is a lot to accomplish, most advisors will want to combine topics even if it means extending the length of a meeting.

We'll get to performance reporting later, so for now we'll simply listen in to the portion of the meeting devoted to the family's investment objectives. Suzy and Billy were unable to attend this portion of the meeting, so it was conducted with Ned, Rose, Ellen (Rose's daughter), and Geoffrey (Ned's son).

THE TITAN FAMILY'S VERSION OF THEIR INVESTMENT OBJECTIVES

Obviously, no portfolio can be designed unless we know what the investor's objectives are. But those objectives have to be consistent with what's possible or likely in the real world of risk and return. Investors who wants to double their money every five years but don't want to take any risk are obviously not living in the real world.

After the last meeting, each member of the Titan family was tasked with drafting his or her own investment objectives. In this part of today's meeting, the Spenser advisors will go over the plain-English versions of the objectives as drafted by the Titans, which Spenser will later convert into investment-ese.

The meeting began by discussing the investment objectives for Ned and Rose, and that discussion was followed by a longer, more elaborate discussion of the objectives for the Grandchildren's Trust.

Carrie: I'm sorry that Suzy and Billy had to leave early. Should Roger and I follow up separately with them?

Rose: I don't think that will be necessary, Carrie. Ned and I will bring them up to speed and they can call you with any questions. Billy's sorry he had to leave, but he has an important meeting in Boston in the morning.

Ned: And Suzy has an important meeting with her boyfriend tonight.

[Laughter.]

Rose: I don't know, Ned. It's none of my business, but I think something serious might be developing there.

Ned: I'm sure I'd be the last to know!

[More laughter. Ned and Rose look inquiringly at Ellen and Geoffrey.]

Ellen: My lips are sealed.

Geoffrey: And no one ever tells me anything!

[Laughter.]

Carrie: Okay! Well, shall we start with you, Ned?

Ned: Sure, somebody has to go first. Here's my draft.

[Ned passes around copies of his draft, which reads as follows:

My investment objectives for my personal money and trusts for my benefit are as follows. First, I believe that I have more assets than I'll likely ever need during my lifetime and I consider myself very fortunate in that regard. In thinking about how to invest my money, I think of the following as objectives to be considered:

- *I wish to be able to support my family's lifestyle at its current level, which I believe to be appropriate relative to our overall capital base.*
- *Over a long period of time—20 years or so—I wish to maintain the real value of my assets, that is, in inflation-adjusted terms, net of my spending, taxes, investment costs, and charitable giving. I fully realize that this will be a challenge.*
- *During my lifetime I would like to make gifts to my foundation sufficient to support annual giving of at least $1 million. The purpose of this objective is to make the foundation large enough so*

that it can be taken seriously as a philanthropic vehicle and can be used to train my children in the art of giving.

- *At the death of the last to die of my wife and me, one-half my estate will go to the foundation and the balance will be distributed to my children outright.*
- *None of the foregoing applies to the trust known as the Grandchildren's Trust, which will have its own investment objectives and terms of distribution.]*

Carrie: That's wonderful, Ned, very useful.

Rose: I'm glad to hear you say that, because Ned and I worked on the language together and my objectives read exactly the same!

Carrie: You're making life easy for us!

Ned: Should we also look at the objectives for the Grandchildren's Trust now, or do you want to wait?

Carrie: Well, sure, let's look at them now. Of course, Roger and I have already seen your draft and we sent you a suggested revision a few weeks ago. However, Ellen and Geoffrey probably haven't seen any of these drafts.

Rose: The draft I'm passing around is the one Spenser sent to us.

[Rose passes around copies of the draft, which reads as follows:

The trust known in the family as the Grandchildren's Trust provides considerable income and estate tax advantages, and offers protection against creditors of family members. Trusts with such advantages can no longer be created under U.S. tax law. Thus, to the extent that family members do not require distributions from the Grandchildren's Trust, it is the policy of the trustees to reinvest all income. Principal distributions under the trust will not be made during the lifetimes of Ned Titan and Rose Wainwright, and possibly not during the lifetimes of their children. Thus, while all living family members are potential beneficiaries of the Grandchildren's Trust, the more likely beneficiaries are unborn future descendants of the family.

Thus, given the lack of spending needs by the Grandchildren's Trust for many years, the investment objectives for the Trust should focus on long-term capital appreciation. It is understood that, consistent with fiduciary considerations, the Trust can tolerate greater illiquidity and price volatility than can the portfolios of other family members.]

QUICK NOTE

Families that have been wealthy for more than two or three generations will often have trusts—and sometimes other vehicles—that can no longer be created under U.S. law. Almost always these vehicles are extremely attractive from an income and/or estate tax perspective and it will be important for advisors and families to maximize these advantages. However, the use of these vehicles can be controversial even within the family. See the following discussion.

Debating the Wisdom of Trusts

Ellen: Well, Geoff, there goes our inheritance!

Geoffrey: I'll say! I wonder if anyone is *ever* going to get this money. I mean, I'm not trying to be greedy, but if I remember it right, the "grandchildren" referred to in the Trust are Dad and Aunt Rose. And, at best, it'll be my kids who eventually get it, or maybe even my grandkids.

Ellen: And mine, and Suzy's and Billy's.

Geoffrey: Right. So how many generations is that that didn't get the money?

Ellen: A lot, that's for sure. Five or six generations, anyway.

Ned: Hold on there, kiddos, are you sure you're not being greedy? I mean, you have your own trusts set up for you by your Grandpa Jake. And you'll get at least half of everything Rose and I have. Isn't that enough?

Ellen: I don't want to put words in Geoff's mouth, but since we talked about this over lunch yesterday, I'll go ahead and do it. Geoff isn't being greedy and neither am I. We're just questioning why this money has to be tied up for so long. I mean, if we could get our hands on the money we might give it all away, so what's greed got to do with it?

Geoffrey: By the time the money is finally distributed, it'll have been in trust for a century!

Rose: Actually, probably more than a century. The—what's that rule called, Ned?

Ned: The Rule Against Perpetuities.

Rose: That's it. The Rule Against Perpetuities requires that the Grandchildren's Trust's assets be distributed ninety-nine years after the death of whoever the youngest family member was who was alive when the Trust was created. Ned, do you remember who that person was?

Ned: I should remember, but I've forgotten. But he or she was just an infant at the time, so if we assume whoever it was lives to be seventy, then the

Trust will have to be distributed one hundred and sixty-nine years after it was created.

Rose: Which was just before World War II.

Geoffrey: Is my math wrong or are we talking something like the year 2100?

Ellen: At the earliest.[1]

Ned: But I'm still not getting the point. The Grandchildren's Trust has a whole lot of tax, estate, and asset protection advantages. Why wouldn't we want to keep it going as long as possible? All I'm hearing is the "greed" part of this.

Geoffrey: Hey, Dad, that's not fair.

Ellen: Geoff told you he wasn't ...

Rose: Everybody calm down, for goodness sakes!

[Silence around the table, but with Ellen and Geoffrey looking a bit sullen.]

Rose: That's better. Look, I agree with Ned about all the advantages the Grandchildren's Trust gives us as a family. But I've never thought of any of our kids as being greedy. So we're obviously talking past each other here. Do you have any thoughts, Carrie?

Carrie: I don't want to get in the middle of a family spat, but let me say a few things I've observed in other families. First, instruments like the Grandchildren's Trust are very rare. You probably have it only because both Jake Jr. and his father, Jake Sr., were both very good lawyers. A lot of families who have similar trusts really think of them as a kind of *endowment* for the family. In other words, if you look at endowments for nonprofit organizations—a college or university, for example—what's the purpose of the endowment? Roger?

Roger: Endowments have a couple of uses. Let's say we're talking about a small college somewhere. That would be more similar to a family. The main purpose of the college's endowment is to provide a steady and, hopefully, growing stream of income to support the operations of the college. But the endowment is also a standby source of funds in the event of a catastrophe or some very bad piece of luck. Instead of going out of business, the endowment provides a cushion that can buy time for the college to recover from whatever the calamity was. Is that what you're looking for, Carrie?

Carrie: Exactly. But a sizeable endowment—sizeable in relation to the operating budget and number of students, for example—also provides a more subtle advantage. It allows the trustees of the college to think long-term, to avoid having to make suboptimal short-term decisions out of financial exigency.

Ned: In other words, it gives the college a kind of true independence, an ability to think and plan for themselves and not be buffeted about by outside forces.

Carrie: That's it exactly. And many families think of large, long-term trusts as offering the family the same kinds of advantages. If you needed the current income, the Grandchildren's Trust would be there to provide it. If you needed principal distributions, the trustees probably have the ability, within limits, to provide that, too. But in the meantime, it sits there as a kind of bulwark for the family, allowing you to operate as you see fit.

Rose: I really like that way of thinking about it.

Carrie: But Ellen and Geoffrey have a point, too. Way too often in my experience, families look at all the advantages of trusts, but don't think about the disadvantages associated with tying the money up for many years.

Ellen: Hear, hear!

Ned: What sort of disadvantages?

Carrie: Does the name Jay Hughes mean anything to you?

Rose: One of you, I think it was Roger, mentioned that name in our last meeting. Something about rice-paddies-to-rice-paddies in three generations.

Carrie: Wow, good memory, Rose! That's right, it was Jay who pointed out that shirtsleeves-to-shirtsleeves in three generations isn't just an American phenomenon. Instead, it's one of those things that is observed in every society.

Ned: But we've ducked the problem so far. Rose and I are G5 and we're not poor yet.

Carrie: Yes, you've really beaten the odds. But back to Jay Hughes. He has pointed out that when we make gifts or set up trusts for other family members, we're not always doing them any favors.

Ned: But if Jake Sr. hadn't put that money in trust, we'd have paid a huge amount in taxes and there wouldn't be much left of it today.

Carrie: Maybe or maybe not, depending on what happened with the money in the hands of whoever inherited it, versus what happened to the money in the hands of the trustees. But my point—Jay Hughes's point, really—is that in Jake Sr.'s mind, and maybe in Jake Jr.'s mind, and maybe even in your and Rose's minds, the gift of the Grandchildren's Trust was an unalloyed good. But in the minds of the next generation, maybe they don't see it that way.

Rose: But are we really doing anything different from what other substantial families are doing?

Carrie: Not at all. By the third or fourth generation, the overwhelming majority of the wealth in most families will be in trust. The tax and other advantages are simply too large for it to be any other way. But that doesn't mean that trusts—much less trust beneficiaries—live in a perfect world.

Roger: In a book that is being published soon,[2] Jay Hughes reminds us that in most parts of the world trusts aren't permitted. I think it was the Napoleonic Code that abolished trusts in Europe.

Rose: Why would they want to do that? Trusts seem like a wonderful idea for the most part.

Carrie: Well, I don't know how deeply you all want to get into this subject.

Ellen: Considering how much of our family's money is tied up in trusts, I'd say we need to go into it *very* deeply!

Geoffrey: Agree!

Rose (looking at her watch): Well, I have all day, but I'm not sure about Carrie and Roger.

Carrie: What could I possibly have to do that would be more important than talking with my clients?

[Laughter.]

Geoffrey: You need to get a life, Carrie!

Ned: I'm not a historian, but I *am* a lawyer, and I can tell you that trusts were invented under English common law a very long time before Napoleon was born.

Carrie: Ned's right about that. In fact, the ideas behind the rise of the trust go all the way back to Aristotle.

Geoffrey: Did you say *Aristotle?* Did the poor guy have all his money tied up in trusts?

[Laughter.]

Carrie: I'm sure I wouldn't know! But Aristotle recognized the distinction between equity—fairness, let's say—and what we might call *blackletter law*. Eventually, English common law developed courts of equity that were completely distinct from courts of law. In effect, these courts …

Ned: The chancery courts, as they were called.

Carrie: Okay, the chancery courts. They dealt with issues of fundamental fairness or equity, even if the blackletter law or the law as understood in the courts of common law seemed to require a different outcome. If you just enforce the law as written, or as it's built up in court decisions, you can end up with some really harsh results. These courts of equity could set aside regular law and enforce fundamental fairness.

Ellen: Okay, that's good, I like the idea that there's a court somewhere that can cut through all the legal niceties and reach a fair outcome. But I don't get what that has to do with trusts.

Ned: By the way, courts of chancery don't exist anymore.[3]

Ellen: Oh, drat!

Carrie: Here's the linkage, Ellen. There can be a gap in the common law—and in the law under the Napoleonic Code or any other sound legal system—between property and obligation. A trustee owns the asset, but unlike other forms of ownership, the trustee can't use the property for his own benefit. He has to use it for the benefit of the beneficiary of the trust. Such an idea is unknown under the Napoleonic Code—you either own the asset and therefore use it for your own benefit, or you don't own the asset.

Ned: And it was the genius of the English common law to recognize that gap and to build a system of rules and understandings around it. That's what we call *fiduciary* law. It was fiduciary law, not the law of property, that the old courts of chancery developed and enforced.

Geoffrey: This is really interesting. You'd think a guy who's getting his Ph.D. in history would know something about this. When did all this start?

[Ned and Carrie look at each other.]

Ned: I'm going to say—don't hold me to this—that these kinds of issues started being dealt with in the 1100s and 1200s.

Ellen: Wow—almost a thousand years ago.

Geoffrey: So what you're saying is that over the centuries, either in these chancery courts or later in the regular courts, a huge body of fiduciary law was built up that has no counterpart anywhere else in the world.

Ned: That's right. Of course, we have it in America, too, because we adopted the British common law. And we should be very glad we followed Britain rather than Napoleon.

Carrie: Technically, it's possible that the idea of the trust was separately invented by Islamic law, possibly even before the idea arose in England.

Ned: Seriously? I never heard that. They have trusts in the Middle East?

Carrie: Yes, they're called a *waqf*, and they seem to date back to about the ninth century. A *waqf* is virtually indistinguishable from the common law trust, and since it seems to be even more ancient, some scholars believe the idea was brought back to England by the Crusaders.[4]

Ned: You're kidding! The Arabs invented the trust?

Carrie: I think that's a controversial idea, but it's possible.

Ellen: But if the idea of the trust is so terrific, and if we have it and the Arabic countries have it, why don't they have it elsewhere, like in Continental Europe?

Carrie: Speaking historically, Jay Hughes points out (in the book Roger just mentioned) that following the French Revolution trusts were banned by the Napoleonic Code. The reasons were that trusts at that time were viewed as a restraint on the economy and as leading to the production of a failed class of people, that is, trust beneficiaries.

Ellen: I understand the "trust-fund-baby" argument—I sure hope my generation isn't a bunch of trust fund babies!—but what do you mean by a restraint on the economy?

Carrie: Trusts in those days were used to tie up large swaths of property—land—in England and France. The beneficiaries of those trusts had no special incentive to manage the land efficiently so it would be productive well into the future. So the productivity of the land declined. Other people, who might have been willing to buy the land and improve it, couldn't do so because the land was tied up in complicated trusts.

Geoffrey: Couldn't they have just reformed the trusts without banning them altogether?

Ned: Remember, this was after the French Revolution and the notion of punishing the rich was very strong. Many people in France simply wanted to destroy anyone who had capital.

Carrie: Clearly, something had to be done. Reform happened in England, but trusts were eliminated in France. Ironically, today they are trying to bring trusts back in France. They are called a *fiducie*, I think because the Latin word for trust is *fiducia*.

QUICK NOTE

This discussion is a good example of the family, or here, the younger generation, hijacking the agenda. Supposedly, this part of the meeting is only about investment objectives. But the younger generation of Titans are clearly uncomfortable having their family money tied up in trusts, and their reasons aren't trivial. The conversation may not have had much to do with investment objectives, but it had a lot to do with getting important generational issues on the table so they could be discussed openly.

The "Affluenza" Disease

Ellen: Well, anyway, it seems to me that the French were right to worry that trusts might create a failed class of people. When a person's money is all tied up in trusts, it's infantilizing. You can't manage the capital yourself—that's delegated to some trustee somewhere—and you get a certain amount of income over which you have no control at all.

Geoffrey: And if you need more money for some reason, you have to go begging on your hands and knees to the trustees to try to get it. Even though it's your own family's money!

Ellen: And people who get large distributions from a trust, for which they didn't have to do anything except be alive, really turn into trust fund babies. Some of these people I swear barely have a pulse.

Rose: That's an awfully broad generalization, Ellen. Some people who are trust beneficiaries are very productive members of their societies. You must see a lot of this on both sides, Carrie.

Carrie: Yes, I do. Frankly, though, people who "barely have a pulse," as Ellen puts it, don't usually go around hiring folks like Spenser. Why is that, Roger?

Roger: "This is a paid commercial announcement." [Laughter.] I think the reason is that it's much easier simply to sit back and clip coupons, as they used to say—to get the income from your bonds and not rock the boat. The idea of looking hard at what the trustees are doing is too much like work.

Ned: In fact, most "trust fund babies," as Ellen calls them, probably wouldn't even know their trustee was doing a lousy job, at least on the investment side.

Rose: Yes, as long as the trustees get the income distributions out on time and serve fine china in their offices, most barely-have-a-pulse beneficiaries would be perfectly happy even if the investment performance was very bad.

Ellen: So the French are right!

Carrie: They were right about some people, certainly. But as I look around at my clients at Spenser, I don't see that kind of thing at all. Most of my clients, I mean the firm's clients, not just mine, are gainfully employed or in school even though they have hundreds of millions of dollars and could simply coast through life. What do you see in your client base, Roger?

Roger: Well, I don't have quite as broad a view as Carrie does, but I agree. And the few people who aren't working, I mean working in the sense of getting a paycheck, are extremely busy volunteering their time to make the world a better place.

Rose: Ellen, are you thinking of specific people you know whom you would view as having failed?

Ellen: Sure. In prep school and at college I knew a lot of kids who were just coasting by on Daddy's money. They didn't study much, didn't play sports, mainly did a lot of drinking and drugs. Now they don't work and are dependent on trust distributions.

Carrie: I guess we all know people like that.

Rose: I don't blame the kids as much as I do the parents.

Ellen: And the grandparents and great-grandparents. When nobody in your family has worked for three generations, it's pretty hard to grow up learning how to hold down a job.

Carrie: That's right. That's the disease of "affluenza," as they call it. It usually strikes in G3 or G4, as Ellen points out, when working and earning your own living has died out as a regular practice in a family.

Rose: Again, I don't mean to justify the trust-fund-baby lifestyle, but let's be realistic. If a kid might, if he's real lucky, get a tough job that pays $35,000 a year, and he's already getting $100,000 a year in trust distributions, what's his incentive to work?

Geoffrey: Is it really any different from people who can make $20,000 on welfare or get a job that pays $20,000? Why work if you can get paid for doing nothing?

Ellen: You're saying trust fund babies are the same as welfare bums?

Geoffrey: I'm just making a point about incentives and human nature.

Rose: You could say the same thing about divorced wives who live on their alimony—welfare bums?

Carrie: Yes, I suppose it's all a very similar phenomenon. The tragedy of it is that human potential is stifled in all those cases. People who might have made something of themselves and made a difference in the world sit around doing nothing. It's probably very damaging to themselves as individuals, but it's also damaging to society, which loses their potential contributions.

Geoffrey: So what do we do about it? I mean, in the trust fund situation?

Carrie: Well, clearly, it isn't trusts per se that cause the problem. In other words, it's not having a lot of money that causes people to fail as productive human beings. If a young person is raised properly, he or she will develop a character that is strong enough to resist the lure of the easy life. Ned and Rose, your kids are all working hard at paying jobs, except for Geoffrey, who's getting his Ph.D. Yet they are all fabulously rich. Money hasn't ruined them.

Ned: So far ...

Geoffrey: Dad!

[Laughter.]

Rose: There's another, very similar phenomenon that goes on in wealthy families and that I think played a role in our own family. It's when someone in the family, often the patriarch, spends every waking moment out making money. At the end of his life he's produced a great fortune, but he may also have produced kids who have been ignored and who are resentful and who tend to turn to money as a substitute for parental love and care.

Ned: Rose is referring to the George Titan branch of the family. The first George was certainly like that—a hard-charging, hardworking guy with an inferiority complex because he was a poor Italian immigrant. But really, Rose, while George Jr. wasn't the "titan" his father was [groans around the table at Ned's pun], he was a pretty competent guy who ran the family company for many years.

Rose: Yes, but that's because his mother, Ellie, was a remarkable woman who did everything she could to make up for the fact that her sons rarely saw their father. George Jr.'s wife—her name was Mary—was a much more ordinary person and George III paid the price. He rarely saw his own father, and his mother wasn't able to fill that void.

Ellen: You don't think a similar thing happened on the Jake side of the family? I mean, on our side?

Rose: No, I don't. Jake Sr. was a Type A personality, to be sure, but he spent a lot of time with Jake Jr. and brought him into the law firm.

Geoffrey: But, still, it's almost like Jake Sr. didn't trust any of us with the family money. He put it in trust so a bunch of trustees could make our decisions for us. We were remote descendants of his whom he didn't know.

Ellen: And maybe didn't even care about.

Rose: I'm sure your great-grandfather had no such thoughts at all. He was just doing what was best from a tax and planning point of view.

Ellen: That's how *he* saw it. That's not necessarily how *we* see it.

Geoffrey: And Great-Grandpa Jake didn't make all that money himself. He made some of it, but the rest he got from old George Titan—his grandfather—who as far as I know left it to him unencumbered by any trust restrictions. So Great-Grandpa got it free and clear, but we get it all tied up in knots.

[Ned and Rose glance at each other.]

Ned (sighing): Well, I guess I'm conflicted on this. Part of me says the kids are looking a gift-horse in the mouth. They ought to be delighted that the Trust is there if they need it. But I'm also beginning to see what they mean about how they view the Trust versus how Jake Sr. viewed it. It's hard to know, several generations in advance, what's best to do and how your descendants are going to think about things.

Rose: It's certainly true that times have changed a lot since the early 1940s, when the Grandchildren's Trust was set up. But what's done is done. We can't go back and undo what Jake Sr. did.

Carrie: That's right, we can't. And, maybe, after the kids have learned more about planning issues and investment issues, they'll change their minds. But let's face it, they have a point. And one way we can respond to the validity of that viewpoint is to get the kids as involved and knowledgeable about the Grandchildren's Trust as possible. That way they might not feel so, well, disenfranchised.

Ellen: By the dead hand of the past!

Geoffrey: We're just puppets of a guy who's been dead for half a century!

[Everyone laughs.]

Geoffrey: Anyway, I like Carrie's idea. If it feels like we have some understanding and influence over the Trust, maybe we'd feel better about it.

Ellen: I'd feel better about it if I had the dough in my hot little hands!

[Laughter.]

Carrie: Okay, can we get back to the investment objectives discussion? I mean, I'm happy to keep pounding on poor old Jake Sr., but …

Ned (laughing): Yes, let's move on—please!

QUICK NOTE

In the case of the Titan family, a discussion of the affluenza disease was relatively straightforward because none of the Titans suffered from it. But in families where the disease is prevalent, the issue will be much more delicate. It's an especially troublesome problem because, once affluenza takes hold, there is no cure. The disease can only be prevented.

Spenser's Version of the Investment and Performance Objectives for the Titan Family

Carrie: Okay. Roger and I discussed the drafts Ned and Rose prepared, and Ned and Rose have seen our draft for how the investment objectives for Ned, Rose, and the Grandchildren's Trust might read in the investment policy statement. But since Geoffrey and Ellen haven't seen them, let me pass them out.

[Carrie passes out drafts. They read as follows:

Investment Objectives for Ned Titan:

Ned is a member of G5 in the Titan family. He is married and has two grown children, Suzy and Geoffrey. His date of birth is 4/26/48.

Ned possesses a substantial asset base that is more than adequate to support his lifestyle. Thus, his primary objective is to continue to support the family's lifestyle at its current level while maintaining the inflation-adjusted value of his assets, net of all spending, measured over a long-term period of 20 years.

Ned also has a secondary, but important, objective, namely to make lifetime gifts to the family foundation sufficient to support annual giving of at least $1 million and to preserve, and to the extent consistent with the primary objective to enhance, the value of his assets to provide further for his children and the foundation after his death.

Performance Objectives for Ned's Assets:

Absolute Return Objectives*: To achieve a long-term annual compound total return, net of taxes and investment expenses, of 3% above the rate of inflation, as measured by the U.S. Consumer Price Index.*

Relative Return Objectives*: To outperform a composite benchmark consisting of the weighted average of the asset class performance benchmarks established for Ned (see below). This objective will be measured pre-tax and net of investment expenses and over rolling three-to-five-year market cycles. In addition, the portfolio is expected to outperform a naïve benchmark consisting of stocks and bonds with the same risk level (as measured by price volatility) as the target portfolio.]*

Carrie: Okay, has everyone had a chance to read through Ned's objectives? Comments, questions?

Geoffrey: Why three percent? I mean, how did you come up with that number?

Roger: We backed into it, Geoffrey. Once you deduct inflation, taxes, and expenses from your return, the three percent is a bit above what your family spends in an average year. So if we hit the three percent target, your family's capital should remain intact and maybe even grow a bit over a longer period of time.

Ellen: Okay, I see that. But can you explain the relative return objectives?

Roger: Sure. Later we'll go through an asset allocation exercise and, I hope, settle on an overall long-term strategy. But just to make it simple, suppose the long-term strategy was to invest fifty percent of Ned's assets in stocks, forty-five percent in bonds, and five percent in cash. The first relative return objective is to beat an index portfolio with that allocation.

Carrie: We would calculate the return on the S&P 500 Index weighted at fifty percent of the asset base, and on, say, the Barclays Capital Municipal Bond Index for forty-five percent, and a cash benchmark for five percent. The actual portfolio should beat that *composite benchmark* over time.

Ellen: What if it doesn't?

Carrie: Then Spenser isn't doing a very good job for you. But keep in mind that the objective says the performance will be measured over a complete market cycle. Short-term underperformance is inevitable.

Roger: Even Warren Buffett underperforms sometimes!

Ned: Yes, I remember that, back in the late 1990s, everybody thought poor Buffett had lost it. He was underperforming the market index by huge amounts.

Geoffrey: It's scary to think of Warren Buffett stinking the place up. But, what's a *naïve benchmark*?

Roger: That's just what we call it. A portfolio designed by a sophisticated investor, or one working with a sophisticated advisor, will be fairly complex, using lots of asset classes and lots of managers. But let's say that, once the complex portfolio has been designed, its risk level, as measured by its price volatility, is eight percent. We can create a very simple portfolio—the so-called *naïve* benchmark—that also has an eight percent risk level by using only stocks and bonds, or sometimes stocks, bonds, and cash.

Ellen: But if you can do that, why wouldn't the simple portfolio be better?

Carrie: Just for that reason: it's too simple. It isn't well-diversified and it has risks embedded in it that aren't necessarily measured by volatility—momentum risk, for example.

Roger: Before you ask, *momentum risk* just means that you are tending to buy whatever's going up, paying higher and higher prices. That's what happens when you own a capitalization-weighted index fund, for example.

Geoffrey: I'm not sure I get that, but let's go on.

Carrie: No, let's stick with your issue for a moment because it's important. An index fund needs to track the market it's indexed to, say, the

S&P 500. So in a bull market, like the one we've been in for several years, the index fund has to keep paying higher and higher prices for stocks. It's setting itself up to get clobbered when the markets turn.

Roger: Let's say the price of Google stock is going up faster than the broad price of the stock market. The index fund has to keep buying more and more Google, even though Google's price might be up there in Cloud Cuckoo Land.

Geoffrey: I'll bet I'm the only one in the room who knows where that phrase, Cloud Cuckoo Land, comes from.

Ellen: That's because Geoff's getting a Ph.D., so he must be smarter than the rest of us.

Geoffrey: You bet. So, okay, any guesses? Anybody know the answer?

Ellen: Alice in Wonderland.

Geoffrey: You're only off by twenty-five-hundred years, Ellen. It's from Aristophanes. In his play, *The Birds*, some of the characters create a perfect city in the clouds called Cloud Cuckoo Land.

Ned: Geoff, I just don't know what we'd do without you!

[Laughter.]

QUICK NOTE

Capitalization-weighted index funds—the Vanguard 500 Index Fund, for example—are a convenient and cheap way for many investors to gain access to the markets. But for more sophisticated investors, cap-weighted index funds will sometimes make sense (when the markets are cheap) and sometimes not (when markets are expensive).

Carrie: Okay, any more questions about Ned's objectives? [No one speaks up.] Great. Let's turn to the Grandchildren's Trust. Here's what we proposed:

Investment Objectives for the Grandchildren's Trust:

The trust known in the family as the "Grandchildren's Trust" was created by Jake Titan Sr. in 1940 and is not expected to begin making distributions until at least the year 2100. Income in the Trust can, at the discretion of the trustees, be distributed out for the support of Ned Titan and/or Rose Wainwright during their lifetimes, and after their deaths to their children. Income not distributed is reinvested in the Trust corpus. Principal distributions may also be made at the discretion of the trustees to the same group of people.

In addition to income tax and estate planning advantages, the Trust assets are also protected against claims of creditors of individual family members.

Since it is not anticipated that the Trust will be distributing income or principal for a very long time, it is able to bear more price volatility and illiquidity than most other family assets. This is an important advantage of the Trust over other investors, and it should be used in designing and implementing the Trust's portfolio. Thus, the investment objective of the Trust is to increase its real value—that is, net of the effects of inflation—over a long-term period of time.

Performance Objectives for the Trust's Assets:

Absolute Return Objectives: *To achieve a long-term annual compound total return, net of taxes and investment expenses, of 4% above the rate of inflation, as measured by the U.S. Consumer Price Index.*

Relative Return Objectives: *To outperform a composite benchmark consisting of the weighted average of the asset class performance benchmarks established for the Trust (see below). This objective will be measured pre-tax and net of investment expenses and over rolling three-to-five-year market cycles. In addition, the portfolio is expected to outperform a naïve benchmark consisting of stocks and bonds with the same risk level (as measured by price volatility) as the target portfolio.*

Carrie: Comments, questions?

Geoffrey: Ellen, since we've been popping off about the Grandchildren's Trust, we better have some good questions!

Ellen: I was counting on you, Geoff!

How Aggressively Should the Family Invest?

Ned: I can help out. I have a question. The target long-term return for the Trust is four percent. That's only one percent better than the target return for my personal assets. Yet, the Trust has a longer time horizon, can withstand more risk, and can bear more illiquidity. Shouldn't the target return for the Trust be higher?

Carrie: Well, keep in mind that because the Grandchildren's Trust has no spending obligations, it will grow pretty rapidly if we can hit that return target. You are spending from your portfolio and making gifts. Beyond that, the trouble with shooting for even higher returns is, we're bumping up against the maximum returns investors can expect to get in the real world over longer periods of time, at least without taking on way too much risk. Consider that the return on an all-stock portfolio over the long-term will be about ten percent. But an all-stock portfolio is far too risky, so getting a long-term return of ten percent on the overall portfolio is highly unlikely.

Roger: Right. Let's say inflation is going to be three percent per year over the long-term. If investment expenses average one percent, then getting four percent above inflation means we're already needing eight percent just to stay even. (That's three percent inflation, plus four percent over inflation, plus one percent for investment expenses.) And we haven't taken taxes or variance drain into account yet.

Ellen: What about things like venture capital. Can't you get a better return there?

Roger: Theoretically, yes. A really well-constructed portfolio of venture capital partnerships might get you a return in the mid-to-high teens. But it's enormously difficult to build a well-constructed venture portfolio, for a couple of reasons. The main one is that the good returns aren't widely distributed among the venture firms. In fact, if you can't invest with the very best firms, the ones at the very top of the industry, it's not worth investing in venture at all.

Rose: Yes, I've heard that. But I assume Spenser knows who the best firms are.

Roger: Well, we *hope* we do!

Carrie: What Roger means is that we certainly know which firms have produced the best returns in the past. But the senior partners in those firms aren't spring chickens anymore, and who knows how hard they're working now, or whether the younger people working under them are any good.

Roger: But even if we knew for sure which firms would be producing the best returns in the future, it's pretty much impossible to invest with them.

Geoffrey: But isn't that what they're in business for? To take our money and invest it in good entrepreneurial ideas?

Carrie: Absolutely. But no firm can produce good returns with unlimited amounts of money. The bandwidth of the partners is only so wide, and the deal flow is only so big. So the best firms limit the amount of capital they'll raise and almost all of it is allocated to the investors in their earlier funds. Those early investors are the Harvards and Yales of the world, not the Titans of the world.

Ellen: You mean, they won't take our money?

Roger: They won't even take your call!

Geoffrey: So we won't be investing in venture capital after all? We're just frozen out?

Carrie: Well, it's not quite that bad. But, basically, you have to go through an access vehicle, a *fund of funds* as they're called. There are a very few really good funds of funds that have relationships with the best venture firms. So a venture firm might give the fund of funds an allocation of, say, fifty million dollars, and then, through Spenser's relationship with the fund of funds, we might be able to get you an allocation of, say, one million dollars.

Ned: One million dollars sounds like a lot of money, but on our asset base it's not going to move the needle much, even if we got a twenty percent return.

Carrie: You're exactly right, Ned, which is another of the problems with venture capital.

QUICK NOTE

The reality is that, attractive as the top-line returns can be in venture capital, most investors should give the asset class a pass. As Carrie Knowlton pointed out, if you're not invested with the tiny group of firms at the very top of the business, the returns you'll get won't be worth the risk, especially including the long-term illiquidity of these funds. Clients, especially wealthy families, who are used to getting preferred access, don't like to hear this, of course. But they don't pay their advisors to agree with them; they pay us to tell them the truth.

Ellen: Oh, brother. Are there other assets that could increase the Trust's return?

Roger: Private real estate, buyout funds, that sort of thing.

Geoffrey: And we'll be investing in those things?

Carrie: You bet. And the Grandchildren's Trust will be investing in more of them than Ned and Rose. Not sure about the next generation, since we haven't gone through those portfolios yet.

Rose: What do you mean by *private real estate*, Roger? Isn't all real estate more or less privately held?

Roger: I just meant, as opposed to real estate investments that the general public can invest in, like REITs. You buy a REIT like you buy a stock. And there are mutual funds that buy REITs. But when I say "private" real estate, I mean real estate that is bought by private investment funds—hedge funds or private-equity-like funds.

Carrie: And, often, those kinds of funds are buying quirky kinds of real estate. Maybe troubled properties that need capital and expertise to be turned around. Maybe nichey kinds of things like student housing, storage facilities, boat marinas.

Accredited versus Unaccredited Investors

Roger: The kinds of funds that buy that sort of real estate aren't available to public investors, by which I mean retail, mainstream investors. They're only available to so-called *accredited* investors. People who meet certain asset and income standards. People like the Titans.

Ellen: *Whoa!* You mean ordinary people aren't allowed to invest in these funds? It's against the law?

Carrie: I'm afraid so, Ellen.

Ellen: That's an outrage!

Rose: Now, Ellen, the government's just trying to protect people who tend to be unsophisticated when it comes to investing.

Ellen: Protect them from what? Getting good returns?

Ned: Securities regulation isn't my specialty, but as I understand it, in a broad sense ordinary folks are encouraged to invest in things that have daily liquidity and that are reasonably easy to understand. Wealthier people are assumed to be more sophisticated, but also more able to bear the risk of investments that might be illiquid or risky from other points of view. Isn't that more or less right, Carrie?

Carrie: Yes. All these restrictions go back to the Great Depression, when a lot of ordinary people lost huge amounts of money investing in things they didn't understand. Congress passed a bunch of laws designed to protect investors. The Securities Act of 1933, the Securities Exchange Act of 1934, the Investment Advisors Act of 1940.

Geoffrey: I agree with Ellen. That was a million years ago, and people are a lot smarter and better educated now. Does the government really take the position that only rich people are good investors? Who is the government to say someone can't invest in venture capital or "private real estate"?

Ned: That's a very long and complicated discussion, kids. But just to make one correction, the government isn't really saying that rich people are better investors than middle-class people. They're simply saying that if they lose a lot of money, they can afford to lose it, while other investors can't. Anyway, we have work to do to finish up our investment objectives. If you don't like the way the laws work, write your congressperson.

Ellen: Maybe I will.

Geoffrey: Getting back to the main point, it sounds to me like it's going to be really hard to grow our money. I mean, our target returns are barely above our spending, except in the Grandchildren's Trust.

Carrie: Unfortunately, that's true, Geoffrey. For a wealthy family to grow or even just maintain its capital over time they pretty much have to do everything right.

Geoffrey: It's a miracle anyone ever gets rich in the first place!

Carrie: Well, almost nobody gets rich just investing in the markets. Warren Buffett's an exception, but let's face it, if you want to *get* rich you need to start your own company and make a success of it. That's what George Titan did, and also Jake Sr. But starting your own company is also a good way to get poor; most startups don't make it. Investing in the markets isn't really a good way to get rich; it's a good way to *stay* rich.

Ellen: So if we do everything right, the best-case outcome is, we'll be roughly as rich twenty years from now as we are today?

Carrie: Or maybe a little richer. But, really, Ellen, if your family is as rich twenty years from now as it is today, and especially if it's as rich a couple of generations from now, that's a major homerun. Almost no families manage to do it.

Geoffrey: I can see why. The difference between success and failure is a razor's edge!

Rose: Well, it's not an all-or-nothing proposition, I don't think. If we do well, we'll be a little wealthier. If we do a little less well, we'll be less wealthy, but still rich. It's only if we really screw it up—and I understand that most families really screw it up—that things will turn out badly for us.

How to Blow a Billion Dollars

Carrie: That's right. I know we've talked about the shirtsleeves-to-shirtsleeves phenomenon before, but it's worth repeating. Families can make terrible investment mistakes like the George Titan III branch of the family. Families can also spend themselves into oblivion. Spenser used to have a client who was worth almost a billion dollars and they managed to spend themselves into a big hole.

Geoffrey: Starting with a billion dollars?

Carrie: I'm afraid so. This might have been before your time, Roger.

Roger: That's good; at least it can't be blamed on me!

[Laughter.]

Ned: This reminds me of the old joke. Do you know how to end up with a million dollars? Start with a billion dollars.

[Groans around the table.]

Carrie: There's a lot of truth in that old joke, I'm afraid. In the case of the Spenser client who spent down their money, I blame myself, at least a bit. This was a family where the father had built a successful company and sold it, very much like the Titan family experience. The family took stock in the buyer as compensation, so they now had about fifty million dollars in cash and two hundred million dollars in stock of the acquiring company.

Geoffrey: Is that the way we did it, Dad? I mean, when Titan Industries was sold, did we take cash or stock or what?

Ned: The family took half the purchase price in cash and half in stock. Then, over the following decade, we gradually sold off the stock.

Carrie: Very wise. Unfortunately, my client kept all the stock. For almost ten years, that looked like a great decision. The stock kept going up and up and was finally worth more than eight hundred million dollars. But along the way, the family started living like billionaires. They built staggeringly expensive homes in New York, Florida, and Spain. They bought a huge jet and hired two teams of pilots so it would always be available. They made large charitable pledges to get themselves invited onto big national boards.

Ned: Ugh. I think I see where this is headed—at some point the price of the stock collapsed.

Carrie: Yes, exactly. In retrospect, what triggered the decline was a fairly minor accounting irregularity. But the markets were very nervous about accounting matters after Enron and the stock lost forty percent of its value.

Ellen: Those poor people! Now they only had six hundred million dollars!

[Laughter.]

Carrie: You might think so, but actually it was much worse. The stock was margined, that is, the family had borrowed against it to support their lifestyle. When the value of the stock went way down, the family received what's called a *margin call.* A margin call occurs when the brokerage firm that lent the money simply seizes the stock and sells it to pay down the debt.

Geoffrey: They can do that?

Carrie: You bet. My client had to sell the huge houses they'd built and, because they had to sell them in a hurry, they lost money on them. Then they had to sell the jet and lay off the pilots. Finally, in what was probably the most humiliating thing of all, they had to renege on their charitable pledges. They had to resign from those boards and one of the nonprofits actually filed a lawsuit against them for reneging. Really ugly.

Rose: Do grantees actually sue you if you don't fulfill a pledge? I never heard of such a thing.

Carrie: I think it's rare. But sometimes the grantee has used the big pledge to convince other donors to make similar pledges. Then, when the main pledge backs out, there's a danger that everyone else will, too.

Rose: Because they feel like they were conned.

Carrie: Yes. In other words, was the first pledge real, or was it just cooked up to get other donors to give.

Ned: Did the family actually have to declare personal bankruptcy?

Carrie: No, they escaped that humiliation. But the family unit was destroyed. Two of the daughters sued their own mother for mismanaging the family money. The son took the mother's side and, let's just say it was hideous. To this day the daughters don't speak to the mother or their brother, and both of the young women ended up getting divorced in the process.

Ned: And all because they got greedy. If they'd gradually sold off the stock they got in the sale and diversified their portfolio, they'd still be rich. But I suppose that no matter how well a portfolio is managed, a greedy family can spend their way through it.

Carrie: Very true, Ned, although in my experience families who take the trouble to build very strong investment portfolios don't tend to overspend. They understand both the portfolio management side and the spending side.

Roger: And let's don't forget that it isn't just that the family Carrie mentioned is no longer *rich*. They are also no longer *happy*. When money is really badly mismanaged, or when spending is out of control, often the worst consequence is the destruction of the family's happiness.

Rose: Well-said, Roger. I assume Spenser recommended diversifying the concentrated position and the family wouldn't do it.

Carrie: That's right. And when I said I partly blame myself, it's because I could never find a way to convince them to do the sensible thing. Every time it seemed like they might be considering diversifying some of the stock, the price would go up again and they'd change their mind.

Ned: Like I said—greed.

Geoffrey: Well, greed might be one word for it, Dad, but another word—well, words—would be "human nature." I mean, if you own something and it just keeps getting more and more valuable, why would you sell it?

Ned: Do you want to explain this, Carrie, or should I?

Carrie: Be my guest!

Ned: I'm not speaking as an investment expert now, but as a lawyer and family counselor who has seen similar things happen way too often in my career. When you own one stock, no matter how good that stock seems to be, it's much, much more dangerous than owning a diversified portfolio.

Ellen: In the terms Carrie and Roger talk about, it's much more volatile, right?

Carrie: Well, yes, it's a lot more volatile. But that's not the main point, right, Ned?

Ned: Right. If you own a diversified portfolio, your chances of going bust are essentially zilch. All those companies aren't going to go bankrupt at the same time. But if you own only one stock, your chances of going bust are very high. Think of all the famous corporations that have collapsed over the years, either going out of business or becoming a shadow of their former selves: TWA, Arthur Andersen, Carrie mentioned Enron, Blockbuster, Sears Roebuck, Lehman Brothers, a whole bunch of tech high-flyers that went bust in the early 2000s, like Pets.com, and so on.

Roger: A lot of unsophisticated investors think that if they own just one stock, it'll be very risky but that they'll be compensated for that risk. They're thinking, the more risk you take the more return you get.

Ellen: Are you saying that's wrong?

Roger: Yes, unfortunately, it's wrong. *Some* risks are rewarded in the marketplace, mainly those you can't diversify away from. But if you *can* diversify the risk, say, by selling some of the concentrated stock position and buying other stocks, then the market doesn't compensate you for the huge concentrated risk you're taking.

Carrie: Owning one stock isn't about investing, it's about gambling.

Differing Views on Concentrated Legacy Portfolios

Rose: Can I challenge you on that, Carrie?

Carrie: Go ahead! Roger can bail me out!

[Laughter.]

Rose: I understand that owning one stock, especially when it represents most of your wealth, can be risky. But it often works out quite well. I went to college with a girl whose wealth is almost entirely in DuPont and after all these years she's still very rich. And look at all the people who bought Berkshire Hathaway early on—they're billionaires! Or Federal Express.

Carrie: Roger?

Roger: It's like saying that you know people who've won the lottery, or who made a lot of money in Las Vegas. It's an unrepresentative sample—most people lose money on the lottery and get killed in Vegas.

Ellen: I suppose that's right. We don't know about the people who've gone bust owning one stock because they don't go around bragging about it!

Rose: Okay, I can accept that. But I still think there's more to this issue. There is really something different about a family who owns a big chunk of stock in some important company and a family like ours that owns a liquid portfolio. Even if the wealth is the same, the first family feels connected to the company, may even have a board seat. They know the company executives personally and follow the company's fortunes very closely. It's just different. And I can understand why families like that are reluctant to sell. It's not just greed. Selling out is like, somehow, abandoning the family's legacy.

Carrie: That's a really interesting point, Rose. I hadn't thought of it that way. Maybe if I *had* thought of it, I could have had a more intelligent conversation with my billionaire family that came a cropper.

Ellen: Well, that's at least one risk we don't have to worry about, since we don't own any of the family stocks. They've all been sold, and long ago.

Ned: Which is why we're still rich.

QUICK NOTE

The conversation about legacy stocks is worth keeping in mind. Families who own a legacy position in a large company really are different than families with the same amount of wealth invested in a liquid, diversified portfolio. In cases where the legacy stock needs to be diversified, it's useful to keep this distinction in mind and to deal with it. Otherwise, the chance that the family will diversify will be very low.

SUMMARY

Probably the main point of this chapter is how much time the Spenser advisors devoted to the subject of the family's investment objectives. In this case it was discussed over two meetings, and in addition both the family and Spenser gave considerable thought to the objectives in between the meetings. In my own experience, I've seen families and advisors take more than a year to come to a final conclusion about what the investment objectives were and how they should be articulated.

Of course, the portfolio has to be invested and managed while these discussions are going on. But in a typical case, when a new advisor enters the picture the portfolio will already be invested. That portfolio might not be ideally positioned; recall that Spenser advised the Titans early on to increase their equity exposure. But over a relatively short period of time, six months to a year, a poorly positioned portfolio might well outperform a well-positioned portfolio. Portfolio design is something that acts positively on the capital over a very long period of time, not over periods measured in months.

As is usual with the Titan family, and with most affluent families who are truly engaged in the investment process, this meeting often veered well off-track. But those off-point discussions are often the ones that are the most interesting to the family members. Beyond that, discussions that depart from the formal agenda tell the advisor where there are gaps in the family's understanding of issues and give the advisor the opportunity to fill these gaps. Finally, advisors aren't the sole source of wisdom on investment-related issues, as Rose's comments about owning stock in family companies illustrate.

By the end of the "investment objectives" meeting, the Titan family members better understood the question of how investment objectives get established and why performance objectives are articulated as they are. They grasped the importance of the topic both via the specific conversations and also via the amount of time Spenser was willing to devote to it.

There were also several very useful detours into the role, purpose, and wisdom of using trusts and into the related matter of how unearned wealth can (negatively) affect family members if not properly managed.

Because wealth advisors already understand the importance of getting investment objectives right, and because, at the end of the day, many wealthy families will end up with similar, capital preservation–oriented objectives, there is a strong temptation to gloss over the objectives issue. But whatever objectives a family ends up with, and however similar they might be to other families' objectives, the more time spent on developing and understanding the objectives, the more patient the family is likely to be with the resulting portfolio. That alone is reason enough for advisors to devote significant time to this important subject.

NOTES

1. Note that some states have abolished the Rule Against Perpetuities. As a result, trusts established in those jurisdictions (South Dakota, for example) can theoretically last forever. These so-called "dynasty trusts"

are extremely unpopular with the IRS, however, and it is possible that limits could be placed on their use at some point in the future.

2. Hartley Goldstone, James E. Hughes Jr., and Keith Whitaker, *Family Trusts: A Guide for Beneficiaries, Trustees, Trust Protectors, and Trust Creators* [working title], manuscript draft of May 1, 2015.
3. The English Chancery Courts were merged with the courts of common law late in the nineteenth century.
4. See, e.g., A. Hudson, *Equity and Trusts,* 3rd ed. (London: Cavendish, 2003); and Gilbert Paul Verbit, *The Origins of the Trust* (Bloomington, IN: Xlibris, 2002).

CHAPTER 7

The Titans Grapple with Asset Allocation

PREPARATION AND USE

In this chapter we will observe the meeting between the Spenser advisors and Ned and Rose Titan as they discuss how best to design Ned's and Rose's overall asset allocation strategy. Recall that the Titan family has several different family groupings, each of which is likely to have its own asset allocation strategy.

Advisors are fond of telling clients that the asset allocation strategy they decide on will be the most important determinant of their portfolio's importance. Unfortunately, this statement can be highly misleading. In one sense, it's a truism. Imagine that Alyssa owns a portfolio of 100% bonds, while Susanna owns a portfolio of 100% stocks. Over the next market cycle, it won't matter how good or bad Alyssa's bond manager is or how good or bad Susanna's stock manager is. All that will matter is whether stocks beat bonds or vice versa. So in this extreme case, yes, asset allocation decisions dominate the outcomes.

But let's look at a more realistic case. Assume Bob owns a portfolio that is 60% stocks, 30% bonds, and 10% commodities. Ralph owns a portfolio that is 65% stocks, 25% bonds, and 10% hedge funds, and. These portfolios are similar enough that issues other than asset allocation might well determine the differing outcomes of the two portfolios: manager performance, for example, or the allocation between domestic and international stocks.

The real importance of asset allocation is that (assuming it's done properly) it establishes the correct overall strategy for the client and therefore needs to be implemented and *adhered to*. Clients who depart from their long-term strategies just because a bull or bear market comes along are clients who don't have long-term strategies at all. Their portfolios are simply being swept along with the tides of the markets and their wealth is very much at risk.

Another issue surrounding the asset allocation process is the sense that it is intelligible only to the priesthood of financial advisors. Terms like *mean variance optimization, modern portfolio theory, standard deviation, efficient frontier, Capital Asset Pricing Model,* and so on seem positively designed to make the clients' eyes glaze over.

This might make the advisor seem smart, but it does a grave disservice to the client base. Unless the clients understand why asset allocation is important, they are highly unlikely to stick with their long-term strategies during difficult market environments.

In this chapter we'll listen in as the Spenser advisors walk Ned and Rose Titan through the asset allocation process and try to avoid the abovementioned pitfalls as well as others.

QUICK NOTE

The need to ensure that the client understands what asset allocation is, how it works, and why it's important can't be emphasized enough. But it's also important not to oversell the impact on the portfolio. The issue isn't that two very similar portfolios will have differing outcomes that are always driven by asset allocation. The issue—the crucial importance of asset allocation—has to do with *balancing the risk and return characteristics of the capital to best meet the needs of each individual family*. If the family departs from its asset allocation strategy, its capital is no longer serving its needs.

THE ASSET ALLOCATION MEETING

Like the drafting of the investment policy statement, asset allocation is so important that a good advisor will often dedicate an entire meeting just to that issue, especially when the client relationship is a new one. In this case, since Ned and Rose Titan have worked together over the years on their family's capital, Spenser has decided to combine the asset allocation meetings for Ned, Rose, and the Grandchildren's Trust. Ned and Rose invited all the children to attend, but only Suzy, who was on vacation from her job, and Billy, who was in town for a high school reunion, could attend. Let's see how the meeting goes.

What Is Asset Allocation?

Carrie Knowlton: It's nice to see everybody again, and thanks especially to Suzy for coming back for it.

Suzy: Well, it was either this or a week on the beach at Lauderdale, so ... [Laughter.]

Billy: If you really want to know, Suzy's boyfriend's in Pittsburgh looking for a job. Ergo ...

Carrie: Well, we're just glad you could be here. Oh, and you, too, Billy.

[Laughter.]

Carrie: Ned and Rose, I thought our last meeting, on the investment policy statement, went pretty well.

Rose: I certainly learned a lot.

Ned: Me, too. And I thought the kids were really engaged.

Carrie: That was the best part. Roger and I have been in touch with them since the meeting, and they're beavering away on their "assignments."

Roger Epperson: What Carrie means is that *I've* been in touch with them.

[Laughter.]

Carrie: You're closer to their age and speak their language. Besides, young people should always do most of the work so us older folks can rest our weary bones.

[More laughter.]

Ned: I know we talked briefly about this topic [see Chapter 5, especially the section entitled, "The IPS: Asset Allocation"], but as a reminder can you explain what asset allocation is exactly, and why we should care about it?

Carrie: Good questions! I know my fellow finance professionals tend to overcomplicate this, so let's start simple and we'll get more complex as we go on. Roger, what's the simplest way to describe asset allocation?

The Importance of Diversification

Roger: "Don't put all your eggs in one basket." Oh, wait, I said that at the last meeting.

Carrie: But you can't say it often enough: diversify, diversify, diversify. Asset allocation is simply a smart way to diversify your assets. A family like the Titans, which has spent more than a century accumulating assets, needs to think first and foremost about risk.

Rose: Yes, you mentioned that earlier. And by diversifying our assets, we're diversifying our risks and therefore, I guess, reducing them. But aren't we also reducing our returns by the same amount?

Carrie: Hopefully not. I mean, one way to reduce your risk would be to own only low-risk assets, right? Say, just cash and bonds. But we know that a portfolio like that won't produce enough return even to keep your capital whole, much less grow it.

Ned: Like our cousins' portfolio, the George Titan III branch of the family. They've been in bonds for something like forty years. Not that there's much left now ...

Carrie: Yes, a very unfortunate example. So we know that your family has no choice but to put its assets at risk in order to grow the money net of spending, taxes, inflation, and so on. But we want to do that in the least risky way possible that still gets us where we need to be. There's nothing new about any of this, right, Roger?

Roger: Right. People have been diversifying their risks for thousands of years. Long before the birth of Christ, traders would divide their goods between two different boats as they sent them off across the Mediterranean Sea. That way if one boat was lost to bad weather or pirates, the other one might get through.

QUICK NOTE

Note that the Spenser advisors began their discussion about the complex subject of asset allocation by describing it as a smart form for diversification. Families instinctively understand the concept of diversification, and that tends to get the topic off to a good start.

Asset Classes and Mean Variance Optimization

Carrie: So that's our starting point. We want to diversify the risks your portfolio is exposed to. We begin by looking at all the major investment asset classes you could possibly invest in. You'll remember we talked about this in the meeting we had with you and the kids up in Vermont.

Rose: Yes, I remember, in a general way, that part of the discussion. We talked about what an asset class is and how you go about combining them to get the right mix. But can you do a quick refresher?

Carrie: Absolutely. As I said then, technically, an *asset class* is a group of similar assets that tend to move together in the markets. As we say in the business, they tend to be highly correlated in their pricing behavior. If stocks and bonds behaved exactly alike, there would be no advantage to owning both. But since the behavior of stocks and bonds isn't highly correlated, you can improve your portfolio by owning some of both. That is, you can make your portfolio more *efficient*.

Rose: Meaning what, exactly?

Carrie: A portfolio that's efficient is one that rewards its owner with the maximum return for its risk level.

Roger: Or, saying it differently, allows its owner to experience the minimum risk for the return she's getting.

Carrie: You don't ever want to take more risk than you have to.

Ned: But what is it about correlation—or, I guess, low correlation—that makes a portfolio more efficient?

Carrie: A long time ago, a fellow named Harry Markowitz realized that if you built a portfolio out of assets that weren't well-correlated, you could actually reduce the risk of that portfolio without reducing its return by a similar amount. Since that time, most advisors follow Markowitz's idea by using what's called *mean variance optimization* to design the most efficient portfolios.

Suzy: I hate to ask what mean variance optimization is …

Roger: Actually, it's simple in concept. If you know the expected risk, return, and correlation of a group of assets, you input that data into a computer. The computer will then run, say, a thousand possible portfolios and plot the risk and return of each of them. The portfolios that fall along the so-called *efficient frontier* or the *efficient market line* are all efficient. The resulting chart would look something like this.

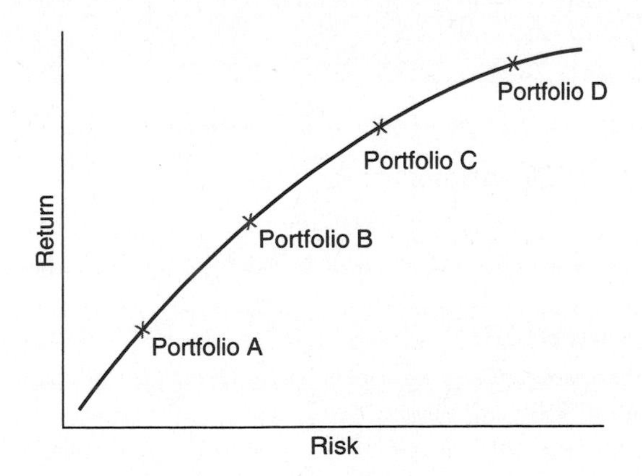

Carrie: Each of the portfolios along the line will have a different risk and return profile, but each will be efficient. You find the right risk level, and there's your portfolio!

Roger: Don't believe her—it's a lot more complicated than that!

Carrie: I'm afraid it is, but I was talking at the eighty-thousand-foot level. One complication is that, obviously, we can't know what the future risks, returns, and correlations are for asset classes; we can only estimate them.

Ned: Which you do how?

Carrie: There are several ways. One is to look at the past. If stocks have tended to return roughly eight to ten percent per year over a very long period of time, we can probably be safe in assuming that they'll continue to do so, at least over a long time horizon.

Roger: And if stocks have had a risk level of, say, sixteen percent over time, then we can probably …

Billy: Sorry to interrupt, but what's a "risk level of sixteen percent" mean?

Roger: Oh, I'm talking about how volatile stocks are.

Billy: Volatile?

Carrie: We're getting way down into the weeds now, but since you seem to be interested in this stuff …

Suzy: Well, it's our money we're talking about!

Billy: So of course we're interested!

Carrie: Well, that's great! Let's keep going. Roger, what's *volatility*?

Roger: It's a measure of how rapidly prices change in any asset. Over time, stocks have exhibited a level of volatility of about sixteen percent. In other words, if the average long-term return of stocks is eight percent, then two-thirds of all returns should fall between twenty-four percent on the upside (eight percent plus sixteen percent) and minus-eight percent on the downside (eight percent minus sixteen percent).

QUICK NOTE

The phenomenon of volatility is crucial to understanding risk and return, but it's hardly an intuitive concept. As we can see, Carrie and Roger keep coming back to it, explaining the idea slightly differently each time.

Carrie: Is everybody still with us?

Rose: I think so.

Billy: I'm hanging on for dear life!

Rose: You said there are several ways to estimate risk and return.

Estimating Risk and Return

Carrie: Right. Looking at past numbers is a good sanity check, but it's a lousy way to proceed. The future is unlikely to look exactly like the past, especially the short- and intermediate-term future. So what's another approach, Roger?

Roger: One approach we use is the *building-block* approach. You estimate what future inflation is likely to be and then you add risk premia to that to get the likely returns of various assets.

Ned: "Risk premia"?

Carrie: Sensible investors won't buy an asset unless they think its return will be commensurate with its risk. Otherwise, you're just gambling with your money. If you invest in a money market fund, let's say, you expect your money to be extremely safe. So you might accept a return more or less equal to the inflation rate.

Ned: Which is about what you'll get, too!

Carrie: Right. But if you buy a bond sold by, say, Microsoft, there are risks involved in owning that bond. One is that Microsoft might default or get into financial trouble and have its bonds downgraded by a rating agency. That's *credit* risk. Another is that you don't get your principal back until the bond matures. In the meantime you only get interest. That's called *duration* risk. If inflation is five percent, you wouldn't buy a Microsoft bond that paid five percent interest; you'd want more, to compensate you for the risk you're taking.

Roger: And if you bought Microsoft *stock*, well, that's a lot more risky, so you'd want even more return than you'd demand on the bond.

Carrie: Over time, we know what the risk premia are that investors demand for owning different kinds of assets, so we add those premia to the inflation rate and, *voila!* We have the expected future returns.

Roger: Should we even mention Black-Litterman?

Carrie (sighing): I guess we should, but only if you folks promise not to ask a bunch of questions, because we'd be here for a week!

Rose: We promise.

Carrie: Okay. Two guys named Black and Litterman, who were working at Goldman Sachs at the time, came up with a different way to do asset allocation.[1] They assume that an investor's asset allocation should be proportional to the market values of all the available investment assets globally. So you use the Black-Litterman model to generate the expected returns for the assets (based on the equilibrium assumptions shown in market pricing) and then use a mean-variance optimizer to come up with the final portfolio.

Billy: Does anyone understand what she just said?

Carrie: You promised no questions!

Roger: Of course, we never just accept the equilibrium values; we impose our own views.

Ned: But why would you do that? Unless I'm misunderstanding, what you call the *equilibrium view* is what thousands or even millions of investors have come up with. Are you saying you're smarter than everybody else?

Roger: Not me! But Carrie is.

[Laughter.]

Carrie: If I was, I wouldn't be here. I'd be sitting on some tropical island surrounded by handsome guys who were doing my cooking and laundry. [More laughter.] But it's a good question, Ned. When we depart from the equilibrium assumptions at Spenser, it's not that we're saying we're smarter than the markets. We're just noticing that pricing is way out of whack in certain categories. If there's a bubble in Asian stocks, for example, we don't assume that's the right starting point.

Ned: Okay, I see that.

Carrie: As you'll see, when we get to the point of designing all the individual portfolios for your family, we'll use all these techniques, plus use a little sound judgment, to get to the "right" portfolio for you.

Roger: And then, as we go along, if we see that you're uncomfortable with that portfolio, we'll adjust it until we get it right.

More on Volatility

Carrie: But back to volatility for a minute. It's important for a couple of reasons. One is that investors don't like volatility. Well, more accurately, investors don't like *downside* volatility. But *vol* (sorry for the jargon), vol is symmetrical—the greater the upswing in value, the greater the downswing will be.

Roger: During the upswing—the bull market—everyone thinks they don't care about vol. But then, when the stomach-churning collapse comes, suddenly everybody cares about vol. And they tend to abandon the markets, as we've discussed.

Rose: Like Uncle George.

Carrie: Correct. But there's another reason vol is a negative. It has to do with the concept of *variance drain*.

Rose: You mentioned that earlier.

Roger: Yes, we spoke about this earlier. What it means is that high vol harms the growth of your capital. The more volatile your portfolio is, the higher the return has to be to grow your capital to the same level.

Rose: Is this that math thing again?

Carrie: It's a close cousin to it. Look at these two lines I've drawn:

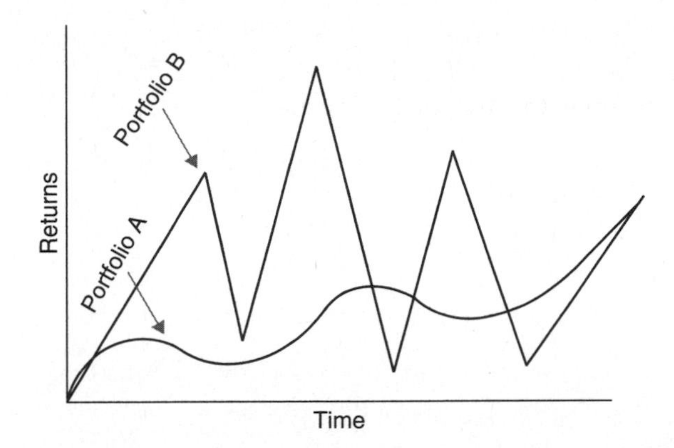

Carrie: The wavy line (marked A) that looks like a snake describes a relatively low-vol portfolio, one whose value doesn't vary terribly widely. The sharp line (marked B) that looks like a rugged mountain chain is a much more volatile portfolio. Let's stipulate that both portfolios result in a long-term return of eight percent.

Roger: But if you calculate the actual growth of capital, as opposed to just the return, the lower vol portfolio will be worth a lot more.

Suzy: That's weird. The portfolios have the same return but the dollars they produce is somehow different?

Roger: Yes. Remember the math we discussed earlier—the more money you lose, the bigger your return has to be to make up for that loss: down fifty percent, up fifty percent, you're down a *net* twenty-five percent.

Carrie: The calculation of variance drain is complicated, but a close approximation can be had by using this formula. [Carrie writes it out on a piece of paper and holds it up: $C = R - \sigma 2/2$.] In the formula, R is the mean return and σ is the variance in the return. The higher the variance number, the lower the terminal capital amount will be.

Billy: Who knew?

Carrie: My point is just that, when we get around to designing your portfolios, we'll be looking for the lowest-vol portfolio that will get us to our target return.

Ned: Okay, where do we start?

Carrie: Well, we actually started at our last meeting when we went through the process of establishing your investment objectives. That was a critical step and one where you, the family members, took the lead role. Now we'll turn to the asset allocation process itself, which is where Spenser takes the lead role, although you'll make the final decisions.

Asset Allocation Modeling: Preliminary Matters

Since the asset allocation process is identical for all the Titan family members and entities, we're only going to observe the portion of the meeting devoted to developing an asset allocation strategy for the Grandchildren's Trust.

Carrie: Fasten your seatbelts, we're ready to plunge into the exciting world of asset allocation!

Suzy: Be still, my heart.

[Laughter.]

Carrie: Laugh if you want, but this is the sort of stuff that gets financial advisors' hearts beating fast. Right, Roger?

Roger: Speak for yourself.

[More laughter.]

Disclaimers and Disclosure

Carrie: There's a lot of material in the books Roger passed out, but let me walk you through it. First, you probably noticed that there are a lot of disclaimers in these books. Did anyone read them? [Dead silence.] I'm not surprised. Nobody ever reads them.

Rose: Which raises the question, why are they there?

Carrie: The short answer is that the regulatory agencies—the SEC, for example—require us to put them in there. But what's the long answer, Roger?

Roger: The long answer is that we, that is, Spenser, are doing it under duress. We think it's a foolish requirement to put in every presentation pages and pages of disclosures no one ever reads. It's required not to help investors, but as a *gotcha*. If there's later a problem, the SEC lawyers can claim your disclosure wasn't good enough. Even though, no matter how good or bad it was, no one ever read it.

Carrie: Did anyone ever hear the phrase, "Sunlight is the best disinfectant?"

[All heads shake, no one has ever heard of it.]

Roger: Well, that's the theory behind long, impenetrable disclaimers. In other words, if a financial advisor discloses obvious things like, "Past results are no guarantee of future returns," people will be smarter investors. In particular, if a financial advisor discloses his conflicts of interest, the idea is that the client will be on high alert and will be very careful about taking the advisor's recommendations.

Rose: But are you saying that it doesn't work that way?

Carrie: It doesn't, for two reasons. In the first place, nobody reads the disclaimers, as we just established. But beyond that, research shows that, when an advisor with conflicts discloses those conflicts, afterward clients tend to *discount* the conflicts instead of focusing on them.[2]

Billy: I get that. The client is thinking, "Hey, this guy's really honest for disclosing all this stuff, so I shouldn't worry about his conflicts of interest."

Roger: Right. And on top of that, the *advisor* is thinking, "Hey, I disclosed my conflicts, so now I can ignore them and do whatever I want."

Carrie: Anyway, I just wanted to make these points. First, no one reads the disclaimers, so they're worthless. Second, if anybody did read them, they'd be worse off than they were before! But enough editorializing. Let's get down to business. Roger, do you want to walk us through the first few pages?

Introductory Materials

[A version of the materials discussed ahead is available on the companion website for this book at www.wiley.com/go/familycapital.]

Roger: Sure. These are disclosures and overall comments that we, I mean Spenser, thinks *are* important, as opposed to the boilerplate regulatory disclosures that aren't. So, first, if you turn past the introductory pages, "Nothing good or bad lasts forever. Markets tend to return to long-term averages over time."

Carrie: And that's very important. Over the course of your investment lifetimes you'll see very strong markets and very weak markets, but those will be outliers. It's important that you keep that in mind as you're enjoying the good markets and suffering through the bad markets. We put that statement in the book because the entire asset allocation process assumes that markets are ultimately mean-reverting, that is, prices eventually move back toward their long-term averages.

Roger: Then we say, "Differential investment performance requires contrary investing."

Carrie: What that means is, if all you do is invest like everybody else, you're going to get the outcomes everybody else gets, which are pretty bad. To do well, you need to think and act *differently* from other investors. That will mean doing things that are occasionally uncomfortable for you—buying assets that are very much out of favor and have performed poorly, for example, or avoiding assets that everybody else loves and that have done quite well. Again, this is important because, once we've agreed on your asset allocation strategies, we'll have targets for each asset class and, periodically, we'll encourage you to rebalance back to those targets, which won't always be what you want to do.

Roger: In other words, we'll be suggesting that you sell, say, stocks, which have done very well, and buy, say, bonds, which haven't done well.

Suzy: It's making me nervous already! Why would I want to buy stuff that's done bad and sell stuff that's done well?

Ned: I think I can answer that one. If you don't, you're driving by looking in the rearview mirror. The first bullet-point said that markets tend to return to long-term averages. So if a particular asset has really outperformed for a while, the likelihood is that it will underperform in the future, in order to get back to its long-term average. Is that right?

Carrie: Correct, Ned. Of course, the *timing* of when an outperforming asset will start to underperform, or vice versa, is tough to get right. But the principle is exactly correct. Go ahead, Roger.

Roger: Next, we say that, "There is no such thing as a good investment, only an investment purchased at a good price or a bad price."

Carrie: For example, it makes no sense to say that Google is a good investment while a rundown apartment building is a bad investment. There's a price at which Google would be a really lousy investment and at which the apartment building would be a terrific investment.

Billy: Interesting. I never thought about it that way.

Suzy: Me, neither. Who'd have thought of a rundown building as a better investment than Google?

Roger: It's really a different way of saying that contrary investing pays.

Carrie: We're on a roll, Roger. What's next?

Roger: "After-tax, net-of-all-fees performance is what matters."

Carrie: In other words, "You can't eat gross returns." Only a portion of those returns actually belongs to you. Uncle Sam is your partner, and Governor Pam is your partner. And in some cities, Mayor Ham is your partner, too.

Roger: So we need to pay close attention to the tax implications of investing your money, and we need to pay close attention to the fees you pay. And those considerations will be built into the asset allocation process, as you'll see in a minute.

Billy: How do we minimize them?

Carrie: Well, we don't actually recommend *minimizing* them; we recommend *optimizing* them. You could minimize your costs by, for example, firing Spenser and doing all this yourself!

Roger: Hey! Don't give them any ideas!

[Laughter.]

Carrie: And you could minimize taxes by never selling anything. But all that would do is allow a huge tax bill to build up inside your portfolio.

Roger: Suppose you buy a stock worth, say, one million dollars, and hold it for twenty years. It's now worth, say, two million. That's actually not a great return over all that time, but because you'd have such a big tax bill if you sold the stock you feel like you're locked in. You don't want to pay all that tax.

Rose: But if you sold the stock gradually over time, wouldn't you pay just as much tax, but not all at once?

Carrie: Possibly, but it would be psychologically easier for you to do the right thing. More important, over that period of time there would be opportunities to reduce the tax bill by offsetting the gain against losses you might have elsewhere in the portfolio.

Rose: Oh, I see. Does everyone understand Carrie's point?

Billy: Not me.

Suzy: Not me. Do I look like an accountant? Don't answer that, Billy!

[Laughter.]

Roger: Without getting down into the weeds too much, if you have an investment position that has a gain, and an investment position that has a loss, generally you can realize both the gain and the loss and offset them against each other.

Carrie: In fact, one of the strategies we like to use is to engage a manager that is constantly harvesting short-term losses as they occur naturally as a result of market action. In effect, they are *banking* those losses to use against gains elsewhere in the portfolio.

Billy: I'm getting it, I think, but only dimly.

QUICK NOTE

This point about optimizing investment expenses and taxes is worth pausing to emphasize. Investors most certainly shouldn't overpay for investment services and they shouldn't pay taxes unnecessarily. But by the same token, if expenses and taxes are absolutely minimized, investors are being pennywise and pound-foolish.

Carrie: We'll come back to this issue a lot. Taxes are important. What's next, Roger?

Roger: This statement: "Maintaining adequate liquidity is crucial to avoiding egregious wealth destruction."

Suzy: That sounds alarming! What does it mean?

Carrie: It means a couple of things. You might design a terrific portfolio that will produce a lot of wealth over the course of many years. But if at any point in time that portfolio fails to cover your living costs, the results could be disastrous.

Roger: The image is this: a guy drowns trying to walk across a river that's on average six inches deep. Trouble is, out in the middle there's a section that's ten feet deep.

Carrie: Also, there's liquidity and then there's liquidity. Stocks are liquid in the sense that you can sell them at any time. But the question is, at what price?

Roger: In very bad market environments, pricing can *gap down*, meaning there are no bids at reasonable prices. You either have to take a lousy price or hold on and hope for the best.

Carrie: Similarly, in long bear markets—and these days there seems to be one or two in every decade—stock prices drop to rock-bottom levels. It's crazy to sell at those prices, but if you don't have enough liquidity in the portfolio (say, in bonds), you have no choice.

Ned: I see that, but how much liquidity is enough? If I understand you, liquid assets—truly liquid assets—would be things like cash and bonds, which don't offer much in the way of returns.

Carrie: That's right, Ned. Owning liquidity comes with a cost, but that cost has to be offset against the alternative, which is ruinous. Roger, what's a good rule of thumb for liquidity?

Roger: At Spenser we like to look at it from a couple of different directions. For example, how much of your annual spending needs should be generated by true *income*—stock dividends and bond interest? Our view is that the number should be at least fifty percent.

Rose: If we spend one million dollars a year—I know that's not the right number, but just to make the math easy—you're saying that dividend and interest income should be about five hundred thousand?

Carrie: Yes. You don't want to have to start selling stocks in a bear market just because you can't meet your income needs. On the other hand, you don't want too much in safe, liquid assets because, as Ned says, they don't produce much in the way of return.

Roger: Another way of looking at liquidity is this: How many years of annual spending should you hold in extremely liquid assets like cash and bonds?

Rose: And the rule is?

Carrie: Well, here there's no real rule, since it depends on the risk tolerance of the client. Let's say a client has fifty million dollars and spends one million each year, all in. I would say that, as an absolute minimum, the client should have four years of spending in very safe, high-quality bonds or cash—in other words, four million dollars, or eight percent of the portfolio. Bear markets don't typically last more than three years, so the family could leave its stocks intact and live on its bond portfolio until the markets recover.

Ned: Eight percent in bonds seems awfully low to me.

Carrie: I agree. Five years of spending is a more typical minimum for a family, so that would be ten percent of the portfolio. And remember, this is the amount in very high-quality bonds. You'll likely have other, lower quality bonds in the portfolio as well.

Rose: Do you mean what they call *junk* bonds?

Carrie: Yes. In case anyone doesn't know what a junk bond is, they are bonds that are below investment-grade quality. Sometimes, when the yield on junk bonds is high enough, we like to buy them as an *opportunistic* investment. Then, when those yields drop and spreads compress, we sell them.

Suzy: "Spreads compress"? Meaning what?

Roger: A *spread* is the difference between the interest rate on the junk bonds and the interest rate you can get on investment-grade securities. If a safe bond, say, a Treasury bond, is yielding three percent and junk bonds are yielding ten, the spread is seven percent.

Suzy: Okay, got it.

Carrie: There are lots of other kinds of bonds that we wouldn't consider appropriate for the sleep-well, liquid portion of a portfolio, and which we wouldn't count as part of the number-of-years-coverage calculation, high-yield municipal bonds, for example, or certain kinds of bond issues that are highly rated but lightly traded. They might be hard to sell out of just when you need to get out of them.

QUICK NOTE

Many investors dislike owning liquid assets, especially during bull markets, because they reduce the portfolio's return. But as Carrie and Roger point out, owning too little liquidity can prove to be disastrous. The two metrics they mention—generating half a family's spending from dividends and interest, and keeping four years of spending in very high-quality bonds—are very useful rules of thumb.

Roger: If there are no more questions about liquidity, can I go on?
Carrie: Go ahead, Roger.
Roger: "All models are wrong, some are useful."
Carrie: A famous mathematician said something like that.[3] In the context of asset allocation it means that we use modeling—like mean-variance optimization—because it's useful, even though we know that the outcomes of the modeling won't be exactly accurate. Now let's summarize the steps we need to go through to develop and maintain a sound investment process. Can we move to the next page?

Elements of a Sound Investment Process

[Carrie holds up her book to show the page that reads as follows:

A sound investment process requires discipline and includes:

1. *Establishing long-term strategic asset allocation policies*
2. *Assessing relative value and current market conditions*
3. *Aligning asset class weights with relative value*
4. *Identifying significant investment opportunities*
5. *Evaluating and selecting managers*
6. *Implementing the changes*
7. *Monitoring and repeating the process*]

Carrie: Number 1 is what we're up to today, of course, but I wanted to put asset allocation in the context of the overall investment process for you.
Rose: Do you mind if we walk through the steps? We don't need to get into a lot of detail, but just to be sure we all understand what the steps are and why they're important.
Carrie: Sure. Roger, what do numbers 2 and 3 mean?
Roger: Once we've gone through the asset allocation process—number 1 on the list both in terms of when we do it and how important it is—we then have to think about where market valuations are *today*. The asset allocation process assumes a steady-state world where market sectors are all fairly valued. But of course that's rarely the case.
Rose: So, just to get specific, let's say our target for U.S. large-company stocks is twenty percent. What Spenser will do is set a range around that target, say, fifteen to twenty-five percent, and the trick is to allocate our money to the right percentage. If those U.S. large-company stocks appear to be way overvalued today, you wouldn't actually put twenty percent of our money in them, right?
Carrie: Right. We might, instead, go only to the minimum allocation of fifteen percent in your example. And then, when prices correct—notice

that I said "when," not "if"—we'll move back toward the twenty percent target or even above it.

Rose: Does everybody see that? One of the things we'll depend on Spenser for is to have strong views about market valuations and relative values as between market sectors.

Roger: Those views can be designed to make you money—as when we think a sector is undervalued and you should overweight it. But the relative value views are especially important to *preserve* your capital. If Spenser thinks U.S. large-company stocks are overvalued, we'll want your allocation to that sector to be relatively low. If we're wrong, the only consequence is that you don't make as much money as you might have. If we're right, it will save your bacon.

QUICK NOTE

Obviously, there is a very fine line between positioning a portfolio to take advantage of valuation anomalies—a sensible idea—and simple market timing—a terrible idea. One difference is the amount of work that a firm like Spenser puts into its valuation analyses. But another difference is that a sound wealth management firm will more typically deploy its valuation views on the downside, that is, to protect its clients' capital, rather than on the upside, to reach for return.

Carrie: The fourth step in the process is for Spenser to look around the world and see if there are any interesting opportunities. I mentioned junk bonds, for example. Maybe a particular client's portfolio won't have an allocation to junk, but if the opportunity is compelling, we'll put some money in junk on an opportunistic basis.

Ned: What would be some other examples, especially of investments we wouldn't otherwise be in?

Carrie: Roger, what would be some examples of opportunistic investments Spenser has recommended over time?

Roger: Well, you might remember that in the summer of 2007 we had a so-called credit crunch.

Rose: Unfortunately, Ned and I remember it all too well. We did some pretty dumb things at that time.

Ned: "Dumb" is a nice word for it.

Roger: Well you were hardly alone. Investors got very nervous about all sorts of credit-related assets, including even investment-grade bonds that were held in closed-end bond funds.

Carrie: Not to get too detailed, but a closed-end fund is different from a normal, open-end mutual fund. A closed-end fund issues a fixed number of shares, sort of like a corporation. You buy those shares on an exchange, just like a stock. The value of the shares normally depends on the value of the underlying portfolio.

Roger: So to take a simplified example, if a closed-end bond fund owns one million dollars' worth of bonds and has ten thousand shares, each share should sell for about a hundred dollars.

Carrie: But in reality the actual price of the shares varies a bit depending on how much investors want to own those assets. So a closed-end bond fund might usually sell at a slight premium to the underlying assets. In Roger's (very simple!) example, the shares might actually sell for one-hundred-four dollars.

Roger: Closed-end bond funds are mainly owned by retail investors, and are mainly sold by stockbrokers, who get a commission on the sale, just like with a stock.

Carrie: Roger is telling you this because it's important to know who owns which assets. Retail investors are subject to panicking at the drop of a hat. So when the credit crunch came along in 2007, they all (well, a lot of them) called their brokers in a panic and demanded that their closed-end bond funds be sold.

Roger: All that sales pressure caused the price of the closed-end bond funds to drop. The prices went from a slight premium, like a hundred-and-four dollars, to a big discount. Some of the funds were selling for (in my example) eighty or eighty-five dollars a share.

Carrie: The bonds the funds owned had also declined in value, but nothing like so much. So we bought—I mean our clients bought—loads of closed-end bond funds and we just held onto them until the panic subsided and the prices went back to rational levels.

Roger: Then we sold them at a very nice profit.

Carrie: The profit was especially nice because we owned very low-risk assets—investment-grade bonds—which normally don't offer that kind of big return.

Ned: Okay, I see the idea. Often, when you're finding what you call *opportunistic* investment ideas it's because other investors are panicking or otherwise behaving badly.

Carrie: Correct, Ned.

Ned: Okay. I see the next step is selecting managers. I think we all know what that involves.

Suzy: But I'd still like to hear Carrie and Roger say a word about it.

Carrie: Sure. I won't go into the details of how we evaluate and select managers; that's for another occasion and, anyway, Ned and Rose have already been all through it during the search process. I'll simply say that Spenser's manager research process is incredibly thorough and careful and that only a tiny minority of managers have any chance of making it through the process successfully. I'll also emphasize that the process is completely objective. We don't get any money or anything else of value from the managers we evaluate or end up working with.

Ned: And I want to be sure Suzy and Billy understand how important that is and how rare it is.

Billy: Important because if a manager is somehow paying the folks at Spenser, we couldn't be sure the manager was any good, right?

Carrie: Exactly, you just couldn't know; there would be too many conflicts going on. And Ned is right that it's very rare for an advisor to be completely independent from and objective with respect to the managers it's recommending to its clients.

Suzy: But why would clients put up with advisors who are—let's call a spade a spade—ripping off their clients?

Carrie: It's a very good question, and all the possible answers reflect very badly on both investors and the financial industry.

Roger: Obviously, we're blowing our own horn here, but we don't want to suggest that there aren't other objective, independent advisors out there. There are. It's just that the conflicted ones have most of the market share, especially when you include retail investors.

QUICK NOTE

Advisors who work mainly with large, institutional clients will typically have vast databases of managers they are following. But advisors who work with families will typically maintain a much smaller, much higher quality list of managers they recommend. This difference reflects how institutional and family investors use managers, it reflects the much smaller number of managers who are tax sensitive, and it reflects the even smaller number of managers who think of the capital they are managing in the same way that families think of that capital. Institutional capital is really "other people's money." Family capital is very much the family's money.

Carrie: Okay, anything else we should say about managers, Roger?

Roger: Well, one thing we might point out is that at Spenser we don't just sit back and evaluate random managers all day. There are thousands and thousands of managers out there; there are, I think, almost eight thousand open-end mutual funds alone and about the same number of hedge funds. What we actually do is, we develop a view on a particular market sector and then we go search for the best managers in that sector.

Ned: I know you said you don't want to get too deeply into this, and I agree, but can you say a word about the process of finding these really good managers?

Carrie: Sure. First, remember that Spenser's been in this business a long time, so even though we might not have been looking for, say, a *mezzanine loan manager*, it's pretty likely that we have a good idea who the best guys are out there.

Roger: And then we ask around. If we know we're working with the best buyout guys, we'll ask them who the best *mezz* guys are. They'll know because they use mezz debt all the time. And then, when we talk with a mezz team, we ask them who their toughest competitors are.

Ned: So you don't use manager databases?

Carrie: I wouldn't say we don't use them—we do. But we don't use them to find the best managers. We use them to get a sense of what other, similar managers out there are doing.

Billy: What does "mezz" mean? I mean, I realize it stands for "mezzanine," but I don't know what a mezzanine manager does.

Roger: Sorry for the jargon. A mezzanine manager is one who makes loans, typically structured as subordinated debt or preferred equity. It's a more expensive form of finance for companies that can't, or don't want to, issue secured or senior debt.

Carrie: A very typical use of mezz debt would be in connection with leveraged buyouts. A buyout fund will use cheaper debt to the extent it's available, but then may turn to the mezz guys to fill a gap in the financing, or to avoid having to put more of their own capital in the deal. So we would expect the return on mezz to fall somewhere in-between the return on secured or senior debt and the returns on equity.

Suzy: Are you sorry you asked, Billy?

Billy: Yes!

[Laughter.]

Carrie: We'd better move on. Next on the list, obviously, is to go ahead and make the changes in the portfolio. That's item number 6. Roger, are there any complexities to that we should be talking about?

Roger: Of course! Everything is complex—that's why our clients pay us the big bucks!

[Laughter.]

Roger: So one complexity involves market timing. If we're moving capital from one market sector to another, we don't want to get whipsawed. In other words, we don't want to take money out of emerging markets stocks and put it in U.S. small-cap stocks just before the former appreciates wildly and the latter collapses.

Carrie: So we will sometimes average-into a sector, averaging out of the other sector.

Roger: And, of course, there is the tax issue. Very often, we're selling down a market sector because the prices have run a lot. But that also means there's a tax cost associated with that sale.

Rose: So I take it you have to decide whether the valuation issues are serious enough to warrant the tax cost.

Roger: Yes, exactly, although sometimes we can mitigate the tax costs, as we discussed earlier.

Carrie: Finally, number 7 is monitoring. We watch the portfolio closely to make sure it's performing as expected. We report to you monthly and quarterly on the performance. We examine what factors are driving returns.

Roger: And then, of course, we recommend changes. These are typically modest. We'd rather nudge the ship a bit now and then rather than risk having to turn it suddenly later on.

Back to Portfolio Modeling

Rose: That was all very useful. But could we go back to the modeling issue for a minute? If I understand it correctly, Spenser is going to present us with some modeling data, based on your assumptions about risks and returns and so on.

Carrie: Exactly right.

Rose: Roger said something like, "All models are wrong, but some of them are useful." Can you explain that?

Carrie: Roger? You're the one who's being quoted.

Roger: That'll teach me to keep my mouth shut. [Laughter.] When we say that all models are wrong, we're really saying two things. First, the inputs that go into the modeling, while they are our best estimates of what the future will look like, are not going to be exactly accurate. If Spenser expects small-cap stocks in the United States to return seven percent over the next cycle, it's highly likely that small caps won't return exactly seven percent. In other words, we were wrong. But our estimate was reasonable and is probably going to be in the ballpark. So the inputs were wrong-but-useful.

Carrie: And on top of that, the model itself will never be exactly right. Mean-variance optimizers, for example, include in their design certain assumptions about return patterns that are simplistic. Otherwise, we'd have to use a supercomputer from the Oak Ridge Laboratory to run the simulations.

Rose: But if we know the inputs are likely to be wrong, and we know the model itself uses simplistic assumptions, are those models really useful?

Carrie: It's a fair question, Rose. Our logic for using these models goes something like this. As investors, we simply have to make decisions about how to invest our money, and therefore about the future. Even if the decision is to convert everything to cash and stash it under your mattress, that's a decision. And that decision will need to be reviewed periodically.

Roger: So the question is, what's the most rational way to think about decisions about a future that's simply unknowable? The way we come up with our inputs, and the models we use, won't be exactly right and can sometimes be alarmingly wrong. But they're rational, reasonable ways to deal with what Donald Rumsfeld called "the known unknowns."

Carrie: And, like it or not, in the markets there will always be "*unknown* unknowns," events we simply can't model because we can't imagine them.

Suzy: Well, that's scary!

Billy: Are there really events like that, I mean events that we simply couldn't imagine but that actually happened?

Carrie: Sure. This was before your time—and Suzy's and Roger's—but Ned and Rose might remember Black Monday, October 19, 1987. On that one day, the Dow dropped almost twenty-three percent.

Billy: *In one day?*

Carrie: Yes. No one ever imagined that such a thing could happen. In fact, if you assume that stock market prices fall into a normal bell curve, the odds against that kind of collapse happening in one day were astronomical. Somebody worked out that if the entire existence of the universe since the Big Bang had been repeated a billion times, that kind of loss would still have been unlikely.[4]

Suzy: Wow. So why *did* it happen? And is it going to happen again?

Carrie: You'd have to ask someone a lot smarter than me that question!

Suzy: Roger?

[Loud laughter.]

Roger: Don't look at me! It's never a good idea to act smarter than your boss!

Carrie: Come on, Roger, take a stab at it. We've talked about this back in the office.

Roger: Well, if I recall correctly, one issue is that markets aren't in fact following a normal bell curve distribution. There are what we call *fat tails*, weird stuff happening way out at the edges of the distribution curve. Those are events that we simply can't know about until they happen.

Carrie: But we know they *will* happen and that the damage to capital from them can be enormous. Yet another reason to be capital-preservation-oriented.

Roger: A related issue is that markets aren't just a bunch of random prices jumping around out there. Markets are driven by human beings, and people react not just rationally, but also irrationally. So once a market starts trending in a bad direction, the actions of millions of investors can drive the trend right over the cliff.

Rose: Okay, that's enough of the scary stuff for me! Can we move on to look at the actual portfolios you've designed for us?

Carrie: Almost, Rose. But before we look at the recommended portfolios, let's let Roger walk us through the process and inputs, just to put things in perspective.

Asset Allocation Modeling: Process and Inputs

Roger: If you turn to the next page, you'll see that it reads as follows:

A strategic asset allocation must:

1. *Accurately address the investor's needs, objectives, and temperament.*
2. *Be fundamentally an exercise in asset–liability management.*
3. *Focus on covering spending needs and maintaining purchasing power.*
4. *Determine the long-term target mix of asset types.*
5. *Set tactical ranges for strategic allocation targets.*

Billy: I get most of that, but what does "asset–liability matching" mean?

Roger: A very simple example would be an investor who knows he has to have a fifty-thousand-dollar down payment to close on a new house in three months, but who invests that money in long-dated assets. Suppose he invests the fifty thousand in very long-maturity corporate bonds. Those bonds are very volatile and, on the date he needs the money, the fifty thousand dollars might be worth only forty thousand. Or he might have invested the fifty thousand in a stock—theoretically, at least, an asset with an infinitely long *maturity*. If the markets crash before the close, he might have only twenty-five thousand dollars.

Suzy: So you're saying what he should have done is to match the—let's see, the *duration* of the asset (his fifty thousand dollars) to the maturity date of his liability (the closing on the house).

Billy: *Whoa!* You're sounding like a financial advisor now!

Roger: That's right, Suzy. He could have matched the asset and liability exactly by buying a Treasury bill that came due the day before the closing. But except in cases of very short liabilities on a known date, we don't necessarily try to match them that closely. It's just that shorter-term needs should be invested in shorter-term assets and long-term needs should be invested in longer-term assets.

Carrie: On the short end, that eliminates the possible funding shortage, and on the long end, it maximizes the return you can get from the assets.

Billy: Okay. And I think I know what you mean by maintaining purchasing power. But just to be sure, that's the business of trying to stay ahead of inflation, right?

Roger: Exactly. Those are the two main goals of portfolio design: make sure your (reasonable) spending needs will be met and, at the same time, ensure that you'll be able to buy at least the same amount of stuff many years into the future.

Carrie: Roger, how about a quick word about tactical ranges? We've mentioned this already.

Roger: Sure. A tactical range is just a band around the asset allocation target within which the portfolio can be allowed to fall. If the target for emerging markets stocks is ten percent, we might set a tactical range of five-to-fifteen percent.

Rose: And the portfolio will be at the low end of the range when those kinds of stocks are unattractive, and at the high end of the range when they are attractive.

Roger: Right. And at target when emerging markets stocks are fairly valued.

Carrie: The next page shows the tax status of the Grandchildren's Trust:

- Federal income tax = 0%
- Federal long-term capital gains tax = 15%
- Federal short-term capital gains tax = 35%
- Federal dividend tax = 0%
- State income tax = 0%
- Local income tax = 0%

Billy: Lots of zeros there! Is that what Dad meant when he said the Trust has income tax advantages?

Ned: That's one of the things I meant. Typically, when income is distributed to a beneficiary …

Suzy: You mean, *if* income is ever distributed to a beneficiary.

Rose: I see that you've been talking to Ellen and Geoff.

Ned: But let's not go back into that morass! When income is distributed, it's taxed in the hands of the beneficiary at the beneficiary's normal rate. Notice that that rate might be lower than what the Trust's rate would have been. Also, if income is accumulated, it isn't taxed at all. And the Trust can even give income away and then no one will ever pay tax on it.

Carrie: So it's a nice vehicle to have. From Spenser's side, it's important for us to know the tax status of the Trust because most assets have tax consequences associated with owning them and we need to take those consequences into account when we design the portfolio.

Roger: And also when we hire managers, but I guess we'll get to that later.

Rose: Can you give us an example of how you take taxes into account when you design the portfolio?

Carrie: Sure. We know that our clients only keep what's left after taxes. So, to take one example, suppose we're looking at a tax-exempt institution. Or, really, even an IRA. We know they aren't taxable, so that means that assets with heavy tax consequences are likely to be more attractive to them than to a taxable investor. So, typically, you'll see more hedge funds in an institutional portfolio than in a family portfolio. Hedge funds are mainly taxed like short-term gains, which is a high tax rate for an individual. But the institution won't pay that tax.

Ned: By the same token, an institution wouldn't own municipal bonds, because the tax-free nature of those bonds is only useful to taxable investors.

Carrie: That's *generally* right, Ned. But sometimes the markets do strange things, and it can make sense for non-taxed investors to own muni bonds or for taxable investors to own corporate bonds. When we're living through an environment like that we often hire a bond manager who can run a so-called *crossover* strategy, buying whichever kind of bonds makes the most sense for the investor at the time.

Ned: So as a family we'll usually own municipal bonds, but sometimes it might pay us, even net of the taxes paid, to own corporates?

Carrie: Correct.

Roger: Next, we show a chart with Spenser's assumptions about *after*-tax returns, risks, and correlations. I should point out that very few financial advisors design portfolios using after-tax assumptions, but almost all of them *should* do it.

Carrie: Otherwise, you'll end up owning a portfolio that is extremely inefficient from a tax point of view and too much of your return will be wasted in unnecessary taxes.

Suzy: These charts are making my eyes go around. Can you quickly walk us through them, especially the top chart?

Roger: Sure. The first column shows the asset classes down the side. Let's just follow U.S. large-cap stocks. The next column shows the risk of U.S. large caps, which Spenser estimates at sixteen percent. Keep in mind that's risk in the sense of price volatility, as we've discussed before. Then we show our assumption that U.S. large caps will return nine percent pre-tax over a long period of time. Then we show a typical management fee for the asset class.

Rose: Zero-point-two percent seems awfully low. That's what, twenty basis points?

Carrie: Yes. But we use that number for the fee because, typically, Spenser will use passive strategies in the U.S. large-cap sector. That's because we don't think active managers can in general outperform net of their higher fees in that sector of the market.

Billy: Why do you show no fee for some of the categories? Do those managers work for nothing?

[Laughter.]

Carrie: No, I can assure that nobody in the financial world works for nothing! For hedge and private equity, the fees are actually very high. Typically, the managers will charge a two percent annual fee and on top of that will cut themselves in for twenty percent of all the profits, sometimes after a hurdle rate has been achieved.

Billy: Pretty sweet!

Carrie: Yes, Roger and I are in the wrong business. [Laughter.] And since it's complicated to show what portion of the fee is the annual fee and what portion is the profit share, we just estimate hedge and P/E returns net of all the fees we expect.

Roger: So then we show the expected annual turnover. In other words, if every stock in the portfolio was sold once in a given year, the annual turnover would be a hundred percent. We worry about turnover because it affects the taxes. So, for example, U.S. large-cap stocks have low turnover (because we're using passive strategies), so the after-tax return is very close to the pre-tax return.

Carrie: If we showed active managers here, the pre-tax return would be lower and the turnover would be higher, so the after-tax return would be much lower.

Roger: You can see, for example, that non-directional hedge funds are expected to have the same pre-tax return as U.S. large-cap stocks—nine percent. But because the turnover is so high—ninety percent—the after-tax return is much lower.

Suzy: Less than seven percent. Why would a taxable investor ever invest in such a thing, given all the other options?

Carrie: It's a good question, Suzy, but a long conversation. We'll have that conversation when we get to manager selection, but for now let me just say that non-directional hedge funds, or what some people prefer to call absolute return–oriented hedge funds, can play a useful role in portfolios because of their low correlation with the returns of other investment assets. Compare municipal bonds, for example. The expected return on munis is very low, but they play a useful role in portfolios nonetheless.

Suzy: Well, I'll take your word for it for now ...

Ned: I'm sure you're going to explain this, but I doubt that any of us knows the difference between the arithmetic after-tax return and the geometric after-tax return. Anybody know?

[Roger raises his hand.]

Carrie: Very funny, Roger. But since your hand is up, perhaps you can explain.

Roger: I should learn never to volunteer. But here's the reason we show both arithmetic and geometric returns. Arithmetic returns are just the average return you get. Let's take a simple example. If you get a seven percent return in one year, a fourteen percent return in the second year, and a minus-five-percent return in year three, what's your average return? It's five-point-three percent, right? [7 + 14 – 5 = 16, 16 ÷ 3 = 5.3.]

Ned: Sounds right, and seems to make sense, given the return stream you specified.

Carrie: Yes. But in fact, if you started with, say, one million dollars and experienced that return stream for three years, you can't compound your return at five-point-three percent and end up with the money you ended up with.

Suzy: Huh? Can you say that in English?

Carrie: Well, I can try! The arithmetic average assumes you got five-point-three percent return every year, but you didn't. That was just the *average* return. And because your actual return differed from year to year, if you run the numbers you get something like this.

[Carrie uses her calculator and then shows the calculations as follows:]

$1,000,000 × 7% = $1,070,000 (end of Year1)
$1,070,000 × 14% = $1,219,800 (end of Year 2)
$1,219,800 × −5% = $1,158,810 (end of Year 3)

Carrie: Okay, everyone with me? [Heads nod.] Good. But look what happens if I start with one million and simply multiply it by five-point-three percent every year:

$1,000,000 × 5.3% = $1,053,000 (end of Year 1)
$1,053,000 × 5.3% = $1,108,809 (end of Year 2)
$1,108,809 × 5.3% = $1,167,576 (end of Year 3)

Suzy: It's higher!
Roger: Yes. The end numbers are different because, in the real world, the underlying capital is growing or shrinking, and it's that growing or shrinking number that the next year's return acts on.
Billy: Price volatility!
Suzy: Variance drain!
Carrie [laughing] Well, yes, more or less. The point is that the geometric return will always be less than the arithmetic return. Let me give you a really impressive example of how this works. The difference between arithmetic and geometric really gets large if you have a few big negative years in the return series. Consider this series of returns:

+90%, + 10%, + 20%, + 30%, and − 90%

Roger, what's the arithmetic average?
Roger: The arithmetic average is a respectable twelve percent.
Carrie: Right. Sounds good! But what's the geometric return?
Roger: Are you sitting down? The geometric return would be *minus*-twenty percent![5]
Suzy: Wow, that makes you think. I guess the lesson is, you really don't want to have a really bad negative year.
Carrie: You sure don't—capital preservation investing again! But, on the other hand, there is no way anyone in this family or any other client of Spenser's is ever going to have a minus-ninety-percent year! Roger was just giving an extreme example to show how different the arithmetic and geometric returns can be.

Constraining the Optimizer

Roger: Okay, so let's move on. On the next page, we show the asset class constraints we used in doing our modeling.

Ned: Constraints? You don't just let the model run?

Carrie: No, we don't, and here's why. The mean-variance process is fraught with issues, and one of them is that if you let the optimizer run on an unconstrained basis, it will come up with weird portfolios nobody would ever own.

Roger: For example, if emerging markets are expected to do very well going forward, and they are also expected to have a low correlation to other assets, the optimizer might select a portfolio that's eighty percent emerging-markets stocks, fifteen percent venture capital, and five percent cash. That's a lunatic portfolio.

Ned: It does sound crazy, but maybe the model is right.

Carrie: Possibly, but it's highly unlikely, Ned. We could be totally wrong about the future of emerging markets. More important, the optimizer doesn't know about any kind of risk except volatility. In emerging markets, you have societies where the rule of law doesn't really apply and where your assets can simply be confiscated. That's happened recently in places like Venezuela, for example.

Roger: And the optimizer doesn't recognize the extreme illiquidity risk associated with investing in venture capital funds.

Ned: I see. You're constraining the model because it takes a very narrow view of what risk is all about.

Carrie: Correct.

Roger: The next page simply shows how the Trust is invested today.

Roger: As you can see, the portfolio isn't well-diversified at present. It's mainly U.S. large-company stocks and municipal bonds. You have a few non-U.S. companies in there. But most of the asset classes we would normally expect to see in a large family portfolio are missing.

Rose: But do we really need all those different kinds of assets?

Carrie: Not necessarily. One important goal of the asset allocation process is to identify asset classes that are additive to the portfolio. If an asset class simply duplicates something we're already getting from another exposure, than we aren't interested in it. As you'll see we think the Trust should be much more broadly diversified than it is today.

The Chhabra Framework and Behavioral Finance

Roger: So on the next page you can see how we map the various asset categories according to a framework devised by a fellow named Ashvin

Chhobra.[6] We think it's a useful way to think about the role assets play in a family portfolio.

Carrie: Dr. Chhabra noticed that the portfolios of most individual investors were poorly diversified, and he believed that this was in part a result of inattention to risk factors. His work is an attempt to merge Modern Portfolio Theory—MPT—with behavioral finance.

Billy: Have we talked about behavioral finance?

Roger: I think we did, briefly. There are two more-or-less opposite approaches to understanding the behavior of markets. One approach, the Modern Portfolio Theory approach, assumes that investors are primarily rational and make thoughtful decisions based on an analysis of risk and return. They are so-called *wealth maximizers*. Behavioral finance suggests that investors are often irrational and make decisions on the basis of emotion, even though the result isn't to maximize their wealth at all.

Suzy: So which is right?

Carrie: Ha! We think both approaches are right. Investors are often quite rational. But normal people aren't automatons who always do the right thing. We do sometimes get carried away by our emotions and by other sorts of unhelpful thinking. How many of us buy lottery tickets, for example, even though the odds are astronomically against winning?

[Rose raises her hand, then quickly pulls it down and covers her mouth laughing and blushing.]

Suzy: Mom! You don't!

Rose: I can't help it! Sometimes I just feel lucky. I'm sure I'm going to win the jackpot. I never do, of course, but that doesn't stop me!

Carrie: There's a perfect example. Rose not only knows, with the rational part of her mind, that her odds of winning are ridiculously low, but she's also had a lot of experience bearing that out. But she buys a lottery ticket, anyway.

Ned: Well, I for one am very surprised at my sister! On the other hand, I never go golfing without wearing my lucky socks!

Carrie: And do you always win your matches?

Ned: Hardly ever!

Carrie: Another perfect example!

Roger: So basically—correct me if I'm wrong, Carrie—Spenser's view is that MPT represents the way markets *ought* to work, and sometimes do work, while behavioral finance represents the way they all-too-often *actually* work.

Carrie: That's right, Roger. And, therefore, a very important part of what we do at Spenser is to help our clients behave a lot more like wealth maximizers and a lot less like people who buy lottery tickets and wear lucky socks.

[Laughter.]

Rose: And you do that how? Remember, you have a tough audience here, at least among the senior generation.

Roger: Fortunately, a lot of work has been done by the behavioral finance guys, so we know what kinds of behavior doesn't work. The most famous of these fellows are Amos Tversky and Daniel Kahneman,[7] who've been studying behavioral finance since back in the 1960s.

Ned: What are some examples of poor decision making that these behavioral finance guys have found?

Roger: Well, for example, they've found that picking stocks while wearing your lucky socks never works.

[Laughter.]

Ned: You made that up!

Carrie: Yes, he did make it up. But here are a few of the key concepts of behavioral finance that all investors should try to avoid and that we try to help our clients avoid:

[Carrie holds up a chart reading as follows:

Prospect theory

Anchoring behavior

Confirmation bias

Gambler's fallacy

Mental accounting

Hindsight bias

Herd behavior

Overconfidence[8]]

Ned: That's a lot of examples!

Carrie: We won't spend a lot of time on this, because you'll get the idea pretty quickly. Roger, what does "prospect theory" refer to?

Roger: It's one of the most famous of the examples in behavioral finance. It refers to the prospect of winning and losing, and how investors sometimes react irrationally to those prospects. The main message is the one we've already talked about here: investors hate losses more than they like gains.

Carrie: But as we've discussed, that usually makes sense because the outcomes for a wealthy family—getting richer versus getting poor—aren't symmetrical. And, also, there's variance drain to worry about. But prospect theory refers to situations where investor preferences make no sense.

Roger: For example, which is better, to win fifty dollars or to win a hundred dollars and then lose fifty?

Suzy: Is this a trick question?

Ned: I see where Roger's going with this. From a rational point of view, the outcomes are exactly the same. But I bet a lot of people prefer to win fifty dollars than to win a hundred and then lose fifty.

Carrie: Exactly. The preference is irrational, but many, many people feel that way. Rather than go through this whole list, are there others you'd especially like to talk about?

Rose: Okay, I'll bite. What's the gambler's fallacy? Thinking that I can win the lottery?

Carrie: Well, I'm afraid that's pretty much it, Rose. The classic example is a lady who sits at the slot machine for hours. She hasn't won but she figures her time is coming. She's lost so many times that her chances of winning must now be very high. But her time is unlikely ever to come, because the machines are programmed to start all over with the same odds every time she plays.

Billy: They *do*? What a ripoff!

Ned: Billy! Do you actually play slot machines?

Billy: I was speaking hypothetically.

[Laughter.]

Carrie: Well, anyway, back to Mr. Chhabra. He believes, and we tend to agree, that it's useful to think about the role certain assets play in your portfolio to make sure you are properly diversified.

Roger: So some assets are best thought of as *protective* assets. These kinds of assets won't make you a lot of money, but they'll protect your portfolio from serious loss, so they play an important role.

Carrie: At the other end of the spectrum, you have *aspirational* assets. These assets hold out the promise of very high return, but they are also very risky. You want some of these assets in your portfolio, but not too many.

Roger: And then, finally, you have the *market* assets. These will represent the core of your portfolio. But all three kinds of assets are important and have their place.

QUICK NOTE

As Carrie points out immediately ahead, "It's the journey that matters." The Spenser advisors have devoted a great deal of attention to explaining what asset allocation is all about and to walking the Titan family though a long presentation. We are only now getting to the actual portfolios Spenser is recommending, but it has been time well spent.

Recommended Portfolios: The Efficient Frontier

Carrie: Finally, we come to the recommended portfolio. I know it's taken us a long time to get here, but it's the journey that matters. Because this is the first time we've gone through the asset allocation process with you, we've gussied up this page to show more than we normally would. But all efficient frontier presentations are basically the same. On the left axis we show compound return, and on the bottom axis we show risk, that is, price volatility as measured by standard deviation. Roger, can you walk us through the page?

Roger: Sure. As you can see, there are several different portfolios shown on this page. Obviously, the ones highest up—to the north, as we say—are the highest returning. The ones to the left—the west—are the least risky. Does anyone notice any relationship between risk and return?

Suzy: *Duh* .... The least risky portfolios have the lowest returns.

Roger: Right, of course. Also, notice that the portfolios we show on the page fall to the right and below the curving line. That line describes what we call the *efficient frontier*.

Carrie: What we're ultimately trying to do is to find portfolios that fall as close as possible to the efficient frontier line. That's because those portfolios have the best combination of risk and return we can get. For example, Portfolio A is a perfectly efficient portfolio, but it happens to be a very low-returning portfolio, so it's unlikely to produce enough return for most investors.

Roger: Portfolios B and C are also efficient and offer more return. These are likely portfolios for the Grandchildren's Trust. Portfolio D is also efficient and offers more return, but it also contains more risk. So if Portfolios B and C offer acceptable rates of return, we wouldn't want to own Portfolio D. We would only opt for that portfolio if, for some reason, we really needed to reach for return.

Carrie: Even if your definition of risk is nothing but volatility, it still makes sense to diversify into more asset classes, rather than fewer. And when you realize that there are other dimensions of risk, that diversification makes even more sense. As you add more asset classes to the portfolio, then as long as those assets aren't perfectly correlated, risk goes down faster than return goes down.

Billy: I know we talked about this once, but can you explain what *correlation* is and why it's important?

Roger: If two assets are correlated, then they tend to move in the same direction at the same time. If U.S. stocks are going up, the likelihood is that non-U.S. stocks will also be going up. Not always, of course—the correlation isn't perfect—and they won't always be going up or down at exactly the same rate. But there will be a correlation, which can be calculated.

Carrie: And as long as the correlation isn't perfect, it will generally make sense to add that asset to the portfolio. Think, for example, of all the investable asset classes in the world. Theoretically, an ideal portfolio would have exposure to all those assets, although there might be practical or other reasons why you wouldn't use them. But the burden should be on the argument to exclude them.

Roger: The degree of correlation is what helps us decide how much of each asset class to include, although there will be other considerations as well. For example, if an asset class is huge, that is, widely invested in, it will likely play a larger role in your portfolio than an obscure asset class, even if the obscure asset has a lower correlation.

Carrie: Note the portfolio designated with an X. That's your current portfolio.

Suzy: Ugly.

[Laughter.]

Carrie: Well, I wouldn't have used that word, exactly, but, it's certainly not very well diversified, at least on the equity side. That's why it falls well below the efficient frontier. Either you are giving up too much return given the risk you are taking, or you are taking too much risk for the return you're getting. Two sides of the same coin.

Roger: So what we're suggesting is that you diversify the equity side of the portfolio into more asset classes, and also, perhaps, a little bit on the bond side as well.

Carrie: On the next page you can see the actual statistics for the various portfolios, including the current one.

Roger: In the column captioned "Allocation," we show all the asset classes we typically use at Spenser. As you can see in the next column, we show the current Trust portfolio, which contains only two asset classes. Then we show various efficient portfolios, along with the specific portfolio we recommend for the Trust.

Rose: Can you quickly walk through the portfolios and talk about what you liked or didn't like about them?

Carrie: Certainly. Portfolio A, as I mentioned earlier, is an efficient portfolio, but it doesn't produce enough return to suit the purposes of the Grandchildren's Trust. The Trust is a long-term vehicle that should emphasize growth.

Roger: Portfolio B offers more return and isn't terribly different from the current portfolio (except better diversified), but, again, we think the Trust could shoot a little higher.

Carrie: I'll skip the Recommended Portfolio for a moment and move to Portfolio D. It offers a bit more return than the Recommended Portfolio, but unfortunately it also carries more risk. Especially in a fiduciary portfolio, we don't want to take any more risk than we really need to take. So, all in all, we like the Recommended Portfolio best.

Roger: As you can see, if you count them up, the Recommended Portfolio contains no fewer than eleven asset classes. It's extremely well diversified.

Carrie: In fact, it might be a little *too* well diversified for some people, simply because a portfolio with so many asset classes is complicated to deal with. But, as I noted, because this is a fiduciary portfolio, we want it to be as well diversified as possible, ensuring that the trustees can never be accused of breaching their fiduciary duties.

Rose: Are you saying that a trustee could be surcharged simply for not being diversified enough?

Carrie: Absolutely. There are cases on point. Typically, I'll admit, they are extreme cases. For example, a trustee might say, look, this is a very long-term portfolio with little or no spending needs, so why not invest it all in stocks and really grow the corpus over the years? Plus, that would be a very simple portfolio to operate.

Billy: Right. Why not?

Carrie: Roger?

Roger: Because trusts aren't desert-island portfolios.

Billy and Suzy: Huh?

Carrie: Let's say a trust doesn't expect to distribute principal for thirty years, and that it will have very modest income distributions over that time. If the trustees truly could send themselves off to a desert island and not even glance at the portfolio for thirty years, an all-stock portfolio might well do okay.

Roger: But it's not certain. At the end of 2008, bonds had beaten stocks over the previous thirty years.

Rose: Seriously? You don't mean beaten them on a risk-adjusted basis?

Roger: No, I mean that bonds beat stocks straight up over that period. On a risk-adjusted basis, it was a slaughter.

Carrie: But we admit that was unusual. More often, over thirty-year periods of time stocks will beat bonds, usually by a lot.

Suzy: But what's the desert island got to do with it?

Carrie: The problem is that trustees can't send themselves off to a desert island and not look at the portfolio for all that time. For one thing, it would be a breach of the trustees' duty of care, right, Ned?

Ned: Absolutely. I'd take that case any day!

Carrie: So what actually happens is, the trustees are watching the trust portfolio constantly.

Roger: And when a really bad bear market comes along and the market starts swooning, the trustees lose their nerve. After all, all they own is stocks, and stocks are getting killed. They're watching the value of the trust corpus decline and decline. They're being screamed at by the beneficiaries. And so they panic and sell out near the bottom.

Billy: Like Uncle George.

Carrie: Exactly. Everybody thinks they have nerves of steel when the market's strong, but almost nobody has nerves of steel when the markets are hemorrhaging. In fact, what we see near the tops of bull markets is that foolish investors move to all-equity portfolios.

Ned: Even in fiduciary portfolios?

Carrie: Even in fiduciary portfolios. It doesn't happen a lot in trusts, I'll admit, but we see it. Especially when the trustee is an individual, not an institution.

Ned: Those trustees are playing with fire. In fact, I don't see how they can win. Eventually, there's going to be a bad bear market. If they try to hold on through it, the beneficiaries will be furious and will likely sue them. If they lose their nerve and bail out, they will permanently damage the portfolio—the Uncle George problem—and they'll get sued for that.

Carrie: We also see it on the other end of the risk spectrum. In fact, I would say, more often. Trustees worry so much about getting sued that they *underexpose* the corpus to risk. They're looking out for the current income beneficiaries, who are happy with this strategy, but they are shortchanging the future beneficiaries.

Ned: You're right. I see that phenomenon in my law practice a lot. In older trusts the beneficiaries today look back and complain bitterly that the trustees years ago owned mostly bonds and a few blue-chip stocks. As a result, the size of the corpus hasn't kept pace with inflation, much less grown any.

Carrie: So what we're trying to do is to avoid both extremes. We'd never in a million years recommend an all-stock portfolio for a fiduciary account, but we also want to have the interests of the future beneficiaries in mind.

Suzy: Especially since we're sitting right here!

[Laughter.]

Carrie: Yes, especially! But even if you weren't here, Spenser would be plugging away for you.

Rose: In the case of the Grandchildren's Trust you could argue that there are no current beneficiaries. I mean, Ned and I could take income from the Trust if we wanted or needed it, but we don't.

Carrie: That's true, Rose. Your family is in the fortunate position of not needing current income, so it's being accumulated. But we can't assume that will always be the case. You or Ned might suffer financial reverses. Or maybe one of the kids will need more help than you can give them from your own assets, and so you would request income from the Trust that you could use to help support the kids.

Rose: I never thought of that angle. I hope it doesn't happen!

Carrie: Well, so far, so good on that point. Three of the four kids are gainfully employed and Geoffrey is well on his way to having a good job.

Billy: If you consider a starving professor to have a good job!

[Laughter.]

Ned: Well, the pay may not be great, but the job security's terrific, at least if you get tenure.

Roger: But back to the presentation—on the next page you can see the targets for each asset class, as well as the ranges we suggest. Keep in mind that, if an asset class falls out of range, the trustees will want to rebalance.

Carrie: Or, if for some reason they don't want to rebalance, the minutes of the trustees' meeting should note that they discussed the matter.

Ned: We're very good at papering up what great fiduciaries we are!

Carrie: I'm glad to hear it! Are there questions about the recommended portfolio?

Rose: Can you tell us how you established the ranges around the target allocations?

Roger: I'm afraid it's more art than science, Rose. We start with the proposition that we want to have ranges, so that the portfolio is never allowed to get too badly out of balance.

Carrie: That's because an unbalanced portfolio is one whose risk profile is different from the risk profile that's right for the investor. In the case of the Grandchildren's Trust, for example, if stocks are going straight up and bonds are just holding their own or going down, the risk level of the portfolio is getting higher and higher. If it's the other way around—bonds going up and stocks going down—the risk level of the portfolio is getting lower and lower. We don't want either of those things to happen.

Roger: So we know need ranges. The next thing we look at is the volatility of the asset class. If an asset is really volatile, like emerging-markets stocks, we might make the range a little wider, so we don't have to be constantly rebalancing just because of ordinary market volatility in that asset. Finally, we look at just how much increased risk—or decreased risk—we're willing to tolerate over the short term.

Carrie: And then, frankly, we just make a judgment.

Billy: Okay, I see all that. But let's look at a specific case. You're showing a target for "U.S. large cap" of twenty percent, with a maximum of twenty-five. Let's say we have a meeting, and our exposure to U.S. large cap is thirty percent. What do we do? Do we rebalance back to twenty-five? Or twenty? Or all the way back to the minimum range of fifteen percent?

Carrie: Very good question, Billy. I only wish I had a really good answer. Basically, here's what I'd say. Everything being equal, you should rebalance back to your target, in this case, twenty percent. But if there are large tax implications to rebalancing, then you should do less. But in no case, well, in hardly any cases, should you do less than rebalance back to the maximum exposure, and hang the taxes. Taxes, after all, will reduce the value of your portfolio, but they'll reduce it less than a big drop in the market will reduce it.

Rose: Speaking now as a fiduciary, can you think of cases where the trustees of the Grandchildren's Trust would be out-of-range but not rebalance?

Carrie: I suppose one example would be if the out-of-balance situation was very small. If it was twenty-six percent, let's say, maybe it wouldn't be worth the trouble.

Roger: Another case might be where the asset you'd be buying to rebalance also isn't attractive.

Carrie: In any case, if the trustees decide not to rebalance, they'll need to make a note in the minutes about the fact and why they made that decision. Unless it's a very extreme case, no court will substitute its judgment for the considered judgment of the trustees made at the time. Or am I wrong about that, Ned?

Ned: No, that's right. Judges don't like to second-guess trustees who've been on the firing line. But, as you say, if the matter gets too extreme, a judge won't hesitate to surcharge.

Suzy: What would be an example of an extreme case, Dad?

Ned: I remember a case in upstate New York, this is going back a few years. The case was being tried by a lawyer from up there, but our firm had been consulted. What happened is that the bank trustee just wasn't paying attention. For years the only current beneficiary had been the son of the grantor of the trust, and that guy, frankly, was a bit of a nut case. He lived on a boat somewhere down in the Everglades and never paid the slightest attention to anything.

Billy: Now there's the life!

[Laughter.]

Ned: So while the son was paying no attention, neither was the bank. The trust portfolio just drifted along with the markets, and since the stock market had been strong, pretty soon the trust was, oh, I don't remember exactly, something like eighty percent stocks. A lot of those stocks were technology companies because the grantor had been in the tech business.

Roger: I think I see where this is heading …

Ned: Right. Along came the tech bust in 2000, and over the next two years the portfolio really got hammered. It lost something like sixty-five percent of its value. Then, right at the bottom, somebody at the bank woke up and said, "Oh, my God! We've got to get out of the markets!"

Roger: So they sold out and immortalized the trust's losses.

Ned: Yep. Naturally, the old fellow died just then—died on his boat, out fishing, hell of a way to go—and his daughter became the beneficiary.

Rose: And she was shocked to see how small the trust was.

Ned: Shocked, indeed. So she hired a lawyer, who filed a one hundred million dollar breach-of-trust action against the bank.

Suzy: I bet that got their attention! What happened, eventually?

Ned: It all got settled out, of course, but only after two weeks of trial that dragged the bank's reputation through the mud.

Carrie: Well, on that happy note, I'd say that Roger and I have seriously overstayed our welcome!

Roger: Actually, for Carrie, she couldn't imagine a happier way to spend four hours than talking about asset allocation!

Carrie: Watch it, buster!

[Laughter.]

Billy: Actually, it wasn't as painful as I'd feared it would be. Not as good as spending the day on a boat in the Everglades, of course.

Ned: But better, as one of my partners used to put it, than a poke in the eye with a sharp stick!

[Laughter.]

Carrie: Then, if there are no more questions, we'll get out of your hair. Our next meeting will be devoted to manager selection—another of my favorites!

QUICK NOTE

Notice that the Spenser advisors often use examples to make their points—the case of the old fellow in the Everglades and his inattentive trustees, for example. This is akin to telling stories. Storytelling is easier to listen to and the points it makes often stick better than simply telling someone what they should be doing.

SUMMARY

Asset allocation is a very complex subject, and unfortunately one that advisors tend to rush through. Unlike Carrie Knowlton, most advisors also think asset allocation is a dry subject, and they are happy to put the topic behind them as quickly as possible.

But, as noted, asset allocation is an extremely important part of the investment process. It's a subject that clients need to understand and feel comfortable with. I'm not suggesting that clients need to become professional financial advisors, but they need to know enough about asset allocation to (a) recognize its importance, (b) understand why it's important, and (c) be willing to be patient with a diversified portfolio even when it doesn't seem to be paying off.

As discussed by the Spenser advisors, there are two main times when clients tend to abandon their long-term portfolios. The first is during strong bull markets, when any braindead index fund will be outperforming a diversified portfolio. The second is during powerful bear markets, when clients want to abandon diversification and move entirely to bonds and cash.

It's much easier for advisors to keep their clients from abandoning their diversified portfolios during extreme periods in the markets if those clients have spent a lot of time and effort understanding the asset allocation process. Rushing through the process early in the engagement may seem like a time-saver, but it can easily cost you a client later on.

The key themes to emphasize at the asset allocation meeting are these:

- Why asset allocation is so important an aspect of the investment process
- What asset allocation is and how it works
- Key concepts in asset allocation
- Issues to be aware of
- Strengths and weaknesses of all models
- The importance of periodic rebalancing

NOTES

1. The Black-Litterman model was published back in 1992, but it was only much later that the approach began to be used widely in the design of real-world portfolios. In fact, most advisors still don't use Black-Litterman. See F. Black and R. Litterman, "Asset Allocation Combining Investor Views with Market Equilibrium," *Journal of Fixed Income*, 1, no. 2 (September 1991): 7–18, and F. Black and R. Litterman, "Global Portfolio Optimization," *Financial Analysts Journal* (September 1992): 28–43.
2. Daylian M. Cain, George Lowenstein, and Don A. Moore, "The Dirt on Coming Clean: Perverse Effects of Disclosing Conflicts of Interest," *Journal of Legal Studies*, 34 (January 2005).
3. George E. P. Box.
4. Jens Carsten Jackwerth and Mark Rubinstein, "Recovering Probability Distributions from Option Prices," *Journal of Finance*, 51, no. 5 (December 1996): 1612.
5. This example is shown by Chris Gallant in Investopedia, available at http://www.investopedia.com/ask/answers/06/geometricmean.asp.
6. See Ashvin B. Chhabra, "Beyond Markowitz: A Comprehensive Wealth Allocation Framework for Individual Investors," *Journal of Wealth Management*, 7, no. 4 (Spring 2005).
7. Kahneman won the Nobel Prize in Economic Sciences in 2002 for his work on behavioral finance. Twersky had died and wasn't eligible for the award.
8. A useful discussion of behavioral finance examples can be found in Investopedia. See Albert Phung, "Behavioral Finance: Key Concepts," available at http://www.investopedia.com/university/behavioral_finance/. Some of the examples in this chapter are taken from Phung's article.

CHAPTER 8

The Manager Search Meeting

PREPARATION AND USE

Following the asset allocation meeting, the Spenser advisors returned to their office and began the manager search process. Like all advisory firms, Spenser maintains a list of managers it has carefully vetted, so the real question was which of the managers to use in the Titan family portfolio. (As with the asset allocation meeting, we'll focus in this chapter on the Grandchildren's Trust.)

However, before managers could be selected, Spenser had to address two preliminary issues. The first was to decide on the relative valuations of the market sectors that were to be included in the Trust's portfolio. This would determine whether, in each sector, the Trust would be positioned at its target allocation or above or below it. As with managers, Spenser had already performed the relative valuation analysis, an exercise the firm went through each quarter and which will be explained to the Titans at the meeting.

The valuation exercise can affect manager selection in several ways. Most obviously, if valuations in a sector are so high that Spenser won't recommend funding any current allocation at all, then no manager would be needed for that sector. (Most market sectors will have a minimum allocation above 0%, but some—high yield debt, for example—might have a 0% minimum.)

Beyond that, if valuations in an efficient market sector like U.S. large caps are within the normal range, Spenser will likely suggest a passive manager. But if valuations are high, that might suggest the use of a value or deep-value manager.

The second preliminary issue was the question whether there might be any market sectors that the Grandchildren's Trust should consider as an opportunistic investment. As explained in what follows, an *opportunistic* investment is one that wouldn't normally have a place in the portfolio but that is compelling enough to own for at least some period of time. If an interesting opportunity appears to be available, a manager or managers will have to be found to manage the allocation to that sector. As we will see as we observe the manager selection meeting, Spenser did in fact have an opportunistic idea for the Trust.

QUICK NOTE

Many wealth managers look at market valuations to position client portfolios and also search for opportunistic investment ideas. But few advisors are as disciplined and focused on the issues as Spenser. By emphasizing these issues in the family meeting, Spenser achieved two goals: showing the Titans how they were adding value to the portfolio, and also illustrating that manager selection itself is the least important value-add.

THE MANAGER SELECTION MEETING

In this meeting, held in Rose's living room rather than at Lawburn (the family office), family members in attendance included Ned, Rose, Suzy, and Billy. Both Suzy and Billy had friends who worked in the asset management field, so they had a special interest in the manager selection process.

Relative Valuations

Carrie Knowlton: Shall we start, Rose? Thank you for inviting us into your lovely home.

Rose: You're very welcome. I thought Suzy and Billy might be more comfortable here than at Lawburn.

Suzy: A school bus would be more comfortable than Lawburn.

Billy: She means that Lawburn doesn't look at all like her punked-out apartment in New York.

[Laughter.]

Carrie: Maybe I'm just showing my age, but I like the slightly old-fashioned look of Lawburn. It exudes a sense of continuity down through the decades.

Suzy: You mean "down through the centuries." I swear the place hasn't been redecorated since the eighteen-hundreds.

Ned: Not true! It was redone when I was a boy, back in the Fifties.

[Laughter, as Suzy throws up her hands in exasperation.]

Rose: We're a frugal family.

Carrie: I'm glad to hear it.

Roger: I'm with Suzy.

[More laughter.]

Ned: Alright, enough with the interior decorating! Let's get on with something important, like manager selection.

Carrie: Go ahead, Roger.

Roger: Before we get to the subject of the managers themselves, we have two preliminary issues to go over with you: relative valuations of the market sectors, and opportunistic investments.

Carrie: We need to talk about those issues first because they will have an impact on which managers we use. Roger, can you distribute the relative valuation chart? [A version of this chart is available on the companion website for this book at www.wiley.com/go/familycapital.]

Carrie: This is a chart we prepare at Spenser every quarter. It looks fairly simple, but a huge amount of work goes into it. The chief investment officer at Spenser and his team put together a long, complex document we call the *relative valuation analysis*. That document is updated every quarter and is heavily data-based, although the senior partners at the firm also use their own judgment in coming to final conclusions about valuations.

Ned: Is the document you're referring to an internal product, or is it something you send out to clients?

Carrie: We don't automatically send out the relative valuation analysis because it's very long and, well …

Roger: Very wonky.

Carrie: Well, yes, wonky. But it's always available to any client who has an interest. We keep a smallish list of clients who want to get it every quarter. Would you like to go on the mailing list?

Ned: Yes, I'd love to see it.

Carrie: Rose? Suzy? Billy?

Billy: Not on your life.

Suzy: I'm with him.

Rose: I'm with her.

Carrie [laughing]: Okay, we'll send it to you, Ned.

QUICK NOTE

The point of the long relative valuation analysis isn't whether clients actually read it—as Carrie points out, few of them do. The point is that it's produced every quarter and represents a weighty and impressive demonstration of intense work Spenser devotes to the subject.

Roger: But the chart I just passed out goes to everybody—in fact, it's included in the performance reports each quarter. Should I walk through it?

Carrie: Well, before you do, let me point out that when you see this chart in your quarterly performance report, there will be several pages in front of it that are designed to put the chart in context. But since we're here in front of you, not just sending you the performance report, we only brought the chart itself.

Roger: Right. So in the first column you see the various asset classes listed, starting with inflation. The next column shows the return on each sector over the past ten years, then Spenser's forecast for the return over the *next* ten years. That's what we call our *strategic* forecast.

Carrie: Let me pause there for a minute. In most cases, if the performance of a market sector over the past ten years has been *below* its long-term performance, then it's likely Spenser's estimate for the next ten years will be for performance *higher* than the last ten. And if the last ten years has been *above* long-term trend, Spencer's forward estimate is likely to be *lower*.

Rose: Those were complicated sentences, but I see what you're saying. This is part of what you mean by markets tending to revert back toward their mean long-term performance.

Carrie: Exactly. There can be exceptions, of course, if we don't feel that conditions are likely to be propitious for a sector, but that's the general rule.

Suzy: Just to be clear—do you mean that your estimate for the next ten years will be higher than the last ten, or will be higher than the long-term performance?

Carrie: Higher than the last ten, and *possibly* higher than long-term. We'll show you some actual examples, but first let's continue to work our way through the chart.

Roger: Okay, so column four shows Spenser's *tactical* forecast, which is our expectations over a shorter, three-year period. Then the next five columns just show how we would position client portfolios now. If our assessment is neutral, clients are likely to be close to their allocation targets. If we're suggesting a strong underweight or a strong overweight, clients would be close to their minimums or maximums, respectively.

Ned: And if you're suggesting a simple over- or underweight, then we would be positioned somewhere in between our targets and our minimum or maximum.

Billy: Wow, Uncle Ned, pretty insightful!

Ned: He sits way over on the other side of the table so I won't strangle him.

[Laughter.]

Carrie: It's usually the advisors whom the clients want to strangle. [More laughter.] Let's look at a few examples on this chart. Take developed markets. It's under Non-U.S. Equities. Everybody with me? Okay. Over the past ten years, developed markets performance has been a snooze—up five-point-four percent. Normally, you would expect those markets to perform more in line with U.S. equities, which were up over eight percent. But Europe and Japan have had a lot of challenges—generally slow economic growth, slow population growth, the financial crisis, deflation in Japan, strains on the Eurozone in Europe.

Roger: So going forward, we expect something of a recovery in developed country equities, about seven percent.

Rose: But that would still be below their long-term performance, right?

Carrie: Correct, Rose. In other words, we expect that Europe and Japan will continue to struggle with the kinds of problems they already have.

Roger: Hopefully, they won't experience another financial crisis like the one in 2008.

Suzy: But you're showing a tactical performance expectation that's higher—almost nine percent.

Carrie: Yes, that's because in both Japan and Europe the central banks are being massively stimulative. They're following in the footsteps of the U.S. Fed.

Roger: And whatever you think of the Fed's effects on the underlying economy, there's no doubt that they drove the prices of risk assets through the ceiling.

Carrie: And also the prices of bonds. So we expect a similar thing to happen in Japan and Europe—stocks will likely go up in the face of the stimulus, though perhaps not so much as in the United States. That will have an impact on the tactical returns—over three years—but then we expect things to settle back down again.

QUICK NOTE

Although it is important for wealth advisors to have tactical—that is, shorter term—market views as well as longer term views, it's also important to keep in mind that the shorter the view the less accurate it's likely to be and, therefore, the less weight the advisor should put on the view.

Billy: I know I'm getting off the point here, but can you explain how the Federal Reserve's actions made stock prices go up so much?

Carrie: Well, that's a long conversation …

Ned: And a controversial one, even inside our family.

Carrie: I'm not surprised. The Fed's policies have been wildly unconventional, and because the effect has been so much more pronounced in the stock markets than in the underlying economy, many people are wondering what the Fed thinks it's doing. On the other hand, many other people think we'd all be much worse off if the Fed hadn't acted as it did.

Roger: But to get back to Billy's question, normally the Fed controls short-term interest rates by setting what's called the *Fed funds rate*. That's the interest rate at which banks lend money to other banks, usually overnight. It's hugely important, because that rate then works its way up through the entire lending system. If the Fed funds rate is low, that's considered stimulative because it encourages borrowing. If the rate is high, that tends to reduce borrowing and to cool off an economy that's growing too fast.

Billy: Okay, I see that, but why would anyone think an economy is growing too fast? Isn't growth good?

Carrie: Yes, up to a point. But any economy, even the U.S. economy, can only grow so fast without all sorts of bad things happening. Inflation can get very high, for example. Capital gets misallocated as investors chase hot sectors in the markets and as companies and individuals worry about the future and hoard capital. Also, asset prices can get into bubble territory, and when those bubbles burst it's very painful.

Suzy: Like the tech bubble.

Carrie: Precisely. Or the housing bubble in 2008. Part of the Fed's mandate is to keep inflation at a reasonable level, which means raising interest rates when the economy starts growing too fast.

Billy: What's the rest of their mandate?

Roger: To try to maintain full employment.

Billy: Sounds weird, if you ask me. I mean, if the economy isn't growing fast enough, then the Fed lowers rates, right? And that's supposed to stimulate borrowing and investing and economic growth. And that, in turn, will improve the employment picture. Am I right so far?

Roger: You're exactly right, Billy.

Billy: But when the economy's growing too fast, the Fed puts on the brakes.

Roger: It's called, "taking the punchbowl away just as the party's getting started."

[Laughter.]

Billy: I like that analogy. The Fed takes the punch bowl away and the economy slows. How's that maintaining full employment?

Roger (looking toward Carrie): Good question.

Carrie: Don't look at me. Frankly, the *full employment* mandate of the Fed makes little sense. You can only have good employment numbers when the economy's doing well, so if the Fed's doing the first part of its job, it's automatically doing the second part of its job. And when the Fed tries to slow the growth rate of the economy, it's obviously not helping employment. My guess is that Congress just wanted to act like it cared about unemployed people, so it added that part of the mandate. This was back in the mid-1970s when conditions were pretty bad in the United States.[1]

Ned: Unfortunately, the "dual mandate" has caused a lot of mischief.

Rose: Uh-oh, here goes Ned, teeing off the Fed again! [Laughter.] Ned thinks the Fed is made up of a bunch of leftwing professors who wouldn't know a robust economy if it bit them in the you-know-what.

[More laughter.]

Ned: Nonsense.

Carrie: Well, anyway, let's go back to the period right after the crisis in 2008. The Fed had already reduced interest rates to a very low level, but that didn't seem to be doing much good. So they tried to come up with other strategies to stimulate the economy.

Billy: Like quantitative easing, whatever that is.

Carrie: Yes, *QE*, as we'll call it, since it's such a mouthful, simply involves having the Fed buy up bonds—government bonds, mortgage bonds, whatever. The Fed prints money and uses that money to buy the bonds. That puts upward price pressure on the bond prices, which means their yields go down.

Rose: Bond price up, bond yield down. Bond price down, bond yield up. I can never remember which is which, though.

Carrie: Most people can't, but you got it right. So as bond yields plummeted, people who owned bonds said to themselves, "Who needs this? I'm getting no return." And they sold their bonds and bought stocks.

Billy: I see. So all that price pressure the Fed was putting on bonds caused bond yields to drop. And then all that price pressure on stocks—as investors sold bonds and bought stocks—caused stock prices to rise.

Suzy: But, wait. Is the Fed in the business of pumping up stock prices? If a normal person did it, wouldn't he go to jail?

Carrie: Yes, manipulating stock prices is illegal, unless you're the government.

Billy: But legal or illegal, and moral or immoral, what was the point? Just to make rich people like us richer?

Carrie: Well, that's the effect it had, although in more recent years ordinary investors have returned to the market, so they're getting richer now, too.

Ned: But not for long. When the retail trade jumps into the stock market, you know it's time for sensible investors to jump out.

Roger: That does tend to be a truism, Ned. But what the Fed is doing is trying to create the *wealth effect*. As the stock market goes up, people feel richer and they spend more. As they spend more, the economy grows faster. As the economy grows faster, people get hired and unemployment goes down.

Carrie: That's how it's supposed to work, anyway.

Suzy: So why is it controversial? If it works, isn't that great? And if it doesn't work, well, at least they tried.

Carrie: It's controversial for a couple of reasons. One is that QE doesn't seem to have had much effect on the underlying economy, so maybe the wealth effect doesn't work. After all, the people who owned the most stocks were already wealthy and their spending didn't change just because the market went up. At the same time, QE has dramatically increased inequality in the United States because as stock prices have skyrocketed, that's mainly helped people who own a lot of stock, that is, wealthier people.

Billy: The rich get richer! I like the sound of that!

[Laughter.]

Suzy: But inequality was already a problem before the Fed adopted QE. Didn't they realize they'd only make the problem worse?

Carrie: I don't know whether they realized it or not, but their thinking went like this. If the wealth effect works, that will improve the lives not just of rich people, but of everybody.

Ned: Except, as you pointed out, it didn't work. The rich got richer but the economy didn't grow anywhere near as much as the Fed predicted. It's the worst of all worlds.

Rose: Now, Ned, it's like Suzy said—at least they tried.

Ned: My point is, nobody elected the Fed to be God. Nobody elected the Fed to be anything, as a matter of fact. They're all professors who were appointed.

Rose: Ned ...

Ned: Now don't you start acting like my wife, Rose! [Laughter.] What the Fed did was wrong. You don't just throw mud against the wall in the hope that some of it will stick. The Fed should have analyzed the harm QE was likely to cause and they should have balanced that against the good it could possibly do.

Rose: While Ned's on his soapbox, I'm going to go check on lunch. I've heard all this before.

[Rose leaves the room.]

Ned: Really, sometimes I find it hard to tell my sister from my wife.

Billy: Go ahead, Uncle Ned, *I* haven't heard all this before.

Ned: Great! A new audience! So, first, the Fed knew, or should have known, that driving stock prices up was going to increase inequality just at a time when that was the last thing we needed. The Fed knew, or should have known, that manipulating stock and bond prices would cause all sorts of serious dislocations in the markets and in the economy.

Billy: What sorts of dislocations?

Ned: Well, the most obvious ones are the bubbles in stock and bond prices. Bond yields in some parts of the world are actually negative. Stock prices, relative to conditions in the broader economy, are in the stratosphere.

Billy: Okay, so there's a bond bubble and a stock bubble.

Ned: Also, capital is being misallocated around the world. Companies aren't spending and hiring, they're issuing bonds at rock-bottom yields that are only propping up weak players who should have gone out of business. They're like the "zombie banks" in Japan.

Roger: I actually agree with Ned about that. [Roger glances carefully toward the kitchen, where Rose is banging pots and pans.] The role of a recession is to squeeze out inefficient players in the economy, companies that are just taking up space and capital that could be much more efficiently used elsewhere. By allowing those kinds of players—like the zombie banks in Japan—to stay alive, the overall efficiency of the economy is being vastly reduced. That's one reason why Japan has been in a two- or three-decade-long slump.

Ned: Exactly. And we're headed down the same miserable path. Also, corporations are hoarding cash—huge amounts of it—and when they do spend it they aren't spending it on productive things like capital expenditures and hiring and research and development. No, they're spending it on stock buybacks and dividend payments.

Roger: Again, Ned is right about that. It's a worrisome phenomenon.

Ned: And what was the upside? Did the Fed cause all this trouble for some good outcome? No! The weakest recovery in U.S. history! Seven years after the crisis in 2008, we're barely growing at two percent. Millions of people have given up and left the workforce. It's shameful. And here's what might be the worst part of all. By engaging in radical experiments with our economy, the Fed has taken all the pressure off Congress to do anything constructive.

Suzy: Boy, when Dad gets wound up, look out! But, anyway, what's wrong with paying dividends and buying back stock? I thought all that was good for shareholders.

Ned: Maybe in the short term. But what are the stockholders going to do with the money they get from dividends and buybacks? Invest it in bonds that yield nothing? Invest it in stocks that are way overpriced? In the long term it would be much better for the companies to keep the cash and invest it productively.

Carrie: Ned is making an interesting point that I hadn't thought of. Normally, when you see a corporation hoarding cash, paying high dividends, buying back its stock, it's because the company is a mature, slow-growing enterprise that can't invest the cash productively itself. These slow-growing, mature companies are known as "cash cows." But these days it seems like all of corporate America is a cash cow—slow growing, nothing useful to invest in, just giving their profits back to the shareholders.

Billy: I have to say that what Uncle Ned says makes a lot of sense. Am I missing something?

Rose (coming back into the room): Yes.

[Everyone turns toward Rose, laughing.]

Suzy: Terrific timing, Aunt Rose!

Rose: Let me guess. Ned's bad-mouthing the Fed because the economy's growing only slowly so many years after the crisis. Plus, they're screwing up incentives in the economy.

Ned: You forgot that they're also increasing inequality.

Suzy: So what's the other side of the story, Aunt Rose?

Rose: Lunch will be ready in a minute. But in the meantime, here's the corrective to the Ned Version of the World.

Ned: Very funny.

Rose: It's true that the economy is still growing slowly. If we'd had the kind of strong recovery we usually have after deep recessions, the country's GDP would be much higher now and many more people would be working.

Ned: That *is* the Ned Version of the World!

Rose: But what Ned's missing is that we didn't come out of a deep recession—we came out of a serious financial crisis, which is a whole other animal.

Ned (pretending to get up out of his chair): I've heard this before. I'll go check on lunch.

[Laughter, as Ned sits back down.]

Rose: Well, *they* haven't heard it before. People have written books about financial crises and how different they are from the normal ebb and flow of expansions and recessions in economies.[2] It's much more difficult for an economy to recover from a financial crisis.

Billy: Why is that, Mom?

Rose: In all honesty, I'm not an expert on financial crises and their aftermath. But the studies show that every economy struggles after such an event. So I think what the Fed was thinking is, if we don't do anything the economy will be awful for a very long time and people will be out of work and things will be really bad. So, instead, we'll try these unconventional policies, like quantitative easing, and maybe they'll turn things around more quickly.

Billy: But did things turn around? Uncle Ned just said the U.S. economy is still growing very slowly and that a lot of people have gotten so discouraged they're not even looking for jobs anymore.

Rose: Well, I agree that the economy isn't great. But maybe it's a lot better than it would have been if the Fed had done nothing but keep interest rates low.

Ned: If Geoff was here, Rose, he'd say you're committing the Parmenides Fallacy.

Suzy: The who?

Ned: Billy?

Billy: Suzy took the words right out of my mouth.

Ned: Hundreds of thousands of dollars of college tuition and our kids are ignorant savages. [Laughter.] Parmenides was an early Greek philosopher, even before Socrates.

Billy: Oh, well, that explains it. I started reading philosophy with Socrates and moved forward.

[Laughter.]

Ned: Sure you did, nephew. Anyway, the Parmenides Fallacy is best explained by an example. Suppose someone says, "The U.S. invasion of Iraq was a disaster. That country is now falling apart and the Islamic State is conquering city after city."

Suzy: Sounds right to me.

Ned: What's wrong with that statement is it doesn't take into account what today might be like if we *hadn't* invaded Iraq. Maybe things would be much, much worse. Maybe Saddam Hussein would have got his nuclear weapons and sent a suitcase bomb to destroy New York City. If that future had happened, the very same people—like Suzy here—would be saying, "What a disaster! We should have invaded Iraq!"

Suzy: Well, I have to admit that I hadn't thought about what would have happened if we *hadn't* invaded.

Ned: Most people commit the Parmenides Fallacy almost every time they open their mouths. That's why you should start reading philosophy *before* Socrates, Billy.

Billy: I'll make a note. But what does the Parmenides Fallacy have to do with the Fed's policies?

Ned: Just this. Your mother is saying that things might have been much worse if the Fed hadn't launched QE. I'm suggesting that things might be much better by now. Monetary conditions are artificial and they have been artificial for a very long time. That's like throwing sand in the gears of the economy.

Rose: I think you just committed the Parmenides Fallacy.

[Everyone laughs, even Ned.]

Billy: What do you think, Carrie?

Carrie: What I think is it would be really dumb of me to take sides! [Laughter.] But in all honesty, I just don't know what to think. Ned and Rose both make good points. But here's one thing we could look at. In Japan and in Europe the central bankers have decided to follow the Fed's example and they're both launching very large QE programs. When we see what happens in those places, it might help us understand better what QE does and doesn't do.

Ned: Fair enough.

Rose: Agreed.

Carrie: Whew! Now we'll go back to the relative valuation chart.

QUICK NOTE

Obviously, the digression on Federal Reserve policies got the meeting well off the agenda. But as I've pointed out before, when it's the family that is hijacking the agenda, it's almost always going to be an important digression. Ned and Rose obviously disagree about the value of quantitative easing, but the discussion proved quite educational to Suzy and Billy—and even to Carrie.

Suzy: Oh! I completely forgot what we were talking about!

Carrie: Where were we, Roger?

Roger: I was giving examples from the chart. So we saw that in non-U.S. developed markets we've had a weak ten years, we expect to have a strong three years looking ahead—due to QE—but then a so-so period over the next seven years, that is, below long-term trend.

Carrie: But now look at emerging markets. We've had an okay ten years, we're expecting a better three years looking forward, and then an even stronger seven years after that, bringing the ten-year forecast up to eleven-point-two percent.

Billy: That's the highest forecast return on the chart, except for private equity.

Carrie: Right. Emerging markets are very much out of vogue right now, but we think that's the place to be. And in bonds, we think the next three years will be pretty dismal, and even the next ten years won't be very good.

QUICK NOTE

At this point in the market cycle—this meeting with the Titans occurred in the summer of 2015—the idea of investing in the emerging markets was anathema to most investors. But Spenser is pointing out—gently—that investing where it feels most uncomfortable is one of the best roads to investment success.

Ned: We've had a very long bull market in bonds—more than thirty years—and I guess you're saying it's over.

Roger: Right, Ned, we think it's over.

Rose: Almost all the numbers on this chart look weak over the next ten years. Why is that?

Carrie: As you probably know, some prominent people, including Larry Summers, the former President of Harvard, have suggested that the United States—and the world—are entering into a period of *secular stagnation.*[3]

Billy: That has a really lousy sound to it! What does it mean?

Carrie: In general, it means a world of much slower growth, slower income gains, lower employment. People and companies save their money but have no place to invest it. So even though inflation and interest rates are very low, which would normally be stimulative, we don't get strong growth.

Roger: Billy and Suzy and I are too young to remember this, but the United States experienced a similar situation back in the 1970s, called *stagflation.* We had high inflation, which is usually accompanied by rapid economic growth, but we had very low growth—hence, stagflation.

Ned: I've heard about this secular stagnation argument. I think Ben Bernanke disagrees with Summers.

Carrie: I think you're right, Ned.

Rose: So are you saying that Spenser is taking the Summers side of the argument, that you also believe we're entering a period of secular stagnation?

Carrie: No, not at all. Spenser hasn't—at least not yet—taken a position on the issue. We're following the arguments and giving the matter a lot of thought and argument in-house.

Rose: But if you haven't bought into secular stagnation, why the low expected returns over ten years?

Carrie: A couple of reasons, Rose. First, we expect the relatively slow recovery from the financial crisis to continue for some time. Second, stock prices are very high and are likely to go higher under central banker stimulus. So from that peak, we expect either a significant correction in the markets or just lower forward-looking returns to bring long-term returns back to sensible levels given economic conditions.

Roger: What Carrie is saying is that we think there are good explanations for low growth and low forward-looking returns without resorting to something like secular stagnation as the explanation.

Carrie: Without prejudicing the possibility that Spenser might at some point embrace the secular stagnation thesis.

> **QUICK NOTE**
>
> Should a wealth management firm be debating issues like secular stagnation? Of course. If the United States is entering a period of secular stagnation, that will have a huge effect on how portfolios are designed and managed. But simply discussing the idea in detail will help the firm and its clients better understand the economic underpinning of the capital markets.

Roger: But just to summarize, if you look at the horizontal bar chart in columns five through nine, you'll see that we're recommending neutral allocations to most market sectors—that is, your portfolio should be roughly at the target allocations. In some sectors, we're recommending underweights. But we don't see anything we would overweight right now.

Ned: So Spenser will adjust our long-term allocation accordingly to fit these recommendations.

Carrie: Correct.

Opportunistic Investments

Carrie: Back to Rose's point about our low expected returns. Even though it's the case that we don't expect robust returns in U.S. equities as a market sector, if we dig down into that sector, we find one small corner of value: *master limited partnerships*, or *MLPs*.

Rose: I don't think I ever even heard the term *MLP*.

Roger: It's an obscure corner of the market. There are certain kinds of assets that are best held not in corporate form, but in partnership form, so that tax benefits can flow through to the owners. By law, an MLP is limited in the kinds of businesses it can be in, mainly to those pertaining to natural resources. These MLPs trade like stocks or closed-end funds.

Ned: What's the tax advantage?

Carrie: An MLP is required to pay quarterly distributions to its partners, and those distributions are typically considerably higher than corporate dividends. But a portion of each distribution is considered to be depreciation, a return of your capital, so you aren't taxed on the entire distribution.

Rose: Sounds like an interesting concept. And you're saying they are currently cheap?

Carrie: Yes, we think they are. As usual, it's irrational investor behavior that has made them cheap.

Roger: As you know, oil prices have plummeted. And, of course, along with them, the prices of oil company stocks have also dropped. Since MLPs are mainly involved in the oil business, investors have punished them as well.

Rose: But?

Carrie: But some MLPs, by no means all, are engaged in operations that aren't closely tied to the price of oil. For example, consider an MLP that runs a pipeline. Oil goes in one end and comes out the other end and the pipeline company charges oil companies on a *throughput* basis. The price of oil might be high or low, but, at least in the short term, the throughput price is the throughput price.

Roger: But, as usually happens, when prices in a sector collapse, investors sell everything indiscriminately. When the dust settles and investors begin to think more clearly, we think the price of these throughput MLPs will recover quickly. And at that point, we'll sell them.

Ned: How do you decide which MLP to buy? There must be more than one.

Carrie: Oh, there are lots of them. But evaluating the desirability of an individual MLP is like evaluating the desirability of a company. It's not really what we do at Spenser. So just as we hire a manager to buy U.S. equities, we hire a manager to buy the best MLPs.

Ned: What sort of position size are you recommending?

Carrie: Well, the position has to be large enough to move the needle, so let's say bigger than one percent. But it's a narrow sector of the market, so it's more risky. I'm thinking a two percent position to start, maybe building it up to three or four percent.

Roger: And, because it's a risky position, we also don't want to be greedy. So as the price of these throughput MLPs begins to approach the normal range, we'll likely sell it.

Ned: Well, I like the idea. With almost all assets either overpriced or fairly priced, it's nice to find something where there might be some value.

Rose: And on that note, here's lunch!

Populating the Portfolio with Managers

In a real client meeting, real managers would be discussed. But in this book, it's not possible to discuss actual managers and their qualifications because, by the time you are reading this, my opinions about those managers could have changed dramatically. This puts us in the slightly awkward position of discussing managers by type without mentioning names. Except for that, the discussion that follows adheres very closely to the discussion that would occur at the actual client meeting.

Carrie: Now that we have the preliminaries out of the way, let's turn to the actual managers we propose to use. Roger, can you pass out the manager recommendations book?

[As noted, we can't actually look at the manager search book Spenser was using, since the recommended managers will be out of date by the time you read this.]

Carrie: When we work with large institutional clients, we don't use "manager recommendation books," we use "manager search books." That's because institutions usually have investment professionals on their staffs and they also have investment committees whose members are also board members and who therefore have fiduciary responsibilities. Institutions therefore like to play an active role in selecting managers, and so we'll propose two or three managers for each sector of the portfolio. The staff and committee will discuss them and possibly interview one or two. Almost always they will interview the finalist before the manager is hired.

Rose: In these recommendation books, you've just suggested a specific manager for each sector.

Carrie: Correct, for a couple of reasons. One is that most families don't employ investment professionals and many families don't even have an investment committee. As a result, the families would have no sensible way to decide among the managers we proposed.

Roger: So we recommend a specific manager—or, sometimes, managers—for each sector of the portfolio and, unless the family objects for some reason, that's the manager we use.

Ned: Why might we object?

Carrie: We rarely hear objections from our family clients. In fact most families want the responsibility to remain on Spenser's shoulders. But when we do get an objection, one common reason is that the family has had experience with that manager in the past and it wasn't a happy relationship. Roger, what else do we hear?

Roger: Sometimes a family can't really understand what it is that a manager is doing—especially when it comes to hedge funds—and that makes them uncomfortable. I remember a few years ago—it was another of your clients, Carrie—we had a situation where the family was simply turned off by a hedge fund manager's activist style.

Billy: What's an *activist* manager?

Roger: They're guys, usually hedge funds, who look at a company and think it could be better managed in some way or other. Usually, the trouble they're focused on is what we call *agency issues*.

Carrie: Before you ask, an agency issue arises when a management team is really working for itself rather than for the shareholders. Very often in life, we have to depend on agents to do things for us. Doctors, lawyers, plumbers, corporate executives, money managers. Very rarely are the agents' interests exactly aligned with the principals' interests, that is, with our interests. A plumber might be working on a really profitable job across town, so he keeps putting your job off.

Roger: A money manager might keep growing his assets under management well beyond his ability to produce good returns just so he can get the increased fees.

Carrie: A corporate management team might want to make a lot of acquisitions because it increases the size of the company and therefore the scale of their compensation, even though the acquisitions don't make sense.

Roger: Or a management team keeps thinking it can fix an underperforming division when they really should sell it or spin it off to the shareholders.

Suzy: Okay, but what does an activist manager do about it?

Carrie: An activist manager—or activist investors, as they're often called—can operate in different ways. In a typical situation the manager will start buying shares in the company he believes needs to be fixed. Under law, an investor can accumulate up to five percent of a publicly held company without any public disclosure.

Billy: When they reach five percent what do they need to do?

Carrie: They need to file with the SEC what's called a Schedule 13D. At that point their holding becomes public knowledge.

Roger: So what will often happen is that the activist will quietly buy up four-point-nine percent of the stock, then more or less simultaneously buy up to five percent and send the company CEO and board chair a letter complaining about whatever they see the problem to be.

Suzy: But is five percent enough to get the company's attention?

Carrie: Oh, yes, almost always. The stock in most companies is very widely held so that even a big institutional shareholder—like a mutual fund—won't hold as much as five percent.

Suzy: But, surely, five percent of the vote couldn't change anything.

Carrie: Not by itself, but what the activist wants to do is to win a seat on the board so he can advocate for whatever the issue is he cares about.

Lots of other investors might be sympathetic to that, especially if they think it will increase the value of the stock they hold.

Rose: So the activist investor is hoping that if he can effect change at the company, then the five percent he's already paid for will be worth a lot more.

Carrie: Right.

Roger: Sometimes, at least in the past, the company would buy out the five percent position, paying a premium to get the activist to go away. That strategy was called *greenmail* (as opposed to blackmail). It really was blackmail, but it converted into a lot of green!

Suzy: Wow, is that legal?

Carrie: A lot of people consider it to be unethical, but it's mostly not technically illegal, as far as I know. However, Congress hated greenmailers and so there's now a provision in the Internal Revenue Code that imposes a fifty percent excise tax on the proceeds of greenmail. The practice has largely gone out of style.

Rose: But you're saying activist investors are different?

Carrie: Yes, an activist is putting his money where his mouth is. If he fails to convince the company to carry out his new plans, he might well lose a lot on the five percent of stock he purchased.

Ned: I can tell you that among the corporate executives we represent at my law firm, activists aren't very popular!

Carrie: I'm sure! And when a family owns a large company, they often don't want to invest with activist managers.

Ned: Well, that's not us, at least anymore. But just don't tell my clients about it!

[Laughter.]

Rose: It's too bad these activist guys weren't around back in the days when Titan Industries was going into decline. Maybe they could have woken up the management and the company could have been saved.

Carrie: I was under the impression that Titan Industries was privately held until the sale.

Rose: Oh! That's right. So even the activists couldn't have saved it!

Carrie: That's one of the problems with a privately held company. But, on the other hand, the agency issues you so often find in public companies tend to be less of a problem in private companies, where the principal and the agent are more or less the same. But to move on, whom are we looking at in the U.S. large-cap sector, Roger?

QUICK NOTE

Agency issues bedevil the investment world and need to be discussed openly with clients. A firm like Spenser has designed itself in a way that presents as few agency issues as possible, and compared to most other kinds of advisors, Spenser has few conflicts of interest. But no firm has *no* conflicts.

Roger: If you turn to the page labeled "U.S. Large Cap Managers," you will see that we're suggesting two managers for the Grandchildren's Trust in this sector. The first is a passive, tax-aware manager benchmarked against a RAFI index.

Billy: RAFI?

Roger: It's an acronym for Research Affiliates Fundamental Index, Research Affiliates being the firm that designed the index.[4] It is a fundamentally weighted index, as opposed to a capitalization-weighted index like you'd find in the Vanguard S&P 500 Index Fund.

Billy: I'm not sure I understand what all that means.

Carrie: Most indexes are capitalization-weighted. That means that very large companies—Apple, Google, GE—account for much more of the index than smaller companies. That makes sense for most purposes. After all, it reflects how capital is invested in the market—many more people own Apple than own a smaller S&P company like, say, DIRECTV. In fact, the one-hundredth largest company in the S&P is less than one-tenth the size of the largest companies in the index.

Billy: I guess I don't know what *market capitalization* means. Sorry!

Carrie: No need to be sorry! Roger and I like to throw around industry jargon so we sound smart. [Laughter.] The market capitalization of a publicly listed corporation is simply the market value of all its outstanding stock. If a company has fifty million shares outstanding and the shares are selling for fifty dollars, then the market cap would be, uh …

Roger: Two-point-five billion dollars.

Carrie: Correct. I was just wondering if you could figure it out.

[Laughter.]

Roger: Uh-huh. By contrast, a fundamentally weighted index uses other factors to decide on how much of a stock to include in the index. Those factors might be revenues, profits, book value, whatever.

Ned: But wouldn't those kinds of factors lead to similar weightings?

Carrie: Sometimes, yes, but not always. One way to think of cap-weighted indexes like the S&P 500 is to view them as *momentum* strategies. The more popular a stock is with the investing public, the heavier a weight it will have in the S&P 500. Since an important way to make money is to avoid following the herd, to be contrarian, simply buying a cap-weighted index isn't always a good idea.

Rose: Wait'll I tell Jack Bogle!

Carrie: Jack wouldn't believe it, anyway. When the stock market is cheap, buying a cap-weighted index fund makes all the sense in the world. But when the stock market is high, maybe even into bubble territory, buying a cap-weighted index fund is like following the "greater fool" theory. You know you're way overpaying for stocks but you hope there's someone out there even dumber than you whom you can sell to.

[Laughter.]

Roger: So when markets begin to get overpriced, we like to use fundamentally weighed indexes to avoid overpaying—or at least, overpaying more than we have to.

Carrie: We're also recommending another manager in the large-cap sector. The passive manager will have the bulk of the capital, as you can see, but about twenty-five percent of it would go to the long/short hedge fund you see listed there.

Suzy: What's a long/short hedge fund?

Carrie: Long/short managers are the granddaddies of the hedge fund industry, Suzy. The very first hedge fund ever formed was a long/short fund.[5] What these kinds of managers do is they both invest long—that is, they go out and buy stocks like anybody else—and they also sell short. Does everyone know what a short sale is?

Suzy: Uh …

Roger: Most investors buy stocks they think will do better than the broad market. But suppose you have an idea that a particular stock will likely *under*perform. How could you capitalize on that idea? I mean make money on it? Well, what you would do is you would borrow that stock from a broker—who got it from one of his clients—and sell it.

Carrie: So let's say you sold the stock at fifty dollars a share. Remember that you only borrowed it—you didn't own it originally, so you have to give it back. It turns out you were right about the company being a lousy investment, and the price declines to twenty-five dollars a share. You simply buy the stock in the market and give it back to the broker you borrowed it from. In the meantime, you made twenty-five a share.

Billy: That is so cool!

Rose: Uh-oh, it looks like we have a budding short seller on our hands! Carrie, you'd better tell him what can go wrong.

Carrie: One of the main things that can go wrong is what's called a *short squeeze*. If a lot of investors have shorted a particular stock and there's a positive development for the company, suddenly all the short sellers want to close out their positions at the same time. Closing out a short position means buying the stock in the open market, so this activity puts even more upward pressure on the stock's price. The remaining short sellers are effectively squeezed out—even if they are ultimately right about how lousy the stock is, they just can't afford to hold on.

Billy: Why not? Why not just be patient and not panic if you really think you're right?

Carrie: The reason is that, unlike a stock you buy long, which can only go to zero (in other words, you lose your entire investment), the loss on a short sale is theoretically unlimited.

Roger: So in the example Carrie just gave, you borrowed the stock and sold it short at fifty dollars a share. Instead of declining to twenty-five a share, it goes to two hundred dollars a share. You just lost one hundred fifty dollars a share on a stock you have fifty dollars invested in.

Billy: Not cool at all!

Carrie: So investors who sell short have to watch their positions very closely and get out quickly if it looks like they were wrong. That's one reason there are hardly any pure short sellers left in the market—if a bull market lasts long enough, eventually they all go broke.

Suzy: So why do people do it?

Carrie: Mostly they do it as part of a larger portfolio that is mostly long—what we call *net long*. So the manager might hold some short positions in companies where he has real conviction that the price is going to drop, but mainly he's buying stocks long just like everybody else. If you net out his long and short positions, he's net long.

Roger: A manager who can both buy long and sell short simply has more tools at his disposal than a manager who only buys long. If a long-only manager doesn't like a stock, he simply doesn't buy it. He might be avoiding a loss, but he's not profiting from his belief that the stock is a lousy investment.

Carrie: One purpose of having a long/short manager in the portfolio is to protect the portfolio on the downside. As prices get higher and higher the manager's short book should get bigger and bigger. Eventually, he'll start shorting indexes—like the S&P 500—instead of individual stocks.

Rose: So if I understand this idea correctly, you're proposing to invest a quarter of the U.S. large-cap allocation with a long/short manager because you think the market is too high. But what if you're wrong?

Carrie: Well, in one sense we *can't* be wrong—trees don't grow to the sky and markets don't go up forever. But we can be wrong in the sense that we're too early. We're like Cassandra, always complaining that the markets are too high. Eventually, we'll be right, but by then nobody will be listening.

Roger: On that note, shall we move to U.S. small cap? In general, we like active managers in the small-cap space. These stocks aren't as efficient as the larger names, so managers have more room to maneuver. Since we think U.S. small caps are even more overpriced than large caps, we're suggesting a value manager for small cap.

Ned: And small-cap value managers do what?

Roger: They buy small-cap value stocks!

Carrie: Thank you for that insight, Roger. [Laughter.] Of course, Roger is right. This manager looks for smaller companies—those that don't make it into the S&P 500—and that are selling at attractive prices.

Ned: But what if the price is attractive for a good reason?

Carrie: Right, that's what they call a *value trap*. The stock looks cheap, but in fact it's cheap for a very good reason. This manager—we hope—is well aware of that issue and avoids it most of the time.

Ned: Okay, so let me see if I understand. This manager buys undervalued companies in the hope that at some point the market will recognize their value and buy them and the price will go up.

Carrie: Well, I don't think it's right to say they *hope* the market will recognize their value. Before the manager buys the stock, he wants to understand exactly what it is that will make the market recognize the value. A *catalyst*, as they call it.

Ned: Well, I'm glad to hear it. Otherwise, it could be a long wait!

Carrie: What's next, Roger?

Roger: International developed markets. This is a sector we semi-like.

Rose: Semi-like!

Carrie: Maybe that needs some explanation. We like the stocks but we hate the currency. So as you can see, the managers we're using are ones that hedge the euro.

Suzy: I'm sorry to sound dumb, but what does "hedge the euro" mean?

Roger: Not dumb at all! If a manager buys the stock of a company based in Europe, he's buying and selling in euros, not dollars. So if the stock goes up ten percent but the euro declines ten percent against the dollar, American investors, who buy and sell in dollars, have gained nothing.

The improvement in the stock price is balanced by the depreciation in the currency.

Suzy: Yes, I see that. An investor in Europe, trading in euros, would be up ten percent, but a dollar investor is flat. But what makes you think the euro is going to keep declining?

Carrie: It won't keep declining forever. Over longer periods of time, currencies tend to even out against each other. But over short-to-intermediate periods of time, some currencies will be strong and some weak. Because quantitative easing is just beginning in Europe, we think the currency will be weak against the dollar for some time to come, especially as the Fed begins to raise rates over here. And we don't want our managers' good stock picks to be offset by a weak euro.

Roger: So for the reasons Carrie mentioned, we're using a core manager for the Europe region who is hedging the euro. We're splitting that allocation with a passive manager. And also, although this guy appears down in the private equity section, we're also using a manager who is buying up credit that is—finally!—beginning to come off the balance sheets of European banks.

Carrie: What Roger is talking about is that, in the United States, banks began shedding poor-quality loans and other assets several years ago under pressure from the banking regulators. But in Europe, matters proceeded much more slowly. Only now are large volumes of assets becoming available.

Ned: I assume you are talking about banks trying to strengthen their balance sheets by selling off underperforming or otherwise troubled assets.

Roger: Correct. Bad loans, for example.

Ned: But if so, why have the Europeans been so slow to move? When a bank is holding a lot of nonperforming loans, doesn't that make it much more difficult for the bank to make new loans? And isn't that what the European Central Bank wants them to do?

Carrie: You're right all along, Ned. Bad loans clog up a bank's balance sheet,[6] making it hard to lend more money. There are a number of reasons why the Europeans have been so slow to come to grips with the problem, but the main one seems to be that the European banks are much larger relative to the economies over there than U.S. banks are to the U.S. economy.

Roger: Europe's biggest banks are as large as or larger than America's biggest banks,[7] but the European countries are only a fraction the size of the United States. France, for example, has two banks roughly the size of JP Morgan, but France's economy is less than one-sixth the size of the United States. So while U.S. regulators pushed our banks hard to unload dodgy assets, in Europe they proceeded more slowly and cautiously.

Ned: Because the consequences of a mistake would have been much larger.

Carrie: Correct.

Ned: But why are you doing this in a private equity fund? Wouldn't a hedge fund format be more appropriate?

Carrie: We used hedge funds in the United States when we were buying bank assets, but the situation in Europe has moved so slowly and uncertainly that we've been reluctant to commit capital.

Roger: In other words, if we were to invest one million dollars of the Grandchildren's Trust's money in this sort of opportunity and do it via a hedge fund, we'd have to put up the entire million now. What if things slow down in Europe again? Your money would just sit there earning nothing while we waited for the banks and regulators to act.

Carrie: And the data we're looking at show bad assets at European banks are still *growing*, not shrinking, even though it's been seven years since the financial crisis. By using a private equity format, where the capital is called down as it's needed, you keep your money until the fund can do something productive with it.

Billy: More stupid questions: why would anyone want to buy bad loans?

Carrie (laughing): It does sound like a dumb thing to do, doesn't it! I once sat beside a guy on a plane and I asked him what business he was in. He told me he was in the business of buying bad investments. When I expressed surprise, he told me the field of buying good investments was way overcrowded, so he'd decided to specialize in bad investments!

Ned: I hope he was pulling your leg!

Carrie: I hope so! But back to why we like bad bank loans in Europe. Roger, why *do* we like bad bank loans in Europe?

[Laughter.]

Roger: As I think we said at an earlier meeting, there's no such thing as a good asset or a bad asset, it all depends on what you paid for it. If the poor-performing loan is worth only fifty cents on the dollar but you can buy it for twenty-five cents, that's a good investment.

Billy: Right, I do remember that conversation now. So you're thinking that you—well, the private equity fund you've selected—can buy these loans for less than they're worth.

Carrie: We certainly hope so!

Billy: Just because your manager is smart?

Carrie: Well, we do think our manager is smart, but the real opportunity is arising because the European banks aren't selling this stuff because they want to, and therefore driving hard bargains. They're selling it because the regulators are forcing them to. That odd—and temporary—inefficiency in the market is something we want to take advantage of.

QUICK NOTE

This discussion shows the complexity of the thought that goes into manager selection. Spenser identified an interesting sector—nonperforming bank loans—and invested in it via hedge funds in the United States. Later, as bad loans (finally!) began coming off bank balance sheets in Europe, Spenser moved to that subsector. But given how slowly those loans were being sold, Spenser decided to use a private equity format rather than a hedge fund format.

Roger: Moving to Japan, we're structuring the allocation a little different. As you can see in the book, we're using a hedge fund manager with deep experience in Japan. And that's very rare these days.

Suzy: Why's it rare? Isn't Japan the third biggest economy in the world?

Roger: It is. But Japan has been in a twenty-five-year bear market until recently, and most managers who were active there in the 1980s are long gone.

Rose: You said, "until recently." I don't follow the Japanese market. Has it been doing better?

Carrie: Oh, yes. You might have seen something in the press about Prime Minister Abe's "three arrows."

Rose: Yes, but I don't really understand what he's up to.

Carrie: Basically, he's trying to reinvigorate the Japanese economy after decades of stagnation. When the real estate markets over there collapsed in 1991, everything went to hell and it's been bad—flat—ever since. Abenomics—that's what the press calls Shinzō Abe's economic stimulus package—is an attempt to get the country back on track. The three arrows are fiscal stimulus, quantitative easing, and regulatory reform of the Japanese economy.

Rose: And you're suggesting it's working, that twenty-five years of stagnation is being turned around?

Carrie: I wouldn't go that far, no. QE in Japan, plus the fiscal stimulus, have had very little effect on the Japanese economy, which remains mired in periodic recession. Incomes are down and inflation remains stubbornly low. What might really help the economy is Abe's third arrow—reforming the labor market over there and also reforming many of the horribly unproductive sectors of the economy, like agriculture. But that's unlikely to happen any time soon because those measures are hugely controversial.

Roger: But whenever you have QE, you can be sure that stock markets will go up, so that's why we like Japanese equities—for now.

Carrie: Let's move on to emerging markets. There, for the core exposure, we like a quasi-passive, structured product. This is a manager who has a rules-based strategy, so it's not actively managed. On the other hand, it differs a lot from a simple index approach to emerging markets. An index approach would heavily weight the big, commodity-driven economies that we think are likely to struggle for the next few years—and maybe longer.

Rose: I've read in the papers something about the "commodity supercycle" being over. What does that mean?

Carrie: The *commodity supercycle* refers to the big rise in commodity prices driven mainly by the rapid economic growth in China. As demand for industrial and agricultural commodities rose, it especially helped commodity exporting countries like Brazil. But now that China's growth has leveled off and is slowing, China's demand for commodities is cooling off. That means that countries like Brazil are in trouble.

Roger: One reason they're in trouble is that during the commodity boom Brazil and similar countries didn't use their good fortune to diversify into other industries.

Rose: What did they do with all that income they were generating through sales to China?

Carrie: Mainly they spent it on social goods, trying to improve the lives of their citizens.

Rose: Oh, well, I guess you can't blame them for that.

Carrie: Yes and no. The best way to improve the lives of the people in your country is to create a strong, sustainable economy. But Brazil, Argentina, and other similar countries adopted crowd-pleasing strategies that allowed their leftwing parties to keep getting reelected. Unfortunately, that mortgaged their countries' future. Everybody knew the commodity boom couldn't last, and now that it's over, places like Brazil are in for a prolonged period of much slower growth and the resulting social instability.

Rose: I suppose that's why the president of Brazil has such low approval ratings. She seems to be very unpopular.

Roger: That's the main reason, Rose, although a big corruption scandal at Petrobras hasn't helped her any. Of course, the extreme example of this is Venezuela. The Chavez regime used oil revenues to essentially buy the votes of the Venezuelan poor. In terms of building a strong economy, Chavez did just about everything wrong you could do. Now he's gone and he has a weak successor and oil prices have collapsed and it's all over for Venezuela.

Carrie: It's not that extreme in other countries, of course, but they mostly did similar things and are now paying the price. So we want to avoid those kinds of economies and focus instead on economies where the middle class is growing, where countries have built a more stable, consumer-driven economy.

Ned: Isn't that what China is trying to do, too?

Carrie: China *has* to do it or it's doomed. An industrial economy can only carry a country so far. At a certain point industry becomes ever less efficient and the economy loses its competitive advantages. Already a lot of the manufacturing activity that used to take place in China is moving to Indonesia, Vietnam, even Mexico.

Rose: I would think the world has a lot at stake on whether China succeeds or not. It's such a huge country—if it fails, economic growth all around the world might slow down or even stop.

Carrie: Well, maybe. I think—and this isn't an official Spenser opinion, so Roger, don't report me to the Management Committee!—but I think China will fail and I don't think the world will go to hell along with it. That's because other large economies—India, for example, plus lots of smaller but rapidly growing economies—will take China's place as the drivers of global economic growth.

Suzy: But why do you think China will fail? In college, all we heard about was how China was going to dominate the world!

Ned: That's because college professors are all leftwing Democrats who have a soft spot for communists.

[Laughter.]

Carrie: Well, China's a long conversation, but in short, a true robust consumer society can only exist in a country where individual consumers have freedom of choice. China is a top-down economic model, which works well in a simple industrial economy. In fact, it probably works better than a free market model. But as a country transitions into a post-industrial, consumer-led economy, top-down doesn't work anymore. Look at the Soviet Union, Cuba, North Korea, Venezuela, Eastern Europe before the fall of the USSR.[8]

Billy: For what it's worth, in the pharmaceuticals business, companies have stopped building plants in China and also stopped outsourcing to Chinese companies. Partly, it's due to what Carrie said—other countries are now more competitive. But it's also because we simply don't trust the Chinese not to steal our products and manufacture them without permission.

QUICK NOTE

The Titan family was obviously interested in the discussion of geopolitical competitiveness and the kinds of mistakes that countries make. But the discussion also pointed up the fact that Spenser has thought deeply about these issues.

Roger: So, anyway, back to managers. The passive, structured manager we're using underweights the big commodity countries and overweights the emerging consumer growth economies, which is what we want. The other emerging markets manager is an active manager who makes big country and sector bets, really focusing intensely on the consumer sectors of emerging markets.

Carrie: Next, we have non-directional hedge funds, or what some people more accurately call *absolute return-oriented* hedge funds. But before I get into this, let me ask Roger a question: Are hedge funds an asset class?

Roger: No.

Carrie: Is that all you have to say?

Roger. No. [Laughter.] We've talked about the definition of an asset class in other meetings—assets that tend to behave like each other. But hedge funds don't fit that definition. The strategies they follow can be as different as night and day, so they can't be an asset class. Really, they're a business model.

Suzy: A *business model*?

Roger: Yes. A hedge fund is a manager that has organized itself as a limited partnership in which the manager is the general partner and the limited partners are the investors. The limiteds pay both an annual management fee and also a percentage of the profits. So, typically, the GP—general partner—will get a two percent annual management fee and twenty percent of the profits he generates.

Billy: Nice work if you can get it!

Carrie: You're telling me! But most people—most managers—can't get it. To convince investors to pay fees like that a manager has to have a proven track record of delivering good investment performance net of all those fees.

Roger: In many cases, the manager will have built his track record by managing internal, proprietary capital for a bank or investment bank. If he's really good, he'll go out on his own and raise a fund. Very often, the bank he worked at will be the largest initial investor.

Rose: What do these—what did you call them, non-directional hedge funds? What do they actually do?

Carrie: We contrast them with *directional* hedge funds. Directional funds are mainly the long/short managers we talked about earlier. A non-directional hedge fund is doing something that isn't necessarily correlated with the direction of the stock markets.

Billy: Which is why you call them *non*-directional.

Carrie: Right. So let's suppose a hedge fund manager is looking at the way a company's preferred stock typically trades relative to its senior secured bonds. If that relationship is currently out of whack, there might be a good reason for it but there might not. If the manager thinks the market's just got it wrong, he might short the preferred and buy the bond, or vice versa. If he's right, he profits whether the broad stock market goes up or down.

Roger: And these funds typically have low volatility compared to stocks or directional hedge funds. More like bonds.

Ned: Carrie, you gave us one example of a non-directional hedge fund strategy. I assume there are others?

Carrie: Oh, yes, many others! Global macro, for example, uses strategies that focus on currencies, interest rates, commodities, and so on. Again, hardly any normal correlation with the equity markets.

Ned: Hardly any *normal* correlation? What does that mean?

Roger: Carrie means that under very stressful market conditions, "all correlations go to one." That means that assets that are not normally highly correlated suddenly *become* correlated.

Ned: Okay, but short of that, the correlations are low and that's why you like—what did you call them? Global macro hedge funds?

Roger: Yes, but the main reason we like them is because their performance has been really, really, bad.

Ned, Rose, Suzy, and Billy: What?

Carrie: I know it sounds ridiculous—in fact, a lot of our clients think we're nuts.

Rose: What kind of performance have they had?

Roger: Dismal, dismal.

Ned: And you want to hire these guys?

Carrie: Well, here's the thing. Over the long term, global macro and similar managers have done really, really well, especially the best of them. But in a world dominated by central banker policy, these managers find it hard to create value. They keep getting whipsawed and the usual market signals they look at don't work when fundamentals aren't driving markets.

Rose: So why invest with them?

Carrie: Because, typically, when very, very smart managers who've had very, very good long-term track records enter a period when their performance is bad, that means they're about to revert to their long-term mean—that is, great performance.

Roger: And in this case we have a catalyst in mind—the U.S. Fed is likely to begin raising rates sometime soon. That should help return the markets to some semblance of normality, meaning that good macro guys should produce great returns again.

Carrie: Or so we hope.

Ned: Well, I guess we hired you guys to make these kinds of hard decisions, so we shouldn't second-guess you.

Carrie: Just promise me you'll be patient. It could take a while for these managers to get their groove back.

Roger: I don't hear anyone promising ...

Rose (laughing): Okay! We promise!

QUICK NOTE

Global macro managers, which include some of the best, most legendary managers on the planet, have been the-skunk-at-the-garden-party since the financial crisis, turning in truly dismal performance. But as can be seen here, Spenser has the courage of their convictions and plans to use at least one global macro hedge fund in the Titan portfolio.

Carrie: There are also event-driven strategies that focus mainly on corporate acquisitions but can invest in other kinds of corporate events. The strategy I mentioned earlier, shorting one security in the capital structure and going long another one, is part of what's called *relative value strategies*.

Roger: There are also multi-strategy hedge funds, those that combine several different strategies in one hedge fund. And, finally, there are hedge funds of funds, organizations that select a group of hedge funds to fill a particular need. For example, some investors want hedge exposure but they aren't large enough to get a diversified exposure. So they can invest in funds of funds.

Ned: I've heard bad things about funds of funds. Why is that?

Carrie: Probably because they cause investors to incur yet another layer of fees. Hedge fund fees are already high—that's the "two-and-twenty" fee format we discussed earlier—and now the fund of funds also has a fee.

Ned: It *does* sound unattractive.

Carrie: In most cases it is. Very few funds of funds can justify their extra fee.

Roger: Also, keep in mind that it's very expensive to identify, select, and monitor hedge funds, to say nothing of maintaining appropriate strategies in hedge. The fund of funds is doing all that work for you.

Carrie: Let's move on to private equity. We're suggesting three kinds of exposures for the Grandchildren's Trust: leveraged buyouts, mezzanine finance, and venture capital. We're also recommending three different approaches for getting those exposures. Roger, can you walk through what these strategies are and how we're recommending that the Trust gain access to them?

Roger: Sure. Let's start with the largest exposure, buyouts. Does everyone know what a leveraged buyout is?

[Some heads nod, others shake.]

Carrie: Maybe you should give us a brief primer on each strategy, Roger.

Roger: Sure. So a leveraged buyout involves the purchase of a company or, more typically, a unit of a company. Most times the management team will remain intact, but sometimes it will be changed or augmented. The buyout fund puts up some cash as equity—that's the money it raises from investors like the Trust—and then borrows the rest. The idea is that, as an independent entity, and with the incentives put in place via the buyout, the company will do better than it did while it was a subsidiary or division of a larger company.

Carrie: Plus, the buyout fund will have a had a lot of experience with this sort of thing, and they will sit on the new company's board and give advice and counsel, bring in seasoned executives as needed, and so on.

Roger: After a few years of operations, and assuming revenues have grown and profits are higher, the company will be sold or go public. When that happens, the Trust will receive a distribution from the buyout fund.

Carrie: A typical buyout fund will invest in a lot of buyouts. Some will fail, some will do okay, and some will do very nicely. We expect that the Trust will get an overall return from its buyout fund that will be higher than investing in the stock market, and rightly so, since buyouts are riskier. It's inherently risky to try to turn a company around or improve its operations, plus you have the illiquidity associated with having your capital called down and then not getting anything back for several years.

Roger: And it's hard to get out of these funds. There is a secondary market for them that you—that is, the Trust—could sell into, but typically you'd have to take a pretty big haircut.

Carrie: And how are we suggesting that the Trust get access to buyouts, Roger?

Roger: Through a combination of individual buyout funds we know well and have worked with for a long time, plus a core position in a buyout fund of funds.

Ned: Why both? Wouldn't it be cheaper just to use the individual buyout funds?

Carrie: Cheaper, yes. But we aren't able to build a full, diversified position in buyouts for the Trust without using a fund of funds. Remember that we want to diversify the Trust's buyout exposure in several ways: by size (the size of the buyout), by industry (not being too concentrated in one industry), by fund (not being too reliant on one or two fund managers), by geography (including outside the United States), and by vintage year.

Roger: And before you ask, *vintage year* means the year that you invested in the buyout fund. Experience has shown that returns in the buyouts space are highly correlated with the year the investment was made.

Ned: That makes sense. Some periods are more conducive to making money in these kinds of deals than others.

Carrie: Exactly. So for Spenser to diversify the Trust's buyouts exposure through all those dimensions, it would take a very large pool of the Trust's capital. By using a fund of funds, we can size the allocation appropriately. Roger, what's a mezzanine fund?

Roger: I mentioned earlier that when a buyout fund buys a company, it puts up some of its own capital and borrows the rest. It will borrow as much as it can from banks and other traditional sources, but often that leaves a gap in the debt structure. The buyout fund might seek *mezzanine* financing to fill the gap.

Carrie: Mezzanine—it's called that because it comes in between the equity tranche and the debt tranche—is basically a loan that allows the lender to convert to equity if the loan isn't paid back. It's usually subordinated to the senior debt.

Roger: Mezz lenders often have to act quickly. Also, they have no collateral for their loan, and as Roger just mentioned, they are subordinated to the senior debt, so they charge a lot.

Ned: In other words, as investors in a mezzanine fund, we can expect pretty good returns.

Roger: Yes, assuming the mezz guys are good at what they do. We think the mezz fund we're recommending is one of the very best. These guys have been in business for a long time, they know all the buyout guys, they're very smart, and they can act fast.

Carrie: Just to put a number on it—don't hold me to this—but under normal conditions we might look at mezz returns in the twenty percent per-annum range. Maybe a little lower under current interest rate conditions.

Ned: As an aside to Rose and the kids, mezzanine debt has an interesting characteristic on the balance sheet of the acquired company. Although it's structured as debt, it's treated on the balance sheet as equity (because of the convertibility feature). That makes it easier for the company to borrow more money if it needs it in the future.

Roger: Interesting, Ned, I didn't know that. I'm sure Carrie did, though.

[Carrie looks pained, everyone laughs.]

Carrie: Let's move to venture capital ...

Roger: I guess everybody knows what this is. People who have ideas for new businesses tend to go through a typical funding process. They max out their own credit cards, then they have the "friends and family round," where they hit up their family and close friends, then they might look to angel investors.

Billy: Angel investors? People who fly down out of the sky and drop money on you?

[Laughter.]

Roger: No such luck!

Ned: Some of my clients are into angel investing, Billy. They are basically guys who built their own companies and now like to work with young entrepreneurs.

Carrie: That's a very good description of an angel investor, Ned. Angels provide funding, but more important, they provide advice and counsel. They've usually built companies themselves, so they know the challenges.

Roger: Once funding needs grow beyond angels—and by this time the company likely has revenues if not profits—the entrepreneurs will look to venture capital firms. These are firms that raise money from investors—like the Trust, though these days mainly institutional investors—and then invest it in new, small firms that are startups or close to it.

Carrie: We tend to divide VC firms (venture capital firms) into early-stage VC and late-stage VC. Obviously, the earlier you invest in a new firm the greater the risk, but also the greater the return. Late-stage VC is attractive to a lot of institutional investors because it seems to offer a nice combination of lower risk but returns that are still quite high.

Ned: So is that what you're recommending for us—late stage?

Carrie: Actually, no. We're recommending a combination, and that you get the exposure via a venture capital fund of funds.

Ned: No individual funds at all?

Carrie: I wish we could do it that way, Ned, but, frankly, it's impossible. There are only a small handful of truly outstanding VC firms—early or late stage—and it's pretty much impossible to invest with them.

Billy: These are the guys who won't return your calls.

Roger: Right. They are already way oversubscribed and basically offer positions only to investors who have been with them for many years. I'm talking about Harvard, Yale, Stanford, and so on.

Ned: But the fund of funds has access?

Carrie: A few of them do, although almost all the VC funds of funds are also invested with VC funds we would consider second tier. But it's the only way to gain access to the top-tier funds.

Ned: And you would rather pay the additional fee layer than invest directly with funds you consider second best?

Carrie: Yes. The return statistics actually demonstrate that if you can't invest with the small handful of VC funds at the top of the business, you probably shouldn't invest in VC at all. The returns produced by second- and third-tier firms don't justify the risk.

Roger: In fact, several studies have shown that more than one hundred percent of the acceptable risk-adjusted returns in the VC space have been produced by no more than a dozen or so top firms. If you can't be invested with those firms, it's best to take your money and go home.

Carrie: Roger, do want to talk briefly about real estate and commodities?

Roger: Sure. Real estate is one of the largest asset classes in the world, and there are many different kinds of real estate. Some of it is much riskier than stocks and some of it is probably safer than bonds.

Carrie: So what we like to do is to find pockets of the real estate market that are currently undervalued and focus our clients' real estate exposure on those sectors. Right now, for example, we feel that most liquid real estate—REITs, things like that—are fairly valued at best, probably overvalued.

Suzy: What's a REIT?

Roger: It stands for real estate investment trust. It's a way to gain exposure to real estate in a fund that offers daily liquidity.

Rose: Daily liquidity sounds good to me!

Carrie: Sure, but at what cost? Most real estate is illiquid, so if you are managing a REIT you have an inherent mismatch between your assets—real estate—and your liabilities—investors who can get in and out every day.

Roger: That's why REITs trade like stocks. As the price goes up and down it doesn't directly affect how the underlying real estate is managed. And the managers don't have to keep cash around to meet redemptions.

Carrie: But even so, there is that inherent mismatch, which in my opinion causes REIT managers to have too short a time horizon.

Roger: In case you're wondering, Carrie doesn't like REITs.

[Laughter.]

Carrie: And I especially don't like them today. What Spenser is recommending for real estate exposure is niche, illiquid stuff where the markets tend to be inefficient. What are some examples, Roger?

Roger: Niche areas would be student housing, storage, marinas, things like that. We also like troubled assets, where we—that is, our managers—can go in and lend with an option to buy. If all goes well and the project turns around, we get a nice return. If the project continues to stumble and the operators can't pay, we go in and foreclose and manage the project until it can be sold.

Carrie: Commodities?

Roger: Commodity investing means buying futures positions in various industrial and agricultural commodities.

Billy: Pork bellies!

Roger: Exactly! There is a school of thought that goes like this. Commodities, as an investment asset, represent a high-volatility, low-returning investment opportunity, so the only reason to own them is because they are completely uncorrelated to other assets. In other words, even an investment—like commodities—that is unattractive itself can make sense in a portfolio because it reduces risk faster than it reduces return. If this approach is correct, and we think it is, then the best way to invest in commodities is to take your position and keep it intact through thick and thin, just rolling positions over as they mature.

Carrie: But there's a problem with that school of thought, namely that almost nobody is willing to own commodities when their price is plunging. People want out. And once they're out, they never get back in at the right time, so the benefit of the low correlation doesn't happen. All that happens is high vol and low returns.

Ned: Ugh. I suppose you have a different idea?

Carrie: We do. It's not a great one, but clients like it better. Basically we try to assess whether aggregate demand for commodities is likely to go up or down in the medium-term future. If it's down, we don't invest at all.

If it's up, we take a position and up- or downsize it as our thesis proves out or doesn't.

Rose: Whatever that meant, I'm all for it!

[Laughter.]

Carrie: Well, that pretty much exhausts the subject of managers for the riskier asset classes. Now let's turn to bonds. Roger?

Roger: I'll start with the riskier fixed income assets—junk bonds, or as the financial world prefers to call them, high-yield bonds.

Carrie: It's easier for firms to sell their clients something called "high-yield bonds" than to sell them something called "junk bonds."

Suzy: What does Spenser call them?

Carrie: Both. Actually, some of these securities aren't spectacularly risky. I'm talking about the world of bonds rated just below investment grade. Say, bonds rated BB. We work with one high-yield bond manager who, as far as I know, has never experienced a default in a bond held in the portfolio.

Roger: But as you go down in quality you get some really speculative issues. Those bonds rated CCC and below, for example, are truly junk bonds. During the tech bust in the early 2000s, for example, almost half of all bonds rated CCC to C defaulted.

Rose: Why would a fiduciary portfolio like the Grandchildren's Trust want to invest in anything like this? Aren't bonds supposed to be safe?

Carrie: We wouldn't use junk bonds in the core bond portfolio in the Trust, Rose, that's for sure. But, like any other investment asset, junk bonds can be a good or a bad investment depending on what you pay for them versus what they're worth.

Rose: Can you give me an example of how you might buy a junk bond and think of it as a good investment?

Carrie: Sure we can, can't we, Roger?

Roger: Uh, sure! Some advisory firms like to maintain a permanent position in junk bonds in their client portfolios, but we prefer to move in and out of junk as spreads widen and narrow.

Rose: Spreads? I think you defined this before, but I've forgotten.

Carrie: The term *spread* refers to the difference in yield between a junk bond and, say, a government bond of the same duration. Or, sometimes, when people are talking about spreads they're talking about the difference in yield between investment-grade bonds and junk bonds.

Roger: So if a ten-year Treasury bond is yielding four percent and a ten-year junk bond is yielding nine percent, the spread is five percent.

Carrie: What we do at Spenser is we look at spreads, and as they widen we begin to take a serious look at the junk bond world. Of course, we have to consider current and potential default rates, but if the spread is wide enough, then our clients are being compensated for the risk they're taking.

Rose: If I'm reading this page in the search book right, you're not recommending an exposure to junk bonds right now.

Carrie: That's right. A while back, we liked junk bonds, but as spreads narrowed we moved out of junk and into bank loans. Then …

Rose: Bank loans?

Carrie: Sorry, these are loans made by banks to the same kinds of companies, that is, relatively weak ones. The loans are bundled up and sold to investors. The nice thing about bank loans is that the interest rate fluctuates with the broad interest rate environment. As you know, if interest rates go up, the value of already-issued junk bonds goes down. But with bank loans the interest rate on the loans also goes up so the value of the loan portfolio stays the same.

Roger: Anyway, after spreads narrowed too much in the junk bond market, we began buying bank loans, using a manager we liked. But a while back even the loan market got too rich for our blood, so we pulled out. But if spreads widen out again, you can expect us to come back and recommend junk bonds or bank loans or maybe both.

Carrie: What about core bonds for the trust, Roger?

Roger: Right now, municipal bonds are reasonably fairly valued, unlike government and corporate bonds, which are way overvalued. So we're recommending that the Trust use the bond manager written up in the book. As you can see, the manager is a very large bank with long experience managing municipal bonds for many different kinds of clients. We like large bond managers for core bonds because they can be more efficient at trading the bonds and costs really matter in the bond world.

Ned: Since the Trust is domesticated in Pennsylvania, will you focus on Pennsylvania bonds?

Carrie: What Ned is getting at is that, if the Trust buys Pennsylvania muni bonds, the interest is tax-free at both the federal and state level. But if the Trust buys, say, New York munis, those are tax-free for federal purposes but not for state tax purposes.

Billy: So you'll only buy Pennsylvania bonds for the Trust?

Carrie: Well, no. Do you want to explain why not, Roger?

Roger: Sure. The Pennsylvania state income tax is fairly low, at least compared to the high rates at the federal level. So we need to balance the small amount of extra tax the Trust would pay if it owns a *national* muni-bond portfolio against the lower risk of a more broadly diversified portfolio.

Carrie: In the case of Pennsylvania, we suggest a home-state-centric portfolio that overweights Pennsylvania issues but that is also diversified into other states. We think that gives you the best balance between tax friction and risk. And it means we won't have to look at weaker issuers just to stay in Pennsylvania.

Roger: And this particular bond manager is also very accessible. We—or you—can talk to them pretty much any time you want.

Carrie: Well, I think that about concludes the manager selection meeting, unless there are other questions.

Suzy: Can I ask one?

Carrie: Of course!

Suzy: Well, I hate to sound like my cousin, Ellen, but when you talk about managers you tend to use the pronoun *he*. Is that just habit, or are all the portfolio managers really men?

Carrie: Well, that's an embarrassing question, Suzy! I try not to use sexist language, but it's sometimes difficult. Like a lot of languages, English doesn't have a gender-neutral singular pronoun. So when I'm thinking about it, I try to use *it* for managers, which are, after all, mainly corporations or partnerships. But I don't think of managers as *its*; I think about them as the human beings who are making the buy and sell decisions. Sometimes I use the plural—*they*. But often this makes the conversation sound stilted or ungrammatical. I do try to be aware of it, though.

Ned: Don't beat yourself up too bad, Carrie, I think what Suzy is really asking is whether the investment management world is a man's game or includes a lot of women as well.

Carrie: Unfortunately Suzy, the answer is that women aren't very well represented in the money management profession. They're not wholly absent, of course. There are some terrific female managers out there, and in the bond space a few women have been real pioneers. But at the really elite levels of the profession, the best hedge funds, for example, or the top-tier venture capital funds, women are almost invisible.

Suzy: I wonder why that is. Is there discrimination against women in the business, or do women just not like to work in it?

Carrie: Probably a bit of both. At the top of the profession the level of competition is intense, the stress level is very high, and it never lets up. And there is incessant travel. Not many *men* want to face that every day and the number of women who aspire to it is probably a lot lower.

Suzy: It doesn't sound like a job that's compatible with having kids.

Roger: Just to give you a sense for the numbers, the top twenty-five hedge funds—by size—have very high profiles and account for a very substantial percentage of all the hedge fund assets. Not one of those funds is headed by a woman.

Suzy: They're all alpha males, I suppose.

Roger: That would be a fair description; these are guys who routinely earn one billion dollars a year.

Billy: *What?* Did you say one billion dollars *a year*?

Roger: Yes, a year. There's no reason why there couldn't be alpha females who run huge hedge funds and make that kind of money, but for whatever reason there aren't any. Same with the top venture funds. There are no more than a dozen or so, but they're all run by men.

Rose: I don't doubt that it would be hard for a young woman to make her way in that world, but I also agree that very few of them would want to. It's like long-haul truck driving. A lot of working-class men really love that kind of work, like they're modern-day cowboys or something. But most working-class women would rather eat nails. [Laughter.] And on that note, let's have lunch.

SUMMARY

As noted in the abstract at the beginning of the chapter, many investors are more fascinated with money managers than is appropriate given the limited—and likely negative—impact of managers on their portfolios. One way for advisors to mitigate this issue is to underplay the manager selection process. As we observed in the foregoing meeting between Spenser and the Titans, the advisors devoted large portions of the meeting to two preliminary issues: relative market sector valuations (which would affect how close to the target allocations the portfolio would be) and an opportunistic investment Spenser was recommending. Only at the very end did the subject of actual manager selection come up, and even then Spenser devoted a considerable period of time to a discussion of the agency issues presented by money managers. Finally, Spenser presented the recommended managers more or less as a fait accompli, emphasizing the importance of keeping the responsibility for manager selection on Spenser.

Many advisors like to encourage their clients to have input into the manager selection process. Unfortunately, that blurs the ultimate responsibility for how the managers perform, allowing the advisor to duck culpability. This is wrong in two ways. First, it assumes the client actually knows something about manager selection, which is unlikely. Second, as noted, it allows the advisor to transfer some of the responsibility for poor manager performance to the client.

Of course, there's a fine line between accepting responsibility and dogmatically shoving managers down the client's throat. If there's a good reason why a client is uncomfortable with a particular manager, that firm has no place in the portfolio. And what about managers the client brings up? Unfortunately, an advisor needs to take a look at client-recommended managers even though it's time-consuming and expensive. In most cases, the defects in the manager will become quickly apparent, but in some cases you might find that you've stumbled onto a very interesting manager you wouldn't otherwise have come across.

At the end of the day, manager selection is all about damage control. Randomly selected managers will detract a great deal from a client's returns. But even very carefully selected managers are unlikely to add much to the returns. All that work checking a manager out 12 ways from Sunday won't ensure that he'll outperform, but it should go a long way toward ensuring that he won't sink the ship.

Here is an example of how difficult manager selection is. There is a very high-quality, hardworking fund of funds manager on the West Coast who has been in business for more than two decades. A few years ago, looking back over the first 20 years of the fund—which, by the way, had produced excellent performance—the manager decided to look at how many of the hedge funds he'd picked had worked out and how many hadn't.

Over those 20 years, the fund had been invested with 51 managers; 26 had worked out and 25 had been terminated for cause. That's pretty much chance. Granted, even the hedge funds that were terminated for cause were head-and-shoulders above the run-of-the-mill hedge fund. I only bring up this experience because it shows, first, that manager selection is *very* hard work. And it shows, second, that portfolios can perform quite well in spite of the fact that a lot of the managers will disappoint.

NOTES

1. In 1977, Congress amended the Federal Reserve Act to read in part as follows:

   > *The Board of Governors of the Federal Reserve System and the Federal Open Market Committee shall maintain long run growth of the monetary and credit aggregates commensurate with the economy's long run potential to increase production, so as to promote effectively the goals of maximum employment, stable prices and moderate long-term interest rates.*

2. The most prominent of these books is the classic, *This Time Is Different: Eight Centuries of Financial Folly*, by Carmen M. Reinhart and Kenneth Rogoff (Princeton: Princeton University Press, 2009).

3. See, e.g., Lawrence H. Summers, "Why Stagnation Might Prove to Be the New Normal," December 15, 2013, available at http://larrysummers.com/2013/12/15/why-stagnation-might-prove-to-be-the-new-normal/.
4. Research Affiliates was founded by Rob Arnott. See http://www.researchaffiliates.com/.
5. Most people agree that the first hedge fund was formed by Alfred W. Jones in 1949.
6. More specifically, bad loans make it difficult for banks to make more loans because the banks have to set aside reserves to cover possible losses, the loans generate little by way of interest income, and the troubled loans take up a lot of staff time and often incur legal expenses.
7. The five largest banks in Europe and the United States, ranked by assets, are: HSBC (Britain), JP Morgan (U.S.), BNP Paribas (France), Crédit Agricole (France), and Barclays (Britain).
8. This argument is made in a more elaborate way in Gregory Curtis, *The Stewardship of Wealth: Successful Private Wealth Management for Investors and Their Advisors* (Hoboken, NJ: John Wiley & Sons, 2013), 15–17.

CHAPTER 9

Reviewing the Performance of the Investment Accounts

PREPARATION AND USE

In the investment world quarterly performance—by markets or managers—means essentially nothing. Yet, virtually every client wants to meet on a quarterly basis to review performance. Setting up these meetings and fitting them into the schedules of busy clients and advisors is a challenging matter. And to imagine that at the actual meeting nothing of importance will be done, no big decisions made, seems absurd. Yet, that is precisely what should happen at virtually every quarterly performance review meeting—nothing.

Of course it's important for advisors and clients to monitor how the portfolio is doing, but the benefits of ongoing monitoring are all too often undermined by the downsides of short-term thinking, of making long-term portfolio decisions on the basis of one or two quarters' worth of performance.

Consequently, thoughtful advisors have tried to identify strategies that will permit close monitoring of the portfolio without encouraging short-term decision making. Some of those strategies include:

- Scheduling meetings at times during the year that don't correspond to the end of calendar quarters
- Utilizing an investment committee operating manual
- Adopting a policy that any decision taken at a quarterly meeting will not be acted upon until at least the following meeting
- Constantly reminding clients that acting on the basis of short-term results is not in their best interests

In the following meeting between Spenser Advisors and the Titan family, we will watch as Spenser employs most of these strategies to try to keep the client and the Spenser advisors themselves focused on the long term.

THE PERFORMANCE REPORTING MEETING

This performance reporting meeting, for the first quarter of the year, was convened, at Spenser's insistence, not near the end of the quarter but in early July—in other words, long after the quarter had ended on March 31, but before the results were in for the quarter ended June 30. By that time, of course, the results for the first quarter were quite stale. Even a family tempted to make short-term decisions wouldn't want to act on the basis of stale data—and this was precisely why Spenser scheduled the meeting in midsummer.

Carrie Knowlton: It's nice to see everyone again. I'm glad the whole family could make it.
Ellen: Nobody would want to miss Uncle Ned's Fourth of July barbecue! [Laughter.] Even though we have to sit in this awful conference room.

[The meeting was being held in the Titan family office, Lawburn. As noted in earlier chapters, little money had been spent on the office over the years.]

Billy: What, you don't like ugly?
Ellen: *Ugh.*
Suzy: You know, some family offices fairly reek of money. Ours reeks of poverty.
Geoffrey: Actually, I think I'm changing my mind about it. Lawburn's so old and musty it's starting to seem cool. I mean, check out the Art Deco lamps.
Billy: And the big worn parts in the carpet.
Ned: All right, all right! We all know how the wet-behind-the-ears generation feels about the décor at Lawburn! But we're here to find out how our portfolio is doing. Where would you like to start, Carrie?
Carrie: If it's okay with everyone, we'd like to start with the Grandchildren's Trust and then move on to the individual portfolios.
Ellen: I think we're cool with that. After all, our great-great-grandchildren might actually see some of the Trust's money.

[Laughter.]

Rose: Let's don't go there again.
Carrie: Okay, since this is our first meeting to go over the performance of the family's various accounts, I wanted to spend a moment walking you through the performance books so you'll understand how they're organized. Roger?

The Monthly Flash Report

Roger Epperson: Thanks, Carrie. As you all know, Spenser Advisors sends its clients several kinds of performance reports. Every month, for example, you've been receiving what we call our monthly flash reports.

[Roger passes out copies of the most recent flash report, which is for the month of May. A version of this report is available on the companion website for this book at www.wiley.com/go/familycapital.]

Billy: Wait! This data is for the end of May! That's only a few weeks ago—aren't you afraid we'll make short-term decisions?

[Laughter.]

Carrie: Well, I hope not. As you can see, these flash reports aren't full performance reports; they just show how each of your managers is doing. We haven't rolled the manager performance and the cash and so on up into a full report.

Roger: That's right. Notice that each manager's return is shown for the month of May and also for the year to date, along with the positive or negative tracking error versus the manager's benchmark. A month is obviously a very short period of time when we're looking at investment performance, and even the year-to-date numbers are too short to matter much.

Geoffrey: Okay, so why do you send this out to your clients?

Carrie: In all honesty, we do it because clients want to see it. They can quickly run down the list of managers and see if anyone is doing especially well or poorly and then, in effect, put that manager on their personal watch-list.

Roger: But these reports also play an important role at Spenser. You can't see it on these reports, but embedded in the spreadsheet is a calculation that shows us whether the manager is performing within our expectations. So, if a manager's tracking error against the benchmark is normally, say, fifty basis points a month, we want to know if this month's performance is more than one standard deviation away from what's normal.

Carrie: And keep in mind that the deviation can be positive or negative. Either way, we promptly contact the manager to see what's going on.

Ellen: I can see why you'd call the manager if the performance was bad, but if it's good, why worry?

Billy: Don't look a gift horse in the mouth!

Roger: The worry is that the manager is doing something he's not supposed to be doing. Suppose it's a small-cap growth manager and he's consistently doing much better than the small-cap growth benchmark. That might be because he's actually buying mid-cap stocks.

Ellen: Okay, but if mid-cap stocks, whatever they are, are doing better than small-cap stocks, why wouldn't we want our manager to buy them?

Carrie: Because that's not why we hired him. If we wanted a specific manager dedicated to mid-caps, we'd hire such a manager. If our small-cap manager is buying mid-cap stocks, he's not giving us the small-cap exposure we want. It's also quite likely that the manager doesn't know what he's doing in the mid-cap space. So while he might look good against the small-cap benchmark, he might look awful compared to a good mid-cap manager.

Roger: Any small-cap manager can end up owning a few mid-cap stocks, of course. We categorize small-cap stocks as companies with a market capitalization of less than two billion dollars. If the manager bought a company with a one-point-five-billion-dollar market cap, and the stock went up strongly, the company could now technically be a mid-cap stock. But the manager won't necessarily sell it until the fundamentals deteriorate.

Carrie: Right. That's not what we're worried about. We're worried about the small-cap manager who's constantly buying bigger companies because it's making his performance look good. We're very likely to terminate such a manager, even though his performance might look great.

Ned: How long will you stick with a manager who is doing what you expected him to do, but whose performance is bad?

Carrie: It's a very good question, Ned, and the answer is, "Generally, too long."

Ned: Why is that?

Roger: The typical mistake investors make is to fire a manager *too soon*, at exactly the wrong time—after a period of two or three years of underperformance. Then they go out and hire a guy or gal who has two or three years of good performance. Over the next cycle, the fired manager significantly outperforms the hired manager.

Rose: That's what you were talking about earlier—people chasing returns instead of being patient.

Ned: And managers tending to revert to the mean.

Carrie: Exactly. And remember that before we use a manager in client portfolios, we've spent a huge amount of time and money evaluating him or her. We *like* the managers we use and we have a lot of respect for them. So even several years of underperformance won't usually cause us to terminate a manager.

Rose: But you said you generally wait too long.

Carrie: Well, that's the characteristic mistake we make at Spenser. Most investors are much too impatient with managers, but when we make a mistake it's because we've been too patient.

Ned: So back to my original question—how long does the underperformance have to last before you pull the plug?

Carrie: The technical answer, Ned, is that if the manager has underperformed for a complete market cycle, we will likely—but not certainly—take him off our recommended list. The problem is that a market cycle might last three years and it might last ten years. You really don't know until it's complete. Obviously ten years of underperformance would be cause for termination, but three years probably wouldn't be. At the end of the day it's a matter of judgment.

Roger: But in reality, most manager terminations happen for reasons other than performance. For example, if there's a major change at the manager's shop—an important person has left or died, for example, or the manager is changing the way it manages money in some important respect.

Carrie: Or we may simply think that the market isn't going to reward a manager's style any time soon, so we'll take client money away but we won't remove him from our recommended list.

Rose: Can you give an example, Carrie?

Carrie: Sure. I mentioned at an earlier meeting that we don't usually have a permanent position in junk bonds in our client portfolios. But, obviously, we need to have a good junk bond manager or two standing by for those occasions when we want to invest in junk. So we'll fund those managers when we like junk and defund them when we don't. But we don't remove them from our recommended list.

Roger: Before we move on, are there other questions about the flash report?

Ned: I notice that some of the returns are asterisked and others are missing entirely.

Roger: Yes, a few hedge fund managers don't report their monthly results in time to make it on to the flash report, so we're reporting their results a month late. And some funds of funds take even longer to report. Since that particular fund of funds was just hired, we don't have a prior month return, so it's missing. Any other questions?

The Quarterly Performance Report

Carrie: Okay, let's move on to the main quarterly performance report. This report has a number of component parts. Why don't you walk us through them, Roger.

[A sample quarterly investment performance report is available on the companion website for this book at www.wiley.com/go/familycapital.]

The Cover Letter to the Client

Roger: We'll skip the table of contents and look briefly at the transmittal letter on page four. The letter shows everyone who is receiving a copy of the performance report. If you had an investment committee, every member of the committee would be shown here. So it's a good idea to take a quick look at this page to make sure the right people are getting the letter.

Suzy: That letter only has Dad and Aunt Rose listed. But we have copies.

Ned: That's because I asked Spenser to send three copies to me and three to Rose. At the time, Rose and I weren't sure each of you wanted your own copy.

Suzy: I'm still not sure I want one. I wouldn't want it lying around our apartment.

Ellen: Agree.

Geoffrey: And since I'm the loser kid still living at home, I can use Dad's copy.

[Laughter.]

Billy: Well, I'd like my own copy, if nobody minds.

Rose: That's fine with me. Carrie, can you add Billy to the distribution list?

Carrie: Will do. Go on, Roger.

Roger: The meat of the report begins with the executive summary. Since we've already gone over this in some detail [see Chapter 4, "Performance Reporting"], I'll just note that this section includes charts and graphs illustrating the most important aspects of current market conditions along with some performance attribution and a manager watch-list. Then we have a section containing a fairly brief take on how the markets in general performed that quarter. As you can see, it's not detailed or in-depth, but just a quick overview of the most important developments along with any thoughts we might have about them.

Carrie: Sometimes we can be pretty opinionated in that section, but other times it's just a straightforward recitation of what happened.

Rose: Do you write it, Carrie?

Carrie: No, a draft is prepared by our chief investment officer and then a couple of us look it over. But we don't typically make many changes.

[There follows a pause while everyone reads the section called Market Performance.]

Carrie: Questions about that section?

Geoffrey: My bet is there are lots of questions, but most of us don't know enough about the markets to really understand what's being said.

Carrie: Well, if there's really something that's confusing, we can try to clear it up.

Ellen: You use the phrase, "Don't fight the Fed." I've heard that before, but I don't know what it means.

Carrie: It means that the Federal Reserve Bank has an unlimited checkbook and can pretty much get its way, at least in the short term. We had a long discussion about quantitative easing at an earlier meeting, so in that context, "Don't fight the Fed" means that if the Fed wants to push investors out of safe assets and force them to buy riskier assets, that's very likely to happen. It might be wise or unwise, and in the long term it might all unwind on the Fed. But in the meantime it would be foolish to fight the Fed by, say, shorting risk assets like stocks.

Rose: As you know, Ned is very negative about quantitative easing. But you're saying that no matter how you feel about what the Fed is doing, you should go along with them?

Ned: Never!

[Laughter.]

Carrie: No, that's not exactly what I'm saying. I think it would be very dangerous for Ned, or anybody else, to bet against the Fed directly by shorting the assets the Fed is trying to boost. But lots of people who are worried about the Fed's unconventional policies are taking a—well, don't take this wrong, Ned—a passive-aggressive approach.

Rose: Passive-aggressive is one thing Ned isn't. Aggressive-aggressive would be more like it.

[Laughter.]

Ned: Who, me? I'm a Casper Milquetoast, at least compared to my father.

Rose: Who was, as I understand it, a Casper Milquetoast compared to *his* father.

Geoffrey: *Whoa*, that's a scary thought.

[More laughter.]

Roger: What Carrie means by "passive-aggressive" is that people who are worried about Fed policies aren't directly fighting the Fed but instead are simply keeping their exposure to stocks at the low end of their range or possibly avoiding stocks altogether.

Carrie: That's right. Some of you may know the name Mohammed El-Erian, who was a very senior guy at PIMCO for a while.

Billy: And before that he was running the Harvard endowment.

Carrie: That's the guy. He has gone public with the fact that he's avoiding stocks.

Suzy: But stocks have done great, haven't they?

Carrie: Yes, so far. So Mr. El-Erian has missed out on some good returns. But a lot of people worry less about missing out on good returns and worry a lot more about getting in on bad returns.

Ned: In other words, the game isn't over yet.

Roger: That's right. It's entirely possible that people who own a lot of stocks could see all their gains—and more—go away. But who knows?

Carrie: The next section in the letter is entitled "Portfolio Performance." This is a really important part of the performance report because it explains in plain English how your portfolio did that quarter.

Rose: I noticed that section immediately, Carrie. I've never actually seen anyone explain to us in English how we did. They send us pages and pages of numbers, but not everybody is—what's the word? Numerate.

Carrie: I'm glad you like that section, Rose, because it takes us a long time to write it. It would be much simpler and cheaper just to send you the numbers.

QUICK NOTE

Although more and more wealth advisors are taking the time to write plain-English descriptions of how their clients' portfolios have performed, it's still very much a minority practice. But clients love it and it forces the advisor to look hard at the returns and what drove them.

Roger: As you can see when you look at it, these paragraphs start at the portfolio-wide level and describe how the capital performed overall, usually measured against a benchmark. Almost all clients have a benchmark that we refer to as a *custom benchmark*. I think we've discussed this before, but it's basically a benchmark showing how the portfolio would have performed if it had been positioned exactly at its target allocation and if all sectors had performed in line with the sector indexes.

Carrie: Of course, there are some market sectors—hedge and private equity, for example—that don't have true indexes. Also, note that even in sectors that have indexes, those indexes don't bear any fees or costs, so were not really comparing doughnuts-to-doughnuts. Finally, it's important to keep in mind that the custom benchmark already incorporates a lot of value the advisor has brought to the table, since it begins with the target asset allocation.

Suzy: Can you say that last part again?

Carrie: Sure. A very important part of the work any advisor does is to make sure you own the right portfolio for your needs as a family, or in this case, for the needs and objectives of the Grandchildren's Trust. That portfolio design work is crucial to everything. When you look at the return of the custom benchmark, that return already incorporates the design of the portfolio.

Roger: So when a client says, "My portfolio underperformed the custom benchmark," the advisor is often thinking to herself, "Well, it could underperform the custom benchmark by a hell of a lot and we'd still be bringing huge value to you."

Carrie: "Herself?"

[Laughter.]

Roger: Just being nonsexist.

Carrie: Uh- huh. But Roger's right. Whether the advisor is thinking that to herself or not, the reality is that a huge amount of value is imbedded in the custom benchmark.

Roger: Some clients also like to see a *naïve* benchmark, which we've also discussed before and which is a simple stock-bond-cash allocation that has the same risk level—as measured by price volatility—as the target allocation.

Carrie: After discussing the performance of the overall portfolio, this section of the letter then walks through each market sector and discusses performance in that sector against a benchmark, as well as manager performance. Note that we don't always mention every manager in this part of the letter, but only those who particularly outperformed or underperformed.

[There follows a pause while everyone reads the section called Portfolio Performance.]

Roger: Questions?

Ned: Well, my question is this. I think I understand most of what is being said in these paragraphs. And, by the way, I agree with Rose—this is a huge improvement over the usual performance reports financial firms produce, which were just columns of numbers. But, still, what should we take away from this? The overall portfolio beat its benchmark for the quarter, but you've already told us that one quarter is too short a period to worry about. Some managers outperformed and some underperformed. Should we be happy or upset?

Carrie: Well, it's a good question, and it goes back to the original thinking behind not focusing on quarterly performance. Basically, you shouldn't really even be thinking about performance over such a short period. Your takeaways should be something like this:

- Is my portfolio performing about like I expected it to perform over the longest period available? In other words, is the mix of risk assets and safe assets and so on giving me roughly the risk-return balance I'm looking for? In the case of the Grandchildren's Trust, we've only just started managing it, so there isn't enough of a track record to look at. But there will be in due course.
- Is the portfolio generating roughly half the income I will need for my spending?
- Over shorter periods of time, is my performance against my benchmarks reasonably okay? Over intermediate periods is my performance very close to the benchmarks? Over a complete market cycle, did I beat my benchmarks? Clearly, this is a very short period, at least in terms of the time frame during which Spenser has managed the portfolio, but I would say, "So far, so good."
- Over longer periods of time, are my managers adding value on a risk-adjusted basis? It's too soon to tell, of course, but as the years go by we will find that some managers are paying their keep and some aren't.
- Finally, as the years go by, how happy are you with the way the capital is performing? Is it meeting your needs? Your expectations? Would you prefer to see higher returns, even if it means higher risk? Would you prefer to see lower risk, even if it means lower returns? Are your income needs being comfortably met?

Rose: Well, I guess we'll just have to watch for these things as time goes by. I just have a fear that I'm going to get lost in the weeds. Quarter after quarter I'll be reading these reports and seeing some good things and some bad things. But does it add up to something that's good or not?

Carrie: One thing that might help you, Rose, is what we call a "Midcourse Checkup." At the fifth anniversary of our relationship with each client—and every fifth anniversary thereafter—we do a complete review of how the portfolio has performed relative to its objectives.

Roger: The Checkup also looks at softer elements of the relationship, like the quality of our communications with you, our responsiveness to inquiries, client service, performance reporting accuracy versus errors, and so on.

Carrie: Again, there will be some good things and some not-so-good things, but it will pose the question: Are we basically on course? If not, we have some major restructuring to do with the portfolio. Also, whenever we find something that's not-so-good, we ask ourselves, "What *should* we have done, and what should we do going forward?" And we propose a plan for improvement.

Rose: That would be a big help to me.

QUICK NOTE

Very few wealth advisory firms offer an automatic midcourse checkup as described by Carrie and Roger. At best, such a review will be conducted only at the insistence of a client—often based on the client's sense that something is amiss. But the regular checkup not only prevents the portfolio from getting too far off course, it also prevents the *client relationship* from getting too far off course.

Ellen: You say you do this every five years for each client. How long does a typical client stay with Spenser?

Carrie: What we *hope* is that a client will stay with us for generations. We've organized our firm that way—we have generations of partners, from senior partners to junior partners to senior investment analysts who are competing to become partners. So while it's true that when your generation takes over responsibility for the portfolio, I'm unlikely to be here, it's also true that Roger *will* be here. And there will be a new "Roger" backing him up.

Roger: But to answer your question specifically, Ellen, we have clients who have been with the firm for three decades—grandchildren who weren't even born when Spenser was first engaged are now beginning to take responsibility for those portfolios.

Carrie: I was eleven years old myself at the time … [Laughter.] So what typically happens is this. If a client is with Spenser for three years, they tend to stay for a *very* long time. During those first three years, both Spenser and the client discover whether the relationship is working.

Suzy: Do you ever fire a client?

Carrie: Well, I wouldn't use that word. We do occasionally resign from an engagement that we see isn't working. But we don't just walk away, we stick around and help to make sure the client lands somewhere happily. I mean, if the client will let us.

Ellen: When Spenser gets fired, what are the usual reasons?

Carrie: Fired? *Us?*

[Laughter.]

Roger: Unfortunately, it does happen. Probably the most common reason is simply that the relationship doesn't click. Whatever the client was looking for, it wasn't what Spenser offered. As Carrie said, this usually crops up in the first few years of the relationship.

Carrie: I agree with that. Those are often the relationships we resign from. But in terms of actually getting terminated by the client, there are two main reasons. The first is a generational shift. So, for example, when Ned and Rose decide to pass responsibility on to the next generation, if we haven't stayed close to the four of you, if you don't know and trust us or don't like the job we're doing, you're likely to want to move on to another advisor.

Roger: Or, sometimes, the portfolio gets divided up and some of the next generation stays with us and some leave.

Carrie: Yes, that certainly happens. The other common way we lose clients is that the client becomes impatient during an extreme market condition. For example, some clients in the past have blamed Spenser for a bear market. Even though the client is doing far better than most investors during the bear, they're unhappy and go elsewhere.

Roger: That "elsewhere" is often just to cash.

Geoffrey: Uncle George again!

Carrie: The same impatience can happen when we underperform during a strong, lengthy bull market.

Roger: I wasn't with the firm in the late 1990s— I was still in college—but I understand that in 1998 and 1999 the firm lost several clients because of underperformance.

Carrie: That's correct, unfortunately. It was a very bad period for us as a firm because we were sure we were doing the right thing for our clients, but some of the clients disagreed.

Billy: What were you doing that they disagreed with, underperforming?

[Laughter.]

Carrie: I'm afraid that's it exactly, Billy. You probably know that in the late 1990s there was a tremendous bull market going on. It had really started way back in 1982, and by the late nineties Spenser was concerned that stock prices were way too high.

Roger: That was also the era of the big tech boom. People were paying huge prices for companies that had no profits at all, and sometimes not even much revenue. They were paying, as the phrase went, "multiples of eyeballs."

Ellen: "Multiples of eyeballs"? What can that mean?

Ned: Ah, to be young and not know about multiples of eyeballs! You see, kids, back in those days it was the beginning of the Internet and everyone was wildly excited by the prospect of selling things at virtually no cost. If a particular Internet company had a website that was being viewed by lots of people—that's where the "eyeballs" came from—then everyone assumed it was only a matter of time before all that traffic could be *monetized* and the company would be worth billions.

Carrie: Right. But it turned out that in most of those cases the eyeballs never turned into dollar bills and the companies people were paying fortunes for turned out to be worthless.

Roger: And on top of that, even when an Internet company managed to get traction, it usually turned out to be a lot more expensive to operate than they'd expected.

Rose: So what you're saying is that Spenser didn't buy into those eyeballs stories.

Carrie: Right. Nor did we buy into the huge multiples people were paying for ordinary growth stocks. Plus, of course, our clients weren't invested in the stock market alone. They also owned bonds, hedge funds, and so on. And *nothing* kept up with tech and growth stocks.

Rose: I see. So some of your clients were looking at the huge returns people were getting on technology stocks and growth stocks and then looking at their portfolios and seeing much lower overall returns.

Carrie: Yes. In one case—it was an endowment client, not a family—I showed up at an investment committee meeting and was instructed by the committee chair to terminate the value manager we'd hired (I think it was Sanford Bernstein) and hire growth and tech managers. I explained why we were doing what we were doing, but of course told the committee that it was their money and they could do as they wished. However, I hoped they would take to heart my fear that prices were way too high and that buying into the growth and tech story now was likely to prove disastrous.

Roger: I've heard this story, it's legendary at Spenser. Carrie had hardly sat down at her desk after she returned from the investment committee meeting when she received a call from the committee chair. She informed Carrie that not only was the value manager being fired, but so was

Spenser. She told Carrie that she wasn't happy about the termination, but that it had to be done because Spenser just didn't "get it."

Carrie: She meant that we had an old-fashioned view of the stock markets that no longer made any sense.

Ned: You and Warren Buffett.

Carrie: Right. Nor were we impressed by P/E ratios of forty times.

Rose: So what happened to the endowment?

Carrie: They went ahead and moved most of their money to two new managers, a then-famous tech manager and a growth stock manager. They kept a bit of money in bonds and enough cash to pay their bills for six months.

Ned: And then the tech boom was followed by the tech bust.

Carrie: Yes, I'm afraid so. The endowment lost sixty-five percent of its value in just under two years. The investment committee chair and the board chair were forced to resign in disgrace and the state attorney general sent the endowment a formal letter demanding that the board members justify what had happened and how their decision making had been consistent with their fiduciary responsibilities. It was a very ugly time.

Rose: And you said there were several other clients who did the same thing.

Carrie: Yes, although that was the most dramatic example. The reason I'm spending so much time on the incident, even though it's fifteen years in the past, is that we're looking at a very similar situation now.

Suzy: I'm not sure what you mean, Carrie.

Roger: Carrie means that we've had a very long bull market and prices are now very high. Spenser is getting more and more defensive, and as a result our clients' results don't look good relative to, say, the returns on U.S. stocks.

Ellen: Has anyone fired you over it?

Carrie: Not yet, but I know of one client who is very unhappy. And two or three other clients are reviewing their relationship with Spenser, supposedly because we've been working together for a long time, but really because their portfolios haven't risen as much as the stock market.

Roger: One of those clients is one that Carrie and I work on together. We're working hard to help them understand why we're doing what we're doing, and we're using the late-1990s experience as a pretty dramatic example of what can happen when investors forget about risk and focus only on return.

Carrie: But in all honesty, I think that at the end of the day we'll lose a few clients. Maybe just one or two, but it depends on how long the bull market keeps running.

QUICK NOTE

Losing a client is always a traumatic event for a wealth management firm, especially if the firm is a boutique and doesn't have hundreds of clients. But losing an occasional client is inevitable, and it is never appropriate for the advisor to knuckle under to unwise client demands just to keep the account.

Roger: Anyway, unless there are more questions, I'll move on. [No one asks a question.] Okay, so the next section just shows actions taken in the portfolio during the quarter and subsequent to quarter-end. We might have terminated a manager—that would be unusual—or we might have received a distribution from a private equity fund. We might have received capital calls from those funds or we might have added money to a manager, perhaps taking it from another manager.

Carrie: And, of course, the client might have withdrawn money from the portfolio for living expenses, taxes, gifts, whatever.

Roger: Right. Then you see a section that sets forth any recommendations we have for that quarter. Of course, if we have an urgent recommendation, we'll communicate that to you in between meetings. But most recommendations aren't time-sensitive and, for nondiscretionary accounts, we like to hold them until the meeting so we can discuss them with the family.

Billy: What do you mean by a *nondiscretionary* account?

Carrie: At Spenser, we have, basically, three kinds of accounts, depending on the size of the client and the client's needs. Roger, can you explain the different kinds of accounts and how they're used?

Roger: Sure. As we've mentioned before, we have a private investment fund called the Spenser Partners Fund. It's called that because the Spenser partners have their own money invested in it. For smaller clients, who can't meet the high minimum account sizes of the best investment managers, the Partners Fund is a terrific alternative to mutual funds.

Carrie: The Partners Fund is also widely used for smaller accounts inside a larger client relationship. For example, in the Titan family there are several *generation-skipping trusts* that have only a couple million dollars in them. The Spenser Partners Fund would be a great investment alternative for those accounts.

Ned: But if it's one overall investment fund, how do you deal with different objectives clients might have?

Roger: What we do, Ned, is to consider the Partners Fund as the *risk asset* portion of a client's portfolio.

Carrie: Every client, or almost every client, will have the core of their money invested in risk assets. Then, depending on how risk averse they are, they'll have a larger or smaller amount in bonds. Finally, unless they are very small or have a short investment time horizon, they'll also have *aspirational* assets—buyouts, venture capital, private real estate, things like that.

Roger: So we'll size all three buckets appropriately for the client: sixty percent in risk assets in the Partners Fund, for example, fifteen percent in aspirational assets, and fifteen percent in bonds.

Billy: Okay, that's one way you have of working with clients, mainly somewhat smaller ones. Then there are two other ways, right?

Carrie: Yes. A nondiscretionary relationship is the one we have with your family. In that arrangement, Spenser makes recommendations and the family considers them and makes all the final decisions.

Roger: And then there are the discretionary relationships. In that arrangement, Spenser makes the decisions and informs the client of what we've done. That way, if the client is uncomfortable with a particular trade, we can unwind it.

Carrie: Just to be clear, Spenser doesn't have complete discretion to do whatever we want in the portfolio. First, the client's objectives are determined and an *investment policy statement* is drawn up, exactly as in a nondiscretionary relationship. Spenser then manages the portfolio in accordance with the terms of the IPS, and especially within the constraints of the asset allocation policy with its targets, minimums, and maximums. If for some reason we want to go outside those constraints, we have to get the client's written permission.

Rose: So how would a client decide which relationship is best? I guess with the Spenser Partners Fund, a very large client would be unlikely to select that. But what about choosing between discretionary and nondiscretionary? And, by the way, kids, I'm asking because Ned and I decided to start with a nondiscretionary account. But that was just to see how comfortable we would be with Carrie and Roger. We're leaning toward moving to a discretionary account at some point.

Carrie: Clients who choose nondiscretionary relationships with us do so for a variety of reasons. Probably the most common is that they are very substantial families who have active investment committees and who operate almost like institutions. Those committees want to see recommendations from us, and sometimes they want to interview managers before they're hired.

Roger: And, of course, there are families who simply like to be directly involved in decision making and who want to talk things over before any trades are made. Or maybe the family just likes to keep control.

Rose: And what about on the discretionary side?

Carrie: Discretionary accounts are the fastest growing kind of business at Spenser. Partly, I think, it's that, after the market collapse in 2008, a lot of families decided that they really didn't understand the markets. They would rather have experts making the decisions, knowing that they can always ask that a trade be unwound.

Ned: But suppose Spenser makes a trade. They let me know about it, and after thinking about it I decide I'm not comfortable. Meanwhile, the market has moved against me so that if I unwind the trade I'll lose money.

Carrie: I'm afraid you're stuck with it, Ned. You can either let the trade stand or you can unwind it and take the loss. I mean why not just wait until you see how every trade works out and then decide whether you're comfortable?

[Laughter.]

Ned: I like that! I'd never lose money!

Roger: A very important reason to have a discretionary account, though it's not often the reason people specify, is to avoid opportunity costs.[1]

Suzy: What's an opportunity cost?

Roger: In this case it refers to the costs you incur via delayed decision making. So let's say that Spenser decides on a trade. We write it up and put it in the recommendations section of your quarterly report. Ned and Rose receive the report, read it over, and then some weeks later we have a meeting and talk about it. No decision is made, maybe because it's a complex issue, maybe because Ned and Rose don't agree, whatever. Time goes by. Eventually, you decide to make the trade. But by then, what was once a great trade is now just an ordinary trade or maybe even a loser. (In which case, of course, we wouldn't do it.) That's opportunity cost.

Ned: In a discretionary account, the trade would have been done and *then* we would have talked about it, argued about it.

Carrie: Right. In a typical recommendation, the opportunity cost might be low, but in some cases it will be high. The real cost, though, is that those opportunity costs add up over the months and years.

Rose: I hadn't thought about the opportunity cost issue. For Ned and me—I hope I'm speaking for Ned—it's more about having the experts making the decisions while we're still watching carefully. Plus, as you say, we're both very busy and can't always respond in a timely way.

Ned: Yes, you're speaking for me as well, Rose. But one issue in my mind is this: If we give discretion to Spenser, will we really be paying as much attention as we should? Will we be learning about managing capital, getting better and better at it as time goes by? Do other clients have that issue, Carrie?

Carrie: Yes, of course they do, Ned. And it's a legitimate concern, especially as the decision makers in a family get older and younger family members start taking over. It's really important that those younger family members be well-schooled in capital management before they have to take responsibility.

Roger: For what it's worth, Ned, we've never noticed any difference in the attention families pay to their portfolios, as between discretionary and nondiscretionary relationships. We are basically on the same meeting schedule and the same reporting schedule for both kinds of arrangements.

Carrie: And as for the educational side, I haven't found that there's any difference between a family that discusses a recommendation before the trade is made or afterward. It's really the same discussion. And investment education is a core part of what a firm like Spenser does, whether it's for the existing decision makers or the younger family members. In any event, we'll be happy to talk about switching to a discretionary model whenever you're ready.

The Liquidity Table

Roger: Moving on, the next section of the performance report is a table showing the liquidity provisions of the various illiquid funds you're invested in. Moving across the columns, we show the manager, the specific fund you're in, the date you committed to the investment, the nature of the lockup (if any), how much notice is required to redeem all or part of the investment, how often you can redeem (monthly, quarterly, annually), when the next exit date is, and, finally, when notice is due if you want to make a redemption.

Billy: I have a dumb question—why are these funds so illiquid in the first place? Why are we locked up?

Carrie: Maybe the best answer is that the funds lock you up because they can.

[Laughter.]

Ned: Refreshing honesty!

Carrie: But there are other reasons as well. These are mostly hedge fund investments we're talking about. Other illiquid funds don't offer any liquidity at all—you get your money back when and if they themselves have a liquidity event. Those are the buyout funds, mezzanine funds, venture funds, some kinds of private real estate funds. In hedge, one very important advantage the hedge fund managers have is that they don't have to stand ready to pay out investors at a moment's notice.

Roger: There are a lot of investment opportunities that take a while to play out and that in the meantime are illiquid. If hedge funds had to offer daily liquidity, like a money market fund or most long-only managers, they would face a much-reduced opportunity set.

Ned: Also, Billy, while I'm not defending hedge fund managers, who I think will take whatever they can get, we don't allocate capital to hedge funds if we think we might need it. So this is longer-term capital we're putting to work, and we expect that we will do better with it than we'll do with short-term capital, at least on a risk-adjusted basis.

Billy: Okay, I can understand that. These hedge fund guys can do a lot more than what Carrie calls a long-only manager can do. And I remember that she told us that, all else being equal, the bigger the opportunity set a manager has, the better he should do.

Roger: Wow—maybe you should work at Spenser.

[Laughter.]

Billy: I'm just parroting what I heard from you guys! But my point is this. When I look at these performance reports, what I see is that the hedge funds have done worse—in some cases much worse—than the funds that offer good liquidity. Am I missing something?

Roger: One thing you might be missing is the *risk-adjusted* performance. Unfortunately, our performance reports—everybody's performance reports—don't show performance on a risk-adjusted basis. We do have a separate report we prepare once a year that shows risk-adjusted performance.

Carrie: Roger is right, But even on a risk-adjusted basis, many of the hedge funds in your portfolio have underperformed long-only funds, especially index funds.

Ellen: Does that tell us something?

Carrie: I'm afraid it tells us that in a strong bull market, long-only funds, and especially index funds will likely outperform hedge funds—and pretty much everything else. But when we design a portfolio we can't assume that we'll always be in a bull market. In a bear market, investors are very glad they own hedge funds.

Roger: And not just in a bear market. Good hedge funds will outperform on a risk-adjusted basis in virtually every kind of market *except* bull markets.

Carrie: As Ned pointed out, defending hedge funds is a tough business. They're mainly overpaid and are often selling what's nothing but beta as though it were alpha. But the best of them play an important role in portfolios, so we use them.

Ellen: I saw recently that even the president of the United States and a couple of the presidential candidates were saying nasty things about hedge funds. They cited a shocking statistic, but I forget what it was.

Geoffrey: I saw that. They claim that the twenty-five highest-paid hedge fund managers made more than all the kindergarten teachers in the country! Can that be true?

Carrie: I don't know whether it's true, Geoffrey, but I wouldn't be surprised. It does sound shocking, but keep in mind that you could say the same thing about the best-paid athletes, the best-paid movie stars, and so on. In a free market economy, people make what other people are willing to pay them. Should a guy who can shoot a basketball be making fifty million dollars a year? It's an unanswerable question. If fans stopped showing up to watch those guys play, their pay would go way down. But I don't see it happening.

Ned: And, again, I'm not defending hedge fund guys, but if investors think they're making too much money, all they have to do is take their money and go away. It's no different from the basketball players. Those statistics you're hearing are just class-warfare baloney during presidential election season.[2]

Geoffrey: Tell us what you really think, Dad!

Rose: How did hedge funds perform during the bad markets in 2008, Carrie? I know we were invested with some, but I don't recall how they did.

Carrie: The answer is, "good and not-so good." Overall, hedge funds did much better than long-only managers and index funds. The market was down nearly forty-five percent, while hedge funds were down about half that much. So that was good. But on the not-so-good side, hedge funds were down more than hedge fund managers suggested they would be down, so many investors were disappointed. And, finally, many hedge funds had been poorly managed in the sense that there was a mismatch between the investments the hedge fund was making and the liquidity they had offered their investors.

Rose: I'm not sure I understand exactly what that means, Carrie. How did it affect their performance?

Carrie: What happened is that, as huge redemptions came in, the hedge funds were forced to sell their most liquid assets. That left only very illiquid positions that could have been sold—if at all—only at huge losses. So many hedge funds simply slammed the door.

Suzy: Slammed the door? Didn't they have to honor redemption requests?

Roger: Technically, no. If you looked at the fine print in the limited partnership agreements, many hedge funds were entitled to raise *gates*. If a certain percentage of limited partners wanted out, the fund could say no.

Carrie: As a result, many investors found that while they thought they had quarterly liquidity, they were actually locked up almost like in a venture fund. Needless to say, they weren't happy.

Geoffrey: I can imagine! I'd have been pretty darned annoyed.

Carrie: Well, keep in mind that the investors who were hurt the most and who were the most angry were those who'd most poorly managed their own portfolios going into the crisis. They owned way too many risk assets and were much more illiquid than they should have been.

Ned: And some of those investors, as I recall, were huge university endowments.

Carrie: You're exactly right, Ned. As we've said many times, institutional investors have a kind of herd mindset. If Yale has sixty percent of its portfolio in illiquid funds, then XYZ University thinks it should have sixty percent. XYZ never actually thought about what that would mean to their day-to-day operations, or their capital plans, in a strong bear market.

Roger: Exactly. As the value of their long-only stocks plummeted, the universities experienced the *denominator effect*. In other words, the denominator (the value of the overall portfolio) went way down, while the numerator (the illiquid assets, which aren't valued regularly) stayed more or less the same. So instead of having a way-too-high sixty percent of its assets in illiquids, XYZ University found that it had something like eighty percent of its endowment in illiquids. They couldn't fund their capital plans, could barely operate on a day-to-day basis.

Carrie: Many universities had to cancel building programs, and some of them had to sell bonds just to meet funding needs.

Rose: Yes, I remember that now. It happened to my own alma mater.

Carrie: And if the truth be known, my own industry, the investment consulting business, was partly at fault. Firms that specialized in endowment accounts knew that those institutions wanted to emulate the Yales of the world. But instead of pointing out all the pitfalls associated with that, they actually encouraged it.

Roger: And one reason they encouraged it is that many consulting firms charged more for private equity and hedge funds than they charged for other kinds of assets. So there was a built-in conflict of interest. The consulting firms were incentivized to put more and more illiquid assets into endowment portfolios.

Billy: What a mess. Does Spenser charge that way?

Carrie: No!

Ned: We looked at how Spenser charges during the search process. The way an advisory firm structures its fee can cause all sorts of problems—conflicts of interest—if you're not careful. But Spenser charges a basis-point fee on the value of the overall portfolio.

The Investment Performance Reports

Roger: And now, finally, we get to the numerical performance numbers. We put this in the back of the report for a reason, namely, that we're trying to minimize client focus on short-term performance. Carrie has mentioned all the reasons, but the fundamental one is that quarterly and even annual performance of a portfolio or a manager is mostly meaningless. Yet, most advisors and their clients spend a huge amount of time looking at and dissecting these numbers. The result is almost always decisions that are wrong. And I mean wrong in the simple sense that the fired manager or abandoned strategy outperforms the new manager or strategy over the next market cycle.

Carrie: And so as we go through these performance numbers, we won't be saying things like, "Oh, this manager underperformed this quarter and here's why and here's what we're going to do about it." Instead, we'll look at unusual performance—good or bad—and explain why we *aren't* worried about it. We think that's the most educational way to look at the performance reports and the best way to avoid short-term decision making.

Roger: So the first page is simply a snapshot of the portfolio, showing its current value, how the assets are allocated, and also account flows. That last chart shows how we got to the current market value. We start with the most recent market value, then add (or subtract) net contributions to the portfolio. We then add income the portfolio has earned and add or subtract market appreciation or depreciation.

Carrie: The next few pages show how each sector of the portfolio performed in absolute terms and relative to benchmarks. It also shows the same data for each manager. We'll come back to all this, but go on, Roger.

Roger: The next page to look at shows the current asset allocation of the portfolio. Going across the top of the page, we show the current allocation to each sector, the long-term targets for each sector, the difference, and the minimum and maximum allocations.

Carrie: We look at this chart every meeting, but only to see whether the tactical bets we're making still make sense. We don't want to revisit the long-term strategic allocation at every meeting—that would be crazy. Instead, the long-term strategy should be briefly reviewed annually just to be sure it still makes sense for the client. Well, and also to make sure there haven't been any developments in the capital markets—maybe a new market sector we should be looking at or maybe older market sectors that have become less useful. But just *looking* at this page can be dangerous, am I right, Roger?

Roger: At certain times, yes. Clients who like to think of themselves as patient, long-term investors will look at their asset allocation during a strong bear market and decide that they're really a lot more risk-averse than they originally thought. So they move their target to stocks lower and their target to bonds higher.

Carrie: And those same investors will look at their asset allocation during a strong bull market and decide that they're really able to take a lot more risk than they originally thought. So they move their target to stocks higher and their target to bonds lower.

Rose: I'm not sure I followed all that, but I get the point—investors who look at their long-term asset allocation strategies too frequently end up changing them for the wrong reasons and at the wrong times.

Carrie: Exactly.

Roger: Okay, after the asset allocation chart we have Spenser's detailed market commentary, which some clients like to read but most don't.

[Laughter.]

Carrie: It's sad but true—we love it at Spenser, but we're in a distinct minority. However, I do want to draw your attention to the page where we highlight our tactical opinions. Can you explain this chart, Roger?

Roger: Sure. As we've discussed at earlier meetings, Spenser spends a lot of time developing the firm's opinions about market valuations in the various sectors. I want to emphasize—before Carrie yells at me—that there's a lot of difference between noticing that a sector is over- or undervalued and taking advantage of that fact in managing the portfolio. Markets have momentum and even though they might be overvalued, as they are today, they can get a lot *more* overvalued.

Ned: In other words, if you rotated out of a market sector every time it got overvalued, you'd leave a lot of money on the table.

Carrie: That's right. And if we rotated *into* a market sector as soon as it became *undervalued*, we'd likely come in too soon and take a lot of losses before the markets turned.

Rose: So how do you use this sector valuation information on the chart?

Roger: Carefully! As you can see, we show our long- and short-term return forecasts for each sector. In broad terms, if the short-term forecast is below the long-term forecast, we expect returns to be depressed over the next cycle. If the short-term forecast is higher than the long-term forecast, we expect returns to be good. The bar chart on the right shows this information graphically. As you can see, almost everything these days is either slightly or significantly overvalued in our opinion.

Carrie: So to answer your question, Rose, as a market sector gets more and more out of whack compared to its long-term valuation, we begin to take an interest. If we can't see any good reason for the odd valuation to continue, we'll begin to implement that view in our client portfolios.

Rose: In other words, buying into undervalued markets and selling out of overvalued ones.

Carrie: Yes, but slowly. As Roger said, markets have momentum and we don't want to get whiplash from it.

Ned: So, today, you'd be moving out of stocks?

Carrie (sighing): Well, actually, no.

Ned: But your chart shows all the stock sectors to be way overvalued!

Carrie: I know! But remember I said there might be a reason why valuations are as they are. Notice, further down the chart, that bonds are *also* overvalued. We're living in one of those weird times when both stocks and bonds look unattractive.

Roger: So the obvious trade—sell stocks and buy bonds—won't work.

Ned: Yes, I see that. So what do you do in such a world?

Carrie: We're living in what the investment industry calls a *TINA* world: There Is No Alternative to stocks.[3]

Rose: So we should just go ahead and buy stocks even though we might feel they are way too high-priced?

Carrie: Well, when you put it that way it sounds really dumb, doesn't it? But if I suggested to you that you should just go ahead and buy bonds even though they are way too high-priced, that would be pretty dumb, too.

Roger: So it's a real conundrum. It's something we debate at Spenser all the time. Most of our partners are pretty bearish on risk assets at the moment.

Carrie: The "top of the house" view, if you want to call it that, is to continue to own stocks at roughly your target allocations, but to be very wary. In other words, the consensus view at Spenser, if there is one, is that the equity markets are likely to continue to outperform the bond markets for at least the near-term future.

Suzy: So you're holding your nose and buying stocks?

Carrie: Well, we're holding our nose and *keeping* our stocks. Unless a new client comes to us with a serious under-allocation to equities, we're not likely to be adding to stocks in our client portfolios.

Ned: But, hold on here. I think I'm seeing a—what do you call it?—an agency issue.
Carrie: I was afraid somebody was going to notice that.
Billy: Wait—I don't know what we're talking about.
Carrie (sighing again): We spoke about agency issues at an earlier meeting, but as a reminder, agency issues arise when there is a conflict between the interests of the agent—that's Spenser in this case—and the principal—that's the Titan family.
Billy: I get that. But I don't see where the conflict arises.
Carrie: Do you want to respond, Ned, or should I just make a *mea culpa*?
Ned: Be my guest.
Carrie: By the way, I say *mea culpa* because I'm a senior partner and a literate highbrow. Roger would just say, "my bad."

[Laughter.]

Roger: No, I would say, "*your* bad."

[More laughter.]

Carrie: Anyway, here's the conflict. If you looked at my personal investment portfolio, what you would see is that I am at my absolute minimum exposure to stocks, and even then I own only the most undervalued stocks I can find. I own certain emerging markets stocks and a lot of hedge funds, including a bunch that have performed horribly in recent years, mainly global macro funds. I own bonds, but only short- and intermediate-term bonds. I own commodities. Does anybody (besides Ned) see anything wrong here?

[Roger raises his hand, everybody laughs.]

Rose: Yes, I think I see it. In your own portfolio you're doing what you think is the right thing. But when you're making recommendations to clients, you're recommending different strategies than the ones you yourself are following.
Carrie: I'm afraid that's right, Rose.
Billy: But why would you do that?
Carrie: You answer him, Roger, I'm too embarrassed.
Roger: It's because, in a nutshell, Carrie has a true investment time horizon that's longer than our clients' true investment time horizons.
Ellen: That sounds like obfuscation.
Roger: It was.

[Laughter.]

Carrie: Oh, all right, I'll fess up. What Roger means is that I don't like the looks of the equity markets now, and I don't like the looks of the bond markets, either. So I'm buying and owning assets that haven't been supercharged by central banker policies over the last few years. The result of this is that the performance of my personal portfolio looks bad—especially compared to, say, the performance of the Titan family's portfolio. But that's okay with me. I'm a very long-term investor and I don't like to lose money. I've been invested this way for about two years and I'm happy to stay invested this way for the foreseeable future. But my clients wouldn't like it at all.

Roger: I've seen Carrie's portfolio, and I can tell you that if all our clients were invested like Carrie, many of them—maybe most of them—would fire us.

Suzy: Because of bad performance.

Roger: Yes. But here's the rub—Carrie truly believes that her portfolio will beat yours over the next market cycle. So if she truly believes that—and, honestly, I think most of the senior people at Spenser agree with her and own similar portfolios—shouldn't we recommend those portfolios to the clients and hang the consequences?

Ned: You should. But you're not. That's an agency problem.

Rose: But is it, Ned? On the one hand, I see what you're saying. Spenser Advisors has business interests—not losing all their clients—that are interfering with the long-term quality of the portfolios they're building for those clients. But on the other hand, maybe Spenser is right: most of their clients simply won't tolerate underperformance long enough to allow the kind of portfolio Carrie owns to pay off. So it's not just that the clients might fire Spenser, it's that those clients won't own the correct portfolios under *any* circumstances.

Ned: So, going back to what Roger said a moment ago, the Spenser clients have investment time horizons—*real* investment time horizons, as opposed to the time horizons those clients *think* they have—that are too short to follow the strategy Carrie is following.

Rose: That's what I'm suggesting. Think about it in our own family. Carrie says her own portfolio has underperformed now for two years.

Carrie: Two and half, actually.

Rose: Okay, two and a half years. Let's suppose it takes another two and half years for Carrie's portfolio to pay off. Would we, as a family, tolerate five years of underperformance from Spenser? Or would we be out looking for another advisor?

[The Titans look around at each other, a bit sheepishly.]

Geoffrey: You're right, Mom. We'd be out looking for a new advisor.

Ellen: Even though, if Carrie's right, that would be the exact wrong thing to do. The new advisor would build us a riskier portfolio that might outperform for a while, but then we'd get killed.

Suzy: And I think Carrie *is* right. At least, if I was a betting woman, that's what I'd bet. Carrie's been in the business a long time and she's put her money on the line.

Ned: All right, let's say I agree with all that. But it still means we own the wrong portfolio for the long term. Maybe even the wrong portfolio for the intermediate term. Yet we won't accept the underperformance the right portfolio would have. What the hell should we do?

Rose: Carrie?

Carrie: In all honesty, I think you should do exactly what you're doing. That is, keep your equity allocation at about its target, but use the more cautious managers we've recommended and be ready to get less risky fast.

Rose: I suppose that's the best we can do. Maybe it's the best *any* nonprofessional investor can do. At least we know that Carrie and her partners are highly skeptical of the markets and will be on high alert for anything that would suggest we should start taking risk off the table.

Ned: So the worst idea would be to pile on risk, like a lot of investors, especially the retail crowd, are doing. The second worst idea is to do what we're doing. The best idea doesn't matter because we don't have the stomach for it. I tell you, it's a hell of a world!

QUICK NOTE

Here we have Carrie Knowlton admitting to a conflict of interest, but one that might possibly be unavoidable. As noted earlier, no matter how carefully an advisor designs itself, conflicts are certain to occur. But reducing them to an absolute minimum and acknowledging those that remain is an important best practice.

The Sources and Uses Report

Carrie: I think we've spent enough time walking through the way the quarterly performance reports are organized. Let's turn to what we call the *sources and uses report*. This is simply a very elaborate spreadsheet that shows the same portfolio information we show on the quarterly reports. However, the price data on the *S&U*, as I'll call it, is usually more current. More important, we can show a lot more analytics on the spreadsheets than we can on the performance reports. And these analytics focus especially on risk and risk-adjusted return. Roger, can you walk us through the S&U?

[Roger passes out the S&U for the family, a version of which is available on the companion website for this book at www.wiley.com/go/familycapital.]

Roger: As Carrie said, what's behind these pages is a complicated spreadsheet. The S&U shows the overall family wealth, then each generation's wealth. In your case, since there are two family units—the Ned unit and the Rose unit—there are separate rollups for each unit. We don't, however, roll up the two units into one overall portfolio, although we could certainly do that if desired.

Geoffrey: I actually saw this S&U report a few days ago because I was talking with Roger on the phone and he sent a copy to me. It's a pretty cool report, much more intuitive, at least for me. I like how it shows our overall family, then Dad and Mom, then Suzy, then me. But I don't understand why there has to be two reports. Can't this information be incorporated into the main performance report?

Roger: It depends on what you mean by *incorporated*. If you mean, couldn't we just bind it into the main report, the answer is "sure." But then we'd have to mail it out to you when we send the main report and the pricing wouldn't be updated.

Carrie: But if you mean, why can't the same systems we use for the main report be used to prepare this report, the answer is that it can't. Or rather, that it can't except at great expense, which we'd have to pass on to our clients.

Roger: That's because the analytics we use in the S&U are very special to our kinds of clients, and because we change them from time to time. We could ask our main vendor to program their reports to do this, but it would be expensive and hard to change.

Ellen: Why don't these reports roll the Grandchildren's Trust up with the other portfolios?

Rose: We specifically asked Spenser not to include the Trust, Ellen. We would have had to allocate it somehow between Ned and me, and then again among the four of you. Best to have a separate S&U for the Trust, I think.

Ellen: Fair enough. What about these elaborate cover sheets?

Carrie: They look more complicated than they are, Ellen. Basically, they're just a summary of the key facts for whatever portfolios are underneath them—usually the overall family rollup. We especially focus on the most important risk factors in the portfolio.

Roger: For example, at the top left we show the Asset Allocation Snapshot for the portfolios. As we've discussed, the asset allocation will, more than anything else, determine how the portfolio performs, so we want to focus on that.

Carrie: And note, at the bottom of that box, that we've added up the *market assets* and shown them as a percentage of the portfolio. The higher the percentage of market assets, the riskier the portfolio, all else being equal.

Roger: Then, as we go across the top of the chart we get into more detail on asset allocation. The first column says "Out of Band." That means, does the allocation for each sector fall between the maximum and minimum or is it outside that range? Obviously, unless there is some special rationale, all the sectors should be inside the band.

Carrie: The next columns show the percentage by which the sector allocation is over or under the target. This is useful because the targets can be quite different. For example, if the target for a sector is five percent and the allocation is at four percent, that's only a one percent difference. But it's a twenty percent bet against the target.

Billy: Aha!

Roger: Then we show the specific sector allocations in dollar and percentage terms, and also the target allocations and the minimums and maximums. That's very similar to what's shown in the performance reports, but since the dates, and hence the prices, might be different, we also show it here.

Carrie: I want to draw your attention to the middle box on the left, the one labeled "Protective Asset Coverage." That box shows your annual spending (as a percentage of your portfolio) as well as how many years of spending you have covered by your bonds and cash.

Suzy: And why is that important?

Carrie: Most of the time, the bond and cash allocation is there to help cover your annual spending and to control the price volatility of the portfolio.

Roger: When Carrie says, "help to cover your annual spending" she means that under normal conditions you can spend dividend income and bond interest and can also sell capital assets and spend the proceeds.

Carrie: Right, as long as you don't depend too much on either dividends and income or capital proceeds. But during an extended bear market, the spending coverage becomes very important. As stock prices drop, you don't want to be forced to sell those stocks. You want to hold onto them until the market recovers. This box tells you how long you can spend down your bonds and cash before you would have to start selling stocks.

Rose: You mean, actually selling the bonds, not just clipping the coupons?

Carrie: Correct.

Rose: And you mentioned at an earlier meeting that there is an optimal number of years of spending we should keep in high-quality bonds. Was it four years?

Carrie: I would say four years is the minimum. Except for the Great Depression, we don't see bear markets lasting more than two or three years. Of course, people who get very nervous during bear markets will want to have more years of coverage than people who don't.

Billy: You mean, there are people who *don't* get nervous during bear markets?

[Laughter.]

Roger: Only Carrie.

[More laughter.]

Carrie: It's true! When I see a bear market I think, "Wow, stocks are going on sale! Time to load up!"

Roger: The strange thing is, she's telling the truth. Around Spenser, Carrie is known as "The Undertaker" because she loves bear markets. It's like asking the undertaker how business is going, and he says, "It's terrific! People are dying left and right!"

[Laughter.]

Suzy: I hope somebody is going to explain the bottom box on the left.

Roger: Sure. That box shows, on the top line, the *implied beta* for the overall portfolio. A *beta* simply shows how volatile the portfolio is relative to the equity market. If your portfolio …

Geoffrey: Excuse me, Roger, but what's the difference between beta and implied beta?

Roger: Beta is a measure of past risk, based on historic numbers. Implied beta, on the other hand, is an estimate of what beta will be going forward. So if your portfolio had an implied beta of *one*, that suggests that, looking forward, the portfolio would likely be exactly as risky as the equity market.

Carrie: Then, looking further down the box, you can see that the equity beta in your portfolio is very slightly higher than the beta of the market. The market, by definition, is *one* while your beta is about one-point-one. The beta of your real assets is *higher* than the beta of the stock market, at one-point-three. But your hedge funds and other assets have much lower betas.

Ned: I don't think of real estate as being riskier—more volatile, at least—than stocks.

Carrie: Typically, Ned, REITs tend to correlate more with small-cap stocks than with large caps. We're measuring beta here against the S&P 500—large caps—which tend to have a lower beta than small caps.

Ned: But would that carry over to true real estate assets, I mean office buildings, apartments, that sort of thing?

Carrie: It's a little like private equity. The observed volatility of real estate assets might be low, but that's only because they can't be valued every day. If they could, as with REITs, their actual price volatility would be much higher than their observed vol.

Roger: In the next column you can see the contribution of each of those sectors to the portfolio's overall beta. Your market assets contribute zero-point-nine while the overall beta for the portfolio is zero-point-seven. So, obviously, the cash and bonds are bringing overall beta down.

Carrie: We like to keep an eye on these numbers especially as we make changes to the portfolio. Most of the time, adding a new manager or market sector won't have a huge impact on the overall portfolio beta, but sometimes it does. And beta can creep up, or down, if you don't keep an eye on it.

Roger: And we don't want that to happen. Once we've got your portfolio at the right beta, we want to keep it there unless your objectives change. Otherwise, you'll be owning a portfolio that's too risky or too cautious.

Rose: In other words, there is some implied beta number that you think is right for our portfolios.

Carrie: Yes, and it will be different for different family units. The more risk-averse a particular family member or unit is, the lower we will want the beta to be. And vice versa.

Ned: So the Trust would have a higher beta than Rose and me?

Carrie: Yes. The Trust's market assets have about the same beta as the Ned and Rose portfolios—zero-point-nine, but the overall beta for the Trust is point-eight-four versus point-seven for you and Rose.

QUICK NOTE

Spenser uses a *sources and uses* report—basically, a very elaborate spreadsheet—to get at various risk analytics. Other firms might use different software, but the main point is that wealth advisors need to show clients something more sophisticated than simple time-weighted returns or internal rates of return. How do the returns look on a risk-adjusted basis? Can you show performance attribution?[4]

Risk-Adjusted Returns

Carrie: There's one final report I want to show you. Roger, can you pass out the charts showing risk-adjusted returns?

[Roger passes out the charts, a version of which is available on the companion website for this book at www.wiley.com/go/familycapital.]

Carrie: We mentioned risk-adjusted returns earlier. All too often, investors look at their returns without considering the amount of risk they're taking. During strong markets, standalone return numbers always look pretty good. And then people are shocked—shocked!—to find how poorly their portfolios perform in bad markets.

Roger: So what these charts show is how your portfolios are performing on a risk-adjusted basis. Let's look at the Grandchildren's Trust as an example. On page one of this report you can see that we've plotted the return of the Trust, the return of the Trust's naive benchmark, and the return of the custom benchmark.

Carrie: Does everyone remember the difference between a naïve benchmark and a custom benchmark?

Ellen: I'll take a stab at it. The naïve benchmark is just stocks, bonds, and cash that has the same risk as the actual portfolio. The custom benchmark is made up of indexes in exactly the same allocation as the target allocation of the Trust.

Carrie: Wow, gold star for Ellen!

Billy: Are you reading that from somewhere?

[Laughter.]

Suzy: She has a cheat-sheet!

[More laughter.]

Ellen: I do not. It's just that I'm becoming an ace investor.

[Louder laughter.]

Roger: Well, Ellen's right. And as you can see on page one of the chart, the Trust has had about the same return as the custom benchmark over this period—a little below six percent. But the portfolio's risk level is much lower—around nine-point-five percent versus twelve for the benchmark.

Ned: That's pretty darn good—same return, twenty percent less risk.

Roger: Yep. Meanwhile, the naïve benchmark didn't perform as well—a bit under five percent—but had more risk, nearly eleven percent.

Carrie: And let me pause there to pat Spenser on the back. [Laughter.] The importance of a naïve portfolio is that you don't need Spenser to build it for you. You could save our fees and save all the fees you're paying to all the managers we've selected and just buy an S&P 500 index fund, a bond index fund, and open a cash account. You'd allocate among those accounts in a way that gave you the right risk level in terms of price volatility. Then ...

Rose: Hold it right there! How in the world would we know what level of volatility we needed?

Roger: Carrie's being too modest. But, theoretically, you could hire Spenser to design the right portfolio for you, then fire us and index everything at the same level of vol.

Geoffrey: That doesn't sound very ethical! Has anyone ever done it to you?

Carrie: Very rarely, and they never admit it. I remember a case a few years ago when a very smart guy hired us, let us build his portfolio, then got into a big argument with us about why he shouldn't just index everything. Then he fired us and indexed everything.

Geoffrey: At the risk level you'd worked out for him.

Carrie: Yes. But I honestly think that in his own mind he didn't think he was using us that way.

Geoffrey: Harrumph.

Carrie: But back to patting myself on the back—I don't want to forget about that. [Laughter.] As I was saying, you could save a lot on fees by just indexing everything, and the naïve benchmark shows how you would have done if you'd followed that strategy.

Ned: What we might call the Jack Bogle Strategy.

Carrie: Yes, and frankly, I think Mr. Bogle is absolutely right when he says that most investors would be better off doing that. But the Titan family, and families like it, aren't "most investors." You have a lot more at stake and you can afford far better advice. So by comparing the risk and return of the naïve portfolio against the risk and return of the actual portfolio—all on a net-of-fee basis—you can see what a difference good advice makes.

Ned: Have you calculated the actual amount of money we've made using good advice versus simply indexing?

Carrie: I haven't, but I could. Just back-of-the-envelope, I'd guess that over this period of time the Trust has added about thirty million dollars versus a pure index approach.

Suzy: Thirty million! Wow!

Carrie: If Spenser was a hedge fund, we'd get twenty percent of that.

[Laughter.]

Suzy: Even so, we'd be twenty-four million dollars to the good. I'm going to write a nasty letter to Mr. Bogle.

[Laughter.]

Carrie: Finally, I want to point out one other metric on this first page. Note in the numbers at the bottom that we show something called a *Sharpe ratio*.

Ned: I've heard of it. It's a measure of how a portfolio is doing relative to the risk it's taking.

Carrie: That's exactly right, Ned. Speaking more technically, the Sharpe ratio, which was developed by William Sharpe, a Nobel Prize winner,[5] is calculated by first subtracting the risk-free rate of return from the total return. In other words, an investor should be able to get the risk-free rate without taking any risk—just go buy Treasury bills. Then you look at the net return per unit of volatility and that gives you the Sharpe ratio. It's very handy because it's easy to compare Sharpe ratios. Basically, the higher the number, the better.

Roger: As you can see, the Sharpe ratio for the Trust's actual portfolio was about point-forty-three, while the Sharpe ratio of the naïve and custom benchmarks was lower: point-twenty-nine and point-thirty-five, respectively.

Carrie: In this case, the Trust's non-risk-adjusted return was good, higher than either of the benchmarks. But the real value of the risk-adjusted return calculations shows up when the portfolio's return is *lower* than the benchmark. In fact, if market prices remain as high as they are now, or go higher, the Trust is likely to experience returns that are *below* both benchmarks.

Roger: In other words, Spenser is going to get more and more cautious. But as we do, it's important for the client to know that we're still managing the portfolio well. In other words, the portfolio isn't underperforming because we're incompetent; it's underperforming because we are intentionally taking risk off the table. But as long as the Sharpe ratio remains positive, we're doing a good, workmanlike job for you.

Carrie: In other words, you can disagree with our strategy of lightening up on risk, but you can't accuse us of incompetence.

Roger: Just quickly on page two, there are other risk analytics shown. One I want to point out is the very last number on the right, which shows the maximum drawdown over any one year period. All these drawdowns are large, thanks to the financial crisis in 2008, but notice that the custom benchmark once lost thirty-seven percent in one year. The actual portfolio was never down more than about thirty percent in any one year. Saving capital on the downside is very important.

Carrie: By the way, when Roger says "one year," he's not meaning one calendar year. He means any twelve-month period. The Trust's maximum loss in any calendar year was, as I recall, about twenty to twenty-two percent.

Roger: Then, finally, on page three we show graphical representation of the drawdowns of the portfolio and its benchmarks.

Carrie: Okay, I guess that's it. Any questions?

Rose: I really like these risk-adjusted charts. Do you produce them every quarter?

Carrie: I guess we could, but typically we produce them once a year, or on request if a client is questioning why the market is so strong and his returns seem a bit on the tepid side. Did you raise your hand, Suzy?

Suzy: Well, this is sort of an awkward question, but I hope it isn't a stupid one. You were just talking about the market being strong and Spenser Advisors getting nervous, right?

Carrie: Yes. As we usually do when markets get high, especially when we don't see any good fundamental reason for it.

Roger: By *fundamental*, Carrie means that the economy is weak. These days, the markets are being juiced by the central banks.

Suzy: Okay, so what you're doing makes sense to me. But you could be wrong, right?

Carrie: Yes, we could be wrong.

Suzy: So quarters and years go by and your—Spenser's—Sharpe ratio continues to be positive but our returns continue to be low. We could have made a lot more money if Spenser hadn't gotten cautious. How long do we wait? Are you suggesting we should wait until the Sharpe ratio turns negative?

Carrie: Well, that's a hard question to answer, but let me take a stab at it. Yes, one way to know when to stop would be that the Sharpe ratio turns negative and stays there. At that point you would be entitled to conclude that Spenser was just *claiming* that returns were low because we were getting cautious. In reality, returns were low because we weren't managing the portfolio very well.

Geoffrey: But I think Suzy's point is that your Sharpe ratio could stay positive and you would still be managing the portfolio worse than it could have—or maybe should have—been managed.

Roger: That would happen if we got cautious way too early and stayed cautious way too long.

Geoffrey: Yes, I suppose so. How do we know when that's happened?

Carrie: Well, this is a self-serving answer, but I would say you should be very patient with an advisor that is producing positive Sharpe ratios but lower-than-benchmark returns during periods when stock prices are historically high.

Suzy: Because?

Rose: I'll answer that. It's because we are capital-preservation oriented. We don't mind so much missing out on the last increment of good returns during a bull market. What we really mind is losing our capital because we've been too aggressive during those bull markets.

Carrie: I couldn't have said it better myself!

SUMMARY

In this chapter we've reviewed one example of a set of investment performance reports for a wealthy family. Obviously, every wealth advisor will have its own take on what those reports will look like. There's no perfect answer to how performance should be reported on, but there are certainly best practices, and I've tried to illustrate some of them by listening in on Spenser's meeting with the Titan family.

As noted at the beginning of this chapter, one very important job of a wealth advisor is to try to keep its clients' attention focused on the long-term. Very few errors will cause as much harm to a portfolio as short-termism.

Beyond that, performance reports should be easy to understand and intuitive. In this case, Spenser writes plain-English summaries of the portfolios' performance, focusing on what's important and ignoring what isn't (or, in some cases, explaining why something that seems important actually isn't).

Performance reports should also be customized to meet the needs of the client. Too much customization will drive costs up way too high, but short of that extreme there is a lot of customization that can be done to make the client comfortable. Obviously, investors tend to focus on different analytics, and they also differ in terms of whether they prefer text, numbers, or graphical presentations.

Once a client's portfolio has been designed and the investment policy statement drafted, most of the client–advisor interaction will be around performance reporting. It is therefore very important for advisors to give a lot of thought to the organization and presentation of performance reports.

NOTES

1. Gregory Curtis, Greycourt White Paper No. 49: *The Outsourced CIO Model* (October 2010).
2. See, for example, Lawrence Delevingne's column, "Hedge Fund Managers Stung by 'Class Warfare' Rhetoric," posted 5/22/15 at http://www.cnbc.com/id/102700183.
3. The acronym *TINA* was historically associated with British Prime Minister Margaret Thatcher, who often used it to mean that there is no alternative to economic liberalism (democracy, free markets, free trade). In other words, to paraphrase Winston Churchill, economic liberalism is the worst way to organize a society, except for all the other alternatives.
4. That is, why did the portfolio perform differently from the benchmark? Was it manager outperformance? Tactical positioning? Well-selected opportunistic investments? Something else?
5. Sharpe was awarded the Nobel Prize in 1990, primarily for his work in developing the capital asset pricing model (CAPM). Remarkably, Sharpe's paper describing CAPM was initially rejected by the prestigious *Journal of Finance* in 1962 and wasn't published until 1964.

CHAPTER 10

Miscellaneous Investment-Related Discussions

PREPARATION AND USE

In this chapter we will listen in on excerpts of meetings between Spenser and the Titans as they discuss several miscellaneous investment-related matters. Of course, in a sense almost everything that is discussed between an advisor and a family is investment related in some way, but for convenience I've placed more obvious investment issues in this chapter and issues that are more remote from the direct investment world in the next chapter.

FAMILY INVESTMENT EDUCATION

There are few issues more important than ensuring that current and future managers of the family's capital learn their jobs well and become ever-more-effective at them. At some point in virtually every family–advisor relationship, the issue of education will arise. We'll listen in is as the issue arises in the Titan family.

Ned: Kids, Rose and I asked Carrie and Roger to be ready to talk about investment education today. I'm thinking of what we need to do to prepare the four of you to succeed Rose and me as managers of the family's capital, of course. But we're also thinking about ourselves. Rose and I want to get as good at this as possible.

Rose: There was a time when the Titan family members were mainly engaged in managing the family companies: Titan Industries and J. Titan & Partners. Ned, of course, is still the managing partner at the law firm, but I think he would agree with me that he's spending less time doing that as younger lawyers have joined the firm's executive committee. I hope I'm not speaking out of turn, Ned.

Ned: Not at all. I'm really semiretired. My grandfather was a remarkable man, but one thing he did wrong was to consolidate all power unto himself at J. Titan. Gradually, the most capable lawyers left and went elsewhere, some of them building firms that grew to be bigger than J. Titan. Dad and I vowed not to make that mistake, and so over the years I've invited our most talented lawyers to join the executive committee, which Dad established after Grandfather died. Each member of the committee is charged with some aspect of the firm's management, so my only duty is to convene the meetings and make sure everybody's doing his or her job.

Geoffrey: Sounds like a great gig, Dad!

Rose: Well, Ned's worked very hard over the years to build and improve the way the firm is managed, so if he's able to relax a bit now, he's earned it.

Ned: Whether I've earned it or not, I'm doing it! [Laughter.] In any event, Rose and I are both spending more time now at Lawburn, most of it dealing with the investment portfolio. As we've done so, we've realized that we have a lot to learn. And if Rose and I have a lot to learn, I can only imagine the depth of our children's ignorance.

[Laughter.]

Suzy: Hey!

Billy: We all know that Ellen's already an ace investor—because she told us!

Rose: Anyway, the Spenser folks are here today, not to educate us about investment matters, but to tell us how we might *get* educated. Carrie and Roger, you have the floor.

Carrie: Thanks, Ned. First, I want to point out the obvious—Spenser isn't an educational organization. Most of the ones that are, are nonprofit entities, and Spenser certainly isn't a nonprofit. So, typically, we do a couple of things that we're capable of doing and then we refer our clients to firms that are actually good at this stuff.

Ellen: I'm not sure I follow the nonprofit comment.

Carrie: The problem for Spenser is that while we and our clients both think investment education for family members is important, the clients won't pay for it and we won't offer it for free.

Ellen: I see. Is that right, Uncle Ned and Mom, you won't pay for it?

Rose: I think we would pay for it, don't you agree, Ned?

Ned: Of course! I mean, well, it depends on what it would cost …

Carrie: And that's what I'm getting at, really. Educating family members about best investment practices is, well, priceless. Most families run their portfolios into the ground and go broke—or nearly broke. And making sure family members are educated about investment issues is one important way of avoiding that fate. But everybody wants to know what it will cost, and when they find out the price they don't do it.

Ellen: Is it really that expensive?

Carrie: Well, we're investment people and we usually charge by basis points—a percentage of the portfolio. But at the end of the day all we have is our time and our knowledge and experience. And investment education, done right, takes a lot of time and a lot of knowledge and a lot of experience. If we're going to do it at Spenser, and do it right, we'd have to double our fees.

Ned: Ouch! Let's hear about those referrals.

[Laughter.]

Carrie: So let me go back to what I said at first. There are some things we're good at and that we can deliver without additional fees. First, there are these meetings with you. The absolute best way to learn the investment business is to attend these meetings and to participate in them. Ask questions, be skeptical.

Suzy: But a lot of the time what I'm hearing is gobbledygook. I mean, that's the way it comes across to me because I'm operating at such a low level of understanding.

Carrie: Yes, I understand that. But by attending and asking questions, you will *come* to understand it. It's hard work, like anything else that's worthwhile. But as you learn the lingo, it begins to make more and more sense, and pretty soon you're digging down into the weeds.

Ned: Okay, that's fair enough. What else is Spenser good at?

Carrie: We're good at answering questions. Roger and I can't know when what we're saying is making sense to you or not, but once you ask a question we can see what the issue is and resolve it with you. Sometimes that makes the meetings longer and often it gets us way off the subject at hand, but it's very much worth it.

Rose: Yes, I would agree that you've been very good about encouraging questions and answering them in terms we can understand. And we've been very good at getting these meetings way off the main agenda! What else can you do on the education front?

Carrie: We're good at making referrals. [Laughter.] In other words, we know when we've reached the limits of our ability to educate clients without being compensated. And we know people who can do a great job of it. They don't work for free, of course, but they charge only for the education part of it. So you can work with them a lot or a little, whatever you need.

Ned: Let's say we need more education than Spenser can provide—or will provide, anyway, without additional charges. Where do we turn?

Carrie: Roger?

Roger: I would say it depends on what it is you're looking for. If you want to get educated over a period of time, and have some fun and meet a lot of families very much like you, I would suggest that you join several of the affinity groups that exist for wealthy families. For example, and I'm mentioning these groups in alphabetical order:

- In Boston, there is the CCC Alliance. This is a group of very large families, many with net worths in the billions of dollars. They put on several conferences each year and also offer other opportunities for families to collaborate, buy-in-bulk and so on.[1]
- The Family Office Exchange, known as FOX, is based in Chicago. The families represented there are also quite large, and often the attendees will skew toward family office staff rather than principals, but there will always be lots of principals there. FOX is especially useful to families who have a family office.[2]
- There is an organization near Chicago called the Family Wealth Alliance that's really for advisors, not families. We find it very interesting and have been members for a long time.[3]
- I'll mention Fidelity Family Office Services, even though they are a commercial operation, because they've gained some traction in dealing with families who want to reduce costs and still get good reporting. As they've grown, they've also begun to offer peer-to-peer networking and presentations on best practices.[4]
- The Institute for Private Investors, IPI, is based in New York and is one of the granddaddies of the affinity groups. It was founded by Charlotte Beyer years ago but is now run by a firm called Campden.[5]
- There are also local affinity groups in individual cities that Titan could participate in. I'm sure you already know about the ones in Pittsburgh.

Carrie: Thanks, Roger. Many of the families we work with belong to more than one of these organizations. Over time, they may find themselves gravitating to one or the other, depending on their individual needs. We have a lot more information about all these organizations, so don't hesitate to ask if you'd like more information. They are all terrific, but each family will likely find certain ones to be more suited to their needs than others.

Rose: But I take it these groups do a lot more than just investment education, right?

Carrie: Oh, absolutely, Rose, but everything they do is related to making sure your capital sticks around for as many generations as possible. So I consider all that to be investment-related education.

Rose: Was that just a turn of phrase, Carrie, or when you say they want to help us keep our capital for "as many generations as possible" are you suggesting that it's inevitable that at some point our money will go away?

Carrie: I wouldn't use the word *inevitable*, Rose. Is everyone familiar with the term *entropy*? Well, just in case, it refers to a situation where things deteriorate from a condition of order to a condition of disorder. It's the way of the world—it's the way of the universe. And, unfortunately, it's the way most families trend. It's enormously difficult for a family to avoid losing its wealth over time, as we've discussed. There are simply too many centripetal forces at play.

Geoffrey: Shirtsleeves-to-shirtsleeves in three generations!

Ned: We know that's the norm, yes. But eventually almost every family will return to shirtsleeves. All it takes is one weak generation, one foolish generation, one profligate generation, and poof! It's gone.

Suzy: But there are families that have been wealthy for many generations. The Rothschilds, for example.

Carrie: The Rothschilds are a big exception to the rule, but they've done just about everything right.

Rose: Are there lessons there for us? What are they doing right?

Carrie: I don't have any inside information about the family, Rose, but my strong sense is that the Rothschilds have focused heavily on maintaining the emotional and intellectual capital in the family. They figure that, if they do that well, the financial capital will take care of itself.

Rose: Well, that's an important lesson. But back to family education—are there groups that just do education specifically?

Carrie: Of course. Roger?

Roger: I guess I'm the font of all wisdom on investment education.

[Laughter.]

Carrie: That's why I keep you around, Rog.

[More laughter.]

Roger: In terms of specific education, a couple of things come to mind. The Wharton School at the University of Pennsylvania, just across the state from you, puts on a really terrific Private Wealth Management Program in cooperation with IPI. It's held in Philadelphia, of course, but also at other locations around the country. Once you reach a certain level of understanding of investment issues, you might look into it. I'd say that Ned and Rose would find it useful now, and maybe in a few years it would be good for the kids.

Carrie: I hate to mention another option, but many large banks and trust companies offer investment education programs and some of them—I *really* hate to say this—are quite good.

Roger: Carrie sometimes has trouble controlling her competitive instincts.

[Laughter.]

Carrie: They typically run these programs for their clients, but if you're thinking of working with them, you can often wangle an invitation. Or Spenser could get you in.

Rose: Why would we have a relationship with those banks if we're already working with Spenser?

Carrie: There are lots of reasons, Rose. You might have your banking and credit arrangements with one of the large banks, for example. Or you might be using one of them as a corporate trustee. Some of our larger clients have custody, banking, and trustee relationships with a large bank and use Spenser for the investment side. As you know, we'll be looking at custody later this year. In addition to the usual criteria for selecting a custodian, you might want to check on what educational programs they have.

Ned: The banks will handle the traditional banking duties and let Spenser handle the portfolio?

Carrie: Yes. It's a fairly recent development, but the banks understand the attraction of open architecture to clients, and they don't want to lose the other business they have with the family.

Ned: They don't require that the families use the banks' products?

Carrie: Well, it varies. Some banks are totally open to what the family wants to do while others expect that at least some of their own investment products will be used.

Ned: Isn't that an obvious conflict of interest?

Carrie: Yes, but usually it's a small one. Remember that these are very large banks—JP Morgan, Bank of America/US Trust, Citi, Northern Trust, names like that. There will always be products the banks have that we consider to be quite good.

Roger: For example, most of these banks are really good at managing municipal bonds. One key for a bond manager is scale—trading bonds more cheaply, because you're trading in huge volumes, is a big advantage.

Carrie: Also, most of these banks offer index products that are reasonably competitive in price. And, depending on the bank, there may be other options as well.

Rose: What about books on investment issues? Are there any you particularly recommend?

Carrie: Gosh, Rose, there are so many of them that I hardly know where to start. In part, it depends on what level of knowledge you're starting from. For example, if you don't know much about the investment world you might need a pretty elementary book, something like *A Beginner's Guide to Investing*,[6] or maybe one of the *Rich Dad Poor Dad* books.[7] A lot of people enjoy Andrew Tobias's *The Only Investment Guide You'll Ever Need*.[8]

Roger: As you become more knowledgeable, you might look into something like Charles Ellis's *Winning the Loser's Game*,[9] a classic. Then I'd think about David Swensen's book that he wrote for individual investors, *Unconventional Success*.[10] As you probably know, Swensen is the chief investment officer at Yale and his book for institutional investors, *Pioneering Portfolio Management*,[11] is a classic.

Carrie: Amusingly, Swensen's book for individual investors basically says, "Do what I say, not what I do." In other words, if you try to follow what Swensen is doing at Yale you will likely fall flat on your face.

Suzy: Seriously? He doesn't recommend that individuals try to do what Yale is doing?

Roger: Carrie is perfectly serious. For example, Yale uses active managers almost exclusively, but he recommends that individual investors stick with index funds. He doesn't think individual investors should use hedge funds, whereas Yale uses a great many of them. And so on.

Carrie: Once you have a good understanding of the fundamentals of the investment process, there are lots of books that you should read and also keep around for reference. I'm thinking of Charlotte Beyer's recent book, *Wealth Management Unwrapped*.[12] For family office issues, there's Kirby Rosplock's *The Compete Family Office Handbook*.[13] Gregory Curtis's *The Stewardship of Wealth*[14] should be on your desk, along with Jean Brunel's *Goals Based Investing*.[15] There are many more terrific books out there and we have a long list of them if you're interested.

Ned: I've heard of goals-based investing, Carrie, but I don't really know what it means.

Carrie: I wish I was more knowledgeable about it myself, Ned. We're just starting to get our arms around it at Spenser. At bottom, it's an approach to thinking about your capital that tries to blend both Modern Portfolio Theory and behavioral science. As I mentioned at an earlier meeting, at Spenser we believe there is a lot of truth in both approaches.

Ned: Can you just give us an eighty-thousand-foot overview? Then we can buy Jean Brunel's book and look further into it.

Carrie: Sure. Go ahead, Roger.

[Laughter.]

Roger: How did I know that was coming? Basically, goals-based investing suggests that individual investors have a hard time understanding—or, really, internalizing—what is meant by things like *volatility* and other common investment terms. But almost everybody understands that they have various goals for their capital.

Rose: So one of an investor's goals might be to pay for his kids' college education, or buy a house, or retire.

Roger: Right. Or supplement their earned income with portfolio income. Each goal will have its own risk profile and its own time horizon. So you figure out what sort of investment strategy would be right for each of your goals and then you roll those strategies up into an overall portfolio.

Ned: Interesting. I'll take a look at the book and then maybe I could call you, Roger. But back to you, Carrie. It seems to me that you left off some real classics. How about *The Intelligent Investor*[16] and *Security Analysis*,[17] for example?

Carrie: Those are certainly classics, Ned, no doubt about it. [Then speaking to the Titan kids.] What Ned is referring to are two books by Benjamin Graham, often thought of as the "Father of Security Analysis." He was an early value investor and taught Warren Buffett, among others, at Columbia. *Security Analysis* was published in the middle of the Great Depression, and *The Intelligent Investor* came out in the late 1940s, but both are still in print and still very widely read. But those books are mainly useful to people who are buying and selling securities for a living. I highly recommend both books, but they won't be that directly useful to someone charged with overseeing a large pool of capital. At least, not until you become pretty sophisticated.

Rose: This is all extremely helpful, Carrie and Roger. Is there anything else we should be thinking about on the education front?

Carrie: Well, I hate to mention a competitor, so I won't. Roger, can you tell them about the relatively new online learning portal one of our annoying competitors has produced?

Roger (laughing): I assume Carrie is talking about something called Greycourt University. It's an online portal on the Greycourt website[18] designed especially for younger or newer investors. You click on the portal, then select the course you want to take and it launches. The courses are short and easy to get through, but also quite basic. But I understand that they are adding new courses all the time, so users will be able to drill down into subjects that really interest them. Did I get the right competitor, Carrie?

Carrie: I wouldn't know. [Laughter.] One last suggestion. Many families have found it useful to convene an annual family investment boot camp. Usually, it's scheduled around an annual family meeting, which might be held at some nice place. So everyone comes because getting together with the family in a vacation spot will be fun. But while they're there they have to attend the boot camp. The sessions don't have to be long and boring, and their main purpose is that *over the years* they will have an effect. Spenser often participates in these boot camps and we often recommend other speakers or presenters.

Ned: And this is just a guess, but may I assume that the presenters you recommend don't work for your competitors?

Carrie: You can bet your sweet bippy. [Laughter.] But one group I would recommend is an outfit called the Redwoods Initiative.[19] It's up in New York and was founded by a woman named Abby Raphel. Redwoods has a whole faculty of people who can both help educate you and help you think about what education means in your family and how to go about getting it.

Ned: Thank you, Carrie. Oh—and you, too, Roger!

[Laughter.]

Roger: Don't mention it.

QUICK NOTE

The main point of this section is the honesty with which Spenser admits its inadequacies in the education realm. Even if clients were willing to pay Spenser to work with them on investment education, it would take considerable time and preparation for Spenser to get up to speed. Although some wealth management firms claim to offer high-quality educational programs, the best of these programs will be conducted in partnership with firms that specialize in investor education.

ADDING VALUE TO THE TITAN FAMILY PORTFOLIO

Throughout the book we've discussed many ways value is added to family investment portfolios, but at one meeting Ned and Rose asked the Spenser advisors to address the issue directly and in the presence of the kids.

Rose: Kids, we asked Carrie and Roger to set aside some time at today's meeting to talk about how value is added to our portfolio—or subtracted, I guess.

[Laughter.]

Carrie: We're really good at subtracting value—we can do it with our eyes closed.

[More laughter.]

Rose: Most of these strategies will be suggested and implemented by Spenser, with our acknowledgment. But maybe there are some things we should be doing ourselves. How would you like to proceed Carrie?
Carrie: Let's start with the list Roger is passing out. I was just going to walk through them in order, but we can do it any way you like.
Rose: That's fine, Carrie.

[Roger's list is as follows:

- Asset allocation
- Tactical positioning
- Opportunistic investments
- Manager selection
- Transition management
- Rebalancing
- Transition management
- Tax management][20]

Asset Allocation

Carrie: Asset allocation is a subject we've discussed at length, so I won't belabor it. But I want to emphasize one very important point, namely, that the portfolio needs to be designed very specifically for your family and its specific needs, objectives, and family culture.
Billy: You mean, we shouldn't just do whatever Harvard and Yale are doing?

Carrie: I mean exactly that. And I also mean you shouldn't do what the family down the street is doing, or some family you meet at The Breakers.

Ellen: But if somebody else—whether it's Yale or the family at The Breakers (where I've never been in my life, by the way) ...

[Laughter.]

Geoffrey: Poor Ellen! She's lived a stunted life!

[More laughter.]

Ellen: We always went to that dumb place over in Naples that needed a good spiffing up about thirty years ago.

Rose: Hey, I liked that place!

Ned: Can we get back to the subject at hand?

Ellen: Sure, I was just saying that if somebody else—whether it's Yale or some other family—has a portfolio that's doing really well, why shouldn't we borrow what they're doing?

Carrie: I'm not suggesting that the Titans—or Spenser, for that matter—can't learn from what other families are doing. But I'm saying there's no point in trying to copy them wholesale. Can you suggest why that's the case, Roger?

Roger: Sure. I'd say there are two main reasons. The first is that just because some family is experiencing good results recently, that doesn't mean that whatever they're doing has any longer-term value. It's like hiring a manager just after he's put up recent strong numbers. You're likely to be very disappointed over the next cycle. The second reason is that even if the other portfolio is in fact well-thought-out (like Yale's), *you're not Yale*. Your needs are different, your objectives for your capital are different, you're a family, not an institution, and so on.

Carrie: In other words, even though the portfolio is a good one for Yale and its needs, it won't be a good one for the Titans and their needs. You'll end up abandoning it at the wrong time.

Tactical Positioning

Carrie: We've mentioned this before, but I'm not sure everyone was at the meeting. Positioning a portfolio tactically means moving the allocation around inside the ranges we've specified for the portfolio during the asset allocation process. So if your target allocation to U.S. large cap is twenty percent, with a range of fifteen to twenty-five, then all else being equal you would want to be at your target. But if we're concerned that U.S. large cap is seriously overvalued, we might suggest lightening up on large caps by moving down toward your minimum allocation of fifteen percent.

Roger: But not below it.

Carrie: Right. It would be a *very* unusual circumstance for Spenser to recommend going above a maximum or below a minimum in any asset class, although note that some sectors might have a minimum allocation of zero percent.

Rose: And you make these tactical decisions on the basis of market valuations you come up with via some internal process at Spenser, right?

Roger: That's right, Rose. We devote an enormous amount of time to looking at markets and trying to understand whether they are fairly valued, overvalued, or undervalued.

Carrie: And we publish our thoughts every quarter so our clients can see where we're coming from.

Ned: Yes, you showed us your valuation chart earlier, but it might be useful to send copies of it to all the kids.[21]

Carrie: Will do. But I want to emphasize how difficult it is to use market valuations intelligently. We might be quite confident that a particular market sector is undervalued by historical standards, but that doesn't mean we know how to get from here to there.

Roger: In other words, if we piled into every market sector that was undervalued, we would lose a whole lot of money.

Ned: Because undervalued markets can get a lot more undervalued.

Roger: Exactly. But as valuations become more and more compelling, we will definitely ease into them.

Carrie: Or think about it in the other direction. As market sectors become more and more overvalued, even though we know markets have powerful momentum, we will begin easing out of those sectors.

Rose: Which, as I understand it, is what you're doing now.

Carrie: That's right, and we're getting killed. The damn markets just keep going up. So we're underperforming our custom benchmarks in most client portfolios and were especially underperforming the simple, naïve benchmarks. If this keeps up, we won't have any clients left!

[Laughter.]

Geoffrey: I laughed, but this sounds like a really scary issue, Carrie. You're doing what you really believe to be right, but your clients are hating it.

Carrie: Well, not all of them, but certainly a minority of them are not liking it one bit. But if we don't give clients the best advice we can give them, what are we doing in this business, anyway?

Billy: Do you have any thoughts about what might cause a correction in the markets, Carrie? The Fed raising rates, for example?

Carrie: I don't, really, no. I doubt that it will be a Fed rate increase, though. That's been telegraphed and telegraphed, and when it finally happens it will be extremely modest. Also, it could easily be postponed depending on what happens with the U.S. and global economy.

Roger: It's often very difficult to know in advance what's going to cause investors to suddenly wake up and say, "Guess what? The emperor has no clothes!" I mean, back before 2007–2008, whoever heard of subprime loans?

Carrie: Right. So my guess is, it will be something out of the blue, something that in a different context wouldn't have mattered much, would hardly have been noticed by most investors. But because market prices are so high, it turns out to be the tipping point.

Geoffrey: Any idea how bad it will be when it happens?

Carrie: Nope. But the longer we go without even a correction[22]—much less a bear market—the worse it will be.

Rose: Well, that's comforting!

Opportunistic Investing

Carrie: Again, we've talked about this before, but finding interesting opportunities in the markets is a nice way to add value to a portfolio. Typically, these won't be huge investments. We might start at a one or two percent position, for example, and as we gain more confidence that we're right, we'll add to it. But rarely will we go above five percent.

Ned: If I recall correctly, these opportunities often arise because of the actions—especially the panic—of other investors. Can you give the kids an example?

Roger: I think one example we gave at an earlier meeting was junk bonds. When spreads between the yields on junk bonds and the yield on, say, U.S. Treasuries, are very narrow, as they are now, we don't like junk bonds and don't use them. But as spreads widen out, we begin to be buyers.

Carrie: That's certainly an example of an opportunistic investment, but I think Ned was looking for an opportunity that arises specifically because other investors are panicking.

Roger: Oh, right. So think of closed-end bond funds in the middle of 2007. They're owned by retail investors and sold by brokers. When the credit crisis hit, retail investors sold those funds in droves, driving the prices from small premiums above net asset value to substantial discounts.

Carrie: At which point your intrepid advisors at Spenser swooped in and bought them up, making lots of money for our clients. The bottom line is that sometimes we find lots of interesting opportunities in the markets, and other times, like today, we don't. We try not to force it—if the opportunities aren't there, they aren't there.

QUICK NOTE

Carrie makes an important point here: when it comes to identifying opportunistic investment ideas, it's important not to force the issue. The temptation to find a good investment idea when the broad markets are falling rapidly can be very strong. But as Carrie says, "if the opportunities aren't there, they aren't there."

Manager Selection

Carrie: We devoted an entire meeting to manager selection, so I'll try to be brief. I know that Ellen and Geoffrey missed that meeting. Basically, I think of manager selection as a defensive activity, not really a way to add a lot of value to portfolios. What we try to do is to find managers who are extremely competent and who have demonstrated that competence over a long period of time. That doesn't mean they will outperform while our clients are invested with them. They might and they might not. But the clients will get competent management.

Roger: There are always managers who, mainly out of luck, shoot the lights out for a couple of years. Investors flock to these managers and then are disappointed. We tend to avoid "hot" managers like the plague.

Billy: It's interesting to hear you talk like that, because whenever I hear people talking about their investment portfolios they are usually bragging about what a great manager they're invested with.

Carrie: And I'll bet you almost never hear anybody talking about what a lousy experience they had with a manager.

Billy: You're exactly right.

Carrie: People brag about the good ones and quietly forget about the bad ones. But the bad ones are buried in there, contributing to poor long-term performance. What you really want is *competent* managers. If the market isn't going their way, they might not outperform, but they won't really hurt you, either.

Transition Management

Carrie: We'll go over this one quickly. Once a family and its advisor know where they're headed—in terms of asset allocation, tactical positioning, and everything else—the question arises: How do we get from here to there? That's transition management.

Ned: What are the main issues?

Roger: First, there are the taxes, which have to be managed as securities are bought and sold. Then there is market timing, or not getting whipsawed.

Carrie: In other words, if you suddenly move out of a sector that then goes straight up, and into a sector that then goes straight down, you're probably not going to be happy.

Roger: So we tend to go slow. In fact, in some cases, we can take years to get from where we are to where we want to be.

Billy: Did you say *years*?

Carrie: Yes. Think about this situation—which isn't yours, of course. A family has spent many generations building a valuable business. Now they've sold that business and their advisor has designed a new portfolio for them, picked their managers, and so on. How quickly should they fund the new portfolio? [Everyone looks around. No one answers.] The answer might be *very slowly*. Typically, when a family business is sold, the timing of the sale reflects strong markets.

Ned: Because the buyer's stock price is high and/or it has lots of cash from big profits.

Carrie: Correct. So if markets are high, that's probably a *really* bad time to jump into them.

Rose: In effect, you're saying that if a family has just sold its business at a good price, almost by definition that's a bad time to jump into the markets.

Carrie: Right. That family has spent generations building the value. Why risk watching much of it go away in a few years?

Roger: We had this issue with several families who hired us in the late 1990s and again in 2006 or 2007. Those families were eager to invest their cash proceeds, but Spenser's advice was to go slow—in some cases very slow.

Ned: And it turned out to be terrific advice.

Rebalancing and Monitoring

Carrie: I know this sounds really boring, but simply rebalancing the portfolio regularly back to the target weights adds a lot of value over time.

It's better if you're an institution and don't pay taxes, but even for a taxable investor rebalancing is important. Does anyone know why?

Ellen: Uh ...

Rose: This is cheating, because I took notes the last time Carrie mentioned this subject. Basically, as I understand it, rebalancing is all about maintaining the correct risk level in the portfolio.

Carrie: Exactly, right, Rose. If stocks are on a strong run, pretty soon you have a lot more money in stocks than you started with and therefore a lot more risk. If stocks have been lousy, you end up with a lot more in bonds and therefore you don't have enough risk in the portfolio.

Ned: But rebalancing usually means paying taxes.

Roger: That's right, Ned, it usually does. And that's one reason why investors don't do it, at least not as regularly as they should. So they end up saving a few pennies on taxes and losing a lot of dollars when markets decline.

Rose: So how does an investor know when to rebalance—and pay the tax—and when not to? I mean, assuming the investor's portfolio is definitely out of balance.

Carrie: It's not easy—in fact, it's really difficult. So what we recommend is this. When you can rebalance without significant tax consequences, do it. When you can't, do it at least once a year.

Tax Management

Carrie: Taxes are a huge headwind for family investors. We pay federal income taxes, state income taxes, and sometimes we even pay municipal income taxes. Typically, state taxes aren't really high, but there are exceptions. There are some smaller states that have high tax rates: Hawaii, Oregon, Rhode Island, Iowa. But in terms of larger states, really high tax rates can be found in California, New Jersey, and New York. But no matter where you live, managing taxes is important.

Ned: You're talking mainly about not taking short-term gains when you can wait and take long-term gains, right? Plus offsetting gains and losses at the end of the year.

Carrie: I'm talking about that and much more, Ned. Roger, what am I talking about?

[Laughter.]

Roger: Carrie is talking about taking tax consequences into consideration in virtually everything we do. For example, when we put together our estimates for future risks and returns and covariances for the various asset classes, we give those assets a haircut depending on the likely tax consequence of owning and trading them. A simple example would be comparing venture capital and hedge funds. The former tends to result in deferred, long-term capital gains while the latter tends to result in current, short-term gains.

Carrie: When we evaluate managers, we look at them on a net-of-tax basis. How much alpha must a manager produce, for example, to overcome the tax drag of his trading?[23]

Roger: And, yes, we do look at short-term gains and evaluate whether it may be worth holding them long enough to convert them to long-term gains, although typically we rely on our managers to make that decision. And we hire those managers in part on their willingness and ability to make it.

Carrie: And we also try to offset short-term losses against long-term gains across the client's portfolio, as Ned suggested. But we do it all year long, not just in December.

INVESTMENT COMMITTEES

Rose: Carrie, would you explain to the kids what an investment committee is?

Carrie: Sure. These committees are really creatures of institutional board governance. If you look at the websites for leading institutional governance organizations like the Association of Governing Boards for Colleges and Universities,[24] you will see a great deal of information about the important role investment committees play in board governance.

Suzy: Does Spenser work with a lot of institutional clients, Carrie?

Carrie: We do, quite a few, but it's not our real bread-and-butter. We mainly work with families. I was just pointing out where the idea of the investment committee came from. I seem to remember that Ned sits on an investment committee for a nonprofit organization.

Ned: Yep. For the symphony.

Carrie: In the institutional world, the role of the investment committee is to oversee how the endowment is being managed. There might be in-house investment staff and there might not be. If there isn't, the committee will tend to be more proactive.

Ned: That's the way it is at the symphony. We hired a consultant—an institutional version of Spenser Advisors—and the job of the committee is to consider the consultant's recommendations and approve or disapprove.

Carrie: Years ago, some very wealthy families began to borrow the investment committee idea for their own families. They would recruit talented, thoughtful people and those committees would help the family manage its capital.

Roger: But note that there's a difference between the kind of committee a really wealthy family can recruit and the kind of committee smaller families can recruit.

Rose: And we would be a smaller family?

Carrie (laughing): Yes! When I say "very wealthy" families I mean families with at least a billion dollars, and often much more.

Roger: Families like that really are somewhat institutional in nature. And also, some of them are quite famous and people tend to be eager to work with them on their investment committees.

Geoffrey: Bill Gates, for example.

Carrie: That sort of family. And there can be some interesting benefits associated with being on those committees—co-investment opportunities, for example.

Ned: You're suggesting—I think you've already suggested in an earlier meeting—that the Titans are unlikely to be able to attract really good people if we set up an investment committee.

Carrie: I'm afraid so, Ned. Even a small college with no more money than the Titan family will have thousands of alums and many will be highly qualified investment professionals. All those grads are interested in the college and many will be willing to commit their time to serving on an investment committee. Your family doesn't have that kind of fan base.

Ellen: In fact, since we're the "one percent," we don't have any fans at all!

Rose: So should we give up on the idea of forming an investment committee?

Carrie: Not at all! You just need to think beyond the institutional model. For one thing, most families won't want their investment committee to have any actual authority over the capital. The committee should be advisory in nature, with the family having the final say.

Roger: And you may want to limit your search for good committee members to people who already have an interest in the family—lawyers, accountants, trustees, bankers, and so on.

Rose: Even though most of those people aren't investment professionals?

Carrie: Yes. What you want in the room are thoughtful, honest people who have the family's best interests in mind. Many families find that kicking around ideas with a broader group like that really helps.

QUICK NOTE

The real value of an investment committee for a family of Spenser's size is the one Carrie mentions: having other thoughtful people in the room when difficult decisions need to be made. Otherwise, the committee should be advisory only, not very large (maybe three non-family members at most), and no one who has any conflict of interest should be considered.

Geoffrey: Couldn't we offer to pay some big shots to serve on our committee? I know some families pay their investment committee members.

Carrie: You could do that, but I doubt that it would be effective, Geoffrey. The kind of people you want don't need the money and wouldn't be motivated by it.

Roger: That's right, Carrie. It's true that some families pay investment committee members, but that's really almost an honorarium to show the people that their service is valued.

Ned: So, kids, what Rose and I are planning to do is to pull together a master list of possible committee members. We'll show it to you and to Carrie and Roger and see where we end up.

Rose: And Carrie is exactly right—we want the committee to be advisory only.

Roger: I'm not sure I should bring this up—I haven't cleared it with Carrie …

Carrie: No problem, Rog—it's only your career that's at stake.

[Laughter.]

Roger: Uh-oh. What I wanted to put on the table is that many families have hired someone like Carrie. She might serve on the family's investment committee or advisory committee or just be a compensated advisor. Carrie already does this for a couple of families, and while I don't know whether she would do it for a Spenser client, it's something to think about.

Ned: What about it, Carrie?

Carrie: Spenser has a policy of not permitting us to serve as compensated advisors to clients of the firm—I mean, other than the general fee we charge as a firm. I could do it after I retire from Spenser, of course. Today, I only do it for families who aren't clients.

Rose: Are there other "Carries" out there we could consider?

Carrie: You bet. I know of two or three people off the top of my head who would be good, and we can look further into it.

SOCIALLY RESPONSIBLE INVESTING

Rose: I asked Carrie and Roger to talk about socially responsible investing today because Ellen has expressed interest in the subject. And no sooner did it get on the agenda than Suzy and Geoffrey also expressed interest.

Ned: Billy, I guess that leaves you and me as the only sensible people in the room.

Ellen: Hey!

Carrie: Well, this is a very large subject, but it's one that many people are talking about these days. Quite frankly, at Spenser we're a little late out of the gate. For years and years this wasn't a hot topic in our client base, but now suddenly it is, so we're boning up on it.

Ned: Well, let me just get this out on the table. Nobody will be surprised, but I don't want any part of any social investments that will reduce our returns, either on the personal side, the trust side, or the foundation side. As a trustee, I think it would be a breach of fiduciary responsibilities to accept a lower rate of return just to "make the world a better place." As we've already discussed at an earlier meeting, people think they have all the answers, but they don't.

Rose: You're right, Ned—we're not surprised.

[Laughter.]

Ned: Do you disagree with me, Rose?

Rose: I honestly don't know. What I do know is that socially oriented investing has come a long way in recent years. Maybe ten years ago I would have agreed with you for sure, but things have changed. For example, a lot of community foundations are now doing what's called mission-related investing.

Ned: Which is what?

Rose: I should know, because I was on the board of our community foundation. Carrie, can you help out here?

Carrie: A bit, yes. Mission-related investing is a way of looking at all your resources to carry out your mission. In other words, not just your grants budget. So suppose a foundation is making grants to support affordable housing for low-income people. They might also buy bonds issued by the companies that are building the housing.

Ned: I'll bet those bonds don't return as much as more traditional bonds, especially on a risk-adjusted basis.

Carrie: Actually, Ned, sometimes they do, especially if they have a guarantee by a financially sound party. But some foundations doing mission-related investing are willing to accept a lower rate of return because, to them, it's just like making a grant. When you make a grant, you don't expect to get that money back; you just hope it will do some good.

Billy: But, really, a grants budget is different from an investment portfolio. If the portfolio doesn't do well, the grants budget will decline and you won't be doing so much good any more.

Carrie: True enough. You wouldn't want to put your entire endowment in these kinds of investments, but most community foundations that do this sort of thing limit it to, say, ten percent of the endowment. Then, if it works out, they might gradually expand that amount.

Geoffrey: I've heard a lot about all this social investing stuff, but frankly I find it very confusing. There's "socially responsible investing," and there's "mission-related investing," and there's "impact investing," and probably a bunch more I forgot. What's the difference?

Roger: Just to get the discussion started, let me read this definition of "sustainable development" that was prepared by the World Commission on Environment and Development back in 1987:

> *Sustainable development is development that meets the needs of the present without compromising the ability of future generations to meet their own needs. It contains within it two key concepts: The concept of "needs," in particular the essential needs of the world's poor, to which overriding priority should be given; and the idea of limitations imposed by the state of technology and social organization on the environment's ability to meet the present and future needs.*

Ned: Gobbledygook.

Rose: Now, Ned .... Can you parse that for us, Carrie or Roger? How does it translate into socially responsible investing?

Carrie: Well, the basic idea is that investing shouldn't just be about returns, that there should be additional criteria we should be looking at, having to do with the environment, social issues (in other words, issues surrounding poverty and the distribution of wealth, discrimination, and so on), and the way corporations make decisions, that is, governance issues. In the social investment world, this is known as *ESG* investing, investing that considers *environmental, social*, and *governance* factors.

Ned: And which—oh, by the way—makes a nice profit. Not likely.

Carrie: Back to Geoffrey's question, there's no broad agreement on what these social terms mean. In my own experience, socially responsible investing, or *SRI*, usually means screening companies for desirable corporate practices—say, environmental practices, workplace diversity, that sort of thing. SRI can also mean negative screening—not investing in weapons manufacturers, tobacco companies, and so forth.

Roger: Impact investing, by contrast, usually means assembling capital and investing it in ways that make a social, environmental, or other impact. Probably the most famous example is microfinance. People have established venture capital–type funds that make micro-loans to small businesses or individuals in poor countries.

Ellen: I must say, it makes me uncomfortable to think we're investing in firearms companies and things like that.

Ned: You don't believe in the United States Army, Ellen? You think we should disarm ourselves?

Rose: Now, Ned, we're not here to argue about specific kinds of social investing, but only to understand what it is.

Ellen: Before I was interrupted by Uncle Ned, I was about to say that, while those things make me uncomfortable, what I'd really like is to make a positive difference, not just avoid doing something unconstructive.

Suzy: I agree with that.

Billy: I wouldn't necessarily *disagree* with it if it was something I thought could make a difference. Geoff said earlier that he would be interested in helping poor people and underserved people start businesses. I like that idea, too.

Suzy: What about building schools for girls in Afghanistan?

Geoffrey: How would we get a return on that?

Suzy: Afghani charter schools?

[Laughter.]

Billy: You're thinking way outside the box cousin!

Carrie: If you're interested in pursuing this sort of thing further, Spenser could do two things for you. First, we could introduce you to people who do this kind of investing and who can explain what they do and what their returns have been. Second, we can show you SRI and impact investment opportunities as we find them and if they look good.

Rose: When you say, "people who do this sort of thing," what do mean, Carrie? Do you mean people who can show us social investment opportunities? I don't think we're ready for that.

Carrie: Well, as they say in the movies, "it's complicated." A lot of the best people in the social investment world are actual investors, people who are doing real deals. Otherwise, there's a kind of airy-fairy aspect to it all. And, of course, since it's such a rapidly growing field, there are lots of people jumping into it and not all of them are good—or even honest. Roger, whom do we like in this space?

Roger: Well, like Carrie said, we're coming late to this game so our knowledge isn't yet as broad or deep as it should be. That said, we've worked with these firms and respect what they've done for our clients:

- There is a firm called Imprint, which does a great job defining terms, types of SRI, and describing the nature of investment opportunities.[25] Note that Imprint is now owned by Goldman Sachs.
- Aperio also does a good job defining this space. They have helped several of our clients. Basically, they are indexers who have developed a wide range of SRI screens.[26]
- I wouldn't overlook any local resources. In most large cities there are probably investors—maybe on the foundation or institutional side—who've had a lot of experience and are happy to share that experience with you. Some towns have even created advocacy groups that operate in this space.
- There is a group in New York that we are less familiar with but that comes well-recommended. They are called Veris Wealth Partners.[27]

Carrie: What else can we tell you? I can see that Ned is eager to get started with social investing.

[Loud laughter.]

QUICK NOTE

As this discussion shows, socially responsible investing can be a divisive subject even within families—especially between generations. But it is an idea whose time has come and it is incumbent on wealth advisory firms to study ESG and similar kinds of investments and to be ready to discuss them with their clients. ESG managers, like traditional managers, need to be thoroughly vetted and the best of them added to the firms' recommended lists.

SUMMARY

In this chapter we've discussed a number of different issues that families and their advisors grapple with from time to time. I won't rehash the discussions reproduced above but will merely add a few thoughts as follows.

Family Investment Education

Although there are many resources available to advisors and families on the subject of investment education, this is one activity that *needs to be led by the advisor*. There are two reasons for this. The less important reason is that family members will learn much faster if they are learning on their own portfolio. That money is critically important to them and this tends to focus their attention. The second reason is that *it is in the advisor's own interest to lead the educational work*. In the event of the death or disability of the key decision maker(s) in the family, authority over the portfolio will pass to others—the surviving spouse or the children. Advisors who haven't bothered to lead the educational activity are highly likely to find that they've lost the entire account when a sudden decision-making or generational change takes place.

Adding Value to Family Investment Portfolios

This subject has been alluded to in earlier chapters, but it reappears here because of its crucial importance. Families—and, for that matter, advisors themselves—need to be very clear about how value is added to family investment portfolios and how it isn't. As noted, many individual investors imagine that most of the value is added by managers, but this is very much not the case.

Asset allocation. For purposes of this chapter, we haven't focused on the details of how asset allocation is performed, but only on one vital issue: *that the overall strategy for a family portfolio must be designed and managed for the needs and objectives of that family*. The way other families do things, and the way Harvard, Yale, and Stanford do things, may be interesting and informative, but slavishly following someone else's portfolio is a short road to ruin.

Tactical positioning. There is a very fine line between the tactical positioning of a portfolio—which can add value—and market timing—which can't. The main difference is the amount of effort and insight the advisor puts into the sector valuation activity. But in addition, focusing on small adjustments to the portfolio, and especially on adjustments that move the portfolio away from risk—from overvalued sectors—will also be important.

Opportunistic investing. Finding interesting opportunities in the capital markets is something that comes and goes. Sometimes there are so many interesting opportunities that it's impossible to take advantage of all of them. Other times, virtually everything is overvalued. Thus, opportunistic investing requires both judgment and patience. One very interesting aspect of opportunistic investing is that it can keep a client's morale up during difficult market environments. Finding an interesting way to make money while broader markets are negative can show a client that all is not lost.

Manager selection. As noted in the previous discussion, the goal should not be to select managers who will outperform, since this simply can't be reliably done over time frames appropriate for most family portfolios. Instead, what's called for is the engagement of managers who will be competent and predictable in their management of the clients' assets.

Transition management. Simply transitioning the old portfolio to the new portfolio overnight might be the best way to proceed—but that will rarely be the case. Taxes, sector valuations, and costs need to be considered and could slow the transition considerably.

Rebalancing and monitoring. Because of the tax impact, rebalancing won't add as much value to family portfolios as it does to institutional portfolios, but it is still very much worthwhile. The reason it's worthwhile, though, has less to do with improving returns than with controlling the risk level of the portfolio.

Tax management. Tax management needs to be built into the very fiber of a family advisor. Between federal, state, and local income and capital gains taxes, the failure to be attentive to tax issues will cause far too much of the portfolio to be frittered away in unnecessary costs. As noted in the discussion, the management of investment taxes needs to be built into everything the advisor does from the beginning. You simply can't design the portfolio, hire managers, and then look for ways to save on tax costs—by then it's way too late.

Investment Committees

Establishing a family investment committee is a challenge—unlike the situation with institutional investors. But a good investment committee, containing trusted family advisors, can be of inestimable assistance to a family when hard decisions have to be made or when market conditions are bad.

Socially Responsible Investing

SRI and impact investing are here to stay. Many older family members—like Ned Titan—will be uncomfortable with the idea of investing for any reason other than to produce sound risk-adjusted returns. But younger family members will be more engaged in the investment process if at least some sort of social investing can be on the table. Advisors who aren't up-to-speed on social investing need to get up-to-speed quickly.

NOTES

1. CCC Alliance LLC, 10 Liberty Square, 3rd Floor, Boston, MA 02109, 617-457-8368, http://www.cccalliance.com/.
2. Family Office Exchange, Inc., 100 S. Wacker Drive, Suite 900, Chicago, IL 60606, 312-327-1200, https://www.familyoffice.com/.
3. Family Wealth Alliance, 240 E. Willow Avenue, Suite 102, Wheaton, IL 60187, 630-260-1010, http://fwalliance.com/.
4. Fidelity Family Office Services, https://familyoffice.fidelity.com/.
5. Institute for Private Investors, 17 State Street, New York, NY 10004, 212-693-1300, https://www.memberlink.net/content/innovative-investor-education.
6. Alex H Frey and Alex Fre, *A Beginner's Guide to Investing: How to Grow Your Money the Smart and Easy Way* (Seattle: CreateSpace Independent Publishing, 2012).
7. For example, Robert T. Kiyosaki, *Rich Dad Poor Dad: What the Rich Teach Their Kids about Money That the Poor and Middle Class Do Not!* (Scottsdale: Plata, 2011).
8. Andrew Tobias, *The Only Investment Guide You'll Ever Need*, rev. ed. (New York: Mariner Books, 2011).
9. Charles D. Ellis, *Winning the Loser's Game: Timeless Strategies for Successful Investing*, 6th ed. (New York: McGraw Hill, 2013).
10. David Swensen, *Unconventional Success: A Fundamental Approach to Personal Investment* (New York: Free Press, 2005).
11. David Swensen, *Pioneering Portfolio Management: An Unconventional Approach to Institutional Investment*, rev. ed. (New York: Free Press, 2009).
12. Charlotte B. Beyer, *Wealth Management Unwrapped* (New York: RosettaBooks, 2013).
13. Kirby Rosplock, *The Complete Family Office Handbook: A Guide for Affluent Families and the Advisors Who Serve Them* (Hoboken, NJ: Bloomberg Press, 2014).
14. Gregory Curtis, *The Stewardship of Wealth: Successful Private Wealth Management for Investors and Their Advisors* (Hoboken, NJ: John Wiley & Sons, 2013). See also Curtis's *Creative Capital: Managing Private Wealth in a Complex World* (Lincoln, NE: iUniverse Press, 2004).

15. Jean L. P. Brunel, *Goals-Based Wealth Management: An Integrated and Practical Approach to Changing the Structure of Wealth Advisory Practices* (Hoboken, NJ: John Wiley & Sons, 2015).
16. Benjamin Graham, *The Intelligent Investor: The Definitive Book on Value Investing: A Book of Practical Counsel*, rev. ed. (New York: HarperCollins, 2003).
17. Benjamin Graham and David Dodd, *Security Analysis*, rev. ed. (New York: McGraw Hill, 2008).
18. http://www.greycourt.com/greycourt-university/.
19. http://www.redwoodsinitiative.org/.
20. See Greycourt White Paper No. 60, *How Wealth Advisors Add Value* (October 2014), available at http://www.greycourt.com/white-papers/white-papers-by-date/.
21. The valuation chart was discussed in Chapter 8.
22. By convention, a *correction* means a market drop of 10%, while a bear market requires a 20% drop. A *crash*, a less well-defined term, usually refers to a price drop of 10% or more in a very short period of time, often in one day.
23. See Robert H. Jeffrey and Robert Arnott's classic article, "Is Your Alpha Big Enough to Cover Its Taxes?" *Journal of Portfolio Management*, 19, no. 3 (Spring, 1993).
24. http://agb.org/briefs/investment-committees.
25. https://yoursri.com/.
26. https://www.aperiogroup.com/.
27. http://www.veriswp.com/.

CHAPTER 11

Miscellaneous Non-Investment Discussions

PREPARATION AND USE

A wealth advisor must understand not just investments, but wealth itself. No family can manage its capital effectively without understanding and succeeding at many challenges that don't necessarily seem all that directly related to money or investments. And no wealth advisor can expect to succeed in the wealth management business if it understands nothing more than markets. Moreover, despite its one syllable, "wealth" is a very large and very loaded word. In a country where middle income families have struggled for several decades, and where a grave financial crisis caused even more hardship, many wealthy families will wonder about their position in the society. Advisors can't resolve these issues, but they need to be cognizant of them and to be willing to pursue what can sometimes be awkward conversations with their clients.

HIRING A CUSTODIAN

Carrie: Okay, here's a quiz for the kids: What's a custodian?
Billy: Somebody who has custody.

[Laughter.]

Carrie: Well, that's right, Billy, but I was hoping for something a little more specific.
Billy: That's as specific as I can get!

[Laughter.]

Suzy: Give us a hint!

Carrie: Okay, here's a hint. When we go over your investment performance report, what you see is a lot of managers, and those managers own a lot of stocks and bonds (or similar assets). Where exactly are those assets?

Billy: The manager has them.

Carrie: Nope.

Suzy: Some broker has them.

Carrie: Closer. Some kinds of assets, especially hedge fund assets, are usually held at what's called a *prime broker*. But not ordinary stocks and bonds.

Ned: Another hint—it starts with a *B* and isn't a broker.

Suzy and Billy (simultaneously): Bank!

Carrie: Bingo!

Ellen: But what can that mean? We hire managers to buy and sell stocks and bonds. If our stocks and bonds are at a bank somewhere, is the bank really our manager?

Roger: No. Your investment manager is the organization that makes buy–sell decisions for your account, Ellen. The way it works technically is that you sign a limited *power of attorney* with the manager, and that POA gives the manager the right to direct the bank, which actually holds your cash and securities. So the manager can in effect say to the bank, sell IBM and buy Google. The bank then tenders the IBM shares and, once it has the proceeds in hand, buys Google, which it then holds. But the IBM stock never leaves your account at the bank until the cash has been received. And the Google stock never leaves your account until the manager says "sell it" and the bank has received the cash.

Carrie: And this is a very important safeguard. Suppose you had a dishonest manager. That manager takes your cash and claims to be buying and selling stocks, but actually he's buying Ferraris and yachts. The next thing you know, the manager's in Brazil and your money's gone.

Ned: I hope you're joking about that!

Carrie: I wish I was, Ned. But it's happened when people trust their managers to hold their cash and securities. In the case I just mentioned, investors who had their assets held by a bank custodian rather than the investment manager would have two important advantages. First, the bank statements they received would serve as a check on the manager's claims of what he's doing and what returns he's making. Second, when the manager goes to Brazil, he's going without your assets, because those assets are at the bank.

Geoffrey: I'm liking this custodian idea better and better!

Roger: This was before my time, but there was actually a case like this right here in Pennsylvania. A guy was investing money for a bunch of school districts, and he told them all that it would be cheaper to let him custody the assets rather than putting them in bank custody. He then proceeded to spend the money on his own lifestyle. He went to jail, but the clients' money was gone.

Carrie: In other words, it's not just a best practice, it's an essential practice.

Ned: And I hasten to add that we have, and have had for a long time, a bank custodian in place holding our assets.

Suzy: What did we do before that, Dad?

Ned: Our assets were held at a brokerage firm.

Suzy: Is that the same thing? Were our assets safe during that period?

Ned: Carrie?

Carrie: Yes, I think so, Ned. The broker also stood between the manager and your assets, which was good. The slight difference is—I'm getting down into the weeds, now—when your assets are held at a bank, they are segregated from the bank's own assets. If the bank goes bankrupt, your assets aren't subject to the claims of the bank's creditors. It's not quite so clear with a broker.

Roger: With a broker, it's mainly insurance that protects you in the event of a brokerage bankruptcy or fraud. Normally, that insurance is adequate and you'll be made whole. But in the event of a widespread crisis that bankrupts many brokers, query whether the insurance companies wouldn't also go bankrupt. But that's a pretty remote eventuality.

Geoffrey: But today our custodian is a bank, right? So we don't have to worry about insurance.

Rose: That's right, Geoff. But the reason we're having this discussion isn't just for educational purposes. Ned and I have asked Spenser to evaluate our custodian and possibly recommend a new one.

Billy: Why's that, Mom? Are we unhappy with the bank?

Rose: It's a good question, Billy. The answer is, we don't know enough to know whether we should be happy. We picked our current custodian because they were local and we knew about them. But there are lots of other custodians, and we'd like to know we're in the right place.

Ellen: What is it that determines whether a bank is a good custodian? I don't really know what a custodian does. I understand, in general, that they hold our assets, but I'm not sure what exactly that means or what else they do. Carrie?

Carrie: Roger?

Roger: By an amazing coincidence, I happen to have a list of services a master custodian provides.

[Roger distributes the list, which is as follows:

- Provide for safekeeping of the client's investment assets domestically and internationally.
- Maintain accurate and timely records of the client's investments.
- Consolidate assets as necessary for reporting purposes.

- Clear and settle trades made at the direction of the client's money managers.
- Transfer assets as directed only by the client.
- Pay bills for various services (e.g., money manager fees).
- Provide multicurrency reporting for international assets.
- Prepare reports on a cash or accrual basis.
- Report transactions on a trade or settlement date basis.
- Maintain records and processing trades on a tax-lot basis.
- Maintain tax characteristics (interest, dividends, cost basis, etc.).
- Maintain compliance monitoring systems to ensure that managers adhere to whatever investment guidelines the client has put in place.
- Provide unitized accounting and interim valuations.
- Prepare tax returns or prepare the information to be submitted to the client's tax accountant.
- Maintain accounting for family investment partnerships (note that only a few very high-end custodians offer this service).]

Finally, most institutions that offer custodial services also offer many other financial services, including banking, trust services, asset management, credit services, and so on.

Billy: Wow, that's a lot of services! But why did you call it a *master* custodian, Roger?

Roger: Typically, a wealthy family will have more than one custodian working for them. For example, if you have separate account managers buying stocks in Europe or Japan or Latin America, or some such place, you will need a separate custodian in those locations. Your master custodian will already have those subcustody arrangements in place.

Rose: What about mutual fund accounts, Roger? Does the bank hold those as well?

Roger: No. A mutual fund will have its own custodian—State Street or someone like that. It's a legal requirement. Your bank custodian can show the mutual fund account as a line item if you want to see everything in one place on your statements. There might be a small charge and the line item might have stale values sometimes.

Ned: And what about hedge funds? I thought I heard you say they use primary brokers?

Carrie: *Prime* brokers, Ned. A prime broker—it's just a name—provides services to hedge funds similar to custody services, but they are bundled together with other services hedge funds need, such as margin loans, securities borrowing, and so on. Some hedge funds will also have a traditional custodian, while others will bundle custody at the prime broker. Probably the most important service a prime broker provides is centralized securities clearing—in other words, they clear across their client base, not just for this one hedge fund. That way collateral requirements are netted across the prime broker. In any case, hedge funds won't be held at your bank custodian, either, but could be shown as a line item.

Roger: Same with private equity. Venture capital funds, buyout funds, mezzanine funds all call down your cash and then more or less immediately invest it in deals. So they aren't held in custody at your bank.

Ned: So, basically, what's held in true custody is just stocks and bonds.

Carrie: That's pretty much the case. But, of course, stocks and bonds constitute the core of most family portfolios.

Ned: Do we actually use all those services in Roger's list?

Carrie: You use most of them now, Ned, and you'll likely use others in the future. For example, we're going to talk to you about putting together one or more family investment partnerships (or FLPs), so having a bank that can handle the complicated accounting requirements for FLPs could be important.

Rose: What's the process for searching for a new custodian and then comparing the options?

Carrie: It starts with Spenser figuring out what all your needs are. Then we contact a group of banks that can provide those services and we send them an RFP—much like you sent us an RFP when you were searching for a new advisor.

Roger: Each of the banks will respond to the RFP, and we'll then summarize those responses and make a recommendation to you.

Carrie: Typically, we'll narrow it down to two options and suggest that you meet with both, ask questions, and then pick the one you like best.

Ned: We don't just go with the low-cost provider?

Carrie: Cost is certainly an important issue, but quality of service, willingness to work with you to customize reporting, how you like the client-facing people, and so on are probably more important.

Rose: I've heard that switching custodians is a real pain in the you-know-what.

Carrie: I'm afraid it can be, Rose, but we do what we can at Spenser to ease the pain. The real trouble tends to come at the end, when it turns out that not everything got transferred.

Rose: Do you mean that if we had two hundred million dollars at our old bank, when we get to the new bank we might only have one hundred ninety-five million?

Carrie: Hopefully, it won't be that bad, but there are a lot of details and sometimes something gets lost in translation. That's why we don't recommend changing custodians just to do it, or just to save a few bucks. But if you're not getting best-in-class service, maybe a move is in order.[1]

QUICK NOTE

Asset custody is a nasty business—it requires huge capital investment both to enter the business and to remain competitive. At the same time, custody is cheap and the banks who offer the service typically earn narrow profit margins. To make up for the fact that custody is often a loss leader, banks usually insist—or request—that custody clients also use other bank products, including asset management. Wealth advisors thus walk a fine line between (on the one hand) not being able to gain access to the best custodians and (on the other hand) having to use less-than-best-in-class investment products offered by the banks.

FAMILY LIMITED PARTNERSHIPS

Carrie: I'll go through this quickly, because we've mentioned it before and we'll go through it in more detail at a later meeting. A family limited partnership, or FLP, is a way of bundling family assets into larger units that can meet the high minimum account sizes of the best managers.

Roger: Note that we're calling them limited partnerships, but they are more often limited liability companies, or LLCs.

Carrie: Basically, you set up the partnership and several different family members or units contribute capital to it. Then, when we go to a manager to open an account, the partnership is the client, not the individual family members.

Roger: One important thing to remember is that you can't convert an unaccredited investor to an accredited investor just by setting up an FLP. Each limited partner has to be accredited on his or her own.

Carrie: Also, we typically don't like to include charitable foundations in these vehicles, because it raises red flags with the IRS.

Ned: What sort of red flags?

Carrie: The Service is worried that people might mess around with cost basis among the limited partners, essentially passing tax consequences to the foundation, which pays only a very low tax rate.

Ned: Okay. And speaking of taxes, if I understand these vehicles properly, Carrie, there are tax advantages associated with them.

Carrie: Correct. Very important tax advantages. These have mainly to do with sheltering intra-family gifting from gift taxes, which are very high. Suppose you have an asset that you want to gift to your child. By doing it inside an FLP you can sometimes get a double discount on the valuation of the gift. First, the asset itself might be illiquid—say it's an undivided interest in a real estate property. You get a valuation discount because of the illiquidity. Then, when you put it into the FLP, you get another discount because the FLP is itself an illiquid vehicle.

Ned: I see. In other words, a willing buyer wouldn't pay anything like a market price for such an illiquid asset held in such an illiquid manner.

Carrie: That's the argument, yes.

Roger: Some FLPs include all kinds of assets, by which I mean that they represent a complete portfolio. So as various family members and units take pieces of the partnership, they are getting a complete, well-diversified portfolio. But these days, most FLPs are asset specific. You might set up an FLP just for private equity, for example, or just for hedge funds.

Rose: I must say, these vehicles sound awfully attractive. Are you sure all this is legal?

[Laughter.]

Carrie: They're legal this year, Rose, so we should get cracking on setting them up.

Ned: Do you think Congress might outlaw some of the benefits of FLPs, Carrie? Or, heaven help us, all the benefits?

Carrie: In all honesty, Ned, who knows what Congress might do in the future? But my guess is, it isn't Congress we need to worry about—it's the Treasury Department, that is, the IRS. The Service has been threatening for years to eliminate valuation discounts for FLPs not by changes in the law, but by adopting new regulations.[2] That could happen at any time.[3]

FAMILY PHILANTHROPY

Rose: Kids, we've asked Spenser to talk to us about charitable giving. As you know, Ned and I have our own personal giving programs, mainly to local organizations we are close to and care about. But we also have two smallish foundations, one for Ned's branch of the family and one for my branch. So far, we've used these as pass-through foundations, giving money to them in one year and then giving it away out of the foundations in subsequent years.

Ned: But now we're thinking of increasing the size of the foundations and having them operate as normal, endowed family foundations. If we're going to do that, there's a lot we should be thinking about, right, Carrie?

Carrie: That's right, Ned. A personal giving program is something you decide about every year. If you change your mind about priorities or organizations you've been giving to, it's easy to change course. You can even stop giving or significantly enlarge giving as you go along. But once you start endowing foundations at a significant level, you are making a permanent commitment to philanthropy and you need to begin thinking ahead.

Ellen: What do you mean when you say we are making a "permanent commitment," Carrie?

Carrie: When you give money to your family foundation, you get a tax deduction for the gift. Thereafter, that money is permanently dedicated to philanthropy. You can change the donees, but you have to give the money away. In fact you have to give at least five percent of the endowment away every year.

Billy: Really? Even if we don't see anything worthy out there or we haven't made up our minds yet?

Carrie: Well, technically you have to give away five percent a year on average over a moving three years. But at the end of those three years, if you haven't given away the five percent per year—fifteen percent over that time frame—the foundation will be fined by the IRS.

Billy: Fined! Wow.

Carrie: This might sound weird, but I've known of families who simply couldn't decide what to do. Then, suddenly the deadline was upon them and they were desperate. In one case a family had to get fifty million dollars out the door in less than thirty days.

Geoffrey: Did you say fifty *million*?

Carrie: I did.

Suzy: What the heck did they do? I wish I'd known about that—my Girl Scout troop was probably looking for money at the time.

[Laughter.]

Ellen: You'd have to sell a lot of Girl Scout Cookies to get to fifty million dollars!

Rose: That might have been hard even for Suzy, who was a world-champion Girl Scout Cookie salesman.

Suzy: Sales*woman*, Aunt Rose!

Ellen: Sales*person*!

Geoffrey: I feel like I just walked into the middle of a really bad play.

[Suzy and Ellen both throw pieces of paper at him.]

Carrie: I forgot what the question was.

Rose: It doesn't matter. The point is, if we're going to put a lot more money into our family foundations, we need to be serious about it and do it right.

Carrie: You do. And doing it right means not just adhering to all the legal requirements—which are voluminous—but also doing it right in terms of the kinds of things your family really cares about. Too many people look back on their foundation giving after many years and find they have little to show for it. Somehow the money got dribbled away and the world—or at least the corners of the world the family really cared about—didn't get any better.

Ellen: So how do we avoid that?

Carrie: The main thing is to think seriously about what you care about in the world. Obviously, even the Bill and Melinda Gates Foundation can't solve all the world's problems, so we can be pretty sure a typical family foundation won't.

Roger: So what Carrie is saying is that you should be thinking, "Okay, we can't help everyone, but given our resources, what *could* we do?"

Carrie: And among the things you *could* do, which of them really grab you? A good way to think about it is this: forget the money coming from the foundation. Would you volunteer your own personal time to help out in that cause?

Ned: I like that formulation, Carrie. For a fortunate family like us, money is nowhere near as precious as our time.

Rose: So, kids, what do you think? What causes would you donate your personal time to?

Ellen: That's easy for me. I already volunteer at the food bank in upper Manhattan.

Suzy: But isn't that because you also work at an organic grocery store?

Ellen: Well, that's how I got started, sure. I'd take surplus food up to the bank. But gradually I learned about hunger issues.

Rose: I think that's the beginning of what Carrie is talking about. But our family foundations can't feed the world. We couldn't even make much of a dent in hunger here in Pittsburgh. If we gave all our foundation money every year to the food bank, would that make us happy?

Billy: It wouldn't make *me* happy. I mean, I see Ellen's point, and I might be willing to help out food banks in some way. But if we're going to take a big portion of our capital and dedicate it permanently to charity, why not learn more about *why* people are hungry and whether we can do something about the root cause of the problem?

Geoffrey: You can either give a man a fish, or you can teach him to fish.

Suzy: Is that from the Bible, Geoff?

Geoffrey: No, I think it's a Chinese proverb.

Ellen: Okay, I hear you, Billy. But here's the problem. As I understand it—and I realize I'm still new at this hunger business—there isn't really any one root cause of hunger that we could focus on. There's a whole complex of issues, and it depends on whether we're talking about hunger in a rich country like America, or hunger in a poor country.

Ned: And not to embarrass anybody [Ned glances meaningfully at Ellen], but some of the things some of us care about would actually *increase* human hunger.

Ellen (sighing): Uncle Ned and I have had this argument only about ten million times already. What he's saying is that my commitment to organically grown food conflicts with my commitment to reducing hunger.

Billy: Because organically grown food is so much more expensive?

Ned: Partly. But the real problem is one of scale. If all the food in the world was grown organically, millions of people would simply starve. What we really need is more GMOs.[4]

Ellen: Dammit, Uncle Ned, you know perfectly well that ...

Rose: *Whoa!* This isn't the place to argue about world hunger and organic food.

Geoffrey: Well, okay, Aunt Rose, but I'm still trying to understand Ellen's point. Are you saying it's impossible to eliminate hunger, or just that it's too big an issue for us to take on? Personally, I'd like to work on getting more minorities and poor people involved in starting their own businesses. Maybe a micro-finance sort of thing.

Suzy: As I mentioned before, what grabs me is all these poor young girls in places like Afghanistan who can't go to school.

Ned: As you can see, Carrie, part of the problem is that, even though we're one family, we all gravitate toward different causes. And some of them are in active conflict with one another. What do we do about that? It must be common in families.

Carrie: It certainly is, although what I've typically seen is that the senior generation generally sets the main giving priorities—often based on a long family association with those causes. But then some portion of the grants budget is set aside for distribution to the causes advocated for by younger family members.

Billy: How about if the younger generation sets the priorities and we set aside a few cents for Mom and Uncle Ned?

[Laughter.]

Ned: Don't hold your breath.

Carrie: By setting aside some of the budget for younger family members, it gives them a chance to cut their teeth on the business of philanthropy. And, believe me, it's a tougher business than it looks.

Billy: Sounds like falling off a log to me!

Carrie: Well, just giving money away is easy, that's for sure. But giving it away wisely? That might be one of the hardest things a human being can do.

Suzy: Seriously? I mean, there are so many good causes out there. Couldn't you almost close your eyes and pick one and be doing good?

Rose: No, I agree with Carrie. Just because something is a good cause, that doesn't mean that the organization working on that issue is doing a good job. Sometimes, even with the best of intentions, they're actually making matters worse.

Ned: Yes, as Rose and I have learned the hard way, an awful lot of philanthropic giving is either outright wasted or at least way less effective than it should be.

Geoffrey: I can see how that would happen, even, as you said, with good intentions. The trouble is, you can never do just one thing. You try to wipe out malaria and you end up launching an AIDS epidemic. You eliminate child labor in Bangladesh and little kids starve to death.

Suzy: You're saying it's easy to focus on accomplishing one thing and feel really good about yourself, but then turn a blind eye to the repercussions of what you've done.

Geoffrey: And, really, on a net-net basis, have you made the world better? Or did you just make one part of it better but another part of it worse?

Rose: Yes, I think the ethics of philanthropy can get very complicated. Suppose you fund a huge project to try to make the schools more effective in an urban district. You completely turn everything that's being done upside down. And then at the end you discover that there were things you didn't understand about how the educational system worked. You've destroyed the old system, which at least was functioning, and what you put in its place was much worse.

Ned: I'm afraid I know exactly what project Rose is talking about. And the foundation that funded that catastrophe simply shrugged and walked away. It was "a learning experience," they said. But what about the lives damaged and destroyed? What about the chaos they left behind?

Geoffrey: Was this something local, Dad?

Ned: Thankfully, no. But we've had our share of local philanthropic debacles. They usually happen when well-intentioned people—what in the old days we'd call "do-gooders"—decide they are smarter than everybody else. In fact, they were just making themselves feel good and they didn't really care about the harm they caused.

Rose: Now, Ned, you know we've argued about this in the past. I don't disagree that there were debacles, and I don't disagree that the people who caused them were well-intentioned. But I disagree that they were merely smug or self-aggrandizing. I think it's more complicated than that.

Ned: *Arrogant* would be a good word.

Rose: Let's don't argue, but at least let me have my say. You're right that people, especially people with lots of money to give away, are often blind to the harm they cause. Being able to write a big check inevitably makes people think they're wiser than they are. But I think it's actually their good intentions that blind them to the trouble. They so badly want to make things better that they can't trouble themselves with nuance. It's as though they've developed a set of moral blinders. But that doesn't make them bad people.

Ned: We'll agree to disagree.

[Silence around the table, as everyone thinks about this argument and what it means for the Titan family's ability to manage philanthropy wisely.]

Carrie: The issue of complexity or nuance is important across-the-board in the charitable arena. Consider that the very nature of the fundraising business means that the effectiveness of nonprofit organizations tends to get wildly exaggerated. Let's face it—to be a good fundraiser you have to be a good salesman—or saleswoman or salesperson.

[Laughter.]

Rose: Quick thinking, Carrie!

Carrie: I've learned that you have to be really nimble around this group. Anyway, sales is all about putting the very best light on the product, and if the product is a nonprofit organization, you're never going to hear about the warts. You'd have to really dig down to find out the truth, but who has that kind of time?

Suzy: Well, this really is a lot more complicated than selling Girl Scout Cookies!

Ellen: Actually, have you ever looked at the ingredients in Girl Scout Cookies? Talk about moral complexity!

[Laughter.]

Ned: If Girl Scout Cookies are morally complicated, I think that nails it—philanthropy is way beyond the talents of this family!

[More laughter.]

Carrie: I think these are exactly the kinds of conversations you need to have before you start giving away large amounts of money. It's just that you should be having them with people who know what they're talking about, not with Spenser. We can tell you that philanthropy is very important and very complicated, and we can talk about vehicles and what other families have done. But beyond that you need to be talking to the experts.

Rose: So who should we be talking to?

Carrie: Well, locally, there are people who are extremely experienced in philanthropy and who can be very helpful, especially if you want to focus on local needs. The community foundation, for example, is a great resource, and there are consultants who know the local nonprofit world very well.

Roger: If you're thinking broader—nationally and internationally—you might want to talk to somebody like Rockefeller Philanthropy Advisors in New York.[5]

Suzy: Are they actually part of the Rockefeller family?

Carrie: I think RPA grew out of the family, but they are now an independent organization.

Ned: A while back you mentioned "voluminous" legal issues, Carrie. Can you mention some of the more important ones? We've been running the foundations for years, and J. Titan & Partners is our legal counsel, so I assume we're all legal, but who knows?

Carrie: Well, we're not lawyers at Spenser and we don't give legal advice, so ...

Roger: Actually, Carrie *is* a lawyer.

Carrie: Correction. I'm a *recovering* lawyer.

Roger: She's on the twelve-step program, she goes to Lawyers Anonymous every week, but she keeps falling off the wagon.

[Laughter.]

Ned: Maybe we should hire her at J. Titan & Partners.

Carrie: Only if your liability policy is paid up. [Laughter.] Regarding legal issues, I've mentioned the five percent distribution requirement. You don't want to screw that one up. What else, Roger?

Roger: Well, when you make grants, you need to distinguish between a grant to a *public charity* and a grant to a *private foundation* or *private operating foundation*.

Billy: That difference being what?

Ned: It's too complicated to go into, but I've been all through it with the lawyers at J. Titan. If it comes up, we can talk more about it.

Roger: There are also issues related to unrelated business income and to *lobbying*.

Billy: I assume this is also too complicated to go into now?

Ned: You bet. But if you're interested, there's a good book on the subject called *Private Foundations: Tax Law and Compliance.*[6] We have a copy at J. Titan if you'd like to borrow it.

Billy: I'll learn to keep my mouth shut.

Roger: There's another book you might look into, that's designed for new trustees and foundation staff members. What's it called, Carrie?

Carrie: You're probably thinking of *The Handbook on Private Foundations.*[7]

Roger: That's it. We have a copy at Spenser if you'd like to take a look at it.

Billy: Why does everybody like to give me reading assignments?

Carrie: Other requirements—I'm sure you know about this, Ned—include the filing of an annual return, called a Form 990-PF and the rules pertaining to dealings with *disqualified persons*, the self-dealing issues.

Ned: Yes, we're aware of those issues, although they can be complicated. For example, kids, suppose Rose commits to make a grant to the Garden Club. Later, she has her foundation make the grant. That's a big no-no. On the other hand, if the foundation committed to make the gift and Rose made it instead, that's okay.

Suzy: Sounds weird, but you're the expert.

Carrie: Finally, and then I'll shut up, there's a strange provision on *jeopardizing investments.*[8]

Geoffrey: Now that sounds like it should be right up Spenser's line.

Carrie: Yes and no. A jeopardizing investment is one that jeopardizes the existence of the foundation, presumably because it's so risky. The problem is that all the examples given by the IRS are investments and strategies that are extremely common. It's as though the rules were written by bureaucrats who had no idea how people actually invest their money. Anyway, just something to be aware of.

Rose: Carrie, you mentioned that setting aside some grant money for the kids to decide about was a way to help them gain experience in philanthropy. Are there other strategies we should think about as well?

Carrie: You could add the kids to the foundation board, or add them when they reach a certain age. But—and this is a bit sensitive—you might want to be careful not to let yourselves be outvoted.

Ellen: Ha! There's four of us and only two of them!

Ned: I see what you mean. [Giving Ellen the gimlet eye.]

Rose: What do we do about that?

Carrie: You could rotate the kids onto and off the board, say for two or three-year terms. You could add a trusted advisor who will always vote with you—an attorney or accountant or close friend.

Roger: Places like the Council on Foundations in Washington, DC,[9] have lots of resources for young trustees. You can join the Council and attend their meetings and conferences, or you can buy their materials.

Ned: Well, we're almost out of time, but let me raise one final issue. Rose and I feel pretty strongly about some of the issues we support, and we've seen other families lose control of their foundations. Suddenly, the foundation is supporting the *opposite* of what the family cares about.

Carrie: You're speaking of the Ford and MacArthur Foundations.

Ned: Exactly, although I'm sure there are other, smaller examples. How do we make sure that doesn't happen?

Carrie: I've seen families take several steps to avoid this issue, Ned. The first step is to be sure you are comfortable with the trustees of your foundation. I assume in your case it will be you, Rose, and the kids.

Ned: Right. But as you know, we don't all see eye-to-eye on philanthropic priorities.

Carrie: No, but that's pretty common in families. The main thing is that you respect each other's opinions and come to some kind of compromise on what you're going to support. As the years go by, this should work itself out. If not, maybe not all the kids should be on the board. You could set up a separate foundation for them and let them do their own thing.

Ned: Okay. What else?

Carrie: Often, when the patriarch or matriarch dies, they leave behind a long letter, addressed to the trustees of the foundation, describing their philanthropic beliefs and how they would like the trustees to carry those beliefs out. The letter isn't binding, of course, but it will carry a lot of moral force.

Ned: It sounds like what we call in my law firm a *letter of wishes*.

Rose: What's a letter of wishes, Ned?

Ned: Well, if you read the language in trust documents, it sounds dry and dull, because that's what it needs to say for legal reasons. For example, many trusts allow distributions of principal for "health, education, maintenance, and support." A letter of wishes fleshes out what the grantor of the trust means by that. The letter isn't binding on the trustee, but, like Carrie says, it contains a lot of moral force. It would be a brave trustee who ignored the letter!

Carrie: That's exactly right, Ned, except that this is a letter to the trustees of your foundation, not the trustees of a private trust.

Rose: Well, this has been a very useful conversation, Carrie and Roger. And, obviously, we'll be having many more shouting matches—excuse me, useful conversations—as we work out our philanthropies.[10]

QUICK NOTE

Nonprofit organizations—or important people connected to them—often try to use wealth advisory firms to get to their wealthy clients. While it's important for advisors to be knowledgeable about philanthropy and, especially, philanthropic vehicles, a sensible advisor will stay far away from getting involved in recommending donees to its clients.

THE FAMILY OFFICE

Ned: I know that the folks at Spenser aren't experts at designing and building family offices, but Rose and I have been thinking about hiring some staff and building out Lawburn a bit. So I've asked Carrie and Roger to give us whatever advice they might have.

Carrie: You're right about one thing, Ned—we're not experts on this topic. But we can refer you to resources. For example, I've mentioned the Family Office Exchange, or FOX, at other meetings. FOX has developed blueprints for different kinds of family offices, depending on the nature of the family and what it is you're trying to accomplish. I also mentioned Kirby Rosplock's book, *The Complete Family Office Handbook*.[11] If you decide to move forward, we can direct you to additional resources, depending on what you want to do.

Rose: That's great, Carrie. But you've worked with lots and lots of families, and you've seen lots and lots of family offices. You must have developed some thoughts about all this.

Carrie: Yes, I have, Rose. One piece of advice I would have is this: go slow. Far too often I've seen families sell their companies and immediately start organizing a complicated family office. They hire a bunch of people and then halfway along they realize they want to go in a different direction. They restructure and let people go. And one thing you really don't want—especially in a smaller city like Pittsburgh—is a bunch of disgruntled former employees who know a lot of confidential things about your family and finances.

Rose: Well, that's good—and scary—advice.

Carrie: Another recommendation: outsource as much as humanly possible, especially at first. Companies that specialize in doing things are likely to be able to do it better and cheaper than you can do it. It minimizes your in-house headcount, which is really important if you're not used to managing employees.

Rose: And I'm certainly not. Ned is, of course, but he's used to managing lawyers, who are a whole other ballgame.

Ned: You can say that again! But Carrie is right—managing employees is a big deal. They take a lot of care and feeding. They need a career path or the best ones will leave and the worst will stay forever.

Carrie: That's exactly right. In any event, you can always bring something in-house if you decide it's better or cheaper. But I would start with outsourcing.

Rose: What about confidentiality?

Carrie: Confidentiality is important, of course, but I think families can easily be too paranoid about it. For the most part, other people aren't all that interested in what you're doing. Even if you have some sort of scandal and it gets in the newspapers, people forget about it very quickly. I would focus your confidentiality attention on technology issues: email, social media, that sort of thing. If someone hacks into your systems, it can be no end of headaches.

Suzy: How do you feel about family members working in the family office?

Rose: Has somebody tossed her hat in the ring?

Ellen: Not to tell tales out of school, but Suzy's boyfriend is probably going to take a job in Cleveland, so I might lose my roomie.

Suzy: If I moved back home, Aunt Rose, I'd be a lot closer to Cleveland. But I'd need to look for a job.

Ned: What's your view about nepotism, Carrie? But be careful—I'm a nepo myself!

Geoffrey: But, Dad, how can you be a—oh, Grandpa Jake hired you.

Ned: Right. And, believe me, I don't recommend it. Everybody at J. Titan & Partners, from the lowliest messenger up to the most senior partners, assumed I was some loser who had to be bailed out by my dad. It took many years for me to build my own reputation in the firm.

Carrie: I'm sure that was a tough situation for you, Ned. But I think a family office is a bit of a different circumstance. People *expect* that family members will work at the family office. In fact, almost all family offices are headed by a family member, with the exception of the very largest ones.

Roger: We often see children of family members working in a family's office. It's a way of training them, of helping them understand what's involved in making the family run.

Rose: I wouldn't have any problem with that at all. What we'd need to watch out for is not allowing Lawburn to become a dumping ground for family members who can't get productive work elsewhere.

Ellen: Well, that leaves you out, Geoff.

[Laughter.]

Geoffrey: Hey! Just because I've been in school all my life, that doesn't mean I'm a total loser!
Billy: It doesn't?

[More laughter.]

Ned: Anyway, before our kids start throwing punches at each other, your advice, as I understand it, is (a) go slow, (b) outsource, and (c) go ahead and hire your loser kids.

[Even more laughter.][12]

HOW MUCH TO LEAVE THE KIDS

Rose: Before we bring the kids into the meeting, we wanted to pose a question that probably has no answer: How much money should we leave them?
Carrie: Well, that's a very personal issue for a family, Rose.
Rose: I know it is, Carrie. But you've worked with many families over the years and you must have developed some thoughts about it.
Carrie: That's true. But my most important thought is that this sort of issue needs to be made by individual families based on their own circumstances.
Ned: Okay, what's your second most important thought?

[Laughter.]

Carrie: Okay, let me approach the subject this way. I'll give you some different examples from my own client base and we can talk about them. How does that sound?
Ned: That works.
Carrie: Let's start with the problem extremely wealthy families have. I have a client on the West Coast who has made more than four billion dollars in one generation. They are planning to leave each of their kids a hundred million and the rest will go to charity. What do you think of that outcome?

[Ned and Rose exchange a glance.]

Rose: I don't like to second-guess other families, but that seems like the worst of all worlds. I mean, one hundred million dollars is a *lot* of money, so the kids will have all the usual challenges of managing wealth. Yet, they're likely to feel that their parents didn't trust them with the whole fortune.

Carrie: Ned?

Ned: I think I see where that family is coming from. They're thinking, hell, a hundred million dollars is more than anyone should ever need, so what's to complain about? Meanwhile, people who really need help will be getting the balance of the billions because the parents are leaving it to charity. By the way, when you say "charity," I'm assuming you mean the family's foundation.

Carrie: Yes, the bulk of the money will go to the foundation, but fairly major grants are going to Cal Berkeley, the UCLA Medical Center, and a nonprofit the family founded that helps kids get to college and stay in.

Ned: It seems like an okay outcome to me. But you don't like it, Rose?

Rose: I could see doing that if you didn't yet know what your kids were going to be like. Some kids might grow up to be disasters, and at least the disastrous kids could only blow a hundred million!

[Laughter.]

Carrie: I think there might be something to that, Rose! The client's kids are still very young. Anyway, here's another example. A client in Missouri is extremely charitably oriented. He and his wife currently plan to leave only very modest sums to their kids, who are already young adults. However, they are monitoring the kids' commitments to philanthropy, that is, how much of their resources they give away versus how much they consume. At some point, they plan to change their estate plan to leave much more to the charitably oriented kids than to the others. Thoughts?

Ned: I hate that idea. I don't think you can bribe kids into being charitable. Their hearts just won't be in it. As soon as the parents are in their graves, those kids will start buying jet airplanes.

Rose: I tend to agree with that, Ned, although we don't know the family Carrie is speaking of. It could be a much more benign situation.

Carrie: Yes, I think it is. The kids in that family know that they're going to end up with a lot of money no matter what. Via gifting and various tax strategies, the kids already have a lot of money. It's just that the parents want to leave the bulk of their wealth to people who will likely continue to give most of it away, and to do so sensibly.

Ned: I suppose it's not much different than leaving your money to your family foundation and appointing only certain of your kids to the board of trustees.

Carrie: Yes, very similar. Let me mention a family that lives just across the state, in Philadelphia. My client made a lot of money early in his life in the tech sector. He got divorced along the way, no children from that marriage. Then, late in life, he married a much younger woman.

Rose: What a surprise!

Ned: Lucky SOB.

Carrie: Anyway, he's now in his sixties and he has three kids under the age of twelve.

Ned: I take it back.

[Laughter.]

Carrie: So what this guy did—and his new wife was on board with it—was to leave the kids modest sums in his will. I mean, this is a guy with four hundred million dollars and each of the kids was getting one million. But here's the interesting part—he reviews his will every five years and he and his wife look at what's happening with their kids' characters. If they like what they see, the amount the kids get is increased. So, as I said, when a child is born, he gets one million. But since the parents like what they see in their twelve-year-old, her inheritance is already up to ten million dollars.

Rose: Very interesting. So let's say the twelve-year-old continues to blossom. By the time she's thirty or forty, she could be getting a very major inheritance.

Carrie: Yes. But if she marries a loser or turns to drugs or …

Ned: Appears in a movie dumping on rich people.

Rose: What in the world are you talking about, Ned?

Carrie: Warren Buffett's granddaughter, Nicole—I think she may be adopted—was disowned by Buffett after she appeared in a film called *The 1%*.[13]

Rose: Oh, wow.

Carrie: One interesting aspect of this family's approach is that the kids know nothing about it. They have no idea how much they're going to inherit and no idea that their character development is going to count for so much.

Ned: So there's no obvious use of money to try to manipulate the kids, right?

Carrie: Right. The parents simply don't want irresponsible kids inheriting a lot of money. Naturally, the parents are working hard to raise the kids up to be decent people, but if they fail, well, at least the irresponsible ones won't be rich.

Rose: Interesting. Any other examples?

Carrie: Well, although you hear a lot about wealthy families not leaving their kids much, I actually don't see it a lot in my client base. I've given you some examples of interesting approaches, but mostly people are leaving their dough to their kids.

Ned: And why not, assuming the parents are working hard, as you said, to raise them right.

Carrie: Yes. In my experience, it isn't money that ruins people. By the time most people inherit, they're grown and their characters are formed. If they're solid citizens, they'll put the money to good use. If they're not, not. But it's the character that matters, not the money.

Rose: Well said, well said.

QUICK NOTE

As Carrie is quick to point out, deciding how much money to leave to your kids is a very personal decision and not one most advisors will want to horn in on. But when asked, as Carrie was, the best way to answer the question is to give actual examples of what families are doing. Many parents in wealthy families worry a great deal about the possibility that money will ruin their children, of course. But as Carrie says, it's rarely money that is the problem.

INEQUALITY AND WEALTH

Rose: Carrie and Roger, if we could change the subject for a minute, I'd like to raise the question of inequality. I happen to know that you've been involved in similar conversations already with other families, so maybe you can help us sort this out. Ellen originally proposed the topic and, to my surprise, Ned agreed that it would be a useful discussion to have.

Ned: Actually, Ned agreed that it *might* be a useful conversation, but only if Ned was present to present the correct side of the argument.

[Laughter.]

Rose: I guess I misspoke!

Ned: The kids have been kicking this issue around a lot, probably because they have so many friends who aren't rich.

Billy: And in some ways I envy those friends. They're not poor, but they're not rich, either.

Suzy: Whenever I'm out with friends, they expect me to pay for everything. If I don't—if I just split the check with everyone else—they think I'm stingy.

Geoffrey: If we're not constantly, totally generous one hundred percent of the time, we're scumbags.

Rose: Yes, I know the problem, but if it's any solace to you, it only gets worse as you get older.

Suzy: Oh, wonderful!

Ned: Every organization that needs money thinks you should be supporting them. And if you don't, you're the proverbial guy with "deep pockets and short arms."

[Laughter.]

Suzy: That's a good one, Dad! But there really are wealthy people who are stingy, I think. You must see it in your client base, Carrie.

Carrie: Actually, we don't. Of course, there is a range of commitment to philanthropy. Some families give away far more than they spend on themselves. We have one client who lives in a small, unremarkable middle-class house and who drives a small, unremarkable middle-class car, but who gives away millions of dollars every year.

Billy: Wow. That family makes the rest of us look like pikers.

Carrie: And, of course, we have clients who give away very little.

Suzy: The stingy ones, you mean.

Carrie: Well, no, I wouldn't call them stingy. They simply look at the world in a different way. A very generous family is one that truly believes in philanthropy, that believes that philanthropy works and makes people's lives better. A family that gives away little might be a stingy family that just wants to spend money on themselves. But more likely they're a family who thinks there are better ways than philanthropy to improve people's lives.

Ellen: Such as?

Ned: Such as by starting and growing businesses, or helping others to do it. If one family is helping to feed hundreds of homeless people, and another is creating hundreds of new jobs, who's to say which one is doing more for society?

Carrie: Most families, of course, try to do a little of both. They believe in giving money away—in giving back to their communities. But they also believe that, as Geoffrey said at an earlier meeting, it's better to teach a man to fish than to keep giving him fishes.

Rose: I think the Titan family, at least the ones in this room, would agree that there's a role for philanthropy and a role for creating jobs and tax revenues. But—to get back to the topic of the day—is that the proper role of a wealthy family in a modern, democratic, free market society? To give money away and invest in new enterprises that create jobs? Why *do* we exist? Or, better put, why does society *allow* us to continue to exist?

[Dead silence around the room.]

Billy: Those are awfully big questions, Mom. Are you suggesting that maybe American society *shouldn't* allow rich people to exist?

Rose: I'm not suggesting anything, Billy. I'm merely asking the question. Obviously enough, some societies are extremely hostile to families of wealth. Communist and socialist societies, for example.

Ned: That new government in Greece, Syriza, hates the rich. They refer to anyone who has money as an "oligarch," and their entire plan to save the Greek economy can be summed up in three words: "soak the rich."

Rose: In any event, I don't expect us to answer these questions today—if they can ever be answered. But what Ned and I want is for us to keep thinking about them, to keep talking about them. They're important questions for American society, and they're especially important questions for us, the wealthy Titans.

Ned: What makes them so delicate, I think, is that not everyone in American society is well-off. If the Titans were exactly as rich as we are, and everyone else was affluent, I don't think we'd be having these discussions. I don't think American society would be having them.

Suzy: But, Dad, there have always been poor people. There are poor people in every country in the world.

Billy: Even Finland?

[Laughter.]

Ned: I think we can forget the Finlands of the world. Those are very tiny, extremely homogeneous countries. Finland is only about twice as big as Pittsburgh, so comparing that country to a country with more than three hundred million very diverse people is silly.

Rose: It's certainly true that the United States looks pretty bad from an equality point of view compared to places like Finland. But compared to large, diverse countries more like us, we look pretty good. Think of China, India, Indonesia.

Ned: Brazil, Pakistan, Nigeria, Russia.

Ellen: But don't we look bad compared to other advanced economies, like in Europe?

Carrie: Does everyone know what a *Gini coefficient* is?

[Geoffrey raises his hand.]

Carrie: Go ahead, Geoffrey.

Geoffrey: I only know this because one of my advisors in my Ph.D. program is really interested in inequality and he's always popping off about Gini coefficients.

Billy: Can you give us the ten-cent answer instead of the ten-dollar answer, Geoff?

[Laughter.]

Geoffrey: There's no ten-cent answer, but I can give you the four-dollar-seventy-five-cent answer. [Laughter.] So the Gini coefficient is a measure of a society's equality or inequality. You can use it with income or wealth. If you had a society with a Gini of one hundred, it would be perfectly unequal.

Suzy: Hold on! How's that possible?

Geoffrey: It's not, really. But if you had a society consisting of only two people and one had all the money and the other had nothing, you'd have a Gini of one hundred.

Billy: The one with all the money better be plenty big and strong!

[Laughter.]

Geoffrey: By the same token, if those two people each had exactly the same amount of money, you'd have a Gini of *one*. Got it? [Heads nod.] So Ellen is generally right—Western European nations typically have better Gini coefficients than the United States. A typical Western European country will have a Gini of around thirty, while the United States—and countries like the UK or Israel—will have a Gini of around forty.

Ellen: So they're really a *lot* better.

Geoffrey: Well, yes and no.

Ned: The problem with a Gini coefficient is that it doesn't tell you whether a country is equal-and-rich or equal-and-poor.

Geoffrey: That's right, Dad. Some countries with Ginis of around thirty would include Afghanistan, Albania, Tajikistan, Serbia, and so on. Equal-but-poor.

Billy: So America is "somewhat unequal but very rich"?

Geoffrey: Right. Nobody would choose to live in a country like Tajikistan just because it's "more equal."

Suzy: Do we know why America is more unequal than other wealthy countries, like Europe?

Ned: It's because America is a much more competitive society. In a competitive society you'll have winners and losers—and semi-winners and semi-losers. But you'll also have much faster economic growth, a much more creative and successful society in general, whether you're looking at economic growth, cultural richness, social diversity, whatever. America dominates the world, while more-equal societies like those in Europe are dying on the vine.

Suzy: So if I was a winner or a semi-winner, I'd want to live in a society like the United States, but if was a loser I'd want to live in Europe.

[Laughter.]

Ned: Well, maybe that's a little strong.

Rose: Ned actually loves Europe. He's an anglophile, a francophile, and an italophile.

Ned: True enough, but that doesn't mean I have any respect for those economies. Well, maybe the UK.

Rose: Ned, do you honestly think that the United States has a worse Gini than Europe because we're a more competitive society?

Ned: I do, although there are other reasons as well. For one thing, America welcomes huge numbers of immigrants, more than any other country in the world, and by a gigantic margin. Does anyone know the statistics? [Heads shake.] The United States has about forty-five million immigrants. The next largest country in the world is Russia, with eleven million. Other large countries have almost none. In China there are less than one million immigrants and in India there are only about five million.

Geoffrey: That's right, Dad. I didn't know the exact statistics, but the fact that the United States welcomes so many immigrants, who tend to be poor, is a major reason for our lower Gini. On the other hand, those immigrants add vigor to a society that might otherwise just be boring and getting old. So, over time, America's economy will be more robust, more powerful—more competitive—than the economies of countries like Europe that don't accept so many immigrants.

Ned: But because the immigrants keep coming, our Gini stays relatively low. But keep in mind that in many ways the Europeans are managing their immigrant populations much worse than we are—it's just that they have so many fewer of them.

Ellen: Are there other reasons for our poor Gini rating?

Rose: Well, obviously America has a terrible legacy of slavery, unlike most other countries. And far too many African-American families are poor even today, one hundred and fifty years after the Civil War.

Ned: We also have very large pockets of stubborn poverty in the hills and rural townships of Appalachia. A lot of those counties are as poor today as they were back in the Sixties, when the War on Poverty was launched.

Carrie: I read a very funny newspaper article a few years ago that poked fun at people's preoccupation with Gini coefficients without looking deeper. The writer was using the Chicago Bulls basketball team as an example of how absurd a Gini can be.

Rose: I remember that article! I think it was in the *Wall Street Journal*.[14]

Carrie: I think that's right, Rose. The writer pointed out that in the mid-1980s the Gini of the Chicago Bulls was terrific—somewhere in the mid-thirties. But the Bulls were also terrible. They qualified for the playoffs only twice between 1976 and 1984. By the late 1990s, the team's Gini had gotten much worse—in the high sixties. Inequality had skyrocketed. Does anybody know why?

Billy and Geoffrey (shouting): Michael Jordan!

Ellen: Who's Michael Jordan?

[Groans from Billy and Geoffrey.]

Carrie (laughing): Michael Jordan was one of the best basketball players ever. He made a huge amount of money with the Bulls, and their Gini coefficient went straight to hell.

Billy: The hell with the Gini coefficient! The Bulls were one of the greatest teams in NBA history!

Geoffrey: Two three-peats!

Suzy: Huh?

Billy: Never mind.[15]

Carrie: The point of the article was, who cared about the Gini coefficient? Not Michael Jordan, obviously. Not his teammates, whose median income had gone up *seven times* over what it was before Jordan came aboard. Not the team's owners, who were coining money. Not the Bulls' fans, who were ecstatic.

Ned: I know who wanted the Bulls to have a better Gini—their competitors in the NBA!

Carrie: I'm sure you're right, Ned.

Ned: So if you substitute "United States of America" for "Chicago Bulls," you have exactly the same phenomenon. America is kicking serious butt around the world and the only people who want us to have a better Gini are our international competitors, who are getting tired of getting their you-know-whats kicked.

Rose: Now, Ned, there are lots of people even in America who are worried about inequality.

Ned: Losers! [Laughter.] Sorry, I couldn't stop myself.

Rose: Let's face it, America has always been a very competitive society, and we've always had legacy-of-slavery problems, high immigration, and stubbornly poor areas in Appalachia. But what seems to be new is the struggles of the middle class. We've always thought of the middle class as the backbone of American society, but that backbone seems to be cracking.

Roger: Incomes of middle-class Americans have been pretty well frozen for close to three decades. That's a scary statistic.

Rose: Especially because the incomes of the "one percent" have gone way up.

Suzy: You're talking about us, aren't you, Aunt Rose? We're the one percent everybody hates.

Ned (laughing): Are you kidding, Suzy? Do the math! We're the one ten-thousandth percent! If you earn four hundred thousand dollars a year, you're in the top one percent. Those aren't rich people, they're just well-off upper-middle-class families. If they hate the one percent, what must they think about us?

Carrie: I'm afraid Ned's right. You guys are off-the-charts in terms of income and wealth distribution. And Rose hit the nail on the head. The problem isn't just that "the rich are getting richer." For that matter, the poor aren't getting poorer. The problem is that the middle class seems to be dividing itself into people who are moving out by moving up—into the upper-middle class—and people who are moving out by moving down—into the lower-middle class or even the working classes.

Ellen: You're saying that the *middle*-middle class, the group that used to be the core of our society, is shrinking at both ends.

Carrie: Yes. And no one knows what the consequences of that development might be.

Suzy: But why is it happening? Are we to blame? Are rich people keeping other people down somehow? That seems to be what you read in the papers.

Carrie: A lot of people on the political left in America would say so.

Suzy: But how? It doesn't make any sense!

Ned: "Rent-seeking behavior."[16]

Suzy: Huh?

Carrie: What Ned is referring to is the fact that powerful entities and powerful people can use their power to stay powerful rather than to create anything useful for society.

Billy: You mean by using their influence?

Carrie: Sure. The classic example would be a regulated company that wines and dines its regulator and makes big campaign contributions to the right politicians. That allows it to increase prices without giving its customers better service.

Ellen: Like the airlines or cable companies!

Carrie: I won't take a position on that one! But, really, we're talking about human—and institutional—nature here. Everyone competes hard and wants to improve their position. People and organizations (like corporations) that are already powerful are just that much more effective at pushing their own interests.

Suzy: So what's wrong with that?

Carrie: Roger?

Roger: Nothing, as long as the person or organization pushing its own interest is making a positive contribution. If they're not, that's why we have antitrust laws.

Carrie: Consider Google. If Google, by competing hard, is making people's lives better, fine. But if it's using its dominant position to freeze out competition and increase its profits without adding anything commensurate, that would be rent-seeking behavior.

Ned: And in the United States, we see Google as—mainly—making our lives better through competition. But in Europe, where they can't compete, the antitrust authorities are trying to cripple Google.

Suzy: But how would we do it? I mean, as a rich family, how would we use our influence to keep middle-class people down?

Carrie: In the family context it tends to be more subtle. But, obviously, wealthy people lobby their Congressional representatives for this and that.

Ned: Lower taxes!

Billy: But, Uncle Ned, everybody wants lower taxes, not just rich people.

Carrie: True enough. And since there are so many more middle-income people than rich people, what you actually see in a democracy like America isn't the rich lowering taxes for themselves, but middle-class people lowering taxes for *themselves*.

Ned: Middle-class rent-seekers!

Rose: Well, technically, I think Carrie's right. Wealthier people pay a huge percentage of all the income taxes in the country.[17]

Billy: So much for rent-seeking behavior! It isn't that rich people aren't trying to do it, it's just that we're really lousy at it.

Carrie: And as long as you're vastly outnumbered by middle-class people—and poorer people—you'll continue to be lousy at it.

Geoffrey: I'm not sure I agree that trying to get your taxes lowered is an example of rent-seeking behavior. Lots of people believe that lower taxes lead to faster and more efficient economic growth. If so, then lower taxes actually lead to more productivity and aren't just an example of rich people—or even middle-class people—trying to get a personal benefit without a broader benefit to society.

Ellen: I'm not sure I agree that lower taxes lead to anything productive, but I won't argue with you about it, Geoff, since I don't really understand the pros and cons. But what I'm interested in is this—what's going wrong with the middle-class in America? If the rich aren't keeping them down, what's the problem?

Carrie: If I had to answer that question in one word—and it's a very good question, Ellen—I'd say *globalization.*

Ellen: Globalization seems to get the blame for almost everything these days. But how does it affect middle-class people?

Carrie: I'll give you an example from my own family. My father was a competent, hardworking guy, but he only had a high school education. But back in those days that was enough. Dad was competing for work in the mills with a bunch of local guys just like himself. And he had a powerful union backing him up. He worked forty years in the same factory and supported his family.

Rose: When are we talking about, Carrie? The 1950s?

Carrie: Yes, right after the war. The U.S. economy was booming and there was big demand for guys like Dad. Now let's fast-forward to today. I have a cousin—his name is Dan—out in Wisconsin who is almost a clone of my father. Dan's a competent, hardworking guy, but he only has a high school education. He has struggled most of his life. He has been laid off many times, factories have closed underneath him. It's a very sad story.

Ellen: I can see that it's a sad story, Carrie, and it's especially sad if it's representative of what's happened to a lot of formerly middle-class people. But what's globalization got to do with it?

Carrie: The problem is that my father was only competing with local guys who wanted to work in the mills. But today my cousin, Dan, is competing with billions of very poor people all over the world. Dad worked in a tubing mill all his life, for example, and Dan started there right out of high school. But the tubing mill moved to Mexico a few years after he started. Poor Dan worked odd jobs until he got work in a foundry near Milwaukee, but that foundry closed and moved production to China.

Geoffrey: Where were the unions while all this was happening?

Ned: I can answer that—they were dying on the vine. The unions were in an awful position—damned if they did and damned if they didn't.

If the union didn't fight for high wages and good working conditions, the workers would decertify it and go with another union. If the union managed to get good wages, the factory wouldn't be competitive on a global basis and would close and move production offshore.

Rose: Ned is right. That exact phenomenon happened in a very big way right here in Pittsburgh with the United Steelworkers Union and the steel companies. At one time Pittsburgh was the biggest center for steel production in the world, but today not one ton of steel is made in the city. It's all gone, mostly to Asia and Mexico.

Ned: We lost a hundred thousand jobs—and they were very well-paid, middle-class jobs—in a period of ten years. It's a miracle the city survived.

Suzy: Carrie, you must be suggesting that globalization didn't hurt affluent families as much as it hurt middle-class families. But doesn't globalization affect everybody?

Carrie: I'm actually saying more than that, Suzy. Globalization *helps* a lot of people. If you're a highly skilled person, well educated, talented, hardworking, globalization is a Godsend for you. In the old days, you could be all of those things and hardly anybody noticed or cared. But today, you'll be in demand globally, with a commensurate rise in your pay.

Ned: I certainly see it in my profession. When I first became a lawyer in the early 1970s, we made very little money. I started at twelve thousand dollars a year, at a time when a steelworker made several times as much.

Suzy: You were in the wrong job, Dad!

Ned: You're telling me! In those days it didn't matter whether you were an average lawyer or a really good lawyer, that's what you made. But, gradually, all that changed. Today, average lawyers still don't make much money, but really good lawyers can practically name their own price. They're in demand all over the world. J. Titan & Partners has clients in London, Paris, Hong Kong, São Paulo, you name it. The best young attorneys start at—are you sitting down?—almost two hundred thousand dollars a year. I don't even want to tell you what the best senior attorneys make.

Carrie: The same thing is true in almost every profession now. The best doctors are in demand globally and make huge sums. Same with the best accountants, the best college professors, the best executives, the best software engineers. Average people don't do so well. Thanks to technology and globalization, everybody all over the world knows who the best talents are and they bid for those talents. I don't even want to tell you what I have to pay Roger.

[Laughter.]

Roger: Whatever it is, I'm worth it.

[More laughter.]

Billy: So, basically, in a global world, people with ordinary skills and talents and education are getting killed while people at the top of every profession or job and getting richly rewarded. And that's driving inequality through the roof.

Carrie: That might be a bit of an exaggeration, Billy, but that's the gist of it. I was looking at a book the other day that pointed out that almost seventy percent of the income inequality in America today is simply the result of the difference in earnings between people with high school degrees and people with college degrees.[18]

Ned: But if we were honest with ourselves, we'd have to admit that even a lot of college degrees are mostly worthless. Maybe *on average* college grads make more, but a lot of higher education is a joke. Nobody would hire those kids. They graduate from college barely able to read and write and they certainly can't think.

Suzy: Tell us what you really think, Dad!

Ellen: But what's the solution? Suppose as a family we wanted to get involved in this issue through our foundations. What could we do to help?

[There follows a long silence around the table.]

Ned: I don't know, Ellen. It seems to me that inequality in the United States is the result of powerful global economic and cultural forces that aren't going to change any time soon. It's no different in other countries; the same forces are at work. What could two small family foundations possibly do about it?

Geoffrey: The Titan family can't fight globalization and I'm not sure we'd want to. After all, it might be hurting America's middle class, but it's helping desperately poor people elsewhere. My guess is that, on a worldwide basis, vastly more people have been helped than hurt by globalization.

Ellen: Maybe so. But how do we help the ones who're being hurt? After all, they are our fellow citizens.

Ned: It's just too vast a problem.

Rose: I'm not sure I agree with that, Ned. Geoff's probably right that, net-net, globalization is a positive. But Ellen's right, too, that it's hurting a lot of innocent people right here in America. And since people don't understand what's driving inequality, they could come up with some really bad solutions.

Ned: You mean like taxing the hell out of successful people so failed people can live high on the hog?

Rose: I won't dignify that with an answer, except to say that, yes, a lot of people are saying that income redistribution is the answer.

Ned: Those people—the Thomas Pikettys of the world[19]—are essentially admitting that there's a large class of people who simply can't compete and who have to be permanently supported by competitive people.

Ellen: No; what they're saying is that there's such a thing as human dignity. If global forces are destroying people's ability to hold down jobs and support their families, that's hardly their fault.

Ned: We'll agree to disagree about whether it's their fault. After all, anybody can get an education; anybody can learn a skill that's in demand. If they won't bother, they've got no kick coming.

Rose: That's pretty harsh, Ned.

[Another long silence around the table.]

Ned: Well, maybe you're right, Rose. I take it back.

Rose: Let me say this. Maybe there's a kernel of truth to what Ned was saying. He put it in terms of *fault*, implying that people under pressure from global economic forces are somehow responsible for their own plight. But if we leave fault out of it, what could or should these people be doing? And why aren't they doing it? Suppose it was our kids who were being harmed. What would we recommend that they do?

Ellen: And even if we knew the answers to those questions, what about the plight of those people in the meantime? They can't just change overnight.

Rose: Here's a thought experiment. Suppose our family foundations were to sponsor research into this issue. Or maybe the research has already been done and it just needs to be collected and understood. Suppose the outcome of that research was that people needed more and better education, more and better skills training. Couldn't we advocate for that? Couldn't we even underwrite pilot programs on a small scale to see if they might help people who were at risk of being left behind by the global economy?

Ellen: I really like that idea, Mom.

Ned: I'm skeptical, I guess, but I wouldn't stand in the way of at least looking into these things.

Carrie: The Titan family solves the problem of inequality in America!

Rose: Hardly! But if we could make a small dent in the problem, that's at least something.

Roger: I have an idea for improving inequality in a small, local way.

[Everyone turns toward Roger.]

Rose: You do? Let's hear it!
Roger: Effective immediately, I should be paid the same as Carrie.

[Loud laughter.]

QUICK NOTE

I've put this long conversation about inequality and wealth in the book—and right at the end—not because many wealth advisors are going to be talking about these issues with their clients. No, I put it in because many wealthy families, and especially younger members of such families, think and worry about these issues all the time. The issues may not be right out on the table, but they're there, all right.

SUMMARY

In this chapter we've discussed several issues that aren't directly related to the management of capital, but without which the management of capital is likely to fail.

Hiring a Custodian

The discussion of hiring a custodian was intentionally nontechnical. Many families are unsure what an asset custodian does or why it's an important job. At the end of the day, a good custodian makes a family's investment life work smoothly—and an advisor's life, too. A bad custodian, or one with old or creaky technology, causes endless problems. Life is just too short to deal with a poor custodian.

Family Limited Partnerships

Family limited partnerships offer so many advantages that the default position should be to set them up wherever possible. The only downside is complexity, and, unfortunately, FLPs do in fact bring with them a level of complexity that sometimes seems to beg the question of their usefulness. However, most of the complexity associated with FLPs can be handed off to custodians, tax accountants, and family office personnel. As noted, FLPs are controversial with the tax authorities and their future as tax-reducing mechanisms may be uncertain.

Family Philanthropy

Obviously, philanthropy is a very personal choice, both as to whether to engage in it and as to a family's charitable priorities. But in a democratic, egalitarian society, most families will come to the conclusion that giving back to the society that allowed them to become wealthy is a sound policy. Wealth advisors differ in the depth of their understanding of philanthropy and philanthropic techniques, but the discussion should at least be on the table.

The Family Office

Most advisors won't be terribly knowledgeable about the business of establishing and managing family offices, but we should all be ready with resources to suggest to clients thinking of moving in that direction. Wealth advisors spend a great deal of their time working with a family offices, not just with the family principals, and they should have developed opinions about which family office practices work well and which don't.

How Much to Leave the Kids

Obviously, this is a very personal decision for any family. But since parents worry incessantly about it, anything an advisor to do to help should be considered. The main point—aside from the personal nature of the decision—is that money may well ruin a person with a weak character, but otherwise parents tend to over-worry about the problem.

Inequality and Wealth

The subject of inequality in America is being widely debated, but nowhere is it more delicate than among wealth families. Most people in the 1% are high-earning professionals who have worked and studied hard to get where they are, and very few of them feel guilty about their income-earning ability. But many wealthy families simply inherited their money and, as noted in the previous conversation, they aren't in the 1%, but in a tiny *fraction* of the 1%. These discussions can be very difficult, and often heated, but for many families they will prove to be worthwhile.

NOTES

1. For more information about custodians and what they do, see Gregory Curtis, *The Stewardship of Wealth: Successful Private Wealth Management for Investors and Their Advisors* (Hoboken, NJ: John Wiley & Sons, 2013), especially Chapter 22.

2. See, for example, UBS Advanced Planning Group, *UBS Wealth Planning Alert*, July 2015.
3. For more information about FLPs, see Curtis, op. cit., note 1, Chapter 22.
4. Genetically modified organisms, that is, food grown from organisms whose DNA has been modified by genetic engineering.
5. http://rockpa.org/.
6. Bruce R. Hopkins and Jody Blazek, *Private Foundations: Tax Law and Compliance* (Hoboken, NJ: John Wiley & Sons, 2014).
7. David F. Freeman and John A. Edie, *The Handbook on Private Foundations* (Washington, DC: Council on Foundations, 2005).
8. Internal Revenue Code §4944.
9. http://www.cof.org/.
10. For more information about philanthropy, see Curtis, op. cit., note 1, Chapter 22.
11. Kirby Rosplock, *The Complete Family Office Handbook: A Guide for Affluent Families and the Advisors Who Serve Them* (Hoboken, NJ, Bloomberg Press, 2014).
12. For more information about family offices, see Curtis, op. cit., note 1, Chapter 22.
13. *The 1%* is a documentary film about the wealth inequality in America, made by an heir to the Johnson & Johnson fortune. See the discussion of "Inequality and Wealth" later in this chapter.
14. Michael Schoenfeld, "Air Jordan and the 1%," *Wall Street Journal* (July 10, 2012). This article is also discussed in "Greycourt White Paper No. 56: Being Rich" (February 2013), available at http://www.greycourt.com/white-papers/white-papers-by-date/.
15. A three-peat means that the team won the NBA title three years in a row. The Chicago Bulls accomplished this remarkable feat twice, in 1991–1993 and again in 1995–1998.
16. Although the ideas behind rent-seeking behavior reach far back into classical economics, the concept was articulated in the modern era by Gordon Tullock in a seminal paper in 1967. See "The Welfare Costs of Tariffs, Monopolies, and Theft," *Western Economic Journal*, 5, no. 3 (1967): 224–232.
17. Recent data show that taxpayers who fall into the top 1% of all taxpayers by income pay more in taxes than the bottom 90% of taxpayers. See Andrew Lundeen, "The Top 1 Percent Pays More in Taxes than the Bottom 90 Percent," Tax Policy Blog, available at http://taxfoundation.org/blog/top-1-percent-pays-more-taxes-bottom-90-percent.
18. Claudia Goldin and Lawrence Katz, *The Race between Education and Technology* (Harvard University Press, 2010).

19. Thomas Piketty's book, *Capital in the Twenty-First Century* (Cambridge, MA: Belknap Press, 2014), was a major publishing sensation when it first appeared in America. In essence, Piketty argues that the returns to capital are greater than the returns to labor, and therefore advanced societies will become ever more unequal over time. Needless to say, his thesis is extremely controversial.

About the Website

This book includes a companion website, which can be found at www.wiley.com/go/familycapital (password: curtis123). This site includes many examples of materials discussed in the text and is integral to the book. You will find it useful to keep the website open in front of you as you read the book, as the text alludes to the website materials with great frequency.

The materials on the website are arranged by chapter, meaning that you can follow along the discussion in each chapter with different files. You can also see how the principles are applied in actual situations. Although many of the files are copyrighted, most can be easily adapted for use in your own work.

About the Author

Gregory Curtis is chairman and founder of Greycourt & Co., Inc., an open-architecture wealth advisory firm serving substantial families and select endowments on a global basis. Prior to founding Greycourt, Curtis served for many years as president of a Mellon family office and as president of the Laurel Foundation.

Curtis is the author of *The Stewardship of Wealth: Successful Private Wealth Management for Families and Their Advisors*, and *Creative Capital: Managing Private Wealth in a Complex World*. He is has written numerous white papers on a variety of investment topics, and these papers are available free at http://www.greycourt.com/white-papers/white-papers-by-date/. Curtis also writes a weekly investment blog available at http://gregorydcurtis.com/blog/.

Over the years Curtis has served on many investment committees for family and institutional investors, including investment committees for Carnegie Mellon University, the Pittsburgh Foundation, St. John's College, United Educators Insurance Co., Waycrosse, Inc., and Winchester Thurston School, among others.

Curtis is a member of the board of directors of United Educators Insurance Co.; is a past chair of the board of directors of the Pittsburgh Foundation (the community foundation for the Pittsburgh region); is a past chair of the board of St. John's College (Annapolis and Santa Fe); and is a past chair of the board of the Investment Fund for Foundations.

Curtis holds a BA degree from Dartmouth College, *cum laude* with high distinction in English, a JD degree from Harvard Law School, *cum laude*, and he is a graduate of the Endowment Institute at Harvard Business School. He also holds an honorary BA degree from St. John's College.

Curtis has six children and lives in Pittsburgh with his wife, Simin, the founder and CEO of the American Middle East Institute.

Index